W9-CNA-571

THE GHOSTS OF
EDEN PARK

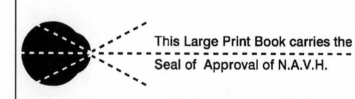

This Large Print Book carries the
Seal of Approval of N.A.V.H.

THE GHOSTS OF EDEN PARK

THE BOOTLEG KING, THE WOMEN WHO PURSUED HIM, AND THE MURDER THAT SHOCKED JAZZ-AGE AMERICA

KAREN ABBOTT

THORNDIKE PRESS
A part of Gale, a Cengage Company

Copyright © 2019 by Karen Abbott.
Thorndike Press, a part of Gale, a Cengage Company.

ALL RIGHTS RESERVED
Thorndike Press® Large Print Nonfiction.
The text of this Large Print edition is unabridged.
Other aspects of the book may vary from the original edition.
Set in 16 pt. Plantin.

LIBRARY OF CONGRESS CIP DATA ON FILE.
CATALOGUING IN PUBLICATION FOR THIS BOOK
IS AVAILABLE FROM THE LIBRARY OF CONGRESS

ISBN-13: 978-1-4328-7703-3 (hardcover alk. paper)

Published in 2020 by arrangement with Crown, an imprint of Random House, a division of Penguin Random House, LLC

Printed in Mexico
Print Number: 01   Print Year: 2020

Spring House Gazebo at Eden Park, Cincinnati, Ohio.

For Katherine Abbott: Tudi
(and in memory of Poe, a brilliant and
wicked bird)

The truth was that Jay Gatsby of West Egg, Long Island, sprang from his Platonic conception of himself. He was a son of God — a phrase which, if it means anything, means just that — and he must be about His Father's business, the service of a vast, vulgar, and meretricious beauty. So he invented just the sort of Jay Gatsby that a seventeen-year-old boy would be likely to invent, and to this conception he was faithful to the end.

— F. SCOTT FITZGERALD,
The Great Gatsby

I will wear my heart upon my sleeve for daws to peck at; I am not what I am.

— WILLIAM SHAKESPEARE,
Othello

CONTENTS

PART III: THE COLOSSAL VITALITY OF HIS ILLUSION

AUTHOR'S NOTE

As strange as this story may seem, this is a work of nonfiction, with no invented dialogue. Everything that appears between quotation marks comes from a government file, archive, diary, letter, newspaper article, book, or, most often, a hearing or trial transcript. One transcript in particular, which numbered 5,500 pages in total, allowed me to accurately depict detailed scenes and entire conversations and to reveal characters' thoughts, gestures, personalities, and histories. For the sake of brevity, some trial testimony has been condensed. A comprehensive list of endnotes and sources (including for each line of dialogue) appears at the end of the book.

PROLOGUE

Reckoning, 1927

He had been waiting for that morning, dreading it, aware it couldn't be stopped. An hour ago he was eating breakfast and now here he was, chasing her through Eden Park. The sun, strong for the season, bludgeoned through his fedora and inflamed his bald head. His silk trousers whisked against his skin. He heard the swish of his wingtips through the grass, the rasping of his breath. On the road nearby a brigade of cars clamored in the rush hour traffic. The throaty engines, the blaring of horns, the people determined to be someplace else. Exhaust fumes burned in his nostrils. Somewhere behind him were his own blue Buick and his driver, abandoned. He'd learned she wanted to kill him. His brain had wandered to a shadowy land, somewhere between sanity and madness.

For two years he had not been right. Friends and associates would attest to the difference, a stark split between then and

17

now. He had long referred to himself in the third person, but such declarations became more frequent; there seemed an odd detaching, as if part of him had crept outside of his skin. With the slightest provocation — just a single, specific word — his face purpled and his features knotted into a ghastly cartoon. He spoke of a halo hovering above his head, whispering to him, marking him wherever he went. He described shooting stars only he could see, their tails imprinting bright, lingering bolts inside his closed eyes. He rambled incessantly about love and betrayal and revenge. He embarked on nationwide searches, hoping to validate every suspicion that tumbled through his mind. He announced, with unwavering conviction, that people from all corners wished him dead: gangsters in St. Louis, a certain woman federal official in Washington, D.C., and — worst of all — his wife, Imogene, who had razed his world to the ground. His Little Imo, his truest and sweetest, his Prime Minister, his centipede, his monkey, his gem; how would he ever forget those old, dead endearments from their past? He just wished to talk to her, he'd insist. Maybe he could stop what she had set in motion. He had little time left.

And there she was, finally, close enough to touch.

She sprinted faster, her black silk dress like a waving flag. He accelerated, everything but the sight of her falling away. They were even now, face-to-face beneath a gazebo, the autumn air just beginning to darken the leaves. He heard her voice, a sound that once upon a time made him mad with a boundless and wild joy. Between them rose a glint of silver and cream: a pearl-handled revolver.

The crack of the bullet shook the birds from the trees.

PART I
THE PURSUED AND
THE PURSUING

ALL THE ROPE HE WANTS

The house seemed out of a Bavarian fairy tale, rambling and turreted, laced with gingerbread cornicing and columns arched like sharp, imperious brows. It was the finest house in Price Hill, the finest neighborhood in Cincinnati, perched high above the Ohio River and its basin of residents and commerce: the downtown business district, the black families in the West End, and the German immigrants in Over-the-Rhine, where Prohibition forced breweries to sell root beer in the hope of surviving the law. Already he envisioned what his "dream palace" would become. A Roman garden, a baseball field, a heated pool, a library stocked with books — presidential biographies, the epic poems of Homer and Milton, tomes of mythology and obscure science that would testify to the surprising depths of his mind. In this house he would once again become someone new, a superior version of himself. In this house the world would come to know his name.

George Remus would be forty-four years old that November of 1920, and had spent the first half of his life gathering momentum for the second. He was the embodiment of the new decade, a harbinger of its grandest excesses and darkest illusions. He endeavored to become the best in the country at his chosen profession — a profession that could not have flourished so dramatically in any other era, nor become so swiftly obsolete. As America reinvented itself Remus would do the same, living in rabid service to his own creation, protecting it at all costs.

The cornerstone of this creation, the fulcrum that would allow him to pivot and rise, was Augusta Imogene Remus, formerly Augusta Imogene Holmes. Imogene, as she preferred, was thirty-five, with dark hair and eyes and a voluptuous figure better suited to the bustles and billowing sleeves of decades past. They'd met five years earlier at his office in downtown Chicago, where Remus had been one of the city's preeminent defense attorneys and Imogene a "dust girl," sweeping the floors and tidying his desk.

She'd confided in him about her divorce, which had been plodding along painfully for years as she and her husband separated ten times before finally going to court. Remus could commiserate. He, too, had suffered marital strife. Lillian — his wife and the mother of his teenaged daughter, Romola —

once filed for divorce charging "cruelty," "pure malice," and a habit of "coming home early in the morning." They had subsequently reconciled, but their union remained tenuous.

Imogene saw her chance.

Remus accepted her as a client and promptly fell in love. He told Imogene everything, sharing long-buried tales of his past, the quirks and compulsions that shaped him now. He recounted his first memory: the journey from Germany to Garden Castle in 1883, when he was six years old, traveling with two sisters and a mother so beleaguered that, when questioned by immigration officials, she couldn't recall the names of four other children who'd died. In America they reunited with Remus's father, Franz (since anglicized to Frank), and settled in Chicago. Remus remembered his father coming home drunk from the corner saloon and evolving, week by week, into a mean and abusive alcoholic; he vowed that he would never drink a drop of alcohol.

When Frank developed rheumatism and could no longer work, Remus quit the eighth grade to take a job at his uncle's pharmacy on the city's West Side, earning $5 per week. As his father's rages worsened, Remus moved into the pharmacy, sleeping on a cot in the stockroom, going for months at a time without seeing his parents and siblings. He called himself a "druggist's devil boy" and in this role experienced a valuable revelation: He could sell anything to anyone under any circumstance, no matter how outrageous his claims or unorthodox his delivery.

At age nineteen he bought the drugstore from his uncle for the charitable price of $10, and during his years in the business he peddled all manner of dubious concoctions: Remus's Cathartic Compound, Remus's Cathartic Pills, a Remus "complexion remedy" containing mercury, Remus's Lydia Pinkham Compound — presumably Lydia's own legendary cocktail, for the relief of menstrual pain, wasn't sufficiently potent — and his specialty, Remus's Nerve Tonic, consisting of fluid extract of celery, sodium bromide, rhubarb, and a dash of a poisonous, hallucinogenic plant called henbane. Although he'd never finished his courses at the Chicago College of Pharmacy, he convinced his customers to call him "Doctor Remus."

When he switched careers and became a lawyer, he brought this salesmanship to his practice. He used the courtroom as an arena, leaping and pacing and prowling the length of the jury box. During the cross-examination of his clients he tore at his remaining rim of hair, sobbing and howling with abandon. Poignant episodes from history lent drama to Remus's closing arguments; one judge was moved to tears by his description of Abraham Lincoln's stint as a bartender. Detractors derided him with a nickname, "the Weeping, Crying Remus," but admirers coined one of their own: "the Napoleon of the Chicago Bar."

In one famous case, Remus defended a husband accused of poisoning his wife. Throughout the trial he kept the poison in question on his table, in full view of the jury. During his closing argument Remus raised the bottle aloft and swiped it slowly across the air, so that the jury got a clear look of the skull and crossbones on its label.

"There has been a lot of talk of poison in this case," he said. "But it is a lot of piffle. Look!"

As the jury gasped, he swallowed the poison and continued with his closing argument, aware that they all expected him to drop dead. When he didn't, the jury returned with an acquittal. Only later did Remus reveal his trick: Drawing on his pharmaceutical background, he had first ingested an elixir that neutralized the poison.

In this same way he sold himself to Imogene Holmes. He would handle her divorce, and she needn't worry about his fee; in fact, she could quit her job as a dust girl and money would be no concern. He would pay the rent on her apartment in Evanston, north of

Chicago, and spend more time there than he did at home with his wife. He would give Imogene allowance money, $100 checks to spend as she wished. He would rescue her from "the gutter" and "make a lady out of her." He would adore her and be true to her. He would protect her and her eleven-year-old daughter, Ruth, from all unsavory people and circumstances.

One evening in the spring of 1919, that promise was tested. A local plumber knocked on Imogene's door claiming he had found the girl's watch and wanting a $15 reward for its return. Imogene thought that $5 would suffice. An argument ensued.

Remus had always enjoyed confrontation, physical or mental. His stout stature — five foot six and 205 pounds — belied his agility and strength. He boasted of his history as a competitive swimmer and how, as a young man, he'd set an endurance record by spending nearly six hours in frigid Lake Michigan. During his stint as a pharmacist he once argued with a customer who complained that a certain liniment had scalded his chest; Remus dragged the man outside and settled the matter by slapping him in the face. When a group of women gathered at his drugstore to protest his "poisonous potions," Remus doused them with ammonia. As a lawyer he had a history of attacking opposing counsel and throwing punches over witness testimony, sometimes ending up in a tangle of limbs on the courtroom floor. His hubris was equaled only by a concern that someone, someday, might get the best of him.

Standing in Imogene's doorway, Remus, wearing slippers, launched himself at the plumber, punched him in the eye, revamped his nose, knocked out a tooth, and chased him onto the lawn.

The plumber pressed charges, and Remus represented himself.

"I acted in self-defense as any red-blooded man with a spark of chivalry would have acted," he argued. "This ruffian of a plumber was disturbing a lady. He was rough housing, loud mouthed, irrelevant, and immaterial about the premises, and I only forcibly applied a perfectly good and legal writ of ejectment."

After five minutes of deliberation, the jury returned a verdict of not guilty.

His wife, Lillian, filed for divorce a second and final time. In her petition she once again accused Remus of cruelty, claiming that on several occasions he beat, punched, struck, choked, and kicked her. Remus agreed to a settlement reflective of his success: a lump sum of $50,000, $25 per week in alimony, and $30,000 in a trust for their daughter, Romola. He moved out of their home for good, allowing Imogene to defend him in the press.

"He is a perfect gentleman," she insisted, "and anything his wife says to the contrary is false. The trouble with modern wives is this: They don't know how to treat their husbands. A husband should be given all the rope he wants . . . he will never hang himself."

In response, Lillian made another disturbing allegation. She claimed to the press that Remus, on several occasions, had ended his affair with Imogene, ordering her to stay away from his office and home. But Imogene persisted, following him down Clark Street during the day and lurking outside their windows at night, flashing a gun and insisting that they were meant to be together.

With a new fiancée, home, and stepdaughter-to-be, Remus once again sought to update his life, discarding any piece of his past that seemed ill fit for his future. He included his career in this evaluation and noticed that his docket had filled with a new type of defendant: men charged with violating the Volstead Act, ratified in January 1920 to enforce the 18th Amendment, which prohibited the manufacture, sale, or transportation of alcohol to, from, or within the United States. Remus considered the law to be unreasonable and nearly impossible to enforce, and his clients were proving him right, making astonishing profits from what he called "petty, hip-pocket bootlegging." They paid retainers in cash right away, fanning the bills across his desk, and never complained about fines imposed by the court, no matter how steep. He noticed that their customers were the "so-called best people," whose primary gripe in life was the difficulty in getting good whiskey. It occurred to him that this demand must be spreading across the country, and that if his clients — "men without any brains at all" — were succeeding, then he himself had "a chance to clean up."

Seeking to launch a large-scale operation, he scoured the Volstead Act, finding a loophole in Title II, Section 6: With a physician's prescription, it was legal to buy and use liquor for "medicinal purposes" — a provision he deemed, in a customary flourish of language, "the greatest comedy, the greatest perversion of justice, that I have ever known of in any civilized country in the world." A plan took shape in his mind. As a licensed pharmacist, he had the knowledge necessary to exploit the law on a national scale. As a criminal defense attorney, he had significant insight into the mindset and machinations of the underworld. As a lifelong teetotaler, he could view the liquor business objectively. And as a risk-taker, he craved the thrill and excitement of outwitting not only his competitors but also the federal government.

He devised his strategy, each step meticulously considered and potential hazards addressed:

1) Close his Chicago law practice and move to Cincinnati, since 80 percent of the country's pre-Prohibition bonded whiskey was stored within 300 miles of the city.
2) Buy distilleries to gain possession of thousands of gallons of that whiskey.
3) Acquire wholesale drug companies, always listing someone else as the owner.
4) Under the guise of these drug companies, obtain withdrawal permits that would allow him to remove whiskey from his warehouses and, in theory, sell it on the medicinal market.
5) Bribe state Prohibition directors to ignore abnormally large withdrawals.
6) Organize a transportation company to provide for distribution and arrange for his own employees to hijack his own trucks — thereby diverting all of that technically legal, curative whiskey into the illicit market at any price he named. Essentially, he would be robbing Remus to pay Remus.

He called this massive octopus of an enterprise "the Circle."

Imogene had sold herself to Remus, too; she was malleable, receptive to his schemes, eager to mold herself into his ideal. She and her daughter, Ruth, would be his new family. She would keep his darkest secrets and uphold all of his lies. She would not tell anyone that Remus had always been terrified of ghosts. She would not divulge that his brother, Herman, had died in an insane asylum. She would not mention that Remus had never officially become an American citizen. She would never repeat the strange story behind his father's death: Frank and Remus's mother, Marie, had engaged in a barroom brawl, which culminated in a bash to his head; he died on the way to the hospital. To protect his mother and to keep her from speaking indiscriminately to the coroner, Remus locked her in the attic for three days, until the inquest was over.

Remus chose to believe that his past was safe with Imogene, to entrust her with his future. En route to Cincinnati, on June 25, 1920, they stopped in Newport, Kentucky, to get married, with Ruth as their witness. Once in the Queen City he rented a suite at the Sinton Hotel, Cincinnati's answer to New York's Hotel Astor, featuring opera concerts, a writing room, and a Louis XVI candy shop.

They would live there until renovations were complete on the Price Hill mansion, which had once belonged to Henry Lackman, proprietor of a now-shuttered brewery. "We must buy the Lackman place," Imogene had urged; it would be a monument to their new start and status, a grandiose barrier to the past. Remus bought the home for $75,000, a record for a residential sale in Cincinnati and a fraction of the amount he'd stashed in a local bank under an alias.

As a surprise for his new bride he put the deed in Imogene's name, one of many decisions he would come to regret.

Q. Did he continue to help the family after

TESTIMONY OF
MARIE REMUS

Q. How long did George Remus live at
home, and what did he do?

A. Until he was about fourteen years old.
Then I took him to the drugstore of my
brother, as he always wanted to make
money to assist the family.

Q. Where was George confirmed?

A. By Reverend Landrech, minister of the
Lutheran Church on the West Side.

Q. Did he continue to work in the drugstore
until he married?

A. My brother had another store and he sent
George there. George ate his meals where
he worked so as to save money and send
the money to me.

Q. What kind of a boy was George, with
reference to looking after his mother and
family?

A. A fine boy. He always sent the money
home. When his father would want money
to buy beer, and I would not give it to him,

George would always give his father the money.

Q. Did he continue to help the family after he was married [to Imogene]?

A. Yes, always. And his wife got mad.

THE CIRCLE

Once settled in Cincinnati, Remus hustled to establish himself. With financing from the Lincoln National Bank, where he kept an account under the name "John P. Alexander," he purchased a retail drugstore downtown and converted it into a wholesale drug company, a transformation that required an additional investment and an intricate sleight of hand. After stocking the shelves with $50,000 worth of drugs and toiletries, he secured a basic permit to withdraw and sell whiskey. As soon as that company had withdrawn as much liquor as it could without attracting suspicion, he closed that drug company, organized another one, and shipped over the initial supply of drugs and toiletries.

He repeated this process and also bought existing wholesale drug companies: two in New York, a few more in Cincinnati, and the Kentucky Drug Company, just across the river in Covington. He also purchased his own distillery, H. E. Pogue in Maysville,

Kentucky, and entered negotiations for several others. He observed that Cincinnati bootleggers conducted business brazenly, without interference from either city police or federal agents — even though Ohio was the headquarters of the Anti-Saloon League (the state conformed to the country-wide tendency for cities to be "wet" and rural counties "dry"). Discreet inquiries revealed the names and prices of local Prohibition officers willing to be "fixed," an expenditure of ten dollars for every case of whiskey withdrawn.

He assembled a diverse group of associates to fulfill specific roles in his organization: "confidential men" to bait law enforcement into accepting bribes; a "traffic man" to assist with transportation; secretaries to falsify paperwork; a personal chauffeur; and a personal cook. George Conners, whom Remus called "the man, Friday," would act as his fearless and savvy lieutenant. Remus met Conners, a lifelong resident of Cincinnati and a local real estate broker, while negotiating for distilleries, and the bootlegger liked him instantly. Finally, there were the "all-around man," Harry Brown, who happened to be Imogene's brother, and Imogene herself, upon whom Remus bestowed the unofficial title of "Prime Minister."

Remus promised she would be his "partner in everything." She would oversee business records and plans that he could not share with anyone else. He would seek her input on potential deals. He would invite her to invest personal funds — meaning her allowance — in his enterprises. There was nobody in the world whom he trusted so fully, and he felt confident in placing both his livelihood and his heart in her lovely and clever hands.

The Circle began to spin. Within the year, Remus would own 35 percent of all the liquor in the United States.

Remus feared neither the police nor Prohibition officials but whiskey pirates, those bands of roving thieves who targeted bootleggers across the country, swooping down on warehouses, binding and gagging the watchmen, cutting telephone wires, and stealing every last barrel inside.

As word of the Circle spread, Remus knew that he would be a target. His fear was realized one night when he and his driver were returning to Cincinnati from Covington, Kentucky, with cases of whiskey piled high in the back of the truck. They were halfway across the bridge when a touring car veered from its lane to block their path. Remus's driver abandoned the truck and fled frantically in the direction of Cincinnati, leaving Remus to fend for himself. Four men leapt onto the running board of Remus's truck, brandishing automatics and shouting a single command: "Stick 'em up high!" Each of them aimed his gun directly at Remus's head.

Remus's driver carried a revolver, but he'd taken it with him when he ran. Remus himself was unarmed. His mind clicked into action, assessing the situation: The location of the holdup was to his advantage, since policemen were typically stationed at either end of the bridge. At the sound of gunfire, they would move to block the pirates' escape.

"Pull your triggers!" Remus dared them. "Shoot, you cowards, and if you do you'll never live to tell the tale!"

He knew he had just a fraction of a second to make a move. He catapulted himself forward with the force and form of a diver. He caught the men by surprise, windmilling his thick arms until he connected with a set of ribs, sending their owner tumbling backward. Then something crashed brutally against the top of his head, as if dropped from several stories above, an impact that folded his body in half and brought him to his knees. He righted himself and swung again, catching another pirate with his boulder of a fist. The butt of an automatic carved a second hole in his scalp, sending him back to the ground. Again he staggered to his feet, blood veiling his eyes. Whirling around, Remus trapped his assailant in his arms, hoisted him above his head, and stumbled to the side of the bridge, intending to heave the pirate into the water below. Instead he collided with the railing and crashed to the ground, stunned.

An uninjured pirate slid behind the wheel of Remus's truck and exhorted his comrades to hurry and join him. One retrieved the dazed pirate, dragging him away from the bridge and into the touring car. Remus battled with the last, swinging his arms wildly, his target barely visible through a sheen of blood. The pirate disengaged and climbed into Remus's truck. Both vehicles started their engines.

But Remus was not ready to yield the fight. He hauled himself up to the running board of his truck and tried to pry his rival from the driver's seat. One last bash on the head hurled him back to the ground, and this time he knew he had lost.

The truck pulled away, the touring car following close behind. Remus swiped the blood from his eyes, crossed the bridge into Cincinnati, and hailed a taxicab to the hospital to get stitches for his wounds. Lesson learned: In the future, all liquor shipments would be accompanied by a convoy of armed guards.

The following week, Remus tracked down the pirates' leader, who surprised him with a compliment: "You have more guts than twenty men and deserved to keep your liquor." Remus laughed and hired a few of the leader's men to drive his trucks, insurance against future attacks. As an extra precaution, he asked his main lieutenant, George Conners, to find him a safer, more secluded storage facility, one that could serve him for years to come.

Conners was Remus's physical and psychological opposite — and therefore his perfect complement. He had a wiry, compact build, with bullet eyes and a reserved nature, as protective of his thoughts and speech as Remus was effusive with his. He was a devoted husband and the father of a baby girl. The son of poor Irish immigrants, Conners had worked for the Democratic State Committee before becoming a real estate agent. He maintained excellent connections with local officials and businessmen; if Remus needed a new facility, Conners could find it.

He soon informed Remus of a perfect location — accessible by trucks and so easily defended that two men could ward off an entire army. Together they drove out toward the small town of Cheviot, ten miles west of the city. They turned down Lick Run Road, a long, twisty passage devoid of any other traffic that narrowed as they approached its end. Hundreds of pear trees touched branches to form a canopy of leaves above them, giving the impression that a forest awaited on the other side.

Instead, a two-story, clapboard farmhouse

came into view, accented by three adjacent barns and a scattering of outbuildings. Amidst this cluster of buildings stood a heavy, unshaven man who looked to be in his mid-fifties. He introduced himself as George Dater and said that he owned the place. He had a small business growing grapes and manufacturing wine, but his profits had plummeted since Prohibition, and he was hoping to rent out the farm for storage privileges. He had one condition: The renters had to be willing and able to remove the liquor at a moment's notice. Remus offered $100 per week, and the deal was done.

The following day Remus and Conners arrived with a truckload of whiskey and began unloading cases — 250 in all. Dater grew unsettled as he watched. He did not live on the farm alone. His hired hand, Johnny Gehrum, occupied a few rooms with his wife and four small children.

"We're all going to get pinched," Dater said, hopping from foot to foot.

"Get out of the way and shut up," Conners responded, and he and Remus continued their work until the space was full.

They began remaking the property into an impregnable fortress. A company of marksmen stood guard at all hours. The property's position at the bottom of the hill helped them monitor traffic; they could see anyone descending the slim path heading to the farm, yet they themselves could not be seen. Every imaginable means of protection — shotguns, pistols, automatics — was stashed at strategic points.

An old voting booth was repurposed as a watchtower and stationed just outside of the entrance, where the guard assessed each potential customer. In the central barn, opposite Dater's farmhouse, armed guards lay prone in the hayloft. The barn itself was connected by an electric buzzer to the second floor of the house, where another guard kept watch during the night. Approved customers proceeded to the yard and dimmed their headlights three times in quick succession. At this signal, the men in the barn pressed the buzzer, and from the second-story window flashed the bold globe of a floodlight, usurping the moon and illuminating everything below.

The compound soon earned the moniker "Death Valley Farm," in honor of the pirates who tried to trespass and were never seen again.

The Circle never once paused. Twenty-four hours, seven days per week, Remus's fleet of 147 trucks blackened the roads. Children playing on Queen City Avenue, along the route to Death Valley, halted their games long enough to cry, "There go the whiskey trucks!" Prohibition had cost thousands of jobs in liquor-related industries, affecting bartenders, waitstaff, truckers, barrel makers, and glass workers. Remus welcomed three thousand men to his payroll, becoming one of the largest employers in the city and a de facto hero — providing not only quality whiskey but also the money to buy it.

Operations grew so complicated that he bought a six-story office building in downtown Cincinnati and spent $74,000 in renovations, complete with custom furniture and mosaic tiles that wove the name "Remus" throughout the lobby floor. Here he held meetings with his depot men and other subordinates, plotting ways to reach his ultimate goal: to gain possession of all of America's whiskey and become the country's sole bootlegger.

Remus embraced his new persona, adding and subtracting traits and nuances, shading and sharpening his lines. He stuffed each sentence until it was filled to bursting, never using one word where a half dozen might do: "I must corral myself together"; "the egregious and excruciating principle at stake"; "from the teeming fullness of my grateful heart." When his temper was cowed he was excessively polite, lacing his speech with such entreaties as "if you please" and "if I may" and "will you pardon my saying" and "may I observe here," certain words tinged with a German accent. He smiled less often than he laughed, a startling, aggressive clatter that invaded both silence and conversation at inopportune times.

He developed a fastidiousness that bordered on phobia. He grew keenly attuned to dirt and disarray; to flaws in schemes not yet hatched; to any threat of restricted freedom in body or mind. Piece by piece he replaced his wardrobe with bespoke suits made of silk, so that it was the only material touching his skin. He could not tolerate the feel of a button at the back of his collar, pressing against his neck. He never wore underwear.

To underscore his importance, he began referring to himself in the third person. "Remus was in the whiskey business," he'd say, "and Remus was the biggest man in the business. Cincinnati was the American mecca for good liquor, and America had to come to Remus to get it." In this way, over time, he developed the ability to consider even the most personal of matters with an objective distance, as if a stranger had stolen his thoughts and fears and decided, unilaterally, how to act upon them.

Although Remus felt invincible, Prohibition officials in Washington had begun to take notice of suspicious activity in Ohio. In the fall of 1920, shortly before the election of President Warren G. Harding, the Treasury Department contacted William Mellin, a thirty-two-year-old professional wiretapper based in New York. They sent him to Cincinnati, where he rented the room in the Sinton Hotel next to Remus's and secured a duplicate of his key.

One morning when Remus, Imogene, and Ruth were out, Mellin let himself in and noted that Remus's telephone extension was 707. In the hotel cellar, he located the terminals for 707 and bridged that extension to the one in his own room. Whenever Remus's phone rang, his would ring, too.

Over the course of one day, Mellin ascertained, a total of forty-four people visited Remus's suite, many of them local Prohibition agents or deputy marshals. Remus paid graft money to each visitor, averaging $1,000 apiece, and coordinated his next shipment: Eighteen freight cars crammed with whiskey were on the way from Covington. After organizing his notes, Mellin contacted a federal official in Cincinnati.

"Here's the dope on Remus," he said. "What do I do now?"

Silently the official read through Mellin's report. Finally, he said, "My boy, come back tomorrow."

Mellin did so and reminded the official that he had information about Remus.

"Son, where is your home office?" the official asked.

"New York," Mellin told him.

"Son," the official said again, "there's times when a man has to be practical in this business. It's only a few weeks to election, and the information you've dug up is political dynamite. The men you spied on — the agents and marshals — are political appointees. Go back to New York and forget about it."

Mellin thought it over and decided, instead, to report his findings to Washington, D.C. As the election results came in and the Harding administration took power, Mellin kept waiting for a response. It never came.

LIFE HAS FEW
PETTED DARLINGS

In the spring of 1921, shortly after Harding's inauguration, Remus received a call from an old Chicago law colleague named Elijah Zoline. Someone in the Department of Justice — a close friend of Attorney General Harry Daugherty, no less — had made it known that the government was willing, even eager, to conduct business with bootleggers. For a certain price, Remus could obtain an unlimited number of genuine government withdrawal permits. Should Remus be interested, Zoline could arrange a meeting on neutral territory, in New York City.

Given the ever-expanding scope of the Circle and its attendant hazards, Remus was interested. With each whiskey withdrawal he took the chance that an honest Prohibition director would discover that subordinates were selling permits. To mitigate this issue, Remus had obtained (for the paltry investment of $1.48) a rubber stamp facsimile of a local Prohibition director's signature, which would allow him to circumvent the standard approval procedure. But large-scale forgery also posed obvious risks. Buying authentic permits directly from the federal government, as Zoline was suggesting, would both streamline the process and diminish its dangers.

On the appointed day Remus and Zoline waited in the lobby of the Commodore Hotel in midtown Manhattan, their table veiled by a phalanx of white marble pillars and cascading ferns. Remus watched the man swing through the doors and approach them. He was an odd-looking character, wide and squat, with a florid complexion and a coarse, bristled moustache that appeared unevenly trimmed. Black wire glasses imprinted on fleshy cheeks. He dressed with monochromatic precision, choosing the same neutral shade for his hat, tie, tweed suit, handkerchief, and silk socks. A diamond and ruby ring provided the lone spot of color.

Zoline made the introductions — George Remus, meet Jess Smith — and left them alone to talk, their words obscured by the soft hush of a nearby fountain.

Smith spoke first, each word launching flecks of spittle into the air between them. He had heard that Remus was a "reasonably large operator" in the whiskey industry. For a "consideration" he would provide Remus with all of the permits he would need to withdraw the pre-Prohibition booze from his warehouses. Moreover, these permits would bear the authentic signatures of various state Prohibition officials who reported to the Justice Department — a bit of insurance if Remus encountered any suspicious authorities. As they both knew, one permit allowed for the withdrawal of one case of liquor, comprised of three gallons. What cut could he expect from Remus?

Remus thought it over. For each permit he would pay Smith $1.50 to $2.50 — a sliding scale, he explained, depending on the size of the shipment. The first permit would name the Central Drug Company in New York, which Remus already owned, and the Fleischmann Distillery in Cincinnati, which he planned to buy imminently.

With that settled, the men moved to the next topic of discussion. Smith offered to use his political clout — in particular, his relationship with Attorney General Daugherty — to protect Remus from legal trouble. If Remus found himself in a "showdown" and was prosecuted for bootlegging, Smith promised that no conviction would come of it. And if for some inexplicable reason Remus *were* convicted, Smith would arrange a *deus ex machina* in the form of a pardon from Daugherty. For this service, Smith would accept $50,000, for starters. Without hesitation, Remus reached into his pockets and produced $50,000, all in $1,000 bills.

The men shook hands, agreeing to meet again soon.

Down the hall from Jess Smith's desk, in Room 501 of the Department of Justice Building, sat Mabel Walker Willebrandt, the assistant attorney general of the United States and the most powerful woman in the country. Just nine months earlier she, along with all other adult female citizens, had been granted the right to vote. She was thirty-two, only five years out of law school, and had yet to prosecute a single criminal case. That soon would change, as she was responsible for all Prohibition-related matters in the country, identifying top bootleggers and bringing them to justice.

Like Remus, Willebrandt had always felt destined for grand and public endeavors. A persistent sense of melancholy had chased her over the years, and leaping into the unknown proved to be the only certain cure. "For all of my life," she wrote, "I have had the most uncanny feeling against which I have often struggled, that seems always to say to me, 'You are marked to step into a crisis some time, as the instrument of God.' It seems that it may mean danger or disgrace, or in some way cause me agony of the heart, but I can't escape it."

A call from an old law professor had led to this new and intriguing path. There was a vacancy at the federal level, he explained: Annette Abbott Adams, the assistant attorney general during Woodrow Wilson's second term, had resigned, and Republicans — eager to curry favor with recently triumphant suffragists — wanted another woman to replace her. Soon after this call came a telegram from Attorney General Daugherty, imploring her to come to Washington to meet President Harding.

For the first time in her life, Willebrandt hesitated.

She certainly had the temperament for the job. Born in a sod dugout on a remote Kansas plain, Willebrandt had come up in the waning decades of the American frontier, a time and place that demanded the same resourcefulness of women as it did of men and that punished them with equal severity if they failed to comply. Her home was a nine-by-twelve-foot tent, pitched and struck on plains in Kansas and Missouri and Oklahoma, her parents fleeing natural disasters and chasing unsustainable dreams. One of her earliest memories was of a flash flood rampaging through their tent, her mother overturning the kitchen table to use as a raft until the waters receded.

Her parents, both descendants of German pioneers, worked tirelessly to shape her character. Once, when she was seven, her father scolded her for "acting like a child," a rebuke she took as a compliment. "He must think of me as bigger, older, and with larger capacities than a child! To what seven-year-old is that no inspiration and challenge!" When she bit a pet cat's ear, her father bit hers in turn. She developed a ruling philosophy, to which she would adhere for the rest of her life: "Look above and beyond the immediate task." Before she milked the cow on their Kansas farm, she carefully arranged the animal toward the west so that she could view the sunset as she worked. "Life has few petted darlings," she always said, and she did not consider herself one of them.

At age thirteen she began formal schooling and cast her mind in all directions, analyzing every fact it caught. After challenging a principal on the doctrine of the virgin birth, she was promptly expelled. When she began her own teaching career in 1908, she assembled a résumé claiming a nearly unfathomable range of expertise: English language, English literature, English composition, grammar, elocution, penmanship, American history, modern history, English history, ancient history, Latin, arithmetic, algebra, geometry, nature study, botany, zoology, biology, physiology, physiography, civics, geography, pedagogy, public school music, freehand drawing, domestic science, household economy, clay modeling, and even gymnastics and baseball. She did not abide disrespect from her students. On one occasion, after threatening to discipline one boy with a rod, he attacked her with a knife. With one deft move, she wrested the weapon from his grasp and delivered what she later termed an "enthusiastic licking."

She moved to South Pasadena, where she not only served as principal and eighth grade teacher at Lincoln Park Elementary School but also attended law school full-time at the University of Southern California. During her last semester, she worked pro bono in the police courts, wielding her ferocious intelligence and fearless demeanor on behalf of her exclusively female client base. As Los Angeles's first female public defender, she argued two thousand cases, with a particular focus on prostitution. Infuriated that "johns" were rarely apprehended and forced to appear in court, she utilized a procedure that enabled her defendants to request jury trials — thereby making the men's presence mandatory. She avoided sentimentality in favor of honest, pragmatic support. When one client, a madam, sought advice about "going straight," Willebrandt assessed the woman's finances, determined that she could retire after six more months, and even loaned her some money to help with her fresh start.

She could have continued in private practice, working on mortgage cases and volunteering as a public defender, but Washington beckoned. Her bank account was so depleted that she had to borrow train fare and a new blouse to wear once she arrived. On the morning of her meeting with Harding, she took her daily ice-cold bath and fastened her hearing aid, on which she'd increasingly depended over the previous few years while straining to hear witnesses and the mutterings of opposing counsel. The bathroom mirror reflected her face, unpainted and unpowdered and dominated by her eyes: large and deeply set, absorbing everything but reflecting little back, collecting secrets while betraying none of her own. For one hour she painstakingly styled her hair so that it concealed the hearing aid and then tucked the batteries into her bosom.

Willebrandt had several misgivings about the position. For one, she had never planned to become a prosecutor, always having enjoyed "being on the other side." Her long-term ambition was to practice civil law, not criminal. She would have to disengage entirely from her private practice, leaving her partners to fend for themselves. Disquieting questions took root in her mind: What if she were a mere token, a woman meant to do nothing but check a box? Would she find herself in a vacuous, toothless government post, catering to cronies rather than upholding the law?

Harding managed to put her at ease. She liked him immediately, finding him "tall, benevolent, interested, and gracious." His "irrepressible friendliness" appeared to be both his greatest strength and most evident weakness. She sensed that he preferred privacy and quiet to the bustle of public life, an inclination she well understood.

The job of assistant attorney general would be like none she'd ever held before; in fact, like no job *anyone* had held before, as it involved an entirely new division of the Justice Department focusing on an entirely new law. She would be in charge of federal income taxes, prisons, and, most important, all issues relating to the Volstead Act. That she herself had not supported Prohibition — and, before its passage, had enjoyed the occasional glass of wine — would not deter her from ruthlessly enforcing it.

She had to prepare herself for the scale of the task. The United States had two long, craggy borders and eighteen thousand miles of coastline, all of it unnervingly porous. Airplane fleets smuggled gallons of liquor from Mexico to San Antonio, Texas, where it was hidden beneath bales of hay and transported by truck. From Canada, eight to ten fleets landed each night at different spots on the Michigan peninsula, guided by searchlights. During their daily dumps in the

Atlantic Ocean, New York garbage scows met with rum ships and hauled spirits back to shore. There were liquor-filled torpedoes landing on Long Island, liquor in bottle-shaped buoys waiting to be collected, ships hauling liquor in dummy smokestacks, specialized "liquor submarines" that raised and lowered out of sight, and seagoing tugs with compartments hiding enough liquor for thirty New Year's Eve parties — all of them slipping past the Coast Guard, whose men were paid to look the other way.

The illicit liquor trade thrived equally within the borders, owing to the staggering quantities of pre-Prohibition alcohol available across the country: More than five hundred distilleries had boasted an annual output of 286 million gallons of spirits of all kinds; more than 1,200 breweries had produced hundreds of millions of gallons of beer. How easy it was to pinpoint loopholes in the law and exploit its exemptions, to re-create your own home as a small-scale distillery, to deliver your product to thousands of thirsty customers through any subversive means. The term *bootlegger,* originally applied to liquor dealers who concealed flasks in their boot tops while trading on Indian reservations, grew in popularity and scope. Now anyone could be a bootlegger, and boots were far from the only vessel employed.

Amputees hid booze in their hollowed

wooden legs. Women tied pints to each string of their corsets. Barbershops stocked whiskey in tonic bottles on their shelves. A raid on a soda parlor in Helena, Montana, uncovered squirt guns with a two-drink capacity. Farmers hid stills in goat barns, cowsheds, and cesspools, with entrances through tunnels. Professional bootleggers, worried about a glut in the market, dropped the price of a pint from $4 to $2.

Competition in the liquor trade was surging — and violence along with it. In Chicago, longtime gangster James "Big Jim" Colosimo was executed in his own restaurant. In Douglas, Arizona, four agents were shot within a week. In Cincinnati, whiskey pirates preyed upon the bootleggers, confrontations that erupted into gun battles and resulted in a significant number of deaths. For Willebrandt to be successful, she would need public support, a force of incorruptible "dry" agents, and a sustained stretch of good luck.

Willebrandt had only one discernible shortcoming, joked President Harding at the conclusion of their meeting: her youth. Laughing, she assured him that she would soon outgrow it.

Her office was dominated by a gleaming mahogany desk the size of a barge, upon which sat a candlestick phone and a rubber stamp facsimile of her signature — a useful tool, considering her wild, erratic scribble, whose sloping trajectory across the page suggested overindulgence of the California clarets she so loved and missed. She unpacked notebooks, legal pads, leather-bound reference tomes with gilt edges and butter-hued pages. On the wall behind her swivel chair she hung a quote by Cotton Mather: "There has been an old complaint that a good lawyer is seldom a good neighbor. You know how to confute it, gentlemen, by making your skill in law a blessing to your neighborhood."

Her personal staff of six — three attorneys, two stenographers, one secretary — stopped by to introduce themselves. They gave her a nickname: "The Queen." Her salary was $7,500 per year, the same amount paid to members of Congress. In long biographical articles, reporters called her the "pretty and young" lawyer and wondered if she would disprove "the age-old adage that woman is governed exclusively by the emotions and not by logic." She insisted to them that women should not be appointed to public office solely because they were women; such a policy would be unfair to the public generally and to women in particular. "At the same time," she clarified, "I am enough of a feminist to hold the opinion that there is no professional or public duty which a woman is not capable of performing."

Willebrandt would learn quickly that bootleggers represented just one facet of the challenge ahead. The other, just as daunting, was politics. None of her bosses had much interest in waging the war on liquor alongside her, from President Harding on down. If they had, a woman just out of law school with no prosecutorial experience would hardly have been their first choice.

During his career as an Ohio senator, Harding was dry in name only, a position adopted solely to avoid the enmity of the Anti-Saloon League. He believed that Prohibition was futile and, unlike Willebrandt, declined to follow the spirit of the law by abstaining in his personal life. One of his first acts as president was to have $1,800 worth of liquor — all purchased before January 16, 1920 — transported from his home on Wyoming Avenue to the White House. Although Harding maintained decorum in the White House's public rooms, he served it openly upstairs during frequent card games with his friends and appointees, including Harry Daugherty and his assistant, Jess Smith.

The secretary of the Treasury, Andrew Mellon, whose department housed the Prohibition Bureau, was an avowed wet who openly loathed the 18th Amendment. Before its ratification the banking mogul had invested millions in the liquor trade, even purchasing the Old Overholt rye distillery, said to produce America's oldest brand of whiskey. Prohibition Commissioner Roy Haynes, a Harding appointee and the country's preeminent dry spokesman, personally ensured that poker parties at the "Little Green House on K Street" — a Victorian townhouse occupied by fellow members of the president's "Ohio Gang" — had plenty of liquor on hand, often sending cases in Wells Fargo wagons driven by armed guards (Willebrandt called Haynes "a politician in sheep's clothing"). Jess Smith visited the Little Green House often, as did numerous bootleggers who needed favors from the federal government, including the withdrawal permits that allowed access to pre-Prohibition whiskey.

Even though Smith's desk was so close to her own, Willebrandt had no idea what he did during the workday or what sort of work he aimed to do. She did know that after Daugherty's wife, Lucie, went to Baltimore's Johns Hopkins Hospital for arthritis treatment, the attorney general and Smith had moved in together, sharing a suite at the Wardman Park Hotel. As far as Willebrandt could tell, Smith seemed to be a "kind of half servant and half glorified valet" who ran errands, buying railroad tickets for the attorney general and carrying his briefcase. Daugherty himself told Willebrandt, "Oh, don't pay any attention to Jess. If I have any directions for you, I will give them to you. There is a telephone on my desk and I will reach you."

Her first assignment, passed along by Daugherty, came in the form of a telegram. Its author was James R. Clark, an Ohio-based federal district attorney who described an "almost unbelievable condition" in Cincinnati. Although his office had successfully prosecuted a number of Prohibition cases, they were now facing "one of such magnitude and so far-reaching" that they needed Washington's assistance. A thorough investigation by capable agents would, in his opinion, "stamp out in this community the so-called 'Whiskey Ring.' "

Willebrandt opened a brown folder labeled "Department of Justice: Mail and Files Division" and slipped the telegram inside. She would soon scrawl one word across the folder, underlined with a heavy hand: *REMUS.*

TESTIMONY OF
A. W. BROCKWAY

Q. What was your business before you were a farm manager?

A. Assistant buyer for Carson, Pirie, Scott & Company at the store at State and Madison.

Q. When did you first become acquainted with [Imogene Remus]?

A. I would say 1917, without being positive. The last year of the war before the Armistice was signed.

Q. How did you become acquainted with her at that time?

A. We were putting on a great drive of washing machines and electric ironers, and she came on to the floor for the purpose of buying one. She was turned over to me, that being my department. It was just being installed under my directions, and I subsequently sold her an ironing machine and a washing machine on the installment plan.

Q. Did she pay for it?

A. She made a few payments, a month or

two months.

Q. Who paid the balance?

A. Mr. Remus finished the payment. Not as payments, but he finished it in a lump sum.

Q. Did you ever have any conversation with her during that period of time about George Remus?

A. On several occasions she told me that he was a good guy, that she would get what he had, that she was going to nick him . . . she said that she was going to "Roll him for his roll." Those were her words. She told me she would get what he had and she would show him how to get more. . . . She said she would marry him if she had to but that she didn't want to.

DADDY

Whenever Imogene wasn't at Death Valley Farm, supervising orders or greeting clients, Remus encouraged her to go shopping for home décor, little trinkets and fixtures that would make their home like none other in the city. She spent afternoons shopping for solid gold service plates and silver cutlery, which she had engraved with the initials "G.R.," in honor of her husband. On one outing, she spotted a pair of stone lions flanking the doors of an antiques store on Edwards Road and ordered her driver to pull over. Alighting from the limousine, she sauntered inside and, without preamble, demanded to purchase them. Informed by a clerk that the lions were not for sale, she called for a manager and insisted he name a price. Thinking quickly, he gave a number multiple times their true value, hoping that Imogene would be deterred. She was not. Nodding, she retrieved her checkbook — a $100,000 diamond winking from her hand — and blithely wrote a check for $4,000. The lions would stand guard at the mansion's entrance, bearing silent witness to everything that happened inside.

Nor did Remus spare any expense for her daughter, Ruth, whom he planned to legally adopt. He and Imogene enrolled the thirteen-year-old in the Sacred Heart Academy, an exclusive boarding school in Cincinnati's Clifton neighborhood operated by an order of cloistered French nuns who, in all likelihood, had no idea who Remus was. For scheduled visits home, the family chauffeur picked Ruth up in a red Pierce-Arrow touring car. Imogene waited in the back seat, reluctant to join the other mothers in conferences with the nuns.

Ruth occupied one of three private rooms and became known for her extravagant possessions: bottles of Guerlain perfume, a genuine muskrat coat, a pale yellow negligee made of satin and trimmed with lace, fit for a bride's trousseau. She gave her favorite classmates diamond-studded gold and platinum figurines that cost $15,000 apiece. Remus called her "Princess."

He of course had nicknames for Imogene, too. In addition to "Prime Minister," he called her his "little honey bunch," his "bunch of sugar," the "apple of his eye — not one, but both," and, simply, "Gene." Imogene had just one nickname for him:

"Daddy."

Remus had never been so content or busy, nor so certain that his life would continue to roll along at such a pleasingly frenetic and productive pace. He crammed work into every minute of every hour, his self-proclaimed photographic memory cataloguing details he refused to commit to paper. There was always a deal to analyze, a meeting to arrange, a train to catch, back and forth to Chicago, New York, Washington, Columbus, Indianapolis, Lexington, St. Louis, and Louisville. He collected new clients and acquaintances — including, according to lore, F. Scott Fitzgerald.

When he stopped to reflect — a rare luxury, these days — even he found the magnitude and intricacies of his own empire staggering, the way its numerous tentacles overlapped and intertwined, taking from one and giving to the next, a system that began and ended with him. His chain of distilleries and drug companies stretched across nine states, from New York to Kansas, some under his name, some under a pseudonym. His clients included the head of the Chicago mob, Johnny Torrio, who bought thousands of cases of Remus's Kentucky bourbon and sold it at his speakeasy, the Four Deuces (managed by his ambitious protégé, Al Capone). Even Remus did not know his exact net worth or the amount of money coursing through his system.

Estimates among Remus's associates fluctuated wildly. Four million dollars, five million, seven million spread across various savings accounts. Deposits that averaged $50,000 a day, in an era when the average salary was $1,400 per year. A $2.8 million deposit for a few months' work. A yearly gross of eighty million, a net of thirty. Daily sales of liquor that ran as high as $74,000. One rum runner paid for a single $200,000 order in one-, two-, and five-dollar bills; it took Conners four hours to count them. The money came in so fast Remus couldn't deposit it all, forcing him to carry as much as $100,000 in his pockets at any given time. For a while he considered opening his own bank.

He continued to meet with Jess Smith for whiskey permits and promises of immunity, paying twenty to thirty thousand dollars at a time, always in cash. With Smith's assurances he felt at ease to operate openly, even brazenly, "milking" distillery after distillery as fast as he could. He bought the Edgewood distillery in Cincinnati for $220,000, ordered his force of bottlers to get to work, and within five days removed 6,500 cases of Old Keller, 500 cases of Johnny Walker, and 250 cases of Gordon's Gin. On the morning of the fifth day, Remus's team finished, put on their coats, and never returned. From the Squibb Distillery in Lawrenceburg, Indiana, they removed 15,000 cases in two weeks; and from the Fleischmann in Cincinnati, 5,000 cases and 250 barrels (equivalent to 10,000 gallons) of rye in seven days. At the same time, liquor arrived from far-flung distilleries by the carload, the deliveries so frequent and massive that Remus's Death Valley storage space quickly began to fill.

He and Conners landed upon a solution. Beneath the floor of the barn, they dug a secret cellar with enough room to hide ten thousand cases at once, accessible through a trapdoor and concealed with hay. Slowly, using a block and tackle, they lowered and raised full barrels of whiskey through the trap. They moved the bottling machine down there for easy access. For a salary of $75 per week, men worked in shifts breaking up and burning the cases, wrapping the finished bottles in newspapers and packing them in the runners' cars.

The runners came from all over the country. Mary Hubbard, whose husband, Elijah, worked as a night watchman for Death Valley, noted the variety of license plates: Ohio, New York, Pennsylvania, Nebraska, Missouri, Michigan, Kentucky, Indiana, Illinois, California. In the early days came streams of Chevrolets and Dodges and Buicks and Studebakers, many of them used. But the runners soon upgraded to Packard Twin Six roadsters and the occasional Rolls-Royce. To avoid suspicion, they equipped their roadsters with limousine springs, which gave a car weighted down with alcohol the appearance of one merely carrying its passengers. They also brought extra supplies of gas, oil, and water to eliminate stops on the road; there were too many cautionary tales of policemen lingering at filling stations, hoping to detect the odor of whiskey or spot a pile of rifles on the floor.

To ensure that his runners remained loyal, Remus treated them as if they were on vacation, making Death Valley as hospitable as a luxury hotel. Upon their arrival, two men were dispatched to wash and polish their cars. The runners had soft cots to sleep on, and Mrs. Gehrum, Johnny's wife, took orders for home-cooked meals. When they were ready to leave, Remus personally handed them a sack of sandwiches, a thermos of milk or coffee, and a few quarts of whiskey, explaining that his runners should never have to drink their own supply on the road. For entertainment, runners were invited to join a game of craps; if they were especially good customers, Remus extended them a line of credit and allowed them to pay it off on their next visit.

From the day Death Valley opened, Remus took precautions to prevent a raid by law enforcement. All of the Cincinnati-based federal officials on his payroll had instructions to alert him should any strange agents come to town. He conducted practice drills so that, in the event of an emergency, his men would be prepared to make the entire operation disappear within moments. At his command, and with the efficiency of battle-tested marines, the men hauled all visible evidence of liquor onto trucks lining the periphery of the property and traveled, convoy-style, to a storage facility a mile away, where they were to wait until the threat passed.

One afternoon, without advance warning, two Prohibition agents arrived at Death Valley, parking next to two idling trucks loaded with whiskey. Conners, alone in the farmhouse, watched as the trucks pulled away and hurried down the long, twisty exit — but he knew he was not in the clear. Under its hay-strewn trapdoor the secret cellar was hiding five thousand cases. He strode toward the agents, aiming to appear casual and unbothered, as if they might be passing motorists who needed directions.

"What do you want?" he asked.

The men held up their badges and said they were Prohibition agents.

"There must be some mistake," Conners said. "Wait while I call up a certain federal official that you know."

He lumbered back into the farmhouse and waited for the operator to make the connection. Quickly he explained the situation and asked, "What does this mean?"

"I'm surprised they're there," the official said. "I understood they were looking for a still somewhere up the road. They haven't found anything, have they?"

"No, but if they start walking around on this hay, they'll damned quick find something, and plenty of it. What are you going to do about it?"

"I think you can handle them," the official assured him. "Go back and see what you can do with them."

Conners hung up, returned to the yard, and called one of the agents aside.

"Now listen," he said. "You fellows are working for a salary, and not a very big salary, at that. What if you did smell around here and find a couple of quarts — what would you get out of it? The fellows up above would take the credit, and you'd get nothing. You wouldn't even get a drink out of it — and you look like you need a drink, too. Why don't you be good fellows about this thing? I'll tell you what I'll do. I'll give you one thousand dollars apiece and a good drink. What do you say?"

The agent considered his offer. "It's all right with me," he said, "but I don't know about my partner. See what he says about it."

Conners nodded, sauntered over to the other agent, and repeated his spiel.

"Well, I don't like to see anybody get in trouble," the agent replied, "but duty is duty. Still, I sure would like to have a drink."

"All right," Conners said. "Come inside and let's all have a little drink. I need one myself."

Together they walked to the farmhouse and sat down. Conners poured glass after glass of whiskey and noticed that the agents' level of inebriation was directly proportional to their belief that he was a "good fellow." When they stood to leave, clutching the back of their chairs to steady themselves, Conners assembled parting gifts: $1,000 each, wrapped in paper, and six bottles of Remus's best rye. He even offered one of his employees as a chauffeur, but the agents insisted that they could drive. Conners watched the men back their car down the winding road, their headlights like eyes in the dark.

MABELMEN

Back in Washington, Willebrandt assembled a team of agents to investigate the situation in Cincinnati, a task that presented a special set of challenges. The Bureau of Investigation, the precursor to the F.B.I., employed about five hundred agents, some of whom were devoted to issues other than Prohibition: economic crimes, violations of the Mann Act (also called the "White Slave Traffic Act," it forbade transporting a person across state lines for "immoral purposes"), and monitoring the speeches and writings of suspected Communists and "alien radicals." Liquor violations were policed by the 1,500 field agents of the Prohibition Unit. Regardless of Willebrandt's feelings on the matter, they would sometimes be called "Mabelmen."

Qualifications to become a field agent were virtually nonexistent — appointees did not have to take a Civil Service exam — and recruitment centered around courthouse gadflies: ex-policemen, bailiffs, deputy sheriffs. Their average starting salary was $1,200 per year, barely a living wage in some parts of the country and a pittance in comparison to the tens of thousands of dollars bootleggers offered in bribes. The chief federal prohibition agent for Cincinnati had worked as a traffic officer before joining the unit and earned a better salary taking bribes from Remus. Another agent, in Norfolk, Virginia, aimed to open a pool hall "in the nigger part of town" in order to entrap and blackmail black bootleggers. A prospective Prohibition agent could even have a record of his own, as in the case of the pseudonymous "Stewart McMullin," the first agent to kill a bootlegger in the line of duty. When McMullin — who had been convicted of murder, falsifying checks, and armed robbery — received his agent badge, he was still doing time in New York's Dannemora State Prison. "The dominant reality," Willebrandt wrote, "is that the whole problem is one of getting the right men in places of power in enforcement — men of creative thought, of courage, those not slaves to political ambition. And by men I mean also women — lots of them." For now, with mounting pressure from Cincinnati, she had to identify and organize the best agents currently at her disposal.

Her first choice for the Cincinnati investigation was thirty-year-old Special Agent Franklin L. Dodge. In addition to sleek dark hair and a deeply cleft chin, Dodge possessed a distinguished pedigree: His father, Franklin L. Dodge Sr., was a prominent Democrat in Michigan, with connections throughout the state and federal government. He and his wife, Abby, a Lansing socialite, regularly entertained Supreme Court justices at their stately mansion on the banks of the Grand River and had once played host to perennial presidential hopeful William Jennings Bryan, soon to reach international infamy for debating Clarence Darrow on the subject of evolution.

With his father's help, Franklin Dodge Jr. got a job as deputy factory inspector for the state labor department, traveling across Michigan to assess the safety of fire escapes and the cleanliness of towels in hotel bathrooms. Only once did he shame the family's name with an arrest for speeding, an offense that merited a brief notice in the local newspaper. Despite this transgression he advanced quickly in his career, becoming a special deputy for the U.S. Marshal Service in 1917, his first federal post. In June of that year, two months after the United States declared war on Germany, Dodge conducted a census of Lansing's "alien enemies," determining that approximately seventy people of German descent lived in the community. In order to avoid arrest, each immigrant had to prepare an application signed by two American

77

citizens and accompanied by a recent photograph. Only if the U.S. Marshal approved the paperwork would the applicant be permitted to stay, and failure to comply meant certain deportation.

Now, as a special agent with the Bureau of Investigation, Dodge was considered a rising star. His most recent triumph was a successful case against a Michigan businessman nabbed for illegally profiteering in sugar. The Remus whiskey ring would be both Willebrandt's and Dodge's first foray into Prohibition. She dispatched Dodge to Cincinnati and hoped the agent would not disappoint.

On the afternoon of October 21, 1921, Remus, relaxing at home with Imogene, received a tip that a strange Prohibition agent was in town — someone from another city in another state, and not on Remus's payroll. For once, he was not alarmed by such news. The night before, a Friday, he had called Johnny Gehrum at Death Valley to ask him to put aside a few bottles of whiskey for some friends.

"There's not a drop in the place," Gehrum told him, "and none coming in before Monday."

Remus, choosing to believe him, did not pass on the warning.

After speaking to Remus, Gehrum picked up

Conners and together they drove to Louisville to bet on the horses. It was sunny, with a slight chill riding the air, and the track at Churchill Downs was "fast" — perfect conditions for a smooth race. After watching Belle of Elizabethtown, Twinkle Blue, and Colonel Taylor gallop to victory, they drove back, exhausted. Gehrum accompanied Conners home and slept on his couch.

The following morning, Conners went to church with his family, then returned home, awakened Gehrum, and suggested they ride out to Death Valley to prepare for Monday's business. They passed the guard post, unoccupied at the moment, and rambled down the incline toward the farm. At the end of the driveway an unfamiliar automobile idled in the yard, two men standing on either side of its doors. Conners cut the engine, and he and Gehrum exited the car, waiting for the intruders to speak.

"Do you want anything?" one of them asked Conners, the words slightly slurred.

"Any what?" Conners said.

"Why, any liquor."

"We aren't looking for any liquor."

The man teetered closer, one hand clutching at Conners's lapel. From those few movements and the labored contortions of his face — eyes compressing into slits, a mouth hastily slackened — Conners could tell the man was pretending to be drunk.

79

"Well, have you got any to sell?" the man asked.

"Listen," Conners said, standing still. "We're not in the liquor business, and we're not interested in it, and if you don't take your hands off me I'll give you a crack in the jaw."

The man was suddenly sober, with wide, alert eyes and crisp reflexes, peeling open his coat to reveal a government badge. "We're Prohibition officers," he announced.

Conners didn't hesitate: "Then we haven't got any business around here — we're just looking for a friend." He turned back to his car and motioned for Gehrum to follow. "Come on, Johnny, let's get out of here."

As soon as Conners spoke those words, he realized he'd committed the "biggest boner" of his life.

"Oh," one officer said, turning to Gehrum. He found a piece of paper in his pocket and unfolded it with a flourish. "So this is Johnny, is it? Johnny, we've been waiting for you. This search warrant calls for a search of your premises."

Conners pressed his foot to the gas and his old Marmon roadster jumped, he later said, "like a race horse at the barrier." He screeched out of Death Valley doing forty-five in second gear, and a glance over his shoulder restored his breathing to normal: No one was following him.

The agents shunted Gehrum between them,

80

led him to the farmhouse, and kicked open the door. Inside, several men were playing cards at a table with a bottle of Old Dearborn whiskey as a centerpiece. At the sight of the agents, George Dater, the owner of Death Valley, leapt through a window, his gut straining against the edges, his feet kicking as if he were on the last leg of a competitive swim. He made it to the other side and huffed up the hill toward the road, tossing an automatic pistol behind him. The approaching footsteps grew louder, closer. There was no use in running. Turning to face the agent, Dater raised his hands and surrendered.

Back inside the farmhouse, Mary Hubbard watched the agents creep from room to room, throwing open every door and drawer, tunneling through each dank stall in the nearby barn. She knew, contrary to what Gehrum had told Remus, that plenty of liquor was stashed on the premises — enough to send all of them to jail. She'd had enough. Her husband's $50-per-week salary was no longer worth the risk of jail time or a fatal altercation with whiskey pirates. It was time for him to tell everything.

By the time Conners reached Remus's house he was again out of breath, his mind spinning. A servant ushered Conners to the library: a dimly lit warren decorated in homage to Remus's former career, where 2,800 legal tomes weighted the bookshelves. Conners told him what had happened, emphasizing that Death Valley was being raided as they spoke.

Remus couldn't believe it. He related Gehrum's insistence that all of the liquor had been cleared out before the weekend.

It was a lie, Conners said. Gehrum was expecting some Toledo runners that very evening.

Remus went quiet and then told Conners he had something to confess: He'd been warned the previous day about a strange agent in town.

Now "madder than a hyena with a split lip," Conners told Remus he was to blame for not delivering the message. For a moment, Remus let his lieutenant rant and scream and then yanked him back to attention with a plan: They'd round up the boys and overpower the officers, locking them up in the basement until they could haul the stuff away. Without hard evidence, they'd have trouble making a case.

Conners picked up the phone and dialed every employee who was not currently under attack by the agents at Death Valley. No one answered. It was Sunday, their day off, and they were out with their wives and sweethearts, their guns left behind.

"All right, Conners," Remus said. "You and I will take it by ourselves." Quickly they gathered shotguns and automatics. As Conners started to back down the driveway, Imogene came sprinting toward the car. She opened the passenger side door, leapt on Remus's lap, and pleaded into his ear: "Don't go, Daddy! Don't go! You'll be killed! Oh, I know you'll be killed, and then what will I do?"

Conners watched as she "blubbered and pawed around" until Remus relented, calling off the surprise intervention at Death Valley.

"That's what happens when you let a skirt get mixed up in your business," Conners thought, but he knew Imogene wasn't going anywhere.

Not if Remus could help it.

Back at Death Valley, agents organized and catalogued the fruits of their search: five hundred gallons of gin, thirteen barrels of whiskey, twelve quarts of champagne, dozens of sacks containing assorted brands of whiskey, gin, and vermouth, and two thousand gallons of wine — not the usual quantity of liquor, but damning enough. They also discovered a cache of pistols, rifles, and shotguns and several record books containing information about the Circle's clients — many of them prominent Cincinnati citizens. One agent appointed himself temporary secretary of the farm and began answering the phone, fielding call after call from customers seeking whiskey for that evening's festivities. Seven showed up in person hoping to buy a few quarts, hustling away once they realized that the dry agents had taken over. The agents unloaded the seized liquor at the Post Office building downtown, where a thousand spectators clogged Walnut Street to count each barrel and sack.

Federal deputies arrested five of Remus's associates, charging them with conspiring to violate the Volstead Act: George Conners, Johnny Gehrum, Harry Brown, and two marksmen. When they descended upon the Remus Building they found the office closed and the lights darkened. They went on to the mansion in Price Hill, where Imogene answered the door. Her husband was out of town, she said, gone to Michigan on business, but she expected a long-distance telephone call from him that evening. She assured them that he would appear in court.

The officers believed her and bade her a good night.

Imogene found her husband in his library, talking with a reporter, and recounted the deputies' visit. "This is an outrage — they'll all get bounced for this," she said. "They better not come around here."

As she spoke she fingered a small pearl-handled revolver.

Three days after the raid on Death Valley, U.S. District Attorney James Clark — who'd first alerted Willebrandt to Remus's operation — sent an encrypted letter to her office: "Devout lager pontoons satyr for bowl of my commoner to go to prism and aquirmate on caterpillar pouted and badigeon qouivwlouam spearman this satyr ramulosed chimney pontoons." For translation, she passed it on to another rising star in the Bureau of Investigation, twenty-six-year-old J. Edgar Hoover.

The forces against Remus began to converge.

TESTIMONY OF
CARLOS CLAPPER

Q. Mr. Clapper, state whether or not you have ever seen Franklin Dodge Jr. and Mrs. Remus together other than the occasions you spoke of this morning?

A. I saw them on Euclid Avenue in a big Pierce Arrow one evening.

Q. Was this after the time they were caught in the room together?

A. Oh, yes.

Q. What were they doing in the car?

A. They just came out and got into the car.

Q. What place did they come from?

A. That I couldn't say. I just saw them getting into the car; in fact I stopped across the street and made sure it was him.

Q. Was it a place of business they came from or a residence?

A. It was in front of a residence along there. . . . I think it is an apartment building right at the corner.

A MAN'S HOME
IS HIS CASTLE

On October 31, ten days after the raid, Remus and Imogene drove downtown to the Custom House, an ornate Victorian building that housed twenty-seven government departments, including the federal court for the Southern District of Ohio. Undaunted by her lack of legal training, Imogene acted as attorney for her brother, Harry Brown, arguing that his arrest was a case of mistaken identity. "Your Honor," she said, "my brother is here only because he is my husband's only brother-in-law bearing the name Brown, and the newspapers stated that the 'H. A. Brown' named in the warrant with my husband is my husband's brother-in-law. He was on a hunting trip in Wisconsin when he read a Cincinnati dispatch in a newspaper, giving an account of the issuance of the warrant. . . . I do not think, in view of his action in coming here, and the probability that he is the wrong man, that you should fix such a heavy bond." As a finishing touch, she insisted that Remus met her brother for the first time only three months earlier.

Despite her plea, the judge set a $15,000 bond for Brown, $12,000 each for Gehrum and Conners, and $50,000 for Remus. Imogene offered to sign the bonds, declaring that she was the owner of a mansion on Price Hill and the grounds opposite the home and had sufficient funds to vouch for everyone. The trial was set for spring of the following year.

Remus continued operating the Circle as though the raid had never occurred. In fact his arrest was a boon to business, as loyal runners and clientele feared that their supply might dry up; what had been an $80 case of whiskey now sold for $110. Considering his history of payments to Harry Daugherty's aide Jess Smith, Remus believed that the trial would result in an easy acquittal, if it happened at all. As insurance, he met with Smith again throughout the fall, finding him at the Hotel Washington in D.C., at the Plaza in New York, and at the Claypool in Indianapolis, pressing thousand-dollar bills into his palm.

In late fall he met with Smith a second time in Indianapolis, spotting him across the domed concourse at Union Station. As Remus approached, he noticed another man clad in a dark gray suit, a cigar pinched between his fingers. Harry Daugherty was block-jawed and fleshy and possessed a remarkable pair of eyes — one brown and one blue, which wandered and focused slightly out of sync, as if controlled by two separate dials. Remus was deciding which eye to focus on, which to catch and hold for the length of a greeting, when the attorney general of the United States walked hastily away, disappearing into the crowd.

December came, bringing holiday festivities and further descent into what historian Frederick Lewis Allen called "a first-class revolt against the accepted American order." Sales ladies at Cincinnati's exclusive Pogue's Department Store grappled with a new type of corset: boneless, made of black velvet, with six elastics loosely fastened to the stockings, leaving the waistline to its natural proportion ("But I look so fat in this corset," one society matron complained. "On the contrary," the saleslady said. "All that flesh is gone from your diaphragm. It no longer makes a ridge over your shoulder blades"). A preacher was arrested and fined $600 for making bathtub gin in his boardinghouse. Essayists analyzed the phenomenon of the "flapper" and her appearance in various recent novels and plays. "She smokes, drinks, and 'damns' about as often as she feels like it," noted the *Minneapolis Tribune,* "which, take it from the authors, is pretty often."

The Remuses of Price Hill planned a

raucous celebration of their own. Renovations on the mansion, totaling $750,000, were at last complete, just in time for a New Year's Eve bash that would be the highlight of the season. "A man's home is his castle, you know," Remus mused. "I really got a castle, haven't I?" The finished house contained thirty-one rooms, each a reflection of their taste, which they'd cultivated together.

The walls in the card room offered a tableau of poker hands, aces in every suit. The pool table in the billiard room stood on carved claw feet the size and heft of Remus's head. Plush leather seats lined the periphery, each one affixed by hinges to the floor. The mahogany doors connecting each room featured windows of exquisitely etched glass. Marble figures of cherubs and warriors and goddesses posed atop every fireplace mantel. Chandeliers splayed across the ceilings like customized constellations. A solid gold piano illuminated the parlor. Oil paintings imported from Europe followed the ascent of each staircase. Persian rugs cushioned every step. Bookshelves displayed a collection of rare *objets d'art,* first editions, and his prized possession: an authentic signature of George Washington's, worth more than $50,000.

Outside, five full-time gardeners shaped and tamed ten acres of holly and flax and sweetbriar and trees that would bloom with fat lemons and limes. Remus's four dogs —

one the brother of President Harding's Airedale terrier, "Laddie Boy" — romped and rolled and chased. A baseball field beckoned the neighborhood kids; Remus planned to play with them, something his own father had been unable and unwilling to do.

Then there was Remus's *pièce de résistance,* which he was certain would impress any guest, regardless of class or position: the Greco-Roman swimming pool, built and perfected for $175,000, to be revealed at the stroke of midnight. The pool had its own heating plant and was housed in a separate backyard building, 115 feet long and 86 feet wide, with a facade of brick and stone perfectly matching the mansion. Scalloped silver sconces gleamed from the white ceiling and walls. At one end stood a variety of Turkish and Swedish needle baths, a style and pressure for every taste, and even electric baths — an early version of a tanning bed, heated by incandescent electric lights and said to make the user "frisky." Around the pool were scattered tables, benches, and chairs of carved marble and statues depicting ancient Greek swimmers. Rookwood tile patterned in terra-cotta circles and pearl-hued squares lined the pool floor. The entire spectacle was wreathed by a Roman garden, with precisely carved topiary and riotous bursts of flowers. He planned to christen the pool "the Imogene Baths" in honor of his wife.

She was "a snappy woman," Remus said, "who wore her clothes and jewels well." He longed to be a social leader, and Imogene knew how to "turn the trick," as he put it. One of his friends appraised her thusly: "The kind of woman that made you think of Turkish harems, oriental dances and Cleopatra. . . . Her long, frizzed brown hair always seemed to be falling about her dusky, olive-tinted face. Long earrings hung free from beneath the folds of her hair. Heavy eyelashes dropped low over her large brown eyes. Her every glance seemed a caress. Although she was voluptuous to the point of stoutness, there was something feline in her every movement."

Imogene was eager to assume the role of hostess, to shake hands with accomplished people, to eavesdrop on conversations about foreign worlds. Her old life, pre-Remus, was spent fighting with her ex-husband, haggling over his carousing and empty wallet. Now, at thirty-seven, she was young in a way she'd never been — a "middle-aged flapper," as the papers called her type: "Not life but movement is what she seeks. It is she who does over the old house or builds a new one — where her husband is deposited while she goes out in search of 'culture.' " She was ready to seek, and to act upon whatever she found.

She oversaw the design of the invitations.

Printed on tea-colored paper tied with red ribbon, they featured boughs of holly around the edges and photographs of her and Remus in profile, captioned "Mrs. Geo. E. Remus" and "Mr. Geo. E. Remus." At the bottom was a cartoon etching of a mother swimming with her baby and the words:

OUR NEW YEARS GREETING
Dive to health
Swim to wealth
Float on happiness
1921–22

Six maids addressed and mailed the invitations to journalists, politicians, judges, captains of industry, and Cincinnati's social elite — family names that were internationally famous: the Longworths, the Sintons, the Tafts. It was a complicated city, one forever escalating the battle against its own inferiority complex; it might not be Boston or New York, but its leading citizens traveled throughout Europe, sent their sons to Harvard and Yale, gave their daughters proper debuts, and married Roosevelts (Alice Roosevelt Longworth, the scandalous eldest daughter of Theodore Roosevelt, dubbed her husband's hometown "Cin-cin-nasty"). It built literary societies, curated art exhibitions, and established music salons. In its quest for respectability it erred on the side of dullness; such flashy extravagance as Remus planned would be commonplace in New York or Chicago, but not here. He would show them what they were missing, and they would welcome him in turn.

On December 31, 1921, the guests began to come, more than one hundred in all, some from as far as San Francisco, the women in metallic fabric and tiers of polished pearls, the men in "Jazz suits," cut thin and pinched at the waist, a trend that would soon become passé. The honeyed notes of a string orchestra whispered across the rooms. Orchids perfumed the air. Servers looped through chattering couples, offering Remus's best whiskey and champagne and gin and vodka and beer, delicacies he would never taste. Models attired in Grecian gowns and towering turbans served *hors d'oeuvres* from silver platters. A representative from the *Cincinnati Times-Star* circled the party with his Aeroscope movie camera, capturing the revelry on film. Remus pulled one guest aside to gossip about Attorney General Harry Daugherty. "He's in a side room," Remus claimed, "and doesn't want to be seen." When Imogene passed by he drew her close, running his thick fingers along her hair. "And I've got Imogene," he boasted, "the truest and squarest and prettiest wife a man ever had." In a gesture emblematic of the times, one that would be remembered with awe decades later, Remus lit guests' cigars with $100 bills.

Remus yanked on a tapestry bell pull, signaling everyone to take a seat at the dining table. One guest found a $1,000 bill tucked beneath his plate, waved it in the air, and lo and behold, the same party favor had been planted for each reveler. But Remus wasn't finished. The Grecian goddesses distributed jewelry boxes, each holding two gifts: a stickpin topped by a knob of diamonds and a gold watch engraved with the letter "R" and the words: "From Mr. and Mrs. Geo. Remus, 1921" — trinkets that thrilled the men and disappointed the women. After a beat, Remus delivered the final surprise: sets of keys. He led his guests to the front door and swung it open. Down the long driveway, past the stone lions and iron gates and around the bend of the avenue, was a chain of brand-new 1922 sedans, one for each lady at the party.

It was time, now, for the evening's highlight. "Swimming is my hobby," Remus told his guests, leading them all to the pool house. "I have dreamed of having my own pool since I was a boy."

There were rumors Remus might fill the pool with whiskey, but tonight it held only water, warm to the touch. His dogs lounged poolside. Gus Schmidt's Band played "The Sheik of Araby," the most popular song of the year:

Well I'm the Sheik of Araby
Your love belongs to me
Well at night when you're asleep
Into your tent I'll creep. . . .

Aquatic nymphs performed synchronized routines underwater, their toes rising and disappearing in unison. Guests used the diving board as a rostrum, making drunken toasts to the New Year. At the stroke of midnight, young Ruth Remus, dressed in a diaphanous gown as the "spirit of the new year," ascended the diving board. "A Happy New Year!" she called before plunging in. Not to be outdone, Imogene, clad in a daring one-piece suit, removed the diamonds, rubies, and emeralds from her hair to perform a graceful dive. "Take a swim," Remus urged the band, and they obliged, soaking their suits and new diamond pins. Remus followed, wearing his tuxedo, his first swim in his own pool. He announced his intention to swim a race along the Ohio River, a hundred miles from the suspension bridge to Madison, Indiana — would anyone like to make a wager?

After he toweled off, he strolled around the pool house, bidding goodnight to each guest. No sign of Cincinnati society, the Longworths and Sintons and Tafts. His world would never align with theirs, no matter how extravagant his home or gifts, how careful his plans, how urgent his wish.

He retreated back to the mansion. From the pool house drifted the sounds of laughter and clinking glasses and the final notes of songs. For Remus, the party was over. He retired to his library, where he sat down with a biography of Abraham Lincoln. A maid fixed him a plate of cold boiled ham — his customary post-swim snack — and a bowl of ice cream. He closed the door and settled into the quiet, spending the rest of the night alone.

TEAR THE HEART OUT OF WASHINGTON

When Willebrandt returned to her office after the holidays, a letter from a Cincinnati resident named William Harrison, addressed to Attorney General Daugherty, waited on her desk. "It is inconceivable," it read, "that you are not fully advised of the operations of the 'Whiskey Kingpin' of Cincinnati, and particularly of the head of that conspiracy against law and order, one Remus, who, notwithstanding his recent indictment and the restraint of a $50,000 bond, is now flagrantly, notoriously and fearlessly violating the very law under which he was indicted and boasts that he is protected by men holding high office positions. I am advised that the wife of this same Remus declares that your own office is not without taint."

Furthermore, the letter continued, all of Cincinnati was well aware that Remus spends lavishly on "riotous living," owns no fewer than forty automobiles, and dispenses enough liquor from his drug companies to "meet the prescriptions of physicians of the whole central United States." Is the attorney general unconcerned that the public holds his office in "utter contempt" and refuses to believe in the sincerity of elected officials? Perhaps he should get in touch with the Revenue Department and ascertain the amount Remus is paying in taxes? Honestly, doesn't the attorney general think it's "about time to get busy?"

"Finally," Harrison concluded, "let me say that I, as a law-abiding citizen, feel unutterable disgust in viewing the present non-enforcement of Prohibition laws. Liquor is flowing freely everywhere; but when pupils in the public schools of Cincinnati of the higher grades are known to carry liquor on their hips — in the name of God, where is this thing to stop?"

The letter was timely, as Willebrandt expected to receive a memo soon from Franklin Dodge and other dry agents in Cincinnati. Remus's trial was fast approaching and she had a tremendous amount of work to do, including preparing indictments against seven additional co-conspirators and requesting Remus's tax returns for 1920 and 1921. Rolling a piece of paper into her typewriter, she tapped out a quick reply, telling Harrison that his letter had been referred to her office. "Appreciation is extended by this Department," she wrote, "for your stand for law enforcement and for the clear statements made in your letter, [which] will be the subject of further consideration." She signed off: "Respectfully, Mabel Walker Willebrandt, Assistant Attorney General."

Within three weeks, her agents sent her an update about the investigation. Numerous Remus customers and employees had signed affidavits about purchasing the bootlegger's liquor or following his orders. Contrary to Imogene's declaration in court, her brother Harry Brown figured prominently in the operation and even served as the president of the Squibbs Distillery in Indiana. Over the course of two months, 180,000 cases of liquor, accessed with medicinal permits, were shipped from Squibbs to recipients who turned out not to exist — proof that Remus was, in fact, shipping all of his "curative" whiskey to himself.

One line in the report gave Willebrandt pause: Informant Elijah Hubbard, a night watchman for Death Valley, "appears recently to have deceased." Agent Dodge had spoken to Hubbard's wife, Mary. Although a coroner listed chronic encephalitis as the official cause of death, Mary believed that her husband had been poisoned to prevent him from testifying at trial. He was killed, she told Dodge, for "knowing too much."

Willebrandt decided to visit Cincinnati herself, buying a ticket on the Baltimore &

Ohio railroad. There, she personally escorted Mary Hubbard — dubbed "Old Mother Hubbard" by the press — to testify before a federal grand jury. During the proceedings Willebrandt barely left her side. "She seemed to me," Hubbard said, "to be more interested in the case than any of the others." Rumors abounded that Hubbard would be kidnapped during the trial; if that was indeed Remus's plan, he'd have to abduct Willebrandt, too.

On April 15, on the strength of Hubbard's testimony, the grand jury returned nine indictments against Remus and his co-defendants. In addition to felony charges for violating Prohibition laws and Internal Revenue statutes, Remus was accused of a misdemeanor: maintaining a "nuisance" at Death Valley Farm, a violation of Title II of the Volstead Act. The trial would begin on May 8 in U.S. District Court in Cincinnati, with Hubbard as the government's star witness. Willebrandt left her witness in Dodge's capable hands and told him to keep an eye on Remus.

Day and night, Dodge parked his sedan at the corner of 8th Street and Hermosa Avenue, watching the bootlegger and his wife come and go.

Every time Remus peered from his window or stepped out his door the agent was there, silent and unmoving. If Remus grew unnerved by the surveillance he kept that sentiment to himself. Instead he boasted that he had "everyone and his brother" in Washington on his payroll. The upcoming trial was "water under the dam" and would "take care of itself." All of the government's purported evidence would be "red-penciled." He made a threat: If he was "crowded too far," he would not hesitate to "tear the heart out of Washington."

And still the agent spied on him, recording every movement.

On the morning of May 8, Remus and Imogene's driver chauffeured them downtown to the federal building. Remus's hands were freshly manicured, soft-skinned and pink-nailed. His thin wreath of hair was trimmed and combed. He was not worried about the prosecution's case, about evidence they'd uncovered, about what Mary Hubbard might say on the stand. He believed Jess Smith's assurances that his money had bought a fast and easy acquittal.

Imogene sat close to him, her dark hair rising from her head in a cumulous cloud of curls. She would be an asset, as she had been in the past. Their first joint court appearance was in 1915, in their early days of dating, after Remus assaulted the plumber who claimed to have found Ruth's watch. Throughout the testimony Imogene had sat in the front row, her face rapt as Remus spoke. Every few moments she shifted her legs, raising and lowering a foot — treating the crowd, according to one reporter, to "a ravishing vision of a silken-clad ankle" that prompted several jurors to wish aloud for brighter lighting in the courtroom.

Emerging from the touring car, Remus and Imogene were greeted by a blaze of flashbulbs and shouted questions. Reporters and curious spectators filled every seat in the courtroom. Imogene carved a space for herself and settled her gaze on her husband. At the government's behest, Judge John Peck had ordered the jury to be sequestered throughout the trial so as to avoid exposure to news, gossip, and bribes. The twelve men who would decide Remus's fate were a diverse group, among them a real estate agent, an accountant, a jeweler, a farmer, a grocer, a druggist, a hardware dealer, and — perhaps fortuitously for Remus — a retired police lieutenant, who likely had comrades on the take.

With a crash of the gavel, it began.

Hoping to set the tone, Remus's team fired an opening salvo, requesting that the government return all of the whiskey and weapons seized at Death Valley Farm.

Overruled.

The government took its turn. Assistant U.S. District Attorney Richard Dickerson outlined what the prosecution aimed to prove: that George Remus (referred to as the "big gentleman") was the "leading spirit" in a bootlegging enterprise; that bootleggers arrived at Death Valley in the middle of the night, loaded up on liquor, and disappeared; and that records found at the farm showed that sums were paid to "G.R." and "Mrs. G.R.," meaning George and Mrs. Remus, with identical sums being deposited on the same days at the Lincoln National Bank.

Spectators swiveled for a glimpse of Imogene.

Mary Hubbard entered the courtroom on the arms of Willebrandt's Mabelmen and proceeded to divulge details she'd learned from her deceased husband. She explained his duties at Death Valley, described the cars that arrived from across the country, named the labels on the cases of whiskey. She walked along the line of defendants and identified familiar faces. She lingered on Harry Brown in particular, recalling that Imogene's brother "was there but didn't do any hard work."

The defense took aim on cross-examination. Remus's legal counsel confirmed that she had been granted immunity in exchange for her testimony and attacked her credibility, wondering how she'd seen certain brands of whiskey that had not been manufactured in twenty-five years. Remus got a break when Judge Peck ruled that the search warrant employed during the Death Valley raid was in fact invalid; Johnny Gehrum's name had been misspelled as "Gerum" and corrected on the spot, rendering it defective. He told the jury that all testimony and evidence based on that raid was now inadmissible and that they must erase it from their minds.

The prosecution rested. Spectators whispered hopeful predictions: Would George Remus testify now? Would he testify at all?

He didn't — what would be the point? Jess Smith had repeatedly assured him there would be no conviction. His lawyers called only four witnesses, whose testimony was deemed so insignificant by the prosecution that it declined to cross-examine. District Attorney Dickerson did, however, spend three hours on his closing argument, concluding with a begrudging compliment: "Whatever else we think of these defendants, we cannot help admiring their audacity and resourcefulness."

The defense played its final card, asking Judge Peck to dismiss the six counts against Remus charged by the Internal Revenue Service for failure to pay income taxes. He agreed, sustaining the motion.

Remus was relieved; he had beaten half of the government's case before deliberations even began.

■ ■ ■ ■

At 8 P.M. on May 16, Judge Peck sent the jury to deliberate, and within two hours they reached a decision. Owing to the late hour only a small crowd remained. Remus and his co-defendants sat in silence as the foreman handed the sealed verdict to the district clerk. He tore the envelope open.

"George Remus — guilty," he said, and paused. One by one he read the other names, each followed by the word "guilty." When he finished the list, Judge Peck asked the defendants to step forward.

"George Remus, have you anything to say?" he asked.

In that moment Remus did not feel like himself, and consequently he failed to act like himself. He did not unfurl a long soliloquy of esoteric words, or shout or weep or tear at his hair, or refer to himself in the third person. Instead he swallowed, and in a voice so thick it barely escaped his throat, he whispered, "I have nothing."

Judge Peck gave him the maximum penalty: two years at the federal penitentiary in Atlanta and a $10,000 fine. For the misdemeanor charge of maintaining a "nuisance" at Death Valley, he received an additional year in the Miami County Jail in Troy, Ohio. His codefendants received varying sentences: a year to eighteen months in Atlanta and fines ranging from $1,000 to $5,000. "The very air seemed a little dryer after the jury announced its verdict," said one observer. "The way of the transgressor is hard, but the way of a thirsty citizen is harder."

Back in Washington, Willebrandt received a telegram from Dickerson's co-counsel, Thomas Morrow, conveying the good news. She sent her own in response: "Congratulations on the splendid manner you and Mr. Dickerson have handled this case. It is a real triumph and occasions intense satisfaction to this Department."

At the same time, she was incensed that Judge Peck had dismissed the charges against Remus for violating Internal Revenue statutes by failing to pay income tax. She composed a separate letter to Morrow, asking him to prepare the paperwork for an appeal and send it to Washington as soon as possible. She hoped to argue her case against Remus before the highest court in the land.

One hour after Remus received his sentence, Imogene, wearing a bold red dress, arrived at the clerk's office to sign the bonds for her husband and his co-defendants. They would all be free until their sentences began, but Remus had no intention of going to prison at all. His mind spun a web of plans. He ordered his lawyers to start work on his own appeal, which he, too, was prepared to take to the Supreme Court. With that underway, he contacted Jess Smith and arranged for an immediate meeting in Washington. Smith had promised that there would be no conviction. Now that he'd been convicted, Remus wanted Smith to deliver on his second promise — that the bootlegger would never spend a day behind bars.

They met again at the Hotel Washington. Smith was waiting for him, dressed in a double-breasted lounge suit accented with a leather money belt. Remus, feeling "not a bit of sentiment" toward Smith, wasted no time on pleasantries.

"The conviction is there," Remus said. "We are likely to go if the Court of Appeals don't reverse the case. What assistance can you give?"

"It doesn't make any difference if the Court of Appeals affirms it," Smith replied. "I'll get you out of it."

Remus remained skeptical. His approach to the trial had been informed by his belief that he would be acquitted, and he wanted Smith to understand the damage that had already been done. "Not one of the boys would have taken the witness stand in the case of U.S. versus Remus," he explained. "I was absolutely sure there would be no conviction. If I had taken the witness stand in my case, I could have thrown out at least eight or nine of the boys that now stand convicted on the theory that the chauffeurs or the office boy that would deposit the money in the banks knew nothing in reference to the criminal effect . . . under those circumstances those men would absolutely have been found not guilty by the jury."

Smith repeated his position. "The court of appeals will undoubtedly reverse the decision of the lower court."

"How do you know that?" Remus pressed.

"On account of my friendship with the general."

Remus considered this. He knew there was talk, both in Washington and in Ohio, that Attorney General Harry Daugherty was a partner in the Circle. To counteract those rumors, Daugherty had to allow Willebrandt and the federal prosecutors in Cincinnati to pursue his case. It made sense that Daugherty would be freer to manipulate the system after a very public trial, calling in favors, making subtle overtures to certain judges, discreetly exercising the power of his office.

Smith waited. An unspoken demand floated between them: This would cost money — more money than the nearly $300,000 Remus had already paid. Remus opened his wallet and counted off twenty $1,000 bills, tucking the wad into Smith's waiting hand.

Remus returned to his hotel suite, worrying that it wasn't enough. It was possible that enough did not exist.

After leaving Remus, Smith walked several blocks north and west, stopping at the Little Green House on K Street. There he met Gaston Means, his partner in collecting graft payments. Formerly a private detective and at present a special agent with the Bureau of Investigation, Means was a controversial figure, a confidence man whose list of transgressions included a murder indictment and accusations of fabricating elaborate plots involving German spies. Still, his murky history did not trouble the current director of the Bureau, William J. Burns, who believed it only enhanced his skills as a sleuth and, when necessary, extortionist.

Means and Smith had developed a system: Means worked mostly behind the scenes, gathering federal files on bootleggers and figuring out whom to shake down for withdrawal permits and protection payments. He then shared this knowledge with Smith, so that the latter could prepare to meet the bootleggers in person, using his connection to Attorney General Daugherty to enhance his credibility. Occasionally Means collected graft payments directly from bootleggers, but only after Smith had made the requisite arrangements.

Means had just returned from one such trip to New York. At the Vanderbilt Hotel in midtown Manhattan, the agent always occupied the same room, number 518. On the table in the center of the room sat a large glass fishbowl, green with currency. Means then adjourned to the adjacent room, 517, and peered into 518 through a peephole he'd drilled. In addition to studying bootleggers' files, Means employed twenty-five "tipsters of the underworld" to deliver reports of profits so he could calculate the appropriate graft. At the appointed hour, bootleggers entered the empty hotel room, approached the fishbowl, and deposited a predetermined amount of money, a sum that in total averaged $60,000 per day.

Back in Washington, Means logged each contribution in his notebook and turned the money over to Smith, who combined it with his own payments from Remus. Smith took a cut for himself, another cut for Prohibition Commissioner Roy Haynes, and went home to the suite he shared with Attorney General Daugherty.

Means also viewed Remus's conviction as an opportunity, a chance to collect graft directly from the biggest bootlegger in the country — without having to share the profits with Smith. He invited Remus to his home. They had met a few times before, always with Smith present, but Means had never seen the bootlegger in such a state: "almost a nervous wreck," crimson-faced and swinging his arms

111

with the urgency of a matador.

Means gave his pitch, arguing that Smith had failed to prevent the conviction and that he himself was best suited to fix Remus's case on appeal. The cost: a modest one-time payment of $125,000. One quarter would go to the Bureau's director, one quarter to Daugherty, one quarter to Supreme Court Chief Justice William Howard Taft, and one quarter to Means himself.

Remus considered the offer. While the director and attorney general might partake in such a scheme, he was certain that Chief Justice Taft would not. If Means did approach Taft, it might only exacerbate his legal concerns. The more likely scenario was that Means planned to tell no one of this deal and pocket all of the money for himself. At this juncture, Remus had no choice but to trust in Jess Smith.

He declined and took the next train back to Cincinnati, eager to get home to Imogene. As he approached the mansion's iron gates, Remus realized that his conviction had had one clear benefit: The Prohibition agent was no longer parked outside his home, watching and waiting.

For now he was out of Remus's mind.

TESTIMONY OF
EMANUEL KESSLER

Q. I will ask you if you ever saw Franklin L. Dodge in New York?

A. I did see him in New York.

Q. Now where did you see Franklin Dodge in New York?

A. He came to my office at 1841 Broadway in New York and told me that he had some whiskey certificates for sale. And I said, "Those are Remus's certificates." And he said, "Yes, I want to sell them; I have got about two hundred thousand dollars' worth."

Q. Did he deny that they were Remus's certificates?

A. He did not.

A Terrible, Terrible Scream

All Remus could do that summer was wait for his lawyers to prepare his appeal. Imogene did her best to distract him, suggesting a trip to Chicago. He agreed, and she, Remus, and Ruth each packed a valise. They took off in a touring car, with their driver at the wheel. Ruth sat shotgun, and Remus climbed with Imogene into the back.

The drive was unsettling. Heat and tension clouded the car. It seemed they crossed a railroad track every few minutes, which made Imogene nervous. She did not like the bumping and jostling or the possibility, no matter how slim, that a train might careen suddenly around the bend, ending their lives in an instant. She asked the driver to slow down and then asked again — pleading now, palms pressed to her cheeks. Remus grew impatient. He did not want to hear another word of complaint. She'd managed to magnify his troubles instead of pushing them away. He said things to Imogene that were "not very

114

nice," Ruth later recalled, and their bickering continued until Remus tapped the driver's shoulder.

"Stop the car," he ordered and uttered curse words that Ruth would not repeat. He turned to Imogene. "Get out," he said, giving her a hard shove. She obeyed. Remus followed and strode to the other side of the car, taking the driver's seat. The driver moved over to shotgun, forcing Ruth from her seat.

Remus screeched off a short way down the road, leaving his wife and stepdaughter behind. The car hurtled along so fast he lost control, until he thrust his feet against the brake, stripping the gears. The car whined into submission. He allowed Imogene and Ruth to approach. He joined Imogene in the back seat and motioned for Ruth to return to the front. The driver took off again, moving slowly this time, and they headed west in silence.

Ruth would catalogue other disturbing memories from that summer. One evening the family was playing cards, and Remus lost the game. He upended the table, spraying the cards across the floor.

Imogene gasped. "Why, George, aren't you ashamed of yourself?"

At that, Remus reached for the first weapon he saw: a five-pound box of Sinton candy set on a table nearby. He hurled the box straight at Imogene, who ducked her head just in time.

Soon after this incident, Remus pulled Imogene aside for a talk. He told her that he wanted to be the official owner of their home, to alter the deed to include his name.

She refused. It was her wedding gift, and belonged to her.

From her room Ruth heard "a terrible, terrible scream," and she ran toward the sound. Remus passed her in the hall without acknowledgment. She would recall finding her mother on the bed, a thin ribbon of blood snaking from her nose.

They reconciled, as they always did.

Some days, Remus was able to tamp down his furious energy and escape from his darkening thoughts. One late-summer afternoon, he came home to find two neighborhood boys standing in the middle of his driveway, gazing at the mansion in awe. They were around the age he'd been when he left school to work in the pharmacy, and he was struck by a desire to talk to them.

He blasted the horn of his sedan and watched the boys jump at the noise. "I'm sorry for scaring you," he said, and suggested they cool off in his pool; they should swim in their underwear and lie in the sun until they were dry. "It was more an order than an invitation," one of the boys later recalled, and they did as they were told.

After an hour Remus fetched them and led them to the house. The walk down a long, narrow hallway to the living room was like wandering into a dream: walls covered in red tapestries and gilded flecks; an army of statues, stark white and life-sized; and a gold piano so bright they averted their eyes. "When my friend and I crossed to the fireplace where Remus was standing," the boy remembered, "I felt as though I were walking through several inches of snow."

Remus tugged on a bell and told the boys to follow him into the dining room, where they sat at a mahogany table the size of a submarine — Remus at the head and a boy on either side. A servant appeared with a platter of turkey sandwiches and a shiny, silver pitcher of milk, which the boys drank from delicate goblets etched with a pattern of flowers and vines. They had hoped for tales of boot-legging and gunmen, but instead Remus lectured them on the intellectual and monetary benefits of a rigorous education. He himself had studied science and medicine and law, and now the grandeur and beauty of his life far exceeded anything he'd dared to imagine when he was their age. "Remus was a poor boy," he told them. "Remus has always been a good student." If they worked hard and applied themselves, he advised, they could be just like him when they grew up.

■ ■ ■

On October 6, 1922, Remus was disbarred by the Illinois Supreme Court on account of his felony conviction. His life had become a feast of indignities, and surely his old colleagues — including Clarence Darrow, with whom he'd partnered on a few cases — took notice of every one. Remus did not believe his punishment was just, because Prohibition was an unjust law. And he broke that law more scrupulously than most; "Remus sold good liquor," as he always said. He disdained those who muddled clean, pure whiskey until it was undrinkable at best and deadly at worst, cutting their supply with sugar or water or wood alcohol, not giving a care if the customer went blind or paralyzed or died or lost his mind. He'd been as skilled a lawyer as he was a bootlegger, and now that piece of his identity had been hacked away for no reason at all.

He waited for a situation to arise that would allow him to corral and aim his rage. Four days after his disbarment, he got it.

He had been in Kentucky on business, and when he returned home in the middle of the night he was surprised to discover that Imogene was not there. A servant told him that she and some friends had accompanied a salesman, one Naseem Shammas, to Indianapolis and would not return until morning.

Remus had heard enough of Shammas to deem him a crook with a bad reputation, someone who peddled shoddy rugs and draperies and cars and whatever else he could convince people to buy. Remus had forbidden Imogene to associate with him, and he was furious at her insolence. He knew exactly where he'd find her: the Claypool Hotel, their favorite in that city. He returned to his touring car and ordered his driver to speed westward. He brought with him a "loaded" cane that was weighted with lead at one end, a gentleman's accessory that could double as a weapon.

When he arrived at the hotel it was four in the morning. Wide awake, bulging with adrenaline, he asked the clerk for Imogene's room number and the room number for Shammas. One small mercy: Imogene was on the fifth floor, her salesman friend on the seventh.

He rode the elevator with the cane clutched tightly in his hand.

Shammas was roused from sleep by a rapping on his door — muffled, at first, but with each successive round growing louder and more violent, a sun shower evolving into a thunderstorm. He forced himself out of bed and cracked open the door. He saw a strange man holding a cane across his chest.

"What do you mean by taking my wife?"

119

the man asked. In the light of the hallway his blue eyes shone like lapis, wide and wild.

"What do you mean?" Shammas replied.

The man wedged a foot against the door so that Shammas couldn't slam it shut.

"What do you mean by taking a married woman up to Indianapolis?" the man asked, tilting the cane forward.

"Well, we have some business matters."

"You know that isn't the manly thing to do."

"Well, I meant no wrong by it," Shammas said, belatedly realizing that his words were only intensifying the man's fury.

"Well, you have no business to," the man said, uprooting his foot and stepping fully into the room. He raised the cane over his head as if it were a sword and lowered it with savage force upon Shammas's skull.

Remus watched Shammas's legs fold in on themselves, like an accordion. His torso flattened to the floor. Remus struck him again. The man groaned, his body flattened and splayed. Remus surveyed the victim at his feet, the tip of the cane slick with blood.

TESTIMONY OF
EMMETT KIRGIN

Q. You talked to Mrs. Remus?

A. We were down to Ragland, Dixon & Williams' office and Mrs. Remus was sitting in the waiting room and I came in and she came over and shook hands with me. I met the lady once before. . . . She said, "I am afraid of this man, I am afraid he is going to kill me. He is so insanely jealous, if he walked in here now and seen me talking to you he would be liable to shoot both of us."

A MIDDLE FINGER OF UNUSUAL PROMINENCE

On the morning of November 29, 1922, preparing for an appearance before the United States Supreme Court, Willebrandt stood at her closet and contemplated what to wear. If she had her way, she wouldn't spend more than a moment thinking about fashion. But from her first day on the job, the press focused on the cut of her dress, the style of her hair, the height of her heels, and the merits of her figure, as though such scrutiny might yield powerful insights about the mercurial state of womanhood in America.

Her eyes were "wide, earnest, truthful [and] brown," according to the *New York Times,* while other publications thought them blue or gray. Her "invariable costume during the day is a strictly tailored suit, worn with a simple and immaculate blouse." Yet at home she preferred "dainty and exquisite dresses, soft drapes, with a flower, at waist or shoulder." She was "essentially feminine," although "she dislikes to think so." She wasn't "exactly pretty," as her features were "too large and too serious for that." Rather, her face was "intelligent." She was "medium-sized" but suffered from "a suggestion of plumpness." At a gala for the Women's Bar Association, she made a "beautiful picture" in "a black spangled gown." At the end of the evening, as attendees lined up to shake her hand, she experienced an infuriating encounter:

a little man came rushing up to the front of the table. His head just came to the top of it, since I was standing on the platform. He reached his hand up and said, "I do want to shake hands with you because I mustn't leave without telling you that you have the most beautiful eyes I have ever seen in a human head. They are perfectly wonderful."

I guess about that time my eyes were expressing a few things at him because he quickly exclaimed, "Oh, don't misjudge me. I'm an old man with four daughters of my own, and am president of the Brooklyn Bar Association of 1,100 members, but I have never seen such remarkable eyes as yours."

I was a little surly, I guess, because I said very promptly, "I wish my eyes would do the talking in these after dinner speeches, I'm not very strong for doing it myself."

Willebrandt hated this "girlie girlie stuff," as she called it, and privately griped to her parents: "Why the devil they have to put that 'girlie girlie' tea party description every time they tell anything a professional woman does, is more than I can see." At the same time, she felt compelled to play along, trying, at least in public, to strike a balance: not too masculine or too feminine; too aggressive or too demure; too indifferent or too emotional; too much or too little of any quality that would highlight her sex instead of her work. "I try not to think of myself as a woman in going before a jury," she told the Washington *Evening Star.* "By this I do not mean that women should be mannish but that they must forget about themselves."

She had "forgotten herself" on many occasions since her appointment, most memorably at a dinner held at the home of Solicitor General James Beck. She had accepted the invitation despite disagreeing with Beck's politics; he was "one of those militant anti-Suffragettes" and "anti-everything that is so progressive." Upon her arrival, she saw twelve colleagues from the Department of Justice but not one of their wives; she was the only woman in the room. "It was a stag party," she realized, "and I was the only doe." Beck had likely invited her out of obligation — and expected her to decline.

She tried to forget herself once again that November morning as she sifted through her wardrobe, selecting her usual tailored suit and loose blouse, and arranged her hair over her hearing aid, which lately had not been much help. Her worsening condition, too, was a prime topic in letters to her parents. "The dread shadow of deafness all but submerges me," she wrote. "For Mama and Papa, dear, when from every quarter and indirectly . . . I hear the most extravagant marvelings at my capacities over the way I handle myself before the court, and when presiding over trying conferences, that surge of bitterness rises even at their praise when I think, 'Damn you, you think that's <u>good</u>, do you know what then I could do if I weren't struggling under the most horrible handicap that you do not guess.' "

She tried to forget herself as she took a taxi from her new apartment on 16th Street to the Capitol Building on First, and as she entered the Old Senate Chamber, with its domed ceiling and tufted leather chairs and gilded eagle ornament, and as she argued before the Supreme Court that George Remus had carried on the business of a liquor dealer without having paid the tax required by law. She insisted that the penalties outlined in revived statutes of internal revenue laws were "highly important in the enforcement of the Prohibition act." She explained that the government, by seeking income taxes from bootleggers, was not "giving its stamp of approval to an illicit business." An unlawful

125

business should not be exempt from paying the taxes that, if legitimate, it would have to pay.

A month later the Court issued its ruling, delivered by Justice Oliver Wendell Holmes. Certain revenue statutes passed before Prohibition had been revived on November 23, 1921. Offenses falling under these statutes, however, could not be prosecuted if committed between the onset of Prohibition and that date. The raid on Death Valley farm and the arrest of George Remus occurred in October 1921; therefore, he was exempt from prosecution for failing to pay income tax. Willebrandt had missed her chance with Remus by a month.

She took solace in the larger victory: The Court agreed with her argument that bootleggers should be taxed. In a letter to her parents, she confessed her admiration for Holmes — "whom I love dearly, from afar" — and her legal triumph. "Since everyone was convinced I couldn't win on that point," she wrote, "it is regarded as a great victory and congratulations have been pouring in."

As for Remus, she planned to do everything in her considerable power to make sure that he went to jail.

In the meantime, she turned her attention to a Southern bootlegging syndicate called the Savannah Four. Its leader, Willie Harr —

known as the "Admiral of the Bootleggers" — owned a fleet of ships that transported liquor from Scotland, France, and Nassau and delivered it for storage inside man-made cement caves along the American coast. There, Harr's employees crated the whiskey, labeled it "fruit" or "potatoes," and loaded it on trucks, trains, and automobiles bound for destinations across the country. Local dry agents in each city were paid to ignore the shipments. So protected and convinced of their invincibility were the Savannah Four, they even dubbed their recreational baseball lineup the "Bootlegger Team."

Willebrandt feared that breaking up this operation would be difficult, given her belief that the U.S. Attorney's Office in Savannah was "worse than useless" and the local Prohibition director "absolutely crooked." Commissioner Roy Haynes had sent his men from the Prohibition Unit, all of whom had either been bought off or made as government officials. "After a few days in the city," she observed, "the bootleggers always warned the agents: 'You had better get out, boys, we know you are Prohibition men.'"

Certain that she could do better, Willebrandt dispatched a team of fifteen Bureau of Investigation agents to work undercover, posing as fellow bootleggers or potential clients. She recalled Franklin Dodge's excellent work in the Remus case, including his

around-the-clock surveillance of the bootlegger's home, and requested that the agent
personally send progress reports to her office. Dodge would be operating under a
pseudonym, F. L. Daly. Willebrandt also had
a nickname for Dodge: her "ace of investigators."

While Willebrandt had complete faith in
Dodge, she harbored a growing concern
about her boss, Harry Daugherty. Recently
the attorney general had faced an onslaught
of accusations from his political rivals: He
was failing to enforce railroad safety. He was
slow in prosecuting war fraud cases and
lackadaisical in prosecuting antitrust cases.
His selection of the controversial William J.
Burns to head the Bureau of Investigation
underscored his poor judgment and crony-
ism. The whole situation had rendered him
emotionally and politically frail. "He is really
in a much more critical condition than
anyone realizes," Willebrandt wrote to her
parents, "and should he remain nominally
still the head of this Department, I would
not feel in conscience or honor, I could resign
and wish upon him the perplexity of choosing a woman substitute."

Like everyone else in Washington, she had
heard rumors that Daugherty was tangentially
involved in Remus's business. Nevertheless,
he'd never hindered her investigations in any

way and often surprised her with his latitude. "Isn't he a peach?" she wrote to her mother. "He sure appreciates loyal service — I don't always do what I think he wants either! He sent a wire about delaying a Prohibition case and I sent a wire to him that unless he *ordered* it I *wouldn't* for I felt it would be a mistake and he told the attorneys — my judgment went!" The attorney general went out of his way to compliment her, once telling suffragist Harriet Taylor Upton that he had "the finest woman assistant. I'll put her up alongside any several men and she comes out ahead from sheer reason and judgment and convinces me, too!"

Knowing she had Daugherty's full support, Willebrandt even allowed herself moments of petty revenge. When Treasury Secretary Andrew Mellon, whom she loathed, requested a delay in an impending indictment in Pittsburgh, she gleefully told him no. She was, she confessed to her mother, "having the devil of a good time."

One morning at the Justice Department, Willebrandt pulled Daugherty aside and asked to look at his palm. She had always been interested in the cosmos and the occult — astrology and tarot cards and other unconventional means of reading character — and she was particularly adept at palmistry. Newspapers frequently noted the striking loveliness of her own hands, admiring her "low set

129

thumb" and "middle finger of unusual prominence," the "strong and elastic" clench and release of her fist. "If you want to lean back in a comfortable porch chair and sip cooling drinks of non-alcoholic qualities, and have that calm, contented feeling that your country is being run satisfactorily, then take a long look at the hand of the assistant attorney general of the United States," wrote the *Atlanta Journal.* "Never have we seen a hand which expressed more energy, common sense and intelligence."

Daugherty complied, offering his hand, palm facing up. Silently, Willebrandt studied his major lines — life, heart, and head — and the minor lines, relationship and intuition and fate. She noted which ones were etched deeply and which barely appeared, how long they traveled and where they stopped, if any of them split into forks and trailed off in different directions, if any resembled stars or crosses or chains.

After a moment, she concluded her forecast. She saw that he was going to be forced out of office, but was too afraid to tell him.

Despite his conviction, Remus sought opportunities to remain in the liquor business — even legally, if need be. His various distilleries across the country still bulged with inventory, and he was desperate to access and sell those reserves. To that end, he invited an old bootlegging associate, "Jew John" Marcus, for a meeting at the Sinton Hotel.

Remus had always been impressed by Marcus's pedigree; he billed himself as one of the first whiskey runners in the United States. Formerly a pickpocket and gambler in Tijuana and Juarez, he had transported liquor from Mexico to dry states in the South before the onset of national Prohibition. In Cincinnati, he worked as an independent contractor who ran whiskey to different cities, making a commission on each case he delivered. Several of his clients were based in St. Louis, and he was well acquainted with the city's crooked politicians. He was also said to be desperate and fearless — and a seasoned killer who, according to one acquaintance, "put many a rival on the spot."

Remus and Marcus requested a table in the Grill Room, reserved exclusively for men, where whorls of cigar smoke fogged the air. Waiters carried trays heavy with larded beef sirloin and the Sinton's signature drink: a $2 sparkling grape juice delivered in a corked bottle. The hotel's manager once predicted that with this concoction, "the problem of Prohibition is almost solved."

Marcus leaned across the table and told Remus he had a tip: The Jack Daniel's distillery in St. Louis, Missouri, could be his for a reasonable sum.

"I'm not interested in buying distilleries,"

Remus told him. "I have enough now. I'm interested in getting the whiskey out of the ones I already own."

"Well, this is one distillery where you can get the whiskey out without any trouble," Marcus said, and offered the backstory. A political connection, Jack Kratz, had approached him about the possibility of "milking" the Jack Daniel's distillery downtown. Marcus said that only one man could handle a job of such magnitude: George Remus of Cincinnati. With a small, discreet group, there would be little risk. Intrigued, Kratz asked Marcus to arrange an introduction.

Remus insisted that Kratz come to Cincinnati. At the meeting, he shared his fears of further legal entanglement. Kratz promised that protection would be arranged through a friend, whom he described as "the biggest Republican politician in St. Louis."

"Are you sure he can be trusted?" Remus asked.

"Absolutely," Kratz said.

"All right," Remus said. "I'll come down in a few days and we'll look over the ground."

Remus left the meeting still uncertain. The whole enterprise struck him as amateurish and unbusinesslike, tainted by personal friendship and political association. If he was going to take part, he needed further reassurances. He met with lawyers, erstwhile whiskey dealers, Democratic and Republican politicians both current and former, tagalongs eager for a piece of the action. All of them made promises: They could "fix" the local collector of internal revenue. Someone's brother would take the place of the usual "gauger" at the warehouse, charged with monitoring the output of whiskey. No need to give a second thought to the police. If Remus put up a certain sum — say, $125,000 — he would receive 60 percent of the profits from the whiskey.

As always, he consulted with Imogene. They had reconciled after the incident in Indianapolis, when Remus had beaten Naseem Shammas nearly to death with a loaded cane. Imogene explained that she'd wished to trade one of her autos for another and that Shammas offered to negotiate the trade. Nothing else was intended; nothing else happened. Remus accepted her explanation and called the evening a "closed incident," filed away to the past. Now, after hearing the details of the Jack Daniel's deal, Imogene decided to make a "personal investment" of $28,000. They were in this together.

Remus was to be in charge of the milking, plotting exactly how the liquor would be removed and over what period of time. He visited the distillery in St. Louis, which was housed inside a dingy brick building at 3960 Duncan Avenue, taking up most of the block.

The warehouse containing all of the barrels was on the second floor. Strolling around the property, he saw how it could be done, each step falling into place.

He would bring in an electric pump from his Fleischmann distillery in Cincinnati. His men could bore a hole through the first floor and run the hose up into the boiler room. The hose would pass out through a window, across a small areaway, and into a garage. One of his men would install a buzzer system; when a truck entered the garage, one buzz would signal the warehouse men to start pumping. Two buzzes would mean the barrels were full.

Because they had no withdrawal permits, they had to remove the whiskey incrementally. He counted 896 barrels, each containing forty gallons. The smart approach would be to siphon about six gallons of whiskey from each barrel at a time, substituting it with water and alcohol to keep the proof up. That would amount to 5,000 gallons of whiskey for each milking, which they could sell for $30 per gallon, which — minus protection payments — would return their investment. At the end of a year, after the liquor had been regauged, he would remove an additional 5,000 gallons. The $150,000 from that sale would be "all velvet," Remus thought, with a personal net of $75,000, and at that point the threat of discovery would be minimal. He was perfectly willing to wait for a year, he confided to a friend. "One must be patient in these matters."

It brought Remus a modicum of comfort to think so far into the future, as if the possibility of prison had ceased to exist and the rest of his life stretched before him, sweeping and unblemished.

He decided to check in with Jess Smith about protection payments one last time.

At 6:30 A.M. on Tuesday, May 29, Jess Smith, wearing pajamas and a dressing gown, knelt by the wastebasket in his bedroom, his head positioned above the opening.

Over the previous year every facet of his life had darkened and diminished. He was fifty-one years old and his body was failing him. His appendix had been removed a year earlier and he had never fully recovered, physically or mentally. His best and truest friend, Harry Daugherty, had observed the changes. Smith was less resilient. Political insults and slights chipped at his psyche in a way they never had before. He had always been proud of his association with Harding, and for years he had boasted that one of the highest honors of his life had been accompanying the president-elect on a trip to Panama just before his inauguration. Smith wanted nothing more than to experience that again, to stand proudly beside the men who made things happen.

Harding planned another trip for June, this time a cross-country trek ending in Alaska, and Smith assumed that he would be invited. Daugherty had a hard time telling him why that would not be the case. The president mentioned rumors that Smith had been engaging in improper conduct, associating with disreputable characters and tarnishing the administration. Harding had enough trouble in that regard; his secretary of the interior, Albert Fall, had been accused of accepting bribes from oil companies and was under investigation, an incident that would come to be known as the Teapot Dome Scandal. Harding also feared scrutiny of his personal life. He had fathered a child out of wedlock with one mistress, Nan Britton, who had met Harding when she was a teenager. Another mistress, Carrie Fulton Phillips (whose vagina Harding christened "Mrs. Pouterson"), collected $5,000 per month in hush money from the Republican National Committee.

Smith seemed disappointed but not surprised. Daugherty suggested that he check himself into a hospital — he did not look well — and Smith agreed. Together they traveled to Ohio. Daugherty got off at Columbus, but Smith continued on to their mutual hometown, about an hour to the south. There he visited his ex-wife and made arrangements to close the department store he'd owned for twenty-three years. He changed his mind about the hospital. Instead the friends returned to Washington, where Daugherty went to the White House and Smith to their suite at the Wardman Park Hotel.

Still concerned about his friend, Daugherty asked one of his special assistants, Warren Martin, to check in on Smith at the suite. The following afternoon, the three men met for a round of golf. Daugherty was relieved to see Smith laughing and joking, a glimpse of his old self peeking through. At sundown, Daugherty said goodbye and returned to the White House, where he planned to stay overnight. Martin and Smith went back to the hotel, where Smith closed his bedroom door at 9 P.M.

Eight and a half hours later, Martin was awakened by a terrifying crash. He hurried to Smith's room and found him — his head buried in the trashcan, a hole in his right temple, and the pistol still dangling from his fingertips.

DYNAMITE

Willebrandt had been looking forward to her summer vacation, a trip out to the West Coast to see her parents and old law partner, Fred Horowitz, who made no secret of his romantic intentions. She enjoyed the flirtation but was unsure where it might lead. The problem wasn't Fred, whom she adored, but marriage itself. When questioned about her marital status she demurred, insisting that it was a "personal matter," which only sparked more speculation: Was Mrs. Willebrandt (always the reporters' preferred title, no matter her marital circumstances) divorced? Was she separated? Did she have a "love-nest hidden away somewhere" that allowed Mr. Willebrandt a comfortable anonymity?

In truth, she and Arthur Willebrandt were still married but had been estranged since 1916, when she left him and moved in with a female law school classmate. Throughout their five-year union she had felt like Joan of Arc, nursing him through tuberculosis, car-

138

ing for his elderly mother, suffering through a painful miscarriage and subsequent surgery, working full-time as a teacher to pay for both of their law degrees, then coming home to cook, clean, and prepare the next day's lessons before attempting a few hours of sleep. When they separated, she lamented that only *she* had made the "necessary adjustments" of marriage. A wife, she wrote, should be concerned with the "preservation of *her* freedom, her self-respect, her intellectual and executive attainments, her economic independence . . . finding the best outlet for her energies, finding the best protection for her spirit, and establishing a basis of mutual understanding with her husband in order to have both a 'child' and a 'job' if she wants both." She wasn't sure that she could risk the constraints of marriage again, even with a man as generous and enlightened as Fred.

As much as she needed the vacation and hated to disappoint Fred, Willebrandt abruptly canceled her plans, at Attorney General Daugherty's request. He'd explained he would "feel very much more comfortable about the Department" if she would not venture quite so far away as the Pacific Ocean. Her boss was so thoroughly devastated by Smith's death that newspapers chastised him posthumously for giving the attorney general "the shock of suicide." Rumors abounded about what exactly was behind Smith's demise. Maybe he and Daugherty had had a falling-out, after which Smith threatened to produce evidence of malfeasance and corruption throughout the entire administration. Maybe, fearing exposure, members of the Ohio Gang had assisted Smith in killing himself. Or maybe it wasn't a suicide at all.

Two weeks after Smith's death, Daugherty summoned Willebrandt for a long talk. He acknowledged the recent turmoil surrounding his office and wished to know if she planned to resign.

"You have done very wonderful work," he said, "and have so far exceeded my expectations of what any woman could possibly do . . . nobody ever lost by sticking by me yet, and you just stay by the ship."

At the moment, Willebrandt had no intention of quitting the Justice Department. Franklin Dodge was sending his daily reports, and they were close to arresting the Savannah Four, her most significant case since Remus. As for the Cincinnati bootlegger, she ordered a coalition of dry agents to monitor him around the clock.

On June 30, 1923, the Federal Court of Appeals upheld Remus's conviction, ruling that he must serve a two-year sentence in the Atlanta Penitentiary and pay a $10,000 fine. But for Remus it wasn't over, even with the appeal denied and Jess Smith, "his ace in the hole," dead. He would file an application for a re-hearing of his appeal, and if that failed, he would appeal to the Supreme Court of the United States, and if that failed, he would appeal to President Harding himself. "George Remus has always met every obligation," he often said — and that included his obligations to George Remus. While his attorneys prepared for the next round, he turned his attention back to business and took a train to St. Louis. It was time to milk the Jack Daniel's distillery and make some money again.

Since Remus first agreed to the deal its circumstances had shifted, acquiring an element of risk he found unsettling. His partners appeared willing to sacrifice competency for haste. They objected to his plan of milking the distillery slowly, over the course of a year, and itched to remove all of the whiskey at once. Remus's approach, they argued, had its own risks: Where would they get enough pure ethanol to substitute for the whiskey?

"It's dynamite," Remus protested. "You'll never get away with it in God's world. I know this business thoroughly, and you fellows are simply trying to break into the penitentiary." He told his partners that he had a source in Philadelphia that could provide the substitute alcohol and produced $6,000 from his own pocket to pay for it — anything to prevent these amateurs from ruining the operation with their own greed.

He traveled back to Cincinnati to pick up Imogene and to tell members of the Circle to meet him in St. Louis. On the morning of August 4, while still at home, Remus picked up a copy of the *Cincinnati Enquirer* and read the headline: PRESIDENT WARREN HARDING DEAD. He had been in San Francisco, a stop on the very cross-country tour that Jess Smith had hoped to join. The official time of death was 7:30 P.M.; the official cause, a "stroke of apoplexy."

As with Smith, rumors suggested a more sinister scenario. While Harding had never been the paragon of health — he had a history of heart disease and was recovering from a bout of influenza — neither had he been in imminent danger. Strange, wasn't it, that the First Lady refused to allow an autopsy? Was she exacting revenge for her husband's infidelity? Then there was the cook at the Seattle Press Club, the site of Harding's last public meal, who claimed that "a few drops of croton oil in the stew or salad" would facilitate a tidy and unprovable murder; by that reasoning, of course, any of Harding's fellow diners might be the culprit. A Sacramento woman took credit for his death and proclaimed herself a sorceress. The Ku Klux Klan cited a papist plot; others blamed the Klan.

Remus was less troubled by the cause of

142

Harding's death than by its effects. Within the span of months, the Ohio Gang, always so generous and accessible to him, was being dismantled, man by man. He thought about his upcoming appeal. He still had powerful friends in Washington, men who owed him a favor or were willing to be owed in turn. When the time came — *if* the time came — he would reach out to Harding's successor, Calvin Coolidge, and expect a favorable response.

For now, Remus had to hasten back to St. Louis. He and Imogene checked into the Chase Hotel on the city's West End. As they settled into their suite they heard an urgent knock on the door: It was Harry Boyd, one of Remus's associates from Cincinnati. He had come to warn Remus that things were not going as planned.

While Remus was out of town, the St. Louis men had begun moving the whiskey out. They hadn't even bothered to secure the replacement alcohol and were blatantly milking the barrels — pumping all day, hauling the liquor out to a nearby farm, and using only water to make up the difference. On top of that, a St. Louis street gang called "Egan's Rats" had heard of the plan and carved a piece of it for themselves. They were a long-established group, dating back fifteen years, and had built a résumé impressive in its brutality — extortion, robbery, and twenty-odd murders for which no one was ever brought to trial. Boyd said that they were a constant and menacing presence on the scene, threatening to pirate all of the whiskey if they were cut out of the deal.

"Tell them to be careful and keep quiet about this," Imogene warned. "We could all get ten years for this job."

Remus thanked Boyd and contemplated this news. For now, he said, he and Imogene "could only sit tight and trust in the Providence that looks after fools and children."

Later that week Boyd returned with an update: The whiskey was still being milked speedily, with little care or regard for who might notice. Panicked, Remus and Imogene abandoned their suite at the Chase Hotel and took an apartment near the distillery. Remus also rented a space in a realtor's office with a clear view of the distillery in order to monitor the job.

Clocking Remus's moves, two of Willebrandt's agents targeted this temporary office. One evening, after Remus had locked it up and returned to his apartment, they broke in and tapped the phone. Another agent set up camp in a building across the street, using opera glasses to amplify every last detail.

Day after day, from the window of the realty office, Remus counted the loitering men, so many strangers contaminating the scene. The view made him nervous. He trusted none of them and regretted the entire situation. When he had to leave town to meet with his lawyers, he appointed a trusted representative of the Circle to look after his interests.

The Mabelmen continued their surveillance and wiretap operation. The operation seemed flawless until the afternoon they plugged into a phone call and heard a Remus employee boldly announce an order of whiskey for the new president, Calvin Coolidge; the head of the Anti-Saloon League; and a prominent clergyman.

They'd been identified as dry agents — but not before gathering incriminating evidence for Willebrandt.

Back in Cincinnati with Imogene, Remus continued to receive dire reports from his men in St. Louis. The stolen whiskey was selling quickly, but Remus received no payment. His partners now owed him about half a million dollars. At the moment, 350 miles away, there was little he could do. Instead he focused on his case, lamenting the verdict from the United States Circuit Court of Appeals, which had denied him a re-hearing. Just after the New Year, the U.S. Supreme Court followed suit, refusing to review records in both of his cases: conspiracy to violate the National Prohibition Act and mainte-

145

nance of the "nuisance" at Death Valley
Farm.

It was time for his final recourse.

Willebrandt followed Remus's appeal as it
wound through the courts, aware of his attempts, she wrote, to carry his influence "up
along the line, from Congressmen and from
public officials in the state of Ohio, and clear
up even to the White House itself." She
needed to quash the bootlegger's hopes of
reopening his case before President Coolidge
could be persuaded to decide otherwise. She
scrolled a piece of paper through her typewriter and began writing, the words coming
faster than her fingers were able to move:

> I am of the emphatic opinion that no respite
> should be given George Remus or any of
> the defendants convicted with him. . . .
> George Remus and his group of coconspira-
> tors are defiant, dangerous lawbreakers. I
> am reliably informed that Remus is now
> engaged in the distribution of illicit liquor in
> St. Louis. In fact, I have under way at the
> present time an investigation as to his activi-
> ties. . . . In all of his conspiracies he has
> exhibited a rare ability to surround himself
> with seemingly respectable and unimport-
> ant citizens while he hides behind their op-
> erations.
>
> In my opinion it would be a grave mistake

to treat these defendants in any manner differently than the thousands of offenders convicted of much lesser crimes under the liquor laws have been and are being treated. I sincerely recommend that you protest the granting of defendant's application for a respite.

Willebrandt was unimpressed by Coolidge, believing him to be as complicit as Daugherty in the mistakes of the Harding administration. After all, Coolidge, as vice president, had sat in on all cabinet meetings. But now, with an election on the horizon, he seemed intent on making Daugherty a sacrificial lamb. In Willebrandt's view, Coolidge was a "yellow-livered, dishonorable craven."

And yet, in the matter of *Remus v. United States,* President Coolidge made the honorable decision. He agreed that the bootlegger's case should not be reopened and that Remus should report to the Atlanta federal penitentiary on January 24, 1924, as originally scheduled.

Heartened by her victory, Willebrandt began work on an incendiary speech for the prestigious Citizen Conference in Washington, D.C., calling the Volstead Act "a puny, little toothless sort of thing." She also dispatched another team of agents to St. Louis, including Franklin Dodge.

147

TESTIMONY OF
HENRY SPILKER

Q. Do you remember when George Remus was sent to the Atlanta penitentiary?

A. Yes.

Q. Did you see Mrs. Remus any time after he was sent to the Atlanta penitentiary?

A. Yes. . . . It was when I had charge one afternoon in a road house. They called it the Delhi House. It is six miles out of Cincinnati.

Q. Who did Mrs. Remus come there with?

A. I never saw that fellow before. . . . He might be lighter than Remus. Much younger. I let them in. It was a secret place for all the dry officials and well-to-do people. So I left them and I never said a word and I sat them in the big dining room. But before I had them seated Mrs. Remus asked me if I didn't have a private room for them. They didn't like to be seen in case someone else should come in. So I took them upstairs and gave them a private room.

Q. How long did they remain in that private room?

A. About an hour.

Q. Did they have anything to drink that day?

A. They didn't get anything off of me. All they got was a bottle of ginger ale.

Q. Did you see them have any liquor that day?

A. They must have had it, but I didn't see it.

Q. How did you happen to come here as a witness?

A. I read in the paper about this case, so I remember the time I saw Mrs. Remus in the road house, and so I thought to myself, "That man has made lots of money and she ought not go out with somebody else while he is in jail." . . . I wanted to tell people that she done something bad that she should not do, and I always figured after that that she will get in trouble sooner or later.

THE BRAINSTORMS

Throughout all of it — the humiliation of arrest, the endless appeals, the disaster in St. Louis, the horror of facing prison, the certainty of another trial — Imogene had been Remus's one constant, the engine that propelled him forward. She knew the insides of all of his deals, the gore and guts, the secrets behind the numbers. He "took her from a hovel" and created her, he said, as surely and as skillfully as he'd created himself.

"Never mind," she comforted him. "When this is all over, we'll go away somewhere together and forget the disgrace."

Remus agreed and added a promise of his own: Before they settled down in anonymity, he would take her on a long trip around the world. They would go to the jungles of Africa and then "live a life of peace."

He began making preparations. He took a short trip to the Burk Springs Distillery in Loretta, Kentucky, and gave instructions to his managers on conducting business in his absence. He checked on the situation in St. Louis, calling one of his more trustworthy contacts, a deputy constable who had been part of the syndicate from the beginning. Would he keep an eye on Remus's interests in the Jack Daniel's deal and collect his share of the money? Remus would pay him well upon his release from prison. The man agreed, promising to "faithfully look after it."

His lawyer prepared a power of attorney that granted Imogene control of his empire. Although he had, in a fit of anger, sought to reclaim the deed to their mansion, he was now glad it was under Imogene's name. He transferred ownership of the Fleischmann distillery in Cincinnati, which he valued at $300,000, and entrusted her with his various bank accounts, $1 million worth of whiskey certificates, and all of his personal jewelry, worth $125,000. Into her hand he dropped the keys for two machines, a Packard and a Jordan. To cover her and Ruth's expenses for two years, he wrote a check for $115,000. He also set up a trust for Romola, his daughter from his first marriage, even though his affection for the girl regularly sent Imogene into an absurd and vengeful rage. At the start of their relationship, back in Chicago, she told a bellboy at the Illinois Athletic Club that she would "kill Remus" if he gave Romola any gifts.

■ ■ ■

At 3 P.M. on January 24, 1924, Remus stood before their bedroom mirror, dressing to go to prison. He selected a pearl gray silk suit with spats to match; his favorite bowler hat, festooned with a petersham ribbon; a diamond stickpin resembling those he doled out to guests as party favors; and as usual, no underwear. He kissed Imogene goodbye at the front door of the mansion. An automobile idled in the driveway, waiting to take him to the federal building downtown. Imogene planned to stay home and prepare a chicken supper and would meet him at the train station that evening.

Remus surrendered and waited for his associates to arrive. They came carrying valises and wearing somber expressions, some accompanied by wives and relatives and others alone. George Conners wept openly on his wife's shoulder. Journalists circled the room, seeking color and comments. They noticed that Remus appeared in good spirits. Would he say something about his experience? About his wife? The room stilled, waiting for him to speak.

His only regret, Remus said, was that he had not been able to obtain executive clemency for his "boys." They had acted upon his advice as an attorney and upon his instructions as their employer, and he "regretted sincerely that no action yet had been taken by the President." He also wished to say a few words about his wife, Imogene. While she was not there at present, she did intend to close the Price Hill mansion during his incarceration and move to Atlanta to be near him. She was absolutely devoted to him, and her presence in Atlanta would be a "great solace," enabling him to maintain his "cheerfulness" during confinement. "The way the courts have handled the case," he concluded, "seems to me one of the greatest travesties on justice that I have ever known."

A reporter raised his hand. "Do you have anything on your hip?" he asked, indicating the spot where one would keep a flask.

Everyone laughed, including Remus. He gave them the truth: "I have never tasted liquor in my life."

Servants arrived from Remus's home, carrying teetering platters piled high with chicken, enough to feed all thirteen prisoners. At 8 P.M., deputies escorted Remus and his boys to the Union Central depot, where they would catch a Cincinnati Southern train. Although Imogene was not allowed to ride with Remus, his lawyer made arrangements for her to be in a public car on the same train.

Remus spotted her on the platform, looking ravishing in a gray sealskin coat. Reporters encircled her, begging for a few words.

She obliged, promising that the Cincinnati mansion would be "kept up" and the water in the Imogene Baths would "sparkle the same as ever."

The train rumbled into motion. Through curls of dingy smoke Remus watched the hills and buildings and river grow smaller, a city in retreat. He tried to maintain his joviality, or at least the appearance of it. He joked that his weight had climbed to 225 pounds, the heaviest he'd ever been, and prison would help him "reduce." He chided an associate for being even stouter, offering to take the upper berth so that his friend wouldn't crash through. He told accompanying reporters that he already missed his valet and regretted having to appear before the warden unkempt and unshaven. He quipped that this was the first "protracted vacation" he'd had in years. "Oh well," he said, shrugging. "I'm reconciled to my fate. I'll be a good soldier and serve my time." In the early morning hours he picked up his copy of *Dante's Inferno,* reading long after everyone else had fallen asleep.

Situated on the southeastern rim of the city, the Atlanta Federal Penitentiary was one of the first federal prisons in the country. Opened in 1902, it was billed as the "finest institution of its kind," with 330 cells to accommodate more than 700 prisoners and every modern convenience, such as sanitary plumbing and electric lights. Remus was not Atlanta's first celebrity resident, nor would he be its last. Others included Eugene V. Debs, the celebrated labor leader and pacifist jailed for opposing World War I; journalist and activist Marcus Garvey; notorious scam artist Charles Ponzi; and gangster Al Capone.

The penitentiary was an elephant of a building, hulking and gray. Bars clamped over windows like gritted teeth. Arms protruded between them, waving eagerly, a silent ovation for its newest and most famous prisoner.

After waving back, Remus removed his gray silk shirt and gave it to the porter as a parting gift. Then he unfastened his diamond pin and placed it in Imogene's palm, curling her fingers over the stone. She began to cry.

Before entering the prison Remus and his boys took one large collective breath, as if hoping to carry the outside in with them. He looked back, his eyes on Imogene until the closing door stole her from his sight.

In America's oldest penitentiary, Eastern State in Philadelphia, officials practiced a "separate system" of incarceration, requiring inmates to wear white cloths over their faces when brought into common areas — the idea being that the less contact they had with each other, the greater their chance of reform. An examiner for the Department of Justice studied this approach, deemed it antiquated, and decided that the congregate system, in which prisoners were free to interact and mingle, produced better results. "If there is a surviving spark of respectability in the heart of a prisoner sent to the Atlanta penitentiary," concluded the *Brooklyn Daily Eagle,* "he has a splendid chance to reform his ways."

Remus was assigned to a private cell in a section of the prison known as "Millionaire's Row." George Conners was placed in another part of the prison, far enough removed to prevent Remus from seeing him day to day. His immediate neighbor was bootlegger Willie Harr, the leader of the notorious Savannah Four bootlegging ring targeted by Willebrandt and Dodge.

Before reporting to prison, Harr and his associates had requested an off-site meeting with Warden A. E. Sartain, a member of the Ohio Gang and an appointee of Attorney General Daugherty. Sartain sent the prison's chaplain as an emissary. In the lobby of an Atlanta hotel, the chaplain and Harr discussed an arrangement. If the bootlegger paid $10,500, Warden Sartain would provide him and his men Atlanta's most comfortable accommodations and coveted jobs — positions in the chief clerk's office, the clothing room, and the radio room. For an extra $5,000, one of Harr's associates was appointed chauffeur for the prison physician.

Remus had a similar setup in mind, starting with a modest $50 donation to the warden and the promise of future "judicious presents." He spent $425 on décor to make his cell "habitable," sending Imogene out for a new mattress, blankets, and a set of fine sheets. An additional $2,500 bought him his own refrigerator, a private bath, a prized job in the library, and the privilege of eating his meals separate from the rest of the inmates. Occasionally Remus invited Harr to dine with him, their feast arranged artfully across a linen tablecloth, a fresh floral centerpiece from Imogene alleviating the gloom. They organized games of high-limit poker, with the minimum bet set at $50.

These comforts did little to assuage his humiliation. Furious thoughts careened through his mind: "Remus, who paid millions to buy his way, was inside prison walls, while those who had made it possible for him to act were enjoying the wealth made by the operations of Remus." He began to suffer from what he called "brainstorms," a word that in recent years had become euphemistic for temporary insanity and that in Remus's case conveyed a strange sensation: powerful zaps of energy that sparked without warning and buzzed like flies inside his skull.

Imogene was his only comfort. She had taken a suite at the opulent Georgian Terrace Hotel but came to see him nearly every day, always bringing flowers or a bit of roast chicken or cake. On days she didn't visit they spoke on the phone, long conversations during which he invented new nicknames: his "little bunch of sweetness" and his "little bunch of nerves." For extra donations, $500 and $1,000 at a time, she was permitted to cook for him and clean his cell, scrubbing the floor on her hands and knees. She had a habit of calling him "Daddy" loud enough for everyone to hear. "How she loves to show off," Remus thought, but secretly he was pleased that the other prisoners noticed her. They called her "the angel of the pen."

There were moments when a brainstorm seized his mind, sparking his synapses, and in that dark, electric cloud his thoughts would turn on her. He was not proud of his behavior — scolding her as if she were a child or a temptress and doling out petty punishments, like choosing to play in a baseball game with Willie Harr and his gang instead of accepting her visit. Their arguments were different from those they'd had before; his rages now came frequently and without warning, each word delivered with a blind and wild vitriol that precisely hit its mark. She often cried as she left his cell, complaining to Harr about her husband's "unkindly remarks" and "fussing" and "abuse."

One evening Remus received a phone call from Imogene's sister.

"Why does my sister cry after she's seen

you?" she asked. "Why is she unable to sleep?"

There was silence as Remus considered his response. "Because she doesn't understand me," he said.

They had a variation of this conversation numerous times.

After these incidents Imogene sometimes traveled back home to Cincinnati, checking on the mansion and daughter Ruth, now sixteen and still attending Sacred Heart. Other times she holed up in her hotel suite, visiting him briefly or abstaining altogether until her anger had quieted. Remus atoned by retreating to his cell to compose effusive letters:

To the only true and sweetest little girl in the whole dear world, to the apple of my eye — not one, but both:

How glorious it feels to know that my sweetheart is cheery again. Little one, you do not know what it means to have you away from me long. The minutes turn into days, the days into months, and the months into years. So therefore the nervous tension under which I labor, my nerves are one mass of tension, you must by all means forgive me for my spontaneous combustion of the mind sweet and dear little one. Nothing more than a brainstorm predicated upon no substantial facts. . . .

Sweet one, I did not know this would be so horrible. I weigh this matter too lightly. I am afraid, little one, and you and only you are at the bottom of this whole thing. I crave you. I would devour you. I care only for you — a human madness. All other matters are infinitesimal against you, and only you, therefore you see how I burst into a human cloud, burst with a vitriolic tongue interspersed.

But bundle of sweetness, forgive the lowly the downtrodden mortal being who has no one to think about but that little bundle of nerves who is all the time looking out for my spiritual and physical welfare. Dear one I have just enjoyed the best feast I have had since I have been in the institution, thanks to you dear one. Chickens, coffee finest, butter milk, great bread, real butter — the grandest and they call this a penitentiary, how ridiculous how absurd how nonsensical. And still so true and why dear great little one I have not you and only you. Imagine what a difference — a loaded stomach when you relish the substance that your tender hands have brought.

Gee Gene, I wish I had you in my arms to squeeze so tightly so dearly so tenderly and how great and glorious it would be. I tremble with emotion you bundle of sweetness. Gene, I want you near me — to hell with the world. If I did not think you were everlasting sincere in my reciprocal condition of mind as to loyalty, dear one, I would be more amazed at the hypocrisy of the human mind.

She had always forgiven his temper, but things were different now. He was trapped and she was free, occupying a world outside of the one they'd created, one he had no power to touch. If their bond changed it would render him someone new and strange, someone desperate to regain what he'd lost.

Testimony of
George L. Winkler

Q. What public position did you occupy?

A. Federal Prohibition agent.

Q. Did you hear [Remus] discuss the relationship that existed between his wife and Franklin L. Dodge?

A. I have.

Q. What would be his attitude and demeanor when he referred to them?

A. Well, he was very indignant, he was very much put out about it.

Q. How would he act on the occasions when he was talking about those two?

A. He would speak in very endearing terms of his wife, he would call her his beautiful Imogene, and the next minute he would be cursing her and calling her names.

Q. I believe you said to me this morning that when he would refer to his wife and Franklin L. Dodge, he acted like a wild man?

A. Well, he would pace the floor. . . .

THE WIELDERS OF THE SOAP

On the morning of March 12, 1924, United States senators and congressmen, Justice Department Officials, witnesses, spectators, and one hundred newspaper reporters gathered in the Senate Office Building for the commencement of the hearings on alleged misconduct in the Department of Justice, focusing specifically on Attorney General Harry Daugherty. Daugherty himself refused to appear before the committee, maintaining that its members were less interested in investigating the department than in putting him personally on trial. As evidence, he pointed to the committee's chairman — Senator Burton K. Wheeler, Democrat of Montana — whom Daugherty had once investigated for a conflict of interest, resulting in an indictment and later acquittal. He was not going to subject himself to Wheeler's grandstanding display of vengeance and trusted that Willebrandt's support would help clear his name, if not save his job.

The third day of testimony featured Gaston Means, Jess Smith's shakedown partner and former agent for the Bureau of Investigation, currently awaiting trial on charges of violating the Volstead Act. Means entered wearing a rumpled linen suit and his customary bow tie, which concealed the multiple folds of his chin. One spectator noted his "somewhat ghoulish smile."

Means spoke readily about the late President Harding's clandestine activities but was reticent on the subject of collecting graft money from bootleggers. When asked of Smith's and Daugherty's involvement, Means offered a terse response: "They knew the game."

Wheeler was about to excuse Means from the stand when Daugherty's attorney held up a hand and said, "I would like to ask one question. . . . How much altogether passed through your hands?"

Means was silent for a long moment, running a hand across his briefcase. "Oh, I don't know," he said. "I guess the largest sum I ever had in my hands at one time was six or seven thousand dollars" — and not in connection with whiskey, Means added, but with a bootleg film of a Jack Dempsey boxing match.

From his cell in Atlanta, Remus followed news of Means's appearance, his outrage intensifying with each new report. The fearless and cunning secret agent was suddenly afraid to divulge the truth about whiskey permits and protection payments? During Imogene's next visit he shared his frustration and assigned her a task: Send a telegram to Senator Wheeler suggesting that he might want to hear from the bootlegger George Remus, who knew well the system of graft payments coordinated by Means and Smith. She should sign the telegram "John Adams," in honor of the nation's second president, known to be an ardent drinker who began every morning with a tankard of hard cider. Imogene did as instructed, and Remus waited for the subpoena to come.

In the meantime, Willebrandt's palmistry prediction came true. Attorney General Daugherty resigned his position on March 28, and was immediately replaced by Harlan Fiske Stone, dean of the Columbia Law School and future Supreme Court justice. Unable to bear the idea of leaving politics behind, Daugherty sought to become a delegate to the Republican convention and asked Willebrandt to support his bid. "In the most pathetic way," she wrote to her parents, "he asked if I would speak at a women's meeting, so they wouldn't feel he had been crooked with my work. He hasn't — and it is my duty to say so — now when he needs it most, but never was I called on to do a more unwelcome thing." Men alone determined when being a "woman lawyer" was a hindrance and when it was an asset, and she yearned for the day when her sex ceased to be a consideration at all.

She traveled to Marion, Ohio, to speak on his behalf. "The Republican Party has no apology to offer for the administration of Mr. Daugherty as Attorney General," she told constituents of the Eighth Congressional District. "His policy was vigorously and fearlessly to enforce the laws of the United States." Three days later, at a dinner for the League of Women Voters, she shifted her focus and tone, encouraging the crowd to keep politics clean by getting involved. "Corruption in high places is only a boil on the body politic; it will recover," she said. "Women always are the wielders of the soap."

At noon on May 15, Remus boarded a train for Washington to testify at the Daugherty hearings, escorted by Warden Sartain and a prison guard. For the occasion he was permitted to exchange his prison grays for his old uniform of a bespoke suit and silk shirt. In the two months since Means's testimony several witnesses had mentioned Remus's name. One, a former president of an Ohio-based drug company, testified that Remus had a deal with the numerous government officials who were on his payroll: If rival bootleggers bought liquor from anyone else, they were to be indicted at once.

Despite his desire to testify, Remus was nervous. He quashed his instinct to refer to himself in the third person and spoke, in the words of the *Chicago Tribune,* "with an intense and trembling earnestness." He confessed that since he entered prison his "mind had not been normal." He declared that all that is "sacred and holy" had been taken from him and chastised America as a nation of hypocrites: "Every person who has one ounce of whiskey in his possession is a bootlegger. Not one scruple of liquor prescribed by physicians is ever used for medicine."

He delivered the answers that the committee wished to hear. He had met with Jess Smith on several occasions to secure whiskey permits and protection from prosecution. He sometimes cashed checks to his own account, marking them with "J.S." in the corner, and then paid Smith in $1,000 bills. In exchange, Smith had promised that Remus would not be molested by law enforcement and, in the case of an emergency, "the general" would intervene.

"You never had any doubt about his influence?" Wheeler asked.

"There was none from my viewpoint," Remus said.

"And you have been double-crossed?"

"I don't know. The dead don't speak."

If the committee were interested, Remus added, he would be happy to produce the checks, currently stored in "good secluded spots" in Cincinnati and Missouri.

Willebrandt had no intention of allowing Remus another sabbatical from prison to gather those checks, telling Attorney General Stone that she was "not favorable to letting him have a two-week trip around the country." Exhausted by the drama surrounding Daugherty and the hearings, she focused instead on the Jack Daniel's case, studying reports from Dodge and other agents in St. Louis. One week after Remus's testimony, Willebrandt issued indictments for seventeen people involved in the purchase and milking of the Jack Daniel's distillery, including Remus — and Imogene.

On the evening of May 21, deputy U.S. marshals knocked on the door of 825 Hermosa Avenue. A servant summoned Imogene, who began plotting her public statement as soon as she realized what was happening. Deputies informed her that she was under arrest for conspiring to violate the Volstead Act, as was the mansion's watchman, William Mueller, who had worked as a guard in St. Louis. She pleaded with the marshals, insisting that she could prove she was at home with Ruth and not at the distillery in St. Louis, but to no avail. She tried again, telling the marshals that she, like other wives, knows "nothing or very little about her husband's business affairs." The marshals remained unmoved.

Imogene dropped her act long enough to sign Mueller's bond, offering her home as collateral, only to be told that the property was encumbered by a tax lien. A nearby property in Price Hill, where she and Remus planned to build a large apartment building, was accepted. She spent a sleepless night, drifting through the mansion's cavernous rooms and sinking beneath the cool stillness of the pool, and issued a statement the following morning. It read, in part:

> I had nothing to do with the alleged conspiracy to purchase the Jack Daniel's Distillery at St. Louis and the warehouse receipts covering 891 barrels of whiskey and their illegal withdrawal, as charged in the indictment. . . . Whatever business transactions I have had, either as to real estate or otherwise, were at the direction of Mr. Remus and, so far as I am concerned, they were all perfectly proper. I regret exceedingly my name was mentioned in the case, for, while Mr. Remus knows I had nothing to do with it, Daddy has trials and tribulations enough without adding this to his burdens.

Willebrandt planned to assist federal prosecutors in St. Louis, but another matter required her immediate attention. She had received troubling reports from Atlanta, all centering on Remus. The bootlegger was not only enjoying special privileges but also obstructing justice in the Jack Daniel's case, threatening potential witnesses in order to keep them quiet. A few of her agents, having heard that some of Remus's old partners were willing to talk, traveled to the penitentiary, only to be told that the prisoners had changed their minds.

She had visited the Atlanta Federal Penitentiary once before, in the spring of 1923, after two inmates managed a sensational escape; both men were caught the following day after a shootout with the police. The prison was clean enough, but she'd been appalled by everything else. "Several men are in the same cell," she recorded. "They sat and stood around the yard and in the halls in squads. The terrible idleness of the institution freezes my blood. Most of them got in prison because they had never learned the joy of an honest sweat and a hard day's work and for the government to continue to encourage such habits is no less than criminal." She had wired advance notice of her visit to Warden Sartain, but nonetheless he "appeared half drunk, and talked most uncouthly."

With Remus intimidating potential witnesses, Willebrandt decided to send Dodge

170

to Atlanta to salvage the investigation. He had studied the bootlegger intently, and would know how to handle him.

The Ace of Investigators

Even with Imogene's home-cooked meals and fresh flowers on the table, Remus did not know how much longer he would last in prison. His troubles had multiplied: Imogene's arrest, an inevitable trial in St. Louis directed by Willebrandt, the government liens on everything he owned. He felt depressed, an unfamiliar and frightening emotion that was amplified by the absence of work. He had come to the hard conclusion that his entire career had been a folly, that he had never been so happy as when he earned $5 a week in the pharmacy, sleeping on a cot in the stockroom, too scared to go home.

An idea came to him, illuminating a possible way out. If he recanted his testimony from the Harry Daugherty hearings, maybe Willebrandt would be appreciative enough to grant him parole. In the warden's office, Remus prepared a signed affidavit stating that he had never met Jess Smith, had never given him money for any purpose, and had never

172

met or communicated with former Attorney General Daugherty, either directly or indirectly. He declared that he had only given such testimony because of the Senate committee's promise to help free him from jail.

He released the letter to the press and sent a copy to Washington. Nothing.

He asked Warden Sartain to follow up with a letter to Willebrandt. In her response, she told the warden that she was "not disposed to do anything for Remus."

He was prepared to give up when fellow inmate Willie Harr revived his hopes. A federal agent had arrived at the penitentiary, purportedly to investigate corruption among prison officials. Harr was familiar with him; the agent had worked undercover as a bootlegger in Savannah, but Harr had recognized the ruse right away. From what Harr understood, the agent was approachable and amenable to bribes. If Remus provided certain information about crooked officials, the agent might reward him in turn.

When Harr pointed out the agent, Remus realized he, too, had seen him before — parked outside of the mansion, day and night, an ominous presence invading his life. Finally Remus learned his name: Franklin Dodge. From behind the bars of his cell Remus appraised Dodge as if he were a potential deal, something to be acquired and put to use. This was his last chance.

He sent a message that the agent was welcome to visit him anytime.

Built like a grand entrance, Dodge had a demeanor both intimidating and inviting. Like Remus, he was flashy in dress and boisterous in conversation. Unlike Remus, he had hair, plentiful and dark and combed with slick precision. There was an ease about the agent, a kind of confidence bestowed only upon those with deep connections and old money, allowing him to wander through life unquestioned and undenied.

Remus spoke in a brusque, conspiratorial whisper meant to convey that he and Dodge were partners, each possessing something the other wanted. He had information that the agent might find useful. As Dodge knew, Remus had been enormously successful in operating the Circle: buying distilleries, obtaining whiskey permits, and using those permits to withdraw whiskey cosigned to his numerous fictitious drug companies. Would Dodge be interested to know that Remus secured these permits from the prohibition director of Ohio? And that several federal officials were complicit in these deals?

Remus could provide Dodge with paperwork that proved this network of graft, and could also speak of rampant corruption inside the Atlanta penitentiary. He understood from Willie Harr that Dodge, under the right

174

circumstances and with proper incentive, would consider a quid pro quo. Remus would be happy to supply more evidence and names in exchange for the agent's influence in Washington — a commutation of his sentence or even a full pardon.

Dodge took notes on the conversation, writing down Remus's names and figures. He couldn't promise anything, but he would be back to talk again.

In the meantime, Remus called upon his secret weapon, his truest and sweetest, his partner in everything. During Imogene's next visit, he confided to her about Dodge and issued an order: "Play up to him, because he is the last chance to help me get out of jail."

She did not have to be asked twice.

TESTIMONY OF
FRIEDA SCHNEIDER

Q. What is your position with the American State Savings Bank of Lansing, Michigan?

A. I am in the Safety Deposit Department of that bank.

Q. Do you know Franklin L. Dodge?

A. I do.

Q. Did you ever see the party who signed the application for Safety Deposit box No. 128, who signed the name of Mrs. A. H. Holmes?

A. Yes, I have waited on her when she was in the vault.

Q. How many different times have you seen her in the Safety Deposit Department of your bank?

A. I think twice.

Q. Who, if anyone, was with her on the two occasions that you have referred to?

A. I think Mr. Dodge was with her.

Q. Did you know Mrs. Holmes by any other name?

A. I did not.

VIGOR AND VIM UNEXCELLED

After talking with Remus, Dodge compiled his notes and prepared a report for his superiors at the Bureau of Investigation. Remus, he wrote, "told me that he secured these withdrawal papers through former Prohibition Director J. E. Russell's office with the assistance of one Fred Schwenck, and that Mr. Schwenck advised Mr. Remus that Mr. M. B. Copeland, an employee in the Prohibition Director's office, cooperated with him in securing the Prohibition Director's approval of these permits for the withdrawal of whiskey at the Hayner Distillery."

He sent the information to the Bureau's new director, twenty-nine-year-old J. Edgar Hoover, who had been promoted at Willebrandt's urging. She had told Attorney General Stone that Hoover was "honest and informed and one who operated like an electric wire, with almost trigger response."

"Everyone says he's too young," Stone replied, "but maybe that's his asset. Apparently he hasn't learned to be afraid of the politicians."

Although Hoover had been deputy chief at the Bureau through the recent scandals — Teapot Dome and the Daugherty investigation — Stone gave him the benefit of the doubt. Hoover had also downplayed his involvement in domestic surveillance operations and promised to disband the intelligence division, responsible for the brutal postwar Palmer Raids in which thousands of suspected anarchists and communists were illegally arrested and detained. He had grand plans to remake and modernize the Bureau, and told Stone he intended to identify and dismiss all crooked agents. "Every effort will be made by employees of the Bureau to strengthen the morale," Hoover vowed, "and to carry out to the letter your policies."

The information Dodge acquired from Remus was enough to indict eleven men for conspiracy to violate the Volstead Act. It seemed to Hoover that Dodge was one of the honest agents, a true asset to the Bureau.

Dodge sent similar updates to Willebrandt, often attaching newspaper articles that had nothing to do with Remus. She opened her mail one day to find a clipping from the *Atlanta Journal,* another paean to the "fascinating prettiness" of her hands and an analysis of her looks: "Much has been written about the lack of paint, powder and lipstick about her person. It is rather the knowledge that these things detract from her appearance than a narrow-minded opinion on their use which keeps them off her shopping list."

The accompanying note was on official Department of Justice letterhead: "Dear Mrs. Willebrandt, I am enclosing herewith a newspaper clipping, which is self-explanatory. I am sure that you will be interested in reading this article." He signed off, "Very truly yours, F. L. Dodge, Special Agent" and marked it "personal."

On December 19, 1924, Remus, Willie Harr, and several members of Harr's gang testified in a closed grand jury hearing against Warden Sartain, revealing all of the various perks and privileges they had enjoyed under his command. Willebrandt summoned the warden to Washington and asked for his resignation, thereby removing the department's final link to Daugherty. She had "done it all," she wrote to her parents. "Firing the men, hunting provisional wardens and choosing permanent appointees." For Sartain's replacement she recruited the warden of the Idaho State Penitentiary, John Snook — a decision she categorized as "clearing out the politicians and getting real prison experts." Fearing that rival prisoners might retaliate against the bootleggers, Willebrandt arranged for Remus and the others to move to the Clarke County

Jail in Athens, Georgia, where they would remain until the situation settled.

Willebrandt was mistaken if she thought the prisoners would face more austere conditions across the state. They were placed in an empty hospital ward, each with his own private two-room suite. Another room in the ward served as a makeshift office, complete with several desks to store the voluminous piles of mail the bootleggers received each day — more, reportedly, than any person or institution in Athens except the University of Georgia library. Guards provided Remus with his own radio set, allowing the entire fleet of bootleggers to listen to President Coolidge's inaugural address.

Remus and Harr hired a uniformed maid to cook and serve their meals. On occasion they held dinner parties in the hospital chapel, inviting the other prisoners as guests. At the appointed hour, they gathered around a long table draped with a lace runner and adorned with vases of fresh flowers, replenished often by Imogene. One visitor described the spread as a "bachelor's apartment," where the prisoners were free to "take life languidly" while they waited to return to Atlanta. When Remus wasn't working at the library, he exercised and read the paper from front to back. He was able to maintain these comforts as long as he continued his regular donations, $500 to $1,000 at a time, with Imogene as his emissary.

In Athens, she was permitted free access to his rooms and an occasional stay overnight. She developed a routine, spending one week a month in Cincinnati to visit Ruth at her boarding school before returning to Athens, where she took a suite at a local hotel. While in Georgia she made time for jaunts to Atlanta, where Dodge was still gathering evidence against Warden Sartain for the upcoming trial.

During her absences Remus called her every night, often keeping her on the line for ninety minutes. He inquired about their plan, asking if she were "cultivating" Dodge.

"Well, Daddy," she assured him, "I think Mr. Dodge will be able to do you some good."

He let his mind conjure scenes of a pardon or early parole, handed down from on high by Washington, stamped with Willebrandt's signature. His upcoming year-long sentence in the Ohio county jail would be canceled. He told Imogene to keep working on Dodge and in the meantime sent adoring letters:

I again sit down to write or scribble and attempt to contort the English language. . . .
You write that I am near you, as you know, always am, always will be, always must be, even after death. You and I, little one, must not be parted. As in the words of the Rubaiyat:

"Yesterday the day's madness did
    prepare,
Tomorrow's silence, triumph or despair,
Think, dear one, for you know not
    whence you come nor why;
Think, loved one, for you know not why
    you go,
Unless for me, nor where."

I can not tell you, Little One, how glorious
it is to know you are so close, so near, so
sweet and always so charming. It seems as
though your very presence kindles a present downtrodden heart (for the present in
me). However not for long, thanks to your
kindly assistance. . . .

Nothing seemed amiss until one evening
when Remus sat down to dinner with Willie
Harr, the two of them alone in the serene
hush of the hospital chapel. As the maid filled
their glasses, Harr leaned forward and said
there was something Remus ought to know.

Remus waited, fork poised in the air.

Harr was direct: He'd heard rumors that
Mrs. Remus had engaged — and was engaging — in "misconduct" with Dodge. Their
bootlegger friends in prison, namely Morris
Sweetwood and Mannie Kessler, had heard
the same. Kessler in particular had a low image of Dodge, believing him to be "insincere."
True, Harr had suggested that Dodge could

be helpful, but Remus might want to reconsider that advice.

Without hesitation, Remus told Harr that he didn't believe him. Imogene was merely doing what he had told her to do.

It was Harr's impression that Remus was in denial: "He doesn't *want* to believe me." Silently he studied Remus's face. A crimson flush spread across his skin.

Remus stood, dropping his linen napkin, and retreated to his room.

He wanted revenge — not on Imogene but on Harr, whether his words were true or not. He picked his opportunity. One day, while Imogene was visiting, a woman of easy virtue entered Harr's room. Remus waited, the confrontation looming in his mind.

As soon as the woman left, Remus barged into Harr's room.

"Your visitor has contaminated the air where my wife is," Remus said.

At that he propelled himself at Harr with the force and velocity of a cannonball, his arms retracting and releasing and fists connecting, that smack of skin, again and again. He wanted to "crack a skull." That was his new favorite saying: "I will crack a skull." He pulled back again, preparing to strike, but felt his limbs pinned behind him. The guards pried him from Harr and hauled him back to his room.

By the following evening Remus had apologized, and the two bootleggers met once again in the prison chapel to share a quiet dinner.

Before Warden Sartain's trial began, Remus, Harr, and three others who had testified at the grand jury were transported back to Atlanta in case they would be needed on the stand. Instead of occupying their old cells in the Atlanta penitentiary, the prisoners were taken to the Robert Fulton Hotel, a hulking facade of brick and terra-cotta that offered circulating ice water and an air-conditioned coffee shop, remarkable luxuries for the day. Imogene took a room at the nearby Ansley Hotel after deputy sheriffs informed her she would not be permitted to stay with Remus.

Willebrandt had ordered three deputy sheriffs from Athens to accompany the prisoners to Atlanta and monitor their movements throughout the hotel. Despite the prisoners' 8 P.M. curfew, Harr and his associates were permitted out at night as though they were on vacation. They could wander down Decatur Street to Atlanta's famous black vaudeville theater, Bailey's 81, which offered special nights for white audiences featuring chorus girls, animal acts, and blues singers who were just finding fame. Country bootleggers came down from the northern counties to sell their moonshine, offering cups to every woman who passed. Their standards fell far short of Remus's; even their "bottled in bond" whiskey was manufactured and stamped with false labels.

But Remus, for reasons unknown, was kept on evening lockdown in his room. The three sheriffs flanked his doorway and would not budge, unmoved by his furious pleas.

"Are you going out at night?" he asked Harr, hoping to confirm his suspicions.

"Yes."

"I don't understand why all of you men can go out at night," Remus said, and Harr promised to ask around for some answers.

After deliberating for sixteen hours, the jury found Warden Sartain guilty, sentencing him to time in the same penitentiary he'd formerly ruled. With the trial concluded, Remus, Harr, and the other bootleggers were escorted back to the county jail in Athens. Imogene took the train home to Cincinnati and stayed longer this time. Remus imagined the minutiae of her days — sitting before the mirror in her boudoir, a splash in the Imogene Baths, a spin in the car with Ruth. Her absence became its own entity, haunting his rooms, conquering his mind.

Feverishly he composed letters, suddenly feeling self-conscious with his wife of nearly five years:

My only wife.

How is it that you are a monkey, you are a centipede, you are a gem, you are a jewel, you are a combination of all the aforesaid in one; if I but had you this very moment I would demonstrate all of the foregoing with a real vigor and vim unexcelled. How about it? You know very well, no matter how often you phone or wire, I do extremely expect a letter in between moments.

I will judiciously obey all of your injunctions and restrictions with an obedience that is alarming even unto you. I see in the *Enquirer* that they are again headlining us. Will we ever get them? It seems not. How is Ruthey? I hope she is home in your beautiful and faithful care as only you can give it. I have just gotten through frying a steak and mushrooms and it boiled on me and is tough as leather; I will give most of it away; also clean the dishes and will retire early tonight after I have talked to you. I only wish that you and I were back again. It seems to me as though it will be much longer than we expected it to be. The weather here continues sunshine all day long and I read and exercise and am feeling very good, only lonesome.

I am debating in my mind whether I should have some coffee tonight, or not; I suppose I will wind up having it although it is much better not to have it, as my nerves are in good shape, but get nervous writing, as you see.

Love, George

At dinner one night Harr told Remus that he'd learned the truth about what happened at the Robert Fulton Hotel: It was Agent Dodge who had ordered the guards to let everyone out at night but Remus. Not only that, but Manny Kessler had spotted Imogene often in Dodge's company: lingering over lunch, sitting side by side in the courtroom, strolling the streets of Atlanta, laughing and taking their time.

Remus put his fork down and aimed his gaze at Harr. He had been so careful with his creation, cultivating Remus the person and Remus the persona until they seemed one and the same, building a world that could accommodate them both. Now, with Imogene's behavior, with so many questions pecking at his mind, there was a loosening — a stitch or two undone, a few more frayed, an unraveling.

"I don't think my wife is treating me right," he said. "I don't know what she is doing."

Testimony of Olive Weber Long

Q. State whether or not you saw Mrs. Remus at your sister's home very often?

A. Well, I saw her there several times.

Q. Now I will ask you if you recall an occasion when you heard Mrs. Remus call somebody in Cincinnati with reference to Mr. Remus?

A. She was at the telephone at the time I entered the room, and she was in bed. She said, "Did you get in touch with my lawyers there? . . . well, I will take care of him. Never mind, don't worry about it, I will take care of him."

Q. Then what did she do?

A. With that she hung up the phone . . . she said [to me] that she had him just exactly where she wanted him, the poor boob . . . she said also that if he kept on fooling around the way he did she would take care of him, and that she could shoot him and then plead self-defense.

Q. After making that statement, what did she

188

next do?

A. Well then she took the telephone and put in a long-distance call to Franklin Dodge, at Lansing, Michigan. . . . She said, "Franklin, do you love me? Are you sure that you love me? How much do you love me?" And she was sitting on the bed and she said, "Say it again," and then she reached over the bed right alongside of me and she put the receiver to my ear. I heard a gentleman's voice say, "You know I love you, dear." So with that after she hung up she said to me, "Don't you think he has a marvelous voice? He is so wonderful." And I said, "Yes, I think he has a marvelous voice."

Q. After hanging up the receiver did she say anything then to you about Franklin L. Dodge?

A. She told me that she was in love with him . . . and she also said that he was now wearing a very fine tie pin, a tie pin that belonged to Mr. Remus, and she said he would be perfectly wild. She went on to say that she had [Remus] where she wanted him because she had him broke. . . . She said that the only thing he could possibly realize on were the whiskey certificates, and they were made out jointly, and she said that she would burn them before she would give him a penny of them.

Q. Did she say anything further in that conversation?

189

A. Well, she repeated many times over again that she had him just where she wanted him because of his brother being in the insane asylum. She could have him judged insane.

A DISTURBANCE IN ROOM 902

At last, after nearly a decade of separation, Willebrandt's divorce was final. The press would detail her husband's complaint, filed back in 1916, that she, "disregarding the solemnity of her marriage vow, willfully and without cause, deserted and abandoned the plaintiff . . . against his will or consent." Reporters descended upon the Los Angeles home where he still lived with his mother, calling him "Mr. Mabel Willebrandt" and asking him for comment. "She has managed things so expertly along other lines that I'm willing for her to explain our divorce, too," he said, peering from behind the door. "Ask her about it if you want to know." As Willebrandt had come to expect, the articles included elaborate physical descriptions and speculated as to how her appearance informed her personality, including her decision to divorce. "Her features reveal the almost grim intensity that characterizes all her actions," read one caption. "Her whole career has been one of self-promotion, of pushing constantly ahead."

When the news broke, she heard from Fred Horowitz. He wanted a future with her, a marriage, but Willebrandt faltered. She still worried that marriage would never be "a private affair in my life the way it was for a man." She reminded herself of Fred's perplexing and irksome habits — why, for instance, did he type instead of write his personal notes? She asked for time, as her life was already in the thick of irrevocable change: She had decided to adopt a child.

"I've been going to orphanages," she told her mother. "Tomorrow I go to a foundling home. A little baby — a wonderful one was found abandoned. . . . There are a great many abandoned babies here. It would be rather nice to take one like that, wouldn't it, providing it were of good health. Life is all a gamble anyway. You and papa drew a lemon. I can't do worse than you did with your own — No? Reaching — always — for stars — and grasping nettles!" Hoping to increase her savings, she invested in one of Fred's real estate projects, a Los Angeles hotel he planned to call the Chateau Marmont. "I hope we *can* make some money," she wrote. "But I'm a poor fish at it. I really can't keep my eye focused on the money end of anything I do — I fear I'll always be more or less of a parasite on my friends and wind up in an old

192

ladies home, but I'll have a fine time on the way there!"

She was also distracted by a troubling situation at work. She had been hearing rumors about possible misconduct on the part of Franklin Dodge — her most skilled and reliable special agent, someone whose character had seemed as impeccable as his performance. Even members of the press, often cynical about the efficacy of Prohibition enforcement, acknowledged his illustrious career. "Dodge is said to be one of the 'star' members of the Department of Justice's Secret Service," the *Cincinnati Enquirer* reported, "and he has had a leading part in virtually every liquor investigation of importance in the United States during the last few years." Some reporters recognized her personal connection with Dodge, calling the agent her "confidant."

It was possible that Dodge was engaging in a variety of unsavory behaviors: conducting business with bootleggers, accepting bribes, even consorting with Remus's wife, whom Willebrandt planned to prosecute in the upcoming Jack Daniel's case. With the blessing of her friend J. Edgar Hoover, she sent one of Dodge's own colleagues, Special Agent E. B. Harrington, to spy on him.

Harrington's first task was to speak with one E. J. Sweeney, convicted of violating the

National Motor Vehicle Theft Act in 1922 and serving a three-year sentence at the Atlanta penitentiary. Dodge had recruited him as an informant during the prison investigation, and the two men spent considerable time together. During Warden Sartain's trial, Sweeney stayed at the Robert Fulton Hotel along with Dodge, Remus, and Harr. He was well acquainted with Remus, and liked him.

Sweeney revealed that Dodge often took Imogene Remus to the federal building in downtown Atlanta, where they would lock themselves in the private office of the U.S. attorney. Sweeney supposed that these closed-door meetings were "conferences with reference to Mr. Remus." After one of these conferences, Imogene pulled Sweeney aside and invited him to a party she'd planned for that night at the Robert Fulton Hotel. The Sartain trial had just concluded, and everyone deserved a celebration. She seemed pleased that Dodge had already accepted.

Sweeney caught up with Dodge alone and advised him not to go.

"Frank, you are getting yourself in a hot spot," he warned. "If George ever finds out that you are mixing up in company with his wife, he will shoot you."

Dodge laughed and slapped him on the shoulder. "Old kid," he said, "if you don't want to come, you don't have to, but I am going."

Reluctantly, Sweeney dropped into the party for a few moments, taking the elevator fifteen flights up to the rooftop of the hotel. Imogene had rented the bungalow, which was tucked into a far corner and impossible to find without prior knowledge of its existence and detailed directions. The space was outfitted with a small living room, a bathroom, and a bedroom. Remus, locked in his room by Dodge's guards, was the lone prisoner forbidden to attend.

The following evening, February 21, 1925, Dodge asked Sweeney to accompany him to Cleveland, where he was to investigate another Prohibition case on Willebrandt's orders. Sweeney had served him well as an aide and informant, and Dodge could use his services again.

Dodge arrived at the Terminal Station first, a half hour before the 6:30 departure time, passing his luggage to a white-gloved porter. As Sweeney approached, he noticed that Dodge seemed to be waiting for someone, looking left and right along the platform, holding two Pullman tickets for the drawing room — a luxurious and spacious sleeping car with three berths, private toilet facilities, and a lush velvet settee.

Sweeney greeted Dodge and motioned toward the tickets. "What do you want the drawing room for?" he asked. "Why would

195

you want to go to the expense of paying for it?"

Dodge smirked and said that the tickets cost him nothing. Mrs. Remus was paying for them.

"Frank, is she going with you?" Sweeney asked.

"Well, I'm not going alone," Dodge said.

Sweeney knew he had to talk quickly; Imogene would be there soon. "Frank, this woman is a scheming woman. She is simply trying to trap you and place you in a position where she can force you to use your influence on behalf of George."

Dodge laughed. Sweeney gave up and exited the platform. Planning on catching a later train to Cleveland, he hoped to talk some sense into Dodge when he arrived.

Agent Harrington took Sweeney's statement about these various encounters with Dodge and sent a report to Willebrandt. Not wanting to rely solely on Sweeney's testimony, she sent Harrington to Cleveland to track Dodge's movements there. Upon arriving, Harrington spoke to two employees of the Hollenden Hotel who recalled seeing Dodge and Imogene on February 26, 1925, just a week after the conclusion of the Sartain trial.

Around 3 A.M. that morning, the night watchman, Fred Yockey, had been making his rounds, checking all twelve floors for signs of any disorder or disturbance. While walking the corridors of the ninth floor, he paused outside of room 902: He had heard a lady's voice, followed by a man's. He knew from the guest ledger that a married couple had not rented that room, and coed visits at such a late hour were against house rules. He pressed his ear against the door. More murmuring — and then the bed creaking on its springs.

He took the elevator back to the lobby and asked the hotel clerk, Carlos Clapper, for the name of the guest in room 902. Clapper checked the book: A "Miss Conan," hailing from Detroit, had taken the room alone.

Later, Agent Harrington was able to determine via photographic evidence that "Miss Conan" was indeed Mrs. Remus.

Yockey and Clapper then returned to room 902. Clapper rapped on the door several times before a man called, "Who is it?" After a moment, the man appeared in the doorway. Clapper recognized him as Franklin Dodge, an agent with the Bureau of Investigation who had frequented the hotel in the past. He assessed Dodge's state of dress: "Mr. Dodge had his trousers on, with his fly all open, and his belt wasn't buckled; he had a shirt on, with no collar or tie, and he didn't have any shoes on, either."

"What are you doing in this room?" Clapper asked.

"I'm in there with my fiancée. She's sick," Dodge said.

"Why didn't you notify the desk if you were going to stay in the girl's room because she was sick? I'll get a doctor for her."

As Clapper turned to go, Dodge stopped him.

"She doesn't need a doctor," Dodge said. "She just has a headache."

"Because she has a headache, you don't have to stay in the room," Clapper pointed out. "Anyone with a headache would go on to bed and go to sleep. Because you are a government official, you're not better than anyone else to be allowed to stay in the room. We treat all the guests the same."

Dodge begged Clapper not to blame the lady; it was all his fault. He promised to return immediately to his own room on the sixth floor.

But Clapper wasn't finished. He stepped around Dodge to assess the room. The woman was still in the double bed, the sheets and pillows "all ruffled up."

"Why did you allow this man to be in your room," he asked, "when you knew it was the order of the hotel not to have any men visit at this hour in the morning?"

The woman did not hesitate with her answer: She intended to marry the man with her — he was her "fellow." She just happened to be in town, and he came over to see her.

198

Clapper told her she must check out by 7 A.M. The couple left together at 7:15, with Dodge paying the bill for both rooms.

Agent Harrington concluded his report with assurance that Clapper had been cooperative and told him everything he knew. Willebrandt commended Harrington for his work and began a file on Franklin Dodge. There was, she suspected, much more to come.

CATALYST

At the end of June 1925, Willebrandt ordered John Snook, the new warden of the Atlanta Federal Penitentiary, to collect the bootleggers from Athens and return them to their original cells across the state. When the announcement filtered down to the inmates, Remus didn't believe it.

"Bet you $200 to $100 we don't go back," he offered Willie Harr.

"You're on," Harr said.

Back in Atlanta, Remus paid up. Under the strict regime of Warden Snook, he had no catered meals, no uniformed maid, no chance of Imogene coming to clean his cell on her hands and knees. More than a year of prison still stretched ahead of him, including his transfer to an Ohio county jail to serve his sentence for the Death Valley Farm "nuisance" charge. He brooded in his cell, pacing and reading the newspapers, tortured by the idea that the world was changing without him.

A new magazine called *The New Yorker* had made its debut, with columnist Lois Long — using "Lipstick" as her nom de plume — reporting on speakeasies and the menacing presence of dry agents: "hawk-eyed men of the federal government stood around respectable night clubs and pounced on patrons who had slid a silver flask under the tablecloth." F. Scott Fitzgerald published *The Great Gatsby* to mixed reviews (it "might just as well be called *Ten Nights on Long Island,*" groused the *St. Louis Post-Dispatch*). Aviator Charles Lindbergh survived a midair collision. High school science teacher John Scopes was arrested for teaching evolution, with Remus's former colleague Clarence Darrow set to defend him. In Chicago, Remus's old customer Johnny Torrio retired and named Al Capone his successor.

One month after the relocation to Atlanta, Remus's bootlegging colleagues won a legal victory that sparked hope for his own case. A federal judge in Cincinnati ruled that five of his partners — including George Conners and Imogene's brother, Harry Brown — had served their sentences for the nuisance charge concurrently with their terms in the Atlanta penitentiary and would be freed imminently. Hoping to be granted the same courtesy, Remus clipped a report about the verdict from the *Cincinnati Enquirer* and sent it, along with a note, to Willebrandt.

Dear Madam. As the date of my release is just around the corner, I am wondering if it would be an unreasonable request to ask if you will not direct the U.S. Dist. Atty. for the Southern Dist. for the State of Ohio to take the necessary steps toward vacating or discharging the <u>One Year Jail Sentence,</u> that is now of record, in that court?

If you would see fit to grant my request and my sentence was vacated or discharged, you can readily see what it would mean for me. It would eliminate the necessity of transferring me to Cincinnati in custody of the U.S. Marshal, thereby saving me a humiliation, embarrassment and unpleasant publicity that is bound to follow if it becomes necessary for me to apply to the Court for relief. . . .

Trusting that you will give careful consideration to my request, and, after due deliberation, you will direct that action be taken along the lines above outlined.

Remus received a personal reply in which Willebrandt addressed him as "Sir." She did not agree with the Cincinnati judge's interpretation of the law, and in fact the government was already planning its appeal. "You can readily understand, therefore, that the Government could not consistently comply with your request." She signed off "Respectfully."

He considered one final possibility: turning state's witness and testifying for the government in the Jack Daniel's case. He had written several letters to Dan O'Neill, the member of the St. Louis syndicate whom he'd asked to look after his interests. He wanted to know if O'Neill had collected any of the money that he was owed. Remus never received a single reply, and he realized that "the St. Louis crowd had made up their minds to double-cross me from start to finish." If he testified, the government might reward him and also drop the charges against Imogene.

Remus had chosen to trust that her behavior, no matter how strange it sometimes seemed, was ultimately for his benefit. She'd always been, in his view, "so considerate, so devoted, so faithful." She was his architect, carrying out his plans. It had been a while since her last visit, but her letters came in bundles, ten and twelve at a time, each one numbered — first, second, third — so that he could read them in order. They cast a lure for him to cling to, pulling him to the surface, throwing sunlight on his mind. "When you return we will have a dear little home somewhere," read one missive, "and I know we will be far happier." In another she enclosed an old photo of the two of them with a handwritten caption: "As we used to be. Love, Imo." Her tone was breezy and newsy. She was busy with

Ruth and working on his behalf; she was preparing for his release and still hoping to eliminate his sentence in Ohio; she loved and missed her Daddy.

He continued to believe her, batting away any doubts, and then — with no explanation or warning — the letters stopped. His telegrams to Cincinnati went unanswered. The operator could never connect his calls.

As Remus kept trying to reach her, Warden John Snook delivered troublesome news. Federal officials in Cincinnati, acting on a tip, were investigating the possibility that Remus might not be a U.S. citizen. If the tip proved true, he faced the threat of deportation to Germany.

He could not bear to consider the likelihood that the two situations were connected.

Agent E. B. Harrington issued a third report to Willebrandt about Franklin Dodge. Another conversation with Sweeney, the prison informant, yielded the information that Dodge had accepted money and whiskey from bootlegger Willie Harr during Sartain's trial. Furthermore, Dodge said that he planned to go into business with Harr as soon as the bootlegger was released from prison.

A young man named William Schneider also told an incriminating story about Dodge. Schneider, who was dating Ruth Remus, met the agent at Remus's mansion in Cincinnati.

Imogene Remus had been there, and she introduced him to "Mr. Dodge."

Schneider was invited inside and saw that Imogene and Dodge were busy, rushing from room to room, lifting paintings from walls, clutching stacks of papers, pushing furniture around, packing boxes. At one point, Dodge called him over and asked for help in carrying a trunk from the second floor to the first. Schneider obliged, heaving the trunk to his chest, shuffling backward down the stairs. Dodge directed him to continue to the rear porch, where they finally lowered it down. Only later did he learn that the trunk contained "Mr. Remus's goods."

After they finished, Ruth asked if he'd like to accompany them to Chicago; he could even drive her stepfather's touring car. They all stayed at the Parkway Hotel, and one night Imogene pulled Schneider aside. She implored him not to mention her association with Mr. Dodge because people might "misunderstand." He was "doing business" for her, she explained, and she did not like people to think she was "going around" with him just for his company. "He is a very nice and well-educated man," Imogene told him. "I think he can be a great assistance to me in a lot of respects."

Willebrandt requested and accepted Dodge's resignation from the Department of Justice,

205

effective August 10, 1925. Publicly, Dodge said that he was taking a position with the Investigation Department of the National Men's Credit Association. The press and public so far remained unaware that he was under investigation, and Willebrandt hoped it would never come to light.

At the time of Dodge's resignation, she had been a mother for only eight days. Dorothy (occasionally called "Mabel Jr.") came from a farm in Michigan; her mother had been a former client of Willebrandt's during her days of private practice in Los Angeles. Willebrandt gave up her apartment and rented a house in Chevy Chase, Maryland, inviting two women friends to live with her — one a fellow lawyer, the other the chief of the Bureau of Home Economics of the Department of Agriculture. The women became Dorothy's honorary "aunts" and intended to help raise her.

Dorothy was, Willebrandt told her parents, "the dearest, wisest little two year old I ever saw," who "honestly, no joking, looks like Papa — the same blue, blue eyes & with quite a similar expression and a mouth with large full lips like all us Walkers are cursed with! And her forehead is like Mama's!" The girl already dressed herself without help and hung up her own clothes. Reflecting the growing interest in the science of parenting, Willebrandt hired five psychiatrists to examine and assess Dorothy; all agreed that she was "an unusual find." Determined that Dorothy would not be spoiled and would evolve into a respectable, responsible, and law-abiding citizen, Willebrandt forced her daughter to join her in the ice-cold bath she still took every morning.

On August 24, ten days before the expiration of Remus's sentence in Atlanta — shortened by three months for good behavior — Imogene visited the prison one last time. Upon arriving at the penitentiary, she went to the office of Warden John Snook and asked to see Remus. During Warden Sartain's tenure, Imogene had been caught giving "tips" to at least three guards in the visiting room, hoping to secure favors for her husband. As a security measure, Snook had instituted a policy that all of Remus's visits must be conducted in his office.

Snook summoned a guard and told him to fetch the prisoner.

Imogene asked if the guard would bring Remus back, or if Remus would be coming alone.

Snook was confused. She knew the prison and was familiar with the protocol. "No," he said. "There isn't any necessity for a guard bringing him in. He will come in all right."

Remus entered the office. Snook sat at his desk, within earshot of the couple.

207

"Why haven't you been staying in Cincinnati where I could reach you by telegram?" Remus asked. "I had telegraphed and was unable to reach you."

Imogene replied that she had gone to Michigan "with others."

"This is important business," Remus said, angry now. "My liberty is at stake. I want you to stay in Cincinnati where I can reach you so that you can handle my business."

Their words came faster, and Snook tried to focus on his work. After a few moments he noticed that Imogene had gotten up from her chair and was now inching backward, approaching his desk. As Remus ranted, Imogene tilted her body and whispered to Snook: "I am afraid of him."

"What are you afraid of?" Snook asked.

"He threatened to strike me."

Snook glanced at Remus, who seemed to be winding down, finally aware that Imogene had exited the conversation. Snook had heard rumors about Imogene Remus — rumors "of such a character" regarding her habit of "traveling around with Dodge." He was reluctant to share them with Remus, lest they "affect his peace of mind." Remus, in Snook's opinion, was "a man of violent temper."

"No, he is not going to strike you," Snook assured her. "He is not threatening to strike you."

"I won't strike you," Remus interjected. "I

have no reason to." He turned down his voice and used his old, familiar endearments: "little honey bunch" and "little bunch of sugar."

Snook turned back to Imogene. "Just go over there and take your seat," he said. "Sit down and finish your conversation and we will close the interview."

Imogene did as she was told, sitting four feet away from her husband. Remus produced a sheath of papers and gave her instructions about various business matters back in Cincinnati. As a portent of good things to come, he pulled a small diamond ring from his pocket and explained that he had bought it from a fellow prisoner. He would be out soon, and their new and quiet life somewhere far away was almost a reality.

She kissed him and walked away. As a guard came to escort Remus back to his cell, Snook followed Imogene down the hall and called her name.

"I think it would be better if you didn't place too much confidence in Franklin Dodge," he told her.

Imogene said nothing. The sway of her figure grew smaller and smaller until she turned the corner and was gone.

Later that afternoon, Snook received a package addressed to Remus. Inside he found a petition for divorce from Imogene. The papers were accompanied by an odd note:

George,

After our conversation today, it is very plain that you have lost confidence in me, and as you told me to go ahead and file, I think I will follow your advice. If at any time I can assist you please let me know.

My heart weighs too heavy to say any more.

— Imo

If Remus had advised his wife to dissolve their marriage, Snook had missed that conversation.

Snook perused the complaint itself. Mrs. Remus claimed that "although she has conducted herself as a dutiful wife to this defendant, the said defendant has been guilty of extreme cruelty toward this plaintiff in this, to wit: that he has on a number of occasions displayed a terrible temper, shouted and yelled at this plaintiff many times and often in the presence of other persons, and further, that he has on more than one occasion threatened and attempted to strike the plaintiff. In particular he was guilty of these specific acts of extreme cruelty on August 24, 1925, at Atlanta, Ga., when this plaintiff visited this defendant, on which occasion said defendant called said plaintiff vile and unmentionable names, threatened her with bodily harm and finally advised this plaintiff to enter suit for divorce." She wished to reclaim "Holmes" as her surname and be granted sole custody of her daughter, Ruth. In conclusion, Mrs. Remus "represents that she is in great fear of being done bodily harm by this defendant, and that she has reason to believe and does sincerely and earnestly believe that he will, if not restrained, do her severe bodily injury."

Snook called Remus to his office. He would have to be the one to deliver the news. His take: Remus was "a very surprised man."

Remus returned to his cell to write a response, attempting to convey calm and assuredness. He believed that she was under the influence of outside forces but thought it beneficial to act as though he respected her decision.

Dear Imo,

I was more than amazed at the abruptness with which you left. . . . You know that large matters are never accomplished in life, unless one has complications and reactions that are not the most agreeable kind, and therefore you should abide with patience and consideration until all matters are amicably and agreeably adjusted without further perplexities.

Whatever future activity is on your mind at this time, by all means you must positively, certainly and specifically hold in abeyance. So that all grave matters of

211

business complications can be adjusted advantageously, harmoniously and without prejudice to either party, to the mutual benefit of you, Ruthie and myself. We know the everlasting clamor for filthy lucre that the outside imaginary friends, posing as such, for their ulterior gains and benefits, are all the time conspiring, conniving and scheming to obtain whatever betterment they can for their own personal selfish motives.

Never have such matters arising between us, that we cannot agreeably mutually and beneficially adjust to our utter satisfaction without the interlocution of others. So, take heart and if there has been a strong nervous mental tension exerted upon you, and myself as well, cover that precipice may it be ever so high, or may it be ever so low, with the same judgment that should be exerted.

With love to you and Ruth. I am sending Ruthie a copy of this letter.

— As Ever Yours, George Remus

Remus marked this moment as the onset of his "diseased mind."

TESTIMONY OF
OSCAR ERNIE MELVIN

Q. Who are you employed by?

A. James E. Burke Transfer Company, of Gary, Indiana.

Q. Did you ever meet Imogene Remus? . . . Tell us what transpired on that occasion.

A. Well, when I first saw her she came into the office and said she had some stuff in there that she wanted taken to Indianapolis, and I went back to look at the stuff that was to go . . . it consisted of marble and oil paintings, mostly. . . . Mrs. Remus came into the office and told my boss that she was taking this stuff to Indianapolis, and I was right there, and when we got out to start on the truck she rode with me.

Q. What happened when you got to 5th and Broadway in Gary, Indiana?

A. She got out of the truck and told me she was going over to the Packard garage to get her own car . . . she told me to go ahead on the road to Michigan City until she overtook me.

Q. While you were driving around with Mrs. Remus, did you have any conversation with her?

A. I did . . . she said her husband was getting out of jail in a couple of days, and she said, "He won't be out long." That is the very words she said. And she said, "I have got about twenty suits of his clothes that I will give to you. He is about the same size you are." That is what she told me.

Q. What, if anything else, did she say?

A. She said when I left, I remember it very well, she said, "You keep your mouth shut now and you won't get into trouble."

Q. Did you see a weapon of any kind on Mrs. Remus?

A. I saw a gun on Mrs. Remus. I saw it there in Kalamazoo, or somewheres between Kalamazoo and Jackson, and then I saw it right in plain sight in Detroit. . . . She had it in her inside coat pocket with her money.

■ ■ ■ ■

PART II
CARELESS PEOPLE

■ ■ ■ ■

Part II
Careless People

A Bolt from the Blue

At noon on September 2, 1925, Remus exited the Atlanta penitentiary and encountered a fleet of reporters. He carried himself with a threadbare swagger. He had lost fifty-three pounds. His cheap gray suit, the same one issued to every departing inmate, wrinkled and bagged at the knees and waist; he feared that it looked like "a Jewish comedian's." His pockets held divorce papers, immigration papers, $36 in cash, and a check from Imogene. In addition to the shock of the divorce, she sent notice that she'd sold the Fleischmann distillery in Cincinnati, which Remus had bought for $197,000 back in 1921. Imogene accepted $80,000 and mailed him a meager $100 as his cut. He did not know what to think about all she had done — the divorce petition, the strange note, the sale of his property, the theft of his money.

Reporters shouted his name, asking for a comment on Imogene's divorce petition.

"Being in jail is the most awful thing that

can happen to anybody," he said. "I have not been able to eat a bite for the last two days. By the way, when do we eat?" That last question was asked "with the enthusiasm of any doughboy," one newspaper man noted, and two deputy marshals ran across the street to a drugstore, returning with a chocolate soda. Remus downed it in one gulp, tilting his head skyward.

"In prison here," he continued, "she was the kindest woman alive. And now comes this suit. Somebody must have brought pressure to bear on her." Tears veiled his eyes, poised to fall. "I can't understand how anyone who had been so faithful and loving during the five years that we have been married, and who has done every act of kindness possible for me since I have been in prison, could have sued for a divorce days before my release."

His voice broke. The crowd stood quiet and motionless while he composed himself.

"She has been a real wife to me in every shape, form and manner, and she has been kind, considerate and loving," he continued. "Her action in bringing suit for a divorce came like a bolt from the blue, leaving me dazed and astounded."

Amid a constellation of flashbulbs, Remus let U.S. Deputy Marshal John Theobald guide him to a waiting car. He asked the deputy if they might run a few errands before catching the train to Ohio, where Remus was to report to the Montgomery County Jail in Dayton to begin the final stretch of his sentence. The previous year, Theobald had escorted Remus from Cincinnati to Atlanta and in the intervening time had occasionally checked on him in the penitentiary. Given Remus's recent difficulties, and the fact that he was under arrest again for his bootlegging activities in St. Louis, the deputy felt inclined to do him a favor.

"All right, George," Theobald said.

First stop: the immigration office downtown, where Remus submitted documents he hoped would prove his citizenship. A copy of his real birth certificate required minor forgery — changing his birth year from 1876 to 1878, to indicate that he'd been a minor when his father was naturalized.

Next they found a haberdasher's shop, where Remus bought a more comfortable suit. At a nearby market, Remus arranged for groceries to be sent to a prisoner friend's family. By the time they boarded the train it was almost four in the afternoon. They traveled in silence until Theobald felt compelled to address the situation with Imogene.

"We're sorry you got into this family trouble," he said, speaking for all of the guards and deputies. "I don't think there is much to it. It is just a little marriage quarrel, like we all get. You will be living with her next month, and you will be all right."

"No," Remus said quickly. "I don't think so." Outside his window thick swaths of kudzu blurred past. Finally he added, "I don't know what to make of it."

Conners visited him at the Montgomery County Jail on September 4. A guard brought Remus from his cell on the second floor to a room off the corridor. The friends hadn't seen each other since the Atlanta penitentiary, but Conners had news about the Jack Daniel's case that would darken their reunion.

"Your bond in St. Louis is fifty thousand," he said.

Remus looked startled. He collected his thoughts. "I had an inkling of it, but did not think it was true," he said. He asked Conners why his bond was so high when the other defendants had bonds ranging from $2,500 to $10,000 each. Conners said he believed that Mabel Walker Willebrandt was behind the discrepancy.

"My God!" Remus said. He stood, waving his arms as he spoke. "They cannot discriminate against me. I do not believe the government would do it."

"I know it to be a fact," Conners said, "and you might as well prepare for it."

Remus started breathing heavily, long deep rasps that alarmed Conners. He tried to calm him, telling Remus that he would work to raise the money on his behalf, but Remus's

220

mind was now on Imogene. She still loved him, he told Conners. In the end she would come through for him and pay the bond; he was sure of it.

Conners didn't respond.

Remus refocused the conversation, steering it away from Imogene. They needed to discuss the Jack Daniel's case and the risk of him becoming a government witness. The Egan's Rats gang and his former business associates might try to prevent him from testifying. "I understand that if they get me to St. Louis I will be killed down there," he said. "Had you heard anything about it?"

"I had," Conners said and promised he would not let it happen.

A moment passed. Conners could see his friend growing anxious again.

"Were you surprised at Mrs. Remus suing me for a divorce?" Remus asked.

"I was not."

"Why?"

"Didn't you know about it?" Conners asked.

"No," Remus admitted.

It would be a difficult conversation, but Conners pressed on. "I know she had approached two lawyers to take that divorce case thirty days previous to that and they refused," he said. The lawyers told her they wouldn't feel "justified" in bringing a suit against a man who was already suffering in prison.

"I know that little woman did not do it of her own free will," Remus said. "There were some other influences at work."

Conners waited for Remus to circle through his thoughts, contemplating possible connections. He noticed the slight uptick of his movements, a quickening pulse that turned his pale skin red.

"My God," Remus said. He sounded shocked, as though a long-buried memory had resurfaced. "I had light before I was released from Atlanta. Dodge and Mrs. Remus were in Detroit and someone called up anonymously and informed me about them." He started pacing the room. "On that day and previous days I had been receiving mail from her from Cincinnati."

Conners shared his theory. "She used to write ten or twelve letters at one time, dating them the first, second, third, etcetera," he said. "Sometimes in your home your mother or sister, whoever would be there, would mail those letters while she was in different parts of the country."

"By God, Conners," Remus said, moving closer. "I picked her up out of the gutter and tried to make a lady out of her, but it was not in her."

And suddenly Remus wasn't Remus but someone else, a stranger to Conners, a man who gripped his old friend by the shoulders and shook him around the room, maneuvering him backward, leading him in an odd and violent dance. Conners tried to steady them both, to look at Remus straight on and bring him back to the moment, but he could not see the pupils of his eyes.

"Control yourself!" Conners snapped. "The situation will work out all right."

Remus released him. Fifteen minutes passed without a word. "Maybe you are right," Remus said finally, and remembered the note Imogene had included with the divorce papers. "When she wrote the note I think she was just kidding."

Within a week Remus found a bondsman who accepted $2,500 and the Remus Building in Cincinnati as security. He was free to live at home until the beginning of the Jack Daniel's trial. A deputy marshal drove him sixty miles from Dayton to Cincinnati, arriving at seven in the morning. The sight of his mansion was both familiar and acutely strange, as though it, too, had changed in his absence. He approached his front door with caution.

There was no sign of Imogene.

He called his servants' names, one by one, making his way through each room. He had no idea if all or any of them were still under his employ. At last one appeared.

"What has become of my wife?" Remus asked.

The servant hesitated. "She has gone away with Dodge."

"With Dodge!" Remus repeated. "Think of it! Oh, my God!"

He considered his plight in the third person. "Remus has been betrayed by everybody he had trusted," he told Conners, "and now, at last, by the one who owed him the most."

Imogene Remus was missing.

With the Jack Daniel's trial fast approaching, Willebrandt was helping St. Louis prosecutors gather evidence and prepare arguments. "The Remus case is not in good shape," one of them told her, and they did not have much time. Imogene was officially a fugitive from justice, and investigators were frantically trying to track her down.

They spoke to George Remus's lawyer, who'd heard that Imogene was with Dodge "at or near the town of Bedford, Ohio," twenty miles from Cleveland. Johnny Gehrum, Remus's old partner at Death Valley, said that he worked briefly for Imogene as a chauffeur after his release from prison and once took her to New York City, where she met with Dodge at the Commodore Hotel. Dodge, he said, had assumed the responsibility of handling her affairs, in particular the sale of Remus's whiskey certificates. Investigators also made inquiries at the Cincinnati Telephone Company and learned that Imogene's mother had made several calls to Dodge's hometown of Lansing, Michigan.

When Willebrandt heard that George Remus wished to meet with her in Washington, she was skeptical but willing to listen; after Imogene's betrayal with Dodge, Remus might be inclined to divulge everything. How surreal it would be to meet him face-to-face — the man she called "the notorious king of the bootleggers" and, in jest, "the gentleman Remus," the subject of her first and most important Prohibition victory. He was "the moving spirit" behind the Jack Daniel's incident and, depending on his mood and whims, could help her build a solid case. For once she and the bootlegger might be on the same side.

A deputy escorted Remus to her office. He looked thinner than he did in photographs. His suit was impeccably tailored and pressed; his shoes polished; his derby stylish and stiff. But he had an anxiety about him, a humming, low-grade panic etched in every gesture. "Take me before a grand jury," he said. "I'll tell them all they want to know about the Jack Daniel's case." He added that he was making this offer at great risk to his own life.

Willebrandt told him that she would make arrangements for him to travel safely to St.

Louis. In the meantime, she and her agents would continue searching for his wife. When the bootlegger left her office she was no more confident of his intention to cooperate, but without him there might be no case at all.

On September 17, deputy marshals transported Remus from Cincinnati to St. Louis, taking him to the office of federal prosecutor Allen Curry. From speaking with Willebrandt, Curry understood that Remus had implicated high-ranking politicians and officials in the Jack Daniel's deal, and Curry wanted all of the details for the upcoming grand jury.

"I am George Remus," Remus said, and Curry motioned for him to sit down.

"Mr. Remus," Curry began, "I have sent for you to go over evidence in the Jack Daniel's distilling case."

"Yes, that is what I came for."

Curry rummaged through his desk to find a pad and a pencil. "Now, Mr. Remus, you can tell me about it."

For the first minute of the interview Remus was focused and direct, describing how he became involved with the Jack Daniel's scheme. Curry scribbled as fast as he could, his head bowed toward the paper, when he was jolted by a bang against his desk. He looked up to see Remus's meaty fist suspended in the air.

"Curry," Remus said, his voice hitching up an octave, "that man Dodge, he has taken the affections of the one thing in this life that is precious to me, my little wife. After I trusted her and gave her everything into her name, power of attorney. That man Franklin Dodge has taken her away from me and ruined my life forever."

In one swift movement Remus bolted up, the chair skipping across the floor. Curry, shocked, watched him: "He walked the floor, he wrung his hands, he pulled his hair, he jabbed himself in the side, tears ran down his cheeks, great drops of sweat stood on his forehead." Curry let him rave this way for fifteen minutes and finally held up a hand.

"Mr. Remus, sit down."

Remus obeyed.

"I want to know about the Jack Daniel's case," Curry said. "I wasn't talking about your troubles with your wife."

"I know that, Curry," Remus replied, chagrined. "I know that."

Curry attempted to refocus the conversation, asking about politicians involved in the Jack Daniel's deal. Remus was not one minute into his response when his voice changed, rising so drastically in pitch it could be mistaken for a child's. "Oh," he cried, "that man Dodge has ruined my life forever."

Again Curry watched Remus flail and twist about the room. The bootlegger's "face was drawn, his muscles were contorted, he had glassy eyes."

Remus kept repeating the same sentence, as if in a trance: "He has taken my wife away from me and taken her affections, the only thing that is precious in my life, and she is gone from me forever."

Curry gave up and told Remus he was free to go.

Remus took a step toward the door and then abruptly stopped, spinning back to face Curry. "I am being watched by detectives," he said. "They have hired gangsters to kill me."

TESTIMONY OF
ORIN WEBER

Q. Where did you become acquainted with [George Remus]?

A. At my father's home . . . at Chicago.

Q. We want to know anything that you told him.

A. I told him they was out to look for him. . . . She was going to take the certificates to Charlotte, Michigan, and then to Lansing. She was going to take them to Franklin Dodge.

Q. Just tell us if you can remember anything else?

A. That she had four bullets and wanted to get Mr. Remus.

NOT MRS. REMUS
ANY LONGER

In an attempt to protect his remaining assets, Remus revoked Imogene's power of attorney and transferred it to Blanche Watson, a whiskey dealer he'd known since the days of the Circle. Even for Watson, a shrewd businesswoman, it was difficult to determine exactly how much Imogene had stolen and how much Remus had left. From the beginning the bootlegger had diversified and scattered his fortune — bank accounts under assumed names, distilleries, whiskey certificates, real estate, furniture, antiques, jewelry, automobiles, and untold sums of loose cash — without keeping cohesive records. Remus himself boasted that he'd "dealt in millions of dollars and never left a scrap of paper anywhere."

The press described Watson as "a woman who is neither young nor pretty, but very much a heroine nevertheless." Remus liked her. More important, he trusted her. She took orders from no one, not even him, but she didn't need orders to make smart and calculated decisions. She was frank about her opinions of Imogene: "She liked to have money and she spent a great deal of it." She was also unimpressed with Remus's business acumen, pointing out that he spent too freely and that from now on he had to be careful "not to squander." She understood that Remus was "broken, and in no condition to take charge of his own affairs." She had connections in the underworld. She called herself a "mastermind." She endeavored to track down every last cent Imogene had hidden or stolen and preserve what was left of Remus's fortune.

When he wasn't consulting with Watson or Conners, Remus roamed the mansion and its grounds, waiting for the Jack Daniel's trial to begin. The government had secured a change of venue from St. Louis to Indiana, since several Missouri politicians were rumored to be exerting their influence over potential jurors (that two of the accused had transported some of the Jack Daniel's liquor to Indiana made the change possible). The mansion felt empty without Imogene, her flamboyant, maddening, intoxicating presence replaced by stark betrayal. He now believed that Dodge had used his connections in the government to ensure Remus's exorbitant bond, with Imogene's blessing. He felt the ghost of Dodge's presence eating at his table

231

and sleeping in his bed.

In recent weeks he'd heard more details about her indiscretions with Dodge. A friend from Atlanta recalled seeing Dodge and Imogene in the warden's office, sprawled along a couch "in a compromising position." A friend from Chicago overheard Imogene address Dodge as "dear" and "honey." Conners told him everything, aware that facts would help restrain Remus's dangerous imagination. Dodge had taken Imogene to a Cleveland hotel, where he was caught, literally, with his pants down. Imogene and Dodge were traveling all over the country trying to sell his whiskey certificates. These certificates were worth $150 to $200 per barrel, and she was unloading them for $50 to get ready cash.

"It looks like now when she gets through with me I won't have railroad fare," Remus interrupted. "I know she has pawned my jewelry and I will never get it back."

Conners pressed on. Imogene had purchased seven automobiles with Remus's money while he was in prison, giving at least one of them to Dodge.

With each revelation Remus suffered another brainstorm. Conners saw him go "starry." His eyelids fluttered like the wings of a wounded bird. His pupils disappeared. "It would be an angel of mercy," he managed to say, "if someone would send a bullet through me." He dropped his head into his hands and went silent for ten minutes. Conners was afraid to disturb him. He sensed that Remus was trying to cry, but he failed to make a sound. Finally Remus rose and pulled at his tie as though it were a noose, holding it up as high as his arm would reach. For ten minutes his face twitched and changed colors, pale to red, red to purple, the hue deepening with each second. Conners was so overwhelmed by the sight that he had to turn away. Remus's voice emerged in a mangled rasp: "My God, just think of that, it is terrible. It is terrible. It is terrible. It is terrible," a grim mantra of three whispered words. Conners counted twenty-five repetitions before Remus lunged at him, grabbed him by his vest and shook him back and forth, their faces inches apart.

"Did you ever think she would do anything like that?" Remus asked, and stopped to let Conners reply.

He'd always thought she would, Conners admitted, as did all of their Cincinnati friends.

Releasing him, Remus said, "I must have been blind."

Conners was there the night Imogene called the house. For Remus's protection, he listened to every phone call on another extension. Imogene's whereabouts were still unknown, and Remus had been working to find her so that he could share her location with Willebrandt. She spoke with a blithe confidence that infuriated Remus.

"Hello, this is Mrs. Remus talking."

"Oh no," Remus said. "It is not Mrs. Remus any longer. Now, Imogene, I am going to file a cross-petition against you Monday morning, and I will let the world know what you are and that parasite you are traveling around the country with. If you and Dodge have got any idea you are going to deplete my fortune and keep my property from me, Imogene, I will follow you to China, and get back what belongs to me."

Remus kept his word, filing a cross-petition for divorce against Imogene and naming Franklin Dodge in the suit. He accused his wife of a litany of offenses: In January 1925, while Remus was in his cell at the Atlanta penitentiary, Imogene had had "improper relations" with Dodge after hours, in the warden's office. She continued these relations later in Cleveland, Ohio, and various other locales. She and Dodge had conspired to deprive him of his liberty by causing him to be arrested and held in prison under excessive bond. She "squandered and dissipated large amounts of his property while consorting with Dodge." Remus denied Imogene's charges of cruelty, physical abuse, and his alleged infliction of "humiliation, mental anguish or embarrassment" and asked that she be denied alimony.

The cross-petition provoked a reaction from Dodge, as Remus had wanted and expected. Speaking about Imogene and Remus publicly for the first time, the former agent issued a statement to the press on October 8. The charges were "absolutely absurd and false." Mrs. Remus was a "very honorable woman," whose conduct had been "above reproach." Mr. Remus was motivated by revenge because it was he, Dodge, who had investigated the bootlegger for violations of the Volstead Act. Since his resignation, he'd been probing "the life and activities" of Mr. Remus. Among other things, he discovered that Remus was disbarred in Chicago and that he is not "mentally responsible." He intended to assist Mrs. Remus in preparing her divorce and alimony case for trial.

Imogene, meanwhile, remained at large.

At the end of October, federal officials summoned Remus to Indianapolis and put him up in a suite at the Claypool Hotel, where years earlier he had beaten a man almost to death for consorting with Imogene. He took a taxi to the federal building and went to the office of John Marshall, the federal prosecutor handling the Jack Daniel's case.

Marshall had spoken about Remus extensively with Willebrandt, who remained suspicious of the bootlegger's intentions. "I would be very reluctant to grant Remus immunity," she wrote. "You are not dealing in this case with the ordinary defendant. Remus has been before the public a long time. His name makes splendid newspaper copy. . . . The Government has had enough experience with Remus to know the character of the man it is dealing with, and it should be very sure of its ground before it grants him any immunity." Marshall promised to heed her advice.

This time Remus was calm and composed, giving detailed and coherent answers about the Jack Daniel's scheme; he was forthcoming about his business partners, the complicit politicians, and his wife and her monetary contribution. He held nothing back about Imogene. He would keep talking until that woman was indicted and behind bars.

On November 1, Marshall sent Willebrandt a report about the interview: "It is of course realized that the success of this case, especially as to some of the more important defendants, depends in a large measure upon the testimony of George Remus. . . . It is my opinion that Remus has made every effort to conform his story to the truth, although he has consented to become a witness for the purpose of saving himself, and in some measure for revenging himself upon his associates." Contrary to Willebrandt's wishes, Remus would have full immunity in exchange for his testimony. "I must say to you that I like the way Remus is acting," he told Willebrandt, "and if he maintains his present attitude he will certainly be a great value." The trial would begin on December 14 in Indianapolis, even if Imogene had yet to be apprehended. To assist in the search, Marshall traveled to Washington, bringing along Remus's description of his wife: "Mrs. Imogene A. Remus, 40 years of age, 5 ft. 6 inches, stout, black hair, sallow complexion, black eyes, flashy dresser." J. Edgar Hoover tracked Imogene's suspected movements, updating Willebrandt with telegrams between field agents and federal authorities:

Detroit, Mich. — McLaughlin, Dept. of Justice, St. Louis. Re: Jack Daniel's Distillery. Is Mrs. George Remus in custody your district if so wire Hennegar Indianapolis District she is wanted there.

Mehegan, Post Office Bldg., Detroit, Mich. — Your telegram re Jack Daniel's Mrs. George Remus not in custody here understand she was here about week ago but left for parts unknown if you have any information as to her being here advise — McLaughlin.

Hoover's next dispatch to Willebrandt, dated November 19, claimed that Imogene was currently in Washington, D.C. A reporter for the *St. Louis Post-Dispatch* named John Rogers heard this news from a government source. Rogers, who was working on a series about Remus's life and career, called him right away. He would meet Remus and Conners in the capital.

In Washington, Remus and Conners took a cab to the Mayflower Hotel. According to Rogers's information, Dodge and Imogene were registered there under "Mr. and Mrs. E. J. Ward" in two adjacent rooms.

Remus took Room 624 and called the Department of Justice. He identified himself and demanded to speak with an agent, explaining that he had important information that the department should act on right away.

Two agents responded to Remus's call and found him in an agitated state.

"Have you seen either your wife or Dodge at the hotel?" one agent asked. "Have you in any manner identified either one of them?"

"I have not," Remus admitted, adding that he believed that the couple were dining in Room 843. He implored the agents to hurry in order to "catch them together" and "nab" his wife.

One of the agents stepped forward. He told Remus that he himself was not personally aware of a fugitive case against Mrs. Remus, and could take no action without explicit orders from the Bureau.

"I will get the house detective and go into the room myself," Remus insisted. "I can hardly keep from choking that man."

The agent told Remus that he could take any action he desired, but he would be acting without the permission of the Justice Department. They left Remus standing alone in the doorway of his room.

He did not stay there long.

Conners and Rogers found Remus on the eighth floor, plunging at the door of Room 843, head lowered, shoulder pitched forward, each contact harder than the last, the wood beginning to split. "He was in a great agonized state of mind," Rogers saw. "His eyes were bulging. He behaved like a wild man . . . he broke out in a great perspiration, puffing like a bull." For an hour the two men battled Remus, securing his arms behind his back and maneuvering him to his room, only for him to wriggle free and bolt down the hall. Finally, they managed to put him to bed and soothe him to sleep, after which they retired to their respective rooms.

Imogene, it turned out, had never been in Room 843. That night, she was eight hundred miles away, in St. Louis. On the advice of her lawyer she had turned herself in to federal authorities and posted $10,000 bond. She would be free until the trial began in Indianapolis, where she would see Remus for the first time in four months.

Time, distance, and Willebrandt's schedule had not diminished Fred Horowitz's ardor. As he practiced law in Los Angeles and built the Chateau Marmont (intent on making it the city's first earthquake-proof building), he hoped that Willebrandt — with young Dorothy in tow — would one day return west so that they could settle down and become a proper family. Fred still wanted to marry her, and Willebrandt had promised him an answer by year's end.

Somehow, since taking her position, she had become not only the most powerful woman in America but also the most famous, excepting movie stars like Lillian Gish and Clara Bow. She received more press than even George Remus; over the previous four years her name had appeared in nearly five thousand newspaper articles. How she longed for "those delicious lazy Sundays," she wrote in her diary, "when one lies in bed until noon and reads with no compunction or concern for lives wasted!" She was working fifteen-hour days, raising a toddler and grappling with a hearing problem, and she realized that she was incapable of reshaping her life to fit with someone else's. Her oldest friend from California was right when she said that Willebrandt "never really belonged to anyone."

Before the start of the Jack Daniel's trial

she composed a response to Fred, her letters jagged and tilting to and fro, as if she'd written from the last car of a speeding train:

Dearest,

The year is up and you rightly ask a final reply. I do not question your demand, but I have put off our date now to give you an answer — for several months I have increasingly known that it must be as it is, dear, No — I am afraid; I cannot feel sure that your love and satisfaction with our marriage will last, given the strain social conditions and other circumstances out of my control will put upon a relationship such as ours — in fact I feel so brokenheartedly sure that however high and sure your faith it will not survive the storms into which we head.

And yes, oh my dear and precious part of me — you in making the high adventure risk little outside the personal heart of disillusion. To break off after five years or ten would add, not detract from your prestige and opportunity for a full life. "Yes, the young unknown man whom Mrs. W married? Must be more to him hidden, but of course he could not remain so tied — have you seen her?"

But oh, for me wretched would be the fruits of all my self repressions and discipline and achievements so far. I'd be broken, safe only financially, and I couldn't bear your pity . . . This year has been more hard than I think you know . . ..

Dear, dear, good night.

THAT SOCIAL PERVERT, THAT SOCIAL LEPER, THAT SOCIAL PARASITE

One morning during the final week of November, John Rogers sat at his desk in the office of the *St. Louis Post-Dispatch,* reading his notes on George Remus. Rogers, forty-four, had been with the newspaper for eight years and had quickly achieved national renown; he had a particular gift for obtaining confessions from criminals. In 1922, while investigating the Ku Klux Klan in northern Louisiana, he received death threats as he uncovered the truth about two missing young men whose bodies had been found in a bayou. In addition to his upcoming series on Remus, he was probing the corrupt activities of a federal judge — a series that would force the judge's impeachment and earn Rogers a Pulitzer Prize. "Unusual things in usual number happened to John T. Rogers," the *Post-Dispatch* noted. Willebrandt anointed him "the greatest correspondent in the world."

The phone trilled on Rogers's desk. He did

not recognize the voice, low and gruff, at the other end, and the caller did not offer his name. He had something to tell Rogers: George Remus was about to be killed in Indianapolis by gangsters.

"Who is this?" Rogers asked.

"That doesn't make any difference."

The journalist wanted to keep him on the line. "How do you know this is going to happen?"

"Because Mrs. Remus and Dodge have paid to have it done," the source said.

"Paid what?"

"Fifteen thousand dollars."

"To whom?" Rogers prompted.

"That is all," the source said, and hung up.

Immediately, Rogers called the Claypool Hotel in Indianapolis and asked for the room of Assistant Attorney General John Marshall. At the sound of Marshall's greeting, Rogers asked where Remus was.

"Remus is here in the room with me," Marshall said.

Rogers recounted the anonymous call.

"We will look out," Marshall promised. "We don't pay much attention to that sort of thing, but thank you for your interest."

Four hours later Rogers's phone rang again. This time it was Marshall.

"There is evidently something to that report which you telephoned this morning," the attorney said, and explained: Remus had planned a short trip to Cincinnati to check on his mansion and bought a ticket for a train departing at noon. When Marshall and Remus arrived at Union Station, they noticed suspicious men — well-known gangsters from Chicago and St. Louis — hiding behind pillars in the waiting room. Upon spotting Remus, the gangsters began to edge closer, following Remus to the platform. The bootlegger became distressed, swinging his arms and flushing from his throat to his scalp. He refused to board the train. He told Marshall that Imogene and Dodge had recruited Mabel Walker Willebrandt, the "czarina of Prohibition matters," in their murderous plot. He believed that Willebrandt "has been intimate" — and perhaps still *was* intimate — with Dodge. They were all out to get him, and he was not safe, and what did the government intend to do about it?

The government couldn't lose Remus as a witness, through either murder or fear. "Now listen," Marshall said, thinking quickly. "You are not going to leave. . . . I shall recommend to the government to pay your flat bill." He rented a private apartment for Remus twenty minutes from Indianapolis proper, paying $125 in advance for two weeks, until the beginning of the trial. He surrounded the apartment with Secret Service men and assured the bootlegger that no one would be able to find him, but Remus remained unconvinced. Dodge had spent most of his career hunting people down, and now he had the benefit of Imogene's knowledge and help.

Remus demanded a gun.

Marshall borrowed a Colt .45 revolver and some bullets from the Prohibition headquarters in Indianapolis. For Remus, this gift carried with it an unspoken understanding — that he was to go ahead and shoot anyone that came near him, with the "full authority of the government." Dodge had encroached on Imogene day by day, an assault of slick promises and vacant words, hijacking Remus's life. Now Remus could put a stop to all of it and lawfully reclaim his rightful place.

"I am his master," Remus said of Dodge. "Physically."

The following week, Rogers and his *Post-Dispatch* colleague Paul Anderson took a train to Indianapolis and went straight to Remus's apartment. They asked hundreds of questions about the bootlegger's life: his childhood in Chicago; his work as a pharmacist and attorney; his graft payments to Jess Smith and his bootlegging empire; his first wife and his affair with Imogene. Remus was receptive and gracious, offering long, rambling answers with copious detail. Anderson drafted the series' flattering opening lines: "If there has ever been a bigger bootlegger than

George Remus of Cincinnati, the fact remains a secret. Remus's operations were by far the most pretentious ever uncovered. His career was short, but not even the prison term which terminated it can extinguish its brilliance and audacity. In the years 1920 and 1921, Remus was to bootlegging what in earlier years Rockefeller had been to oil."

The atmosphere changed when the journalists mentioned Imogene's betrayal with Dodge. "When I returned," Remus said, speaking of his release from prison, "my heart was being eaten out of me because I did love this woman, thought a lot of her." The mere sound of the agent's name stirred Remus into a prolonged rampage that was at once entertaining and alarming. "That pimp Dodge," Remus said. "That social pervert, that social leper, that social parasite." He would "mash" Dodge until he was "flat as a pancake, absolutely."

Remus was simply "cracked" on the subject, Anderson observed. His neck "swelled like a cobra's" and he indulged violent fantasies that invariably began with the words: "If I could get my hands on that pimp Dodge. . . ." Oh, how he wanted to "crack a skull."

"Don't attempt anything like that," Rogers warned. "Don't resort to violence."

Remus spun to face the journalist. "Don't talk to me of violence! Those people have murdered me, in and out of prison every night for the past two years. Don't talk that way to me."

Rogers understood the bootlegger's position. A few months earlier, he had traveled to Atlanta to investigate the allegations that Remus was not a citizen. The immigration inspector confirmed that Imogene and Dodge were the ones who had provided the tip.

The series on Remus would not be complete without comment from Dodge, who had also come to Indianapolis and checked into the Claypool Hotel. Rogers called to make an appointment, and at the specified hour the reporter left Remus's company and ventured into the biting cold. An article in that day's *Indianapolis Star* reported that dry agents along the U.S. northern border, citing the inclement weather, had temporarily ceased enforcement in order to help rum runners and their cargo get safely to land. The wind kicked up swirls of snow and subdued the sounds of the street, every footstep and automobile hushed.

The Claypool's lobby brought a welcome gust of warm air. Rogers took the elevator to the fourth floor, silently rehearsing his questions as the operator worked the switch. Dodge opened the door and invited Rogers inside. The reporter saw another man lying on the bed and recognized him as Imogene's lawyer.

As soon as Rogers took a seat, Dodge pointed at him, keeping his arm steady as he spoke. "I have got the goods on you," he said. "You were present when George Remus gave George Conners twenty-eight thousand dollars to go to St. Louis and pay the Egan gangsters to kill Mrs. Remus."

"You're misinformed of what had happened," Rogers said. "You and Mrs. Remus had gone to St. Louis and offered a murderer fifteen thousand dollars to kill George Remus. It was I who informed Assistant Attorney General John Marshall of that plot, and an investigation by the Department of Justice disclosed there was some foundation for it, that gangsters were seen lying in wait for George Remus at the Union Station."

Dodge was quiet for a moment and then let his large frame relax, sinking an inch in his chair. "Well, we will let it go at that. What is it you wanted to see me about?"

Rogers leaned forward, preparing to watch Dodge's reaction for clues, squints and twitches that would hint at motivations and character. "In view of all the charges and cross charges that have been made, would you care to make a statement of your relations with Mrs. Remus? What they are and what they amount to?"

He glanced at the bed, where Imogene's lawyer still lay motionless, possibly asleep.

Without hesitation Dodge answered,

249

"That's nobody's business but my own."

Rogers tried a different approach. "George Remus looks upon you as having invaded the sanctity of his home."

"Well, if you want to know what I am doing for Mrs. Remus, I am gathering evidence for her in her divorce suit. That is my position in this case, and Remus is a liar and a scoundrel."

"There naturally must be some bad feeling there," Rogers encouraged. "More bad feeling than it seems."

Without warning Dodge rose from his chair and approached. He slid his shirtsleeve up toward his shoulder, exposing his arm, and dangled it an inch from Rogers's face.

"Feel this muscle," Dodge ordered.

Rogers obliged, dragging a finger over the hump of bicep, the muscle tightening under his touch. He retracted his hand.

"I have got this for Remus," Dodge said. "I could crush him like an egg."

Rogers played along. "You are a large man, Mr. Dodge, and Remus is a small man."

"Yes, I weigh two hundred and forty."

Rogers changed the subject, asking a question to which he knew the answer. "Are you still in the Department of Justice?"

"No, I am not. I have resigned."

"As a matter of fact, were you not dismissed from the Department of Justice?"

Dodge stood abruptly. Digging through his

suitcase, he emerged with a letter, which he offered to read aloud. He claimed that it was from none other than Mabel Walker Willebrandt, assistant attorney general of the United States. It commended his work as an agent of the Department of Justice, expressed regret at his decision to resign, and stated that he would be welcome to return at any time.

He did not hand the letter to Rogers so that he could read it for himself. Instead, he tucked it into his pocket and motioned toward his suitcase, where two pistols lay on top of his clothes.

"That is for Remus when he is ready," he said, snapping the suitcase shut. "That is all I have to say. Go back and say that to your friend, with my compliments."

Rogers stood to leave, Dodge's eyes heavy on his back.

Days before the start of the trial, prosecutor John Marshall moved Remus from the private apartment to a room at the Claypool Hotel and took the room next door. He asked Rogers to remain with Remus for the bootlegger's protection. Conners and one of Willebrandt's Mabelmen also kept Remus company, the four of them squeezed into a twelve-by-fifteen-foot space. Remus kept his borrowed government pistol by his side.

At the end of the first day, Rogers gave

Remus an update on the court proceedings. A gauger at the Jack Daniel's distillery testified about his discovery that the barrels were filled with water instead of whiskey. Harry Boyd, Remus's former chauffeur, detailed the milking itself: the whiskey passing through a long rubber hose; the "bung starter" used to pound barrels and spring the wood; the electric buzzer that would sound after the barrels were filled. To Remus's delight, he also implicated Imogene directly, telling the jury, "She had made rum-running trips with me."

The next morning Remus was required to appear in court in case the government needed him on the stand. After breakfast at the Claypool Hotel (during which, thankfully, there was no sight of Dodge), Remus, Conners, Rogers, and the Mabelman started off to the courthouse on foot.

As they turned down Meridian Street, the group noticed Imogene and her attorney walking about a hundred feet ahead. She wore a wool cloche hat and a fur coat Remus had given her, and she spun her head as though she had sensed his presence. At the sight of him Imogene screamed, a piercing siren that halted all movement and conversation along the block: "Daddy, don't kill me! Don't let him hurt me!" She dashed ahead of her lawyer, teetering in her double-strap heels.

Rogers gauged Remus's reaction. The bootlegger did not hasten his pace but merely shook his head and said, "Look what a spectacle she is making of herself. Now she will try to make capital out of this." Moments later, inside the courtroom, Rogers left Remus to take his seat at the press table. Imogene approached the table and addressed every reporter in attendance. She wanted them all to know that her estranged husband, George Remus, was "disappointed at efforts to effect a reconciliation" and had just tried to assassinate her on the street that very morning. Rogers was the lone reporter who declined to print this allegation in the evening editions.

"That's what I get," Remus said, "for being tied up with a bag of filth like that. . . . Now she tries to blacken my reputation through the press."

The government did not call Remus but told him to be prepared to take the stand the next day.

That evening Rogers, Conners, and Remus planned to dine together in the Claypool. Despite the day's excitement Remus was remarkably calm; he even left the pistol in his room. Rogers hoped this tranquillity would last at least through dinner.

The elevator operator pushed the run switch to the right. Fourth floor, third, second, ground. The chime of a bell, the pull of the wrought iron grate, and then the lobby of the hotel spread before them, guests weaving between Roman columns, glimpsing their reflections in mirrored panels. Fifty feet away, a group of men walked in concert toward the dining room, talking and laughing, and as they neared the entrance their faces became visible, the tallest one a head above the rest: Dodge.

Remus tensed and hurtled forward. Conners and Rogers dove after him, grasping the sleeves of his coat and pulling him back as if steadying a listing ship. "It takes two good men to hold Remus when he is in one of those things," Rogers realized. The bootlegger lashed and snarled and writhed. They backed him up to the elevator, one step at a time, their legs wide and their feet planted, pulling and pulling, until the grate closed in front of them, a locked cage. From then on, they ordered every meal to be served in Remus's room.

On the morning of Wednesday, December 16, Imogene made a prediction to reporters that Remus would faint on his way to the stand. Guards stood by every entrance, waiting for his arrival. Rogers watched from the press table, Conners from the spectator benches. Flanked by Mabelmen, Remus walked steadily. He did not faint. He placed his hand on a Bible, swore to tell the truth, and looked directly at Imogene, sitting among twenty-six other defendants.

Before he could speak Imogene's attorney stood and addressed the Court. "We object to Mr. Remus's testimony on the ground that he was the husband of Imogene Remus at the time of the alleged offense," he said, "and is still her husband, and that he is incompetent as a witness."

Remus sat positively still. He expected Imogene's lawyer might try this trick but hoped that the current state of the marriage — with divorce petitions and cross-petitions filed — would work in his favor.

John Marshall's co-prosecutor approached the bench. "We feel," he said, "that there is too much question about this point to permit such an objection going in the records. And for that reason, the Government moves to nolle pros the case as to Mrs. Imogene Remus."

In other words, all charges against Imogene had been dropped, and she was now free to go.

Inside Remus raged but he kept his composure on the stand, answering Marshall's questions about the Jack Daniel's debacle with deliberate calm. Hoping to combat the recent reports that Remus had threatened Imogene, Marshall asked him to comment on the incident.

"It has appeared in the newspapers that I sought a reconciliation with Mrs. Imogene Remus," he said, his voice empty of all emotion. "The woman's statement in this regard is false. I did not attempt at any time, directly or indirectly, a reconciliation. When the article appeared, Mrs. Remus was a defendant in the Jack Daniel's case now being prosecuted here, and I was to be the chief witness for the government in the case. It appeared to me that her statement was designed to influence me in her behalf so as to weaken the government's case. If this was her intention, it failed utterly."

He took a breath. The stenographer clicked her keys.

"If Mrs. Remus has any hopes of reconciliation with me let her put such hopes aside. She has become repulsive to me."

On the strength of Remus's testimony, twenty-four of his former associates were found guilty. "This is going to be a hell of a Christmas for Remus," he said, adding them to his running list of people who wished him dead.

TESTIMONY OF
JOHN S. BERGER

Q. You say you called upon Mrs. Remus?
A. I did . . . I said to Mr. Remus, "Your wife wants nothing whatever to do with you. Your wife is madly in love with Franklin Dodge." I said to Mr. Remus that she would not refund any of his property in any way, nor would she take from Mr. Remus the few hundred thousand dollars that I offered her to return to Mr. Remus his property, and he would agree to let her have a divorce . . . she wanted to keep everything she had because she told me she was madly and greatly in love with Franklin Dodge.
Q. Now, were there any other incidents?
A. The following day I again called on Mrs. Remus. . . . On my second visit there she said that her and her new heavy lover, Franklin Dodge, would kill George Remus at sight, and they had hired some gangsters which were going to get a lot of money to kill George.

257

NONE THE WORSE FOR IT

Willebrandt began 1926 with a Prohibition press conference in Washington, standing alongside an ax-wielding U.S. marshal poised to lower his weapon onto a pyramid of whiskey bottles. "Looks Like Dry New Year," read the wire service photo caption, which no one — especially Willebrandt — believed. Six years after the dawn of the "noble experiment," she could cite a few statistics that signaled progress and success. At the beginning of Prohibition drinking levels plummeted by 70 percent; although drinking had increased since then, the overall trend remained steady. Cirrhosis rates, fatalities from alcohol, and arrests for public drunkenness had all declined. A recent report revealed that arrests for "offenses against chastity" and "foul language" in New York City had fallen 20 percent, a phenomenon that sparked both celebration and ridicule. In a column titled "Sad Decline of Swearing Lamented," the *New York Times* lauded profanity for encouraging "volubility and versatility. Invention is enforced when the supply of ready-made profanity gives out."

But wets skewed these same reports to bolster the notion that Prohibition was at best an abject failure and at worst "the biggest joke that ever happened in this country," as one St. Louis newspaper put it. Although Americans collectively were drinking less, those national statistics didn't account for individual habit; those who *did* drink were consuming more than ever before, overcompensating for those who abstained. Chicago's notoriously corrupt mayor, "Big" Bill Thompson, was running for reelection on the promise that he would not only reopen saloons that had been closed but also open ten thousand new ones. Bootlegging was Detroit's second-largest industry, employing fifty thousand people and garnering more than $2 million in sales annually. The police commissioner of New York City announced that thirty-two thousand speakeasies populated his streets — one for about every 215 New Yorkers, including children (other estimates bumped the number to an even hundred thousand). "There is not less drunkenness in the Republic, but more," wrote H. L. Mencken in the *American Mercury*. "There is not less crime, but more. There is not less insanity, but more."

The decline in arrests for profanity and

lewd behavior had less to do with greater sobriety than with swift and sweeping changes in social mores, including among the police. Thirty-nine percent of American women now engaged in premarital sex (and weren't afraid to admit it), many of them using a new form of contraception called the Dutch cap. They drank with men, smoked, cursed, and invented their own vocabulary: An "embalmer" was a bootlegger; a "petting party" was a social event devoted to kissing and fondling; "dropping the pilot" signified a divorce; and "given the air" was a unisex phrase for being "thrown down" on a date. Willebrandt herself admired their brazenness and envied their freedom. "When I was a girl," she told one reporter, "it was considered a sin to kiss a man before one was engaged. Now this so-called flapper kisses when she likes, and she is none the worse for it."

Both advocates and foes of Prohibition could agree on one indisputable fact: The law had only become more difficult to enforce. Since anyone charged with violating Prohibition laws was entitled to a jury trial, courts were overburdened and, in the larger wet cities, devolved into unruly circuses that only fostered more crime. The scene in Manhattan's federal building was, according to one official, "a seething mob of bartenders, peddlers, waiters, bond runners and fixers," the last group generally found huddled in the bathrooms, waiting to bribe jurors. Arrests didn't always result in indictments, and indictments rarely resulted in convictions, since most Manhattan jurors — often of the same ethnic group as the defendants — didn't believe that violating liquor laws merited any punishment at all.

Funds to fight the liquor traffic diminished each year. Many states had once relied on liquor sale taxes to balance their budgets, and Prohibition erased that revenue. Fewer and fewer states spent any money at all on pursuing bootleggers, choosing instead to devote resources to the enforcement of fishing and hunting laws. At the federal level, the government had suffered a loss of $11 billion in tax revenue while spending $300 million on enforcement; hence Willebrandt's zeal to prosecute bootleggers for tax evasion. Since she'd lost Remus's tax case before the Supreme Court, bootleggers had found another way to combat her efforts: invoking the Fifth Amendment. Being forced to file an income tax form as a bootlegger, thereby admitting illegal enterprise, would violate their rights against self-incrimination.

Willebrandt remained exasperated with the quality of Prohibition agents, many of them as greedy, ruthless, and crooked as the bootleggers they were hired to pursue. A debate raged about including agents under the civil service, which would theoretically eliminate the corrupting influence of politics and ensure merit-based appointments. In the meantime, she marveled at the continuing difficulty in finding honest agents. "I refuse to believe," she wrote, "that out of our one hundred and twenty million population . . . it is impossible to find four thousand men who can not be bought."

All of these factors were on Willebrandt's mind when she received John Marshall's letter. After his success at the Jack Daniel's trial, the Indianapolis prosecutor felt compelled to lobby on behalf of his star witness, who was soon to serve his final sentence.

"My dear Mrs. Willebrandt," he wrote, "I received a wire from Mr. Remus in which he solicits me to lend any influence I might have in relieving him from the jail sentence of one year. . . . No one knows better than myself that Mr. Remus incurred financial loss as well as physical danger as a result of his testimony in the Jack Daniel's case, and this danger is not yet ended. . . . I do feel a considerable appreciation of his services and while I have in no sense obligated myself to him, I would be pleased to do anything I could that would result in the dismissal of this case. I know that it would only be futile and extremely bad taste for me to ask you to set aside your deliberate judgment in these matters but I cannot conceive that there is any harm in expressing myself as I have."

Willebrandt's answer was no — politely to Marshall and more vehemently to an assistant: "If anybody has any notion," she scribbled on an inter-office memo, "that I ever promised to set aside Remus's year sentence let their minds be set at rest! I did not." Instead she began adding newspaper clippings to her Remus file, documenting his accusations against Franklin Dodge and his contentious divorce. "After what my wife has done," Remus said in one article, "she is dead to me."

On March 24, 1926, Republican Fiorello H. La Guardia, the future legendary mayor of New York City, prepared to give a speech on the floor of the House. The topic of debate was Prohibition, and Representative La Guardia's feelings on the matter were well known. In his view, the 18th Amendment represented and encouraged a crusade against American cities and their immigrant communities, something his critics seemed to openly admit. "He's from New York, where there are few real Americans," said one dry official from Maine. "He has the commonest of all foreigners for his constituents — Italian wine-bibbers who have sent him to Congress to recover for them their lost beverage."

La Guardia strode up to the dais carrying a pile of paperwork, given to him privately by George Conners, confidant of the bootlegger

George Remus. He had thirty minutes to illustrate the hypocrisy of dry officials and the futility of trying to enforce such an absurd law. He stood as tall as his five-foot-two frame would allow, the papers held aloft like a weapon.

"Mr. Chairman and gentlemen," he began, his high-pitched voice echoing across the floor. "I do not desire at this time to start a debate on the wet and dry question. We have had a lot of that of late. I have some facts which tend to show a disgraceful disregard for the law on the part of officials who are or were responsible for its enforcement. . . . They came to my knowledge and I deem it my duty to present them to you and to register my protest at the indifference of the Department of Justice and the Prohibition Unit in tolerating conditions which under proper vigilance could not escape their official knowledge."

He paused, checking his paper, fearing he was not skilled at reading aloud.

"When a United States official," he continued, "a prominent investigator in the Department of Justice, who acquired a national reputation as the 'ace' of investigators, leaves the United States Government service in order to go into the bootlegging business and to traffic in the very same goods for which others were convicted and sent to jail, it is about time Congress takes notice and makes some effort to ascertain how general this condition may be and to what degree the departmental conscience has been callused."

John Rankin, Democrat of Mississippi, stood and motioned toward La Guardia. "The gentleman has made a statement there about someone leaving the Department of Justice and going into the bootlegging business. Does not the gentleman think he should name him, if he is going to make such a charge?"

"I will come to that," La Guardia promised. "I will give his name."

Rankin took his seat.

"In the early part of 1922 one George Remus and others were tried and convicted in the city of Cincinnati on an indictment of conspiracy. The conspiracy charge was based on activities of the various defendants in diverting quantities of liquor to unlawful channels. . . . The case was worked up by a Department of Justice agent, one Franklin L. Dodge, who took pride in making himself known as the 'ace' of the Department of Justice. In connection with this case most, if not all, of the defendants were tried and convicted on a separate indictment charging them with maintaining a nuisance in violation of the Prohibition enforcement act."

Thomas Blanton, Democrat of Texas, raised his hand. "Mr. Chairman, will the gentleman yield?"

265

"I will yield later," La Guardia said. "The gentleman from Texas will have plenty of time."

For his remaining twenty minutes he presented his case and raised questions about another conspiracy — not by Remus and his associates but by the Department of Justice. After Remus was sent to the Atlanta penitentiary, La Guardia explained, Dodge investigated corruption in the prison. While gathering information on the warden, he "became very friendly with the wife of the prisoner Remus, and their conduct in the very warden's office is too obscene to relate at this time."

While Remus remained in Atlanta, Dodge — still an agent with the Department of Justice — stole Remus's property, including jewelry and $200,000 in whiskey certificates. He then traveled to New York City and offered to sell all of Remus's whiskey certificates to a potential Manhattan customer. When the customer declined, Dodge was faced with a problem: He needed to "keep Remus in jail and in the clutches of the law" in order to dispose of the bootlegger's certificates.

Was it possible, La Guardia posed, that Dodge — even after he left the Department of Justice — was able to influence the government's legal action against Remus? Why were five of Remus's co-defendants liberated from the "nuisance" conviction? Why was the bail for other defendants in the Jack Daniel's case set at $5,000, while Remus — a government witness, no less — had to pay $50,000? Why was it that the "persecution" of Remus continued, even when the special prosecutor in the Jack Daniel's case lobbied on his behalf?

At this juncture La Guardia read aloud John Marshall's recent letter to Willebrandt.

"I think," he concluded, "that when we have a situation where a Government agent works up a case and puts his man in jail, and while that man is in jail he acquires the very same property for which this man was sent to jail, and succeeds in having the Department of Justice prosecute this man and hold him while cases against others are dismissed — I think it is an outrageous condition, and I think that some action should be taken."

"I wish to ask the gentleman," said Charles Gordon Edwards, Democrat of Georgia, "if he thinks it is going to help the government service and the Department of Justice by making these unfortunate criticisms and whether he thinks those things will help the cause before the country?"

"They are not unfortunate criticisms, but they are the unfortunate conditions which exist in the department," La Guardia countered. "Would not the gentleman have brought such conditions to the knowledge of the House if he had obtained them?"

"No," Edwards said. "I think I would have done the same as the Department of Justice did. Fire the man out."

"Ought we not to hold the infamous liquor traffic responsible," Blanton asked, "for seducing this Government agent and leading him astray?"

"What do you want to do?" La Guardia replied, angry now, voice squeaking. "Do you want to give him a congressional medal for his behavior? I would put him in jail."

"It is the liquor interests that are forever trying to break down this law, and their pernicious efforts lead these agents astray," Blanton argued.

"Surely the gentleman is not going to condone the conduct of agents who are led astray?" La Guardia asked.

"No," Blanton said, his voice etched with sarcasm. "I condemn them just like you do — not."

"I do condemn them," La Guardia said. "I had this knowledge, and I will bring such other knowledge as I obtain to the attention of this House."

With that, his colleagues gave him an ovation.

That same afternoon, Remus, dressed in a fine silk suit and matching bowler, returned home to Chicago for the first time in five years, intending to visit his daughter, Romola, and to save 1,550 cases of rare pre-war bourbon housed in one of his distilleries (a trip that proved futile, as the United States Circuit Court of Appeals for the Seventh Circuit had already ordered the cases to be destroyed). Upon leaving the courthouse he encountered a swarm of reporters, who noted that his "sartorial splendor" belied his foul mood. "He had three or four grievances," observed the *Chicago Tribune,* "the first being his wife, the second being his wife, the third and fourth being his wife."

As the press shouted questions Remus changed his tone, allowing a twinge of optimism. "They are getting wise to this fellow Dodge, though," he said. "Why, today in Congress Representative La Guardia of New York mentioned that Dodge had tried to dispose of $200,000 in whiskey certificates that belong to me. The congressman wants to rip into the crookedness of Prohibition officials and he is making no mistake in investigating Dodge."

He turned dreamy and wistful: If only he hadn't trusted Imogene and given her power of attorney. If only she "had remained true blue." If only he could get his money back he'd be on "easy street." If only he could cordon off the memories of her betrayal and plan for a future where he'd never heard her name. "I'm going to stay in Chicago from now on,"

269

he announced. "Real estate is going to be my line."

And in that moment he let himself believe it.

A PEARL-HANDLED REVOLVER

After John Rogers's series on Remus for the *St. Louis Post-Dispatch* was completed and published, he kept Remus in his life. He now considered the bootlegger a friend and worried about his turbulent moods and violent brainstorms, his despair over being trapped in what he called a "life of hell." Rogers told his editor that Remus had lost his mind. Whenever possible, he traveled to see Remus in Cincinnati or accompanied him on the road. But once Remus got lost in one of his rages, there was little Rogers could do to rescue him. The mere sound of the word "Dodge" seemed to wound him. Raised veins laid tracks across his swollen neck. His voice whisked itself into a fury, the words disjointed in sound and tone.

Did Rogers know exactly what he had suffered at the hands of Dodge and Mrs. Remus? That after Mrs. Remus visited him at the Atlanta penitentiary she would then go to the Robert Fulton Hotel and "have wild drinking

271

parties with that pimp"? They had sought to have him killed and they were still at it, and good God, was there any justice in the world anywhere, that these people were allowed to persecute him as they do?

At least that was the best sense Rogers could make of these speeches, for Remus had begun to speak in broken sentences, words truncated, syllables dropped, leaping from one thought to the next without any connection between the two. Rogers would wait it out, sometimes for hours on end, and eventually Remus would right himself: his pace lessening, his hands no longer pounding his forehead, the color of his skin morphing from red to pink to white. He would sit down across from Rogers, dazed and exhausted, a stranger to that wild lunatic speaking in the third person. In the most gentle, genteel voice, the bootlegger would apologize.

Rogers, George Conners, and accountant Blanche Watson made a pact: Unless absolutely necessary, no one was to mention Imogene's and Dodge's names in the same sentence.

With his final prison sentence looming, Remus continued to search for his missing assets. He filed a lawsuit against Imogene and Dodge in federal court in Cleveland, charging that they had stolen at least $700,000 of his personal property, including $300,000 in whiskey certificates, which covered 4,805 cases in storage at the Pogue Distillery in Maysville, Kentucky. Organizing a fleet of trucks, Remus traveled to Maysville himself to recover the cases, only to be served with a restraining order on behalf of the businessman who'd bought the certificates from Dodge.

Remus shared this latest misfortune with Rogers, and when the journalist next traveled to Cincinnati he expected to find his friend on the verge of another brainstorm. Instead Remus invited him for breakfast at the mansion and a walk through the garden, where men labored with shovels and shears, and thickets of newly bloomed roses shaded their path. Remus seemed in exceptionally good spirits, and Rogers asked what had prompted this mood.

"Imogene is in town and I am in touch with her," Remus said.

"Where is she?" Rogers asked.

"At the Alms Hotel."

They continued walking in silence until 10:30 A.M., when Remus asked if Rogers might like to take a ride. His lawyer had suggested he meet with Imogene in the hope of effecting a cash settlement — a preemptive move to prevent her from selling any more of his property. He hadn't seen Imogene in half a year, since the Jack Daniel's trial the previous November, and a part of him couldn't help feeling excited at the thought. He'd even bought Imogene a box of candy for the occasion.

Rogers agreed, and within minutes a chauffeur was driving to the corner of Victory Parkway and Locust Street. A special entrance through the hotel garage allowed them to avoid the lobby, and they took the elevator directly to Imogene's suite of rooms. Imogene's mother, Julia Brown, opened the door and ushered them in, inviting them to relax in the sitting room, where Ruth and her boyfriend huddled together on a couch. Remus drew a few bills from his wallet and pressed them into Ruth's hand. "Here," he said. "Go and get mother some flowers." She did as she was told and then left again, taking her boyfriend with her.

After a moment Imogene emerged from an adjoining bedroom. Smiling, she greeted Rogers and then turned to Remus, grabbing the lapels of his coat. "Daddy, I am so glad you are here," she said, "and that you have brought Mr. Rogers." She leaned in for a kiss but at the final second Remus turned his head away, letting her graze his cheek.

No one mentioned Dodge, and Rogers noted that Remus seemed calm and collected, his voice steady and his skin its normal hue. He and Imogene sat at a table, a stack of papers fanned out in front of them, and spoke in low, murmuring whispers. Occasionally Rogers caught the phrase "whiskey certificates." Someone unaware of their history might have mistaken them for a couple in the first blush of love, unmoored and unafraid, eager for discovery.

They broke for lunch. White-gloved servers lowered silver platters heavy with salmon mousse and baked ham. They ate in silence, silverware scraping the china, until Rogers felt compelled to speak. He turned to Imogene. "I am glad to see Remus in a good frame of mind," he said. "I hope there will be no untoward incident to disrupt the friendly feeling. There has been so much trouble, and it would be good for all concerned to have a friendly settlement."

Imogene put down her fork and said, quietly, "Everything would be all right if it wasn't for Daddy."

Rogers glanced at Remus, who was trying to maintain composure.

"What is the matter with me?" Remus asked. "What have I done? Mention one incident where I have been mean or cruel to you."

Rogers thought the words were spoken in a "friendly way."

"Well," Imogene said, "I could mention one."

"All right, tell it," Remus challenged. "Now tell it, now that Mr. Rogers is here I would

275

like to have him hear it. Tell him some of the things you have been telling about me. Go ahead and tell it."

Imogene lowered her head. She began to talk, the words barely audible, and then she stopped herself. Remus decided to fill in the gaps, finishing her unspoken thought. "Do you mean about Romola?" he asked. She would understand his inference, as they had fought in the past about his generosity toward his daughter.

Imogene's face yielded nothing. "Yes," she said, as though that response were her only option. "That is it."

"Well, Romola is my daughter and I have a right to be kind to her," he said. "You certainly don't object to my being kind to Romola?"

"Well, that is it."

"Is that all?" Remus asked, triumphant now. "Is that the only incident in your life in connection with me that has caused you trouble?"

"That is enough, isn't it?"

"Well," he said. "We don't discuss that, if that is all."

Wishing to give them privacy, Rogers stood and wandered to a sitting area. Imogene's mother followed. Rogers found her to be "a genteel lady of advanced years." She, too, spoke *sotto voce,* so that only the journalist could hear.

"Mr. Rogers," she said, "Mr. Remus has made a lot of outrageous charges against my daughter, and I understand you have some influence with him. Do you think you could prevail upon him to retract them? If you could do it, we would greatly appreciate it."

"I will do all I can to conciliate the differences between the contending parties," Rogers said.

Mrs. Brown seemed satisfied. "Well, you will be doing us a great service, and I think a good service to Mr. Remus, if you could prevail upon him to withdraw those charges."

As Remus came into the room, Mrs. Brown waved a hand across her lips, halting the conversation. They chatted about nothing — the weather, the décor — until Remus exited again, heading for the bathroom.

Imogene entered the sitting area as Remus was leaving. They did not address each other. She sat on the settee adjacent to Rogers's chair and leaned in close.

"I am awfully glad, Mr. Rogers, that Daddy brought you along," she said. "I understand he listens to you and you may be able to do some good for him and for us."

"I think a disinterested person could help you both," Rogers told her. "But you're in bad company from what I've learned. As long as you have any connection to Franklin L. Dodge, that will tend to keep matters in an unsettled and upset state." He'd been with

Remus on numerous occasions, Rogers continued, when he'd start brooding about their separation, and the wrongs — "real or imaginary" — that he had suffered through his "previous association" with Dodge.

Imogene was quiet, listening, and Rogers decided he had to speak all of his mind, lest he later regret holding back. He took a deep breath and said, "I fear the whole thing will end in a tragedy, unless you do something to put an end to the situation."

She seemed genuinely startled. "What do you mean by that?"

"I am afraid that you will get hurt," Rogers explained, "and I hate to think what would happen if Remus ever met you and Dodge together."

"Oh," she said, relaxing against the settee. "You think you know Daddy, but you don't know him as well as I do. Daddy wouldn't hurt me; Daddy is good to me. But please don't let him hurt Mr. Dodge, please!" She seemed to have tapped into a different mood, one that allowed access to her kindest thoughts of Remus.

"It should be obvious to you that a man like Franklin L. Dodge is reputed to be could only have designs on your money," Rogers warned. "He is the man to whom I referred when I said you were in bad company."

"Well, never mind about that," Imogene said. "Mr. Dodge is our friend."

Throughout this exchange Imogene's mother remained silent.

When Remus appeared in the doorway, Rogers redirected the conversation. "I was just telling Mrs. Remus," he said, turning to the bootlegger, "that I believed that a disinterested person — one who doesn't have designs on your money — could do more to conciliate the situation than someone of whom either side is suspicious."

"Precisely," Remus said, exasperated. "That is the point I am trying to get to her."

He left the negotiations that day with nothing settled, least of all his mind.

The following week Remus invited only Conners and Blanche Watson to the mansion in Price Hill, hoping to draw up a reasonable offer to present to Imogene. They sat at the dining table, going through Remus's papers one page at a time. During a pause in the conversation they heard the front door open, then a pair of heels crossing the wood floor, each step like the tick of a clock. They glanced up to see Imogene, looking aggrieved. She took in all three of them and landed her gaze on Conners.

"What are you people doing here?" Conners heard her ask. "This is my home. I have a right to be here."

"Of course you have," Remus said. "No one asked you to leave. And if you want to stay

279

here, I will go to a hotel." He turned back to Watson and their paperwork.

Conners felt compelled to explain further, telling Imogene that they'd gathered "for the purpose of trying to arrange some kind of settlement."

He watched as she reached inside her purse. He glimpsed a pearl-handled revolver inside her curled fist.

"I will settle this myself," she said.

If Remus heard her he did not react, and instead continued his conversation with Watson. Conners leapt from his seat and pried the gun from Imogene's hand, lowering it back into her bag. She didn't fight him as he took the bag and lay it on the mantel. With his hands on her shoulders, he guided her from the dining room to the library. He closed the door and stood to face her, waiting for her to speak.

Once alone with Conners she grew hysterical, the expression on her face oscillating between fury and gloom. "That man cannot treat me that way," she said and then voiced all of the accusations she'd kept to herself during lunch at the Hotel Alms: He'd abused her, he was cruel and selfish, he had unjustly ruined her reputation.

Conners let her finish and then said, "If you would be reasonable and wanted a divorce you could get it." She could get a better settlement working with Remus directly than by "fooling around" with her lawyers and Dodge.

Without another word she left the room.

Conners followed, pushing past her toward the mantel. Quickly, furtively, he slipped the revolver from her purse.

For now, at least, it belonged to Remus.

TESTIMONY OF
JULIA F. BROWN

Q. You are the mother of Imogene Remus?

A. Yes, sir.

Q. Mrs. Brown, I want to ask you whether or not you were in St. Louis with your daughter, Mrs. Remus, at the time [Remus's friend] John S. Berger called upon Mrs. Remus?

A. Yes, sir.

Q. Did Mrs. Remus at that time or any other time say that she would get ready to kill her husband?

A. Oh, never.

Q. Now, Mrs. Brown, I will ask you whether or not you were present in the Alms Hotel in the month of June 1926, at which time George Remus and John T. Rogers, a reporter, called upon Mrs. Remus?

A. Yes, sir.

Q. Now I will ask you, Mrs. Brown, whether or not at the time Rogers came there to the Hotel Alms with Remus, and was introduced to you and your daughter, whether or not Rogers at that time turned and said to Remus, "These are not the kind of people, George, that you represented them to me to be"?

A. He said it, but later in the conversation.

Q. I will ask you whether or not Rogers upon that occasion made the statement that he would do what he could in the matter of securing a retraction of the charges George Remus had made [against Imogene], and that he then — that is he, Rogers — turned to Remus and said, "You will retract those, won't you George?" and that Remus nodded his head in the affirmative?

A. That he would in case Mrs. Remus would agree to go back and live with him . . . that they would say those charges were lies.

A GHOST AT THE DOOR

On June 7, 1926, the U.S. Supreme Court refused to hear Remus's final appeal — his last hope to avoid his year-long sentence for the Death Valley nuisance conviction. The date marked the court's closing session, and all were present save for Chief Justice William Howard Taft, out with a cold. The assistant U.S. Attorney in Cincinnati sent Willebrandt a letter informing her of the good news, and reported that Remus was to surrender on July 1. He would spend his final year not at the county jail in Dayton, where he was briefly detained after his release from Atlanta, but in Troy, Ohio, twenty miles away.

In the three weeks before his departure Remus worked frantically to recover, hide, and protect any money, whiskey certificates, or property he had left. While in Chicago he arranged for select pieces of furniture to be stored in Romola's apartment. He filed to repossess a Marmon touring car he'd given to Imogene, which Ruth had promptly commandeered and which was now nowhere to be found. He burdened his longtime watchman, William Mueller, with sullen, meandering monologues about his wife's perfidy: "My god," he inevitably began, "could it be possible that this woman would do such terrible things?" To Mueller, he seemed perennially "red and bloated and all puffed up." The watchman considered quitting the job but couldn't bear to leave Remus after seven years. He promised his boss he would monitor the property closely until he came home again.

Remus surrendered fifteen minutes early, arriving at the federal building in Cincinnati at 8:45 A.M. Reporters fixated on one question: There were rumors he and Mrs. Remus were reconciling — was it true? For once, he had no comment.

At the Miami County Jail, after being welcomed by the warden and staff (and warned that no special courtesies would be extended), Remus was led to cell 13, where a guard handed him the necessary supplies: blanket, pillowcase, sheet, towel, and tin cup. A neighboring prisoner pressed his head against the bars of his cell and called out, "Hello, George! Remember me?" Remus actually did remember the man, who had also served time in the Atlanta penitentiary. "Yes,"

Remus responded. "We will renew acquaintance."

From the first day of this confinement Remus's health began to deteriorate. His cell measured four by eight feet and was encased in darkness, save for a sliver of glass etched along the roof, just enough to glimpse what he called "the heavenly bodies above." The visitors' room, lined with wide, unbarred windows, was only slightly more forgiving. "I am sick just being penned up here in this hell hole," he told Conners. He longed to exercise outside.

Conners began to fear for his friend's life. He assessed Remus's sallow skin, the way his once-stout frame now seemed lost in his clothes. Remus declined every meal slid under his cell door; he couldn't stand the sight or scent of the drab, flaccid vegetables and graying meat. The very smell of the steam filled his stomach with gas.

Visits from Conners, Blanche Watson, John Rogers, and occasionally Romola broke up the monotony of his days. Conners visited as many as five times per week. Weighing the desire to protect Remus against the instinct to keep him informed, he often brought unsettling news from the outside, bracing himself for his friend's reaction. In late August, Conners revealed that the government had issued a warrant for Remus's deportation; reporters would be arriving at

Troy for comment.

This deportation action was most "idiotic," Remus told them through the bars. "This was started by my wife and a former Prohibition agent at Cincinnati. The statements made by government officials are untrue." He paused, choosing his next words. "I have been a good citizen. Was admitted to the practice of law in Chicago, in the United States District Court, and in the Supreme Court of the United States. This surely ought to establish my citizenship beyond doubt. My only offense has been to supply a demand of good citizens for good whiskey."

During another visit, Conners presented Remus with a full transcript of Congressman La Guardia's speech on the House floor — proof that at least *someone* in the government had noticed the situation concerning Dodge. "This was the first time the government ever took action in a divorce proceeding," Conners pointed out. And here, too, were the photostatic copies of the whiskey agreements between Dodge and Imogene and their buyers. Because of these agreements, Conners explained, there were various brokers arguing that they had purchased the whiskey in good faith and should have access to the distilleries and warehouses where it was stored. At this Remus tossed his hands in the air and landed them on the crown of his head. "Where am I going to get lawyers to defend these suits all over the country?" he wailed.

Worried about his friend's declining mental state, Conners made an arrangement with the sheriff to screen Remus's mail before it was delivered to him. He was glad that he did. One anonymous letter was laden with incendiary charges: Remus was crazy, and also a murderer. Back in 1923, the letter alleged, while running Jack Daniel's whiskey from St. Louis to Cincinnati, he had killed an Indiana sheriff who'd gotten in his way. The accusations went on: Remus was "a coward, and yellow, and sent everybody he came into contact with to prison." If the sheriff at Troy "put a ghost at Remus's cell door when he was asleep at night," Remus would wake up in the morning and promptly drop dead.

Only two people, Conners and Imogene, knew that Remus harbored an intense fear of ghosts. And now there was a third, Dodge, doubtless the author of this letter.

"That is Dodge's work," Remus said. "Let me see it." He snatched it from Conners's hands. "I know his handwriting. He's a dog. These are the methods they're using, persecuting me in jail." He pummeled his head as he paced the dark square of his cell, his steps quickening, a growl embedded deep in his throat. Before the brainstorm could escalate, Conners summoned a sheriff for assistance.

"Does he always act this way?" the sheriff asked.

In the fall, journalist John Rogers found himself in Washington, D.C., and arranged meetings with politicians and sources who had been helpful in the past. At the top of his list was Willebrandt. In her office at the Department of Justice, she and Rogers enjoyed a long and informal chat. She'd noticed his newspaper's recent photograph of her with her daughter. Dorothy was doing well, thank you very much; she was a strong-willed child, with an "infinite capacity for naughtiness." Willebrandt was currently hunting for a rigorous nursery school that would mold her "marvelous" mind.

Rogers told her that on his way to Washington, he'd taken a detour to visit George Remus in the Troy jail.

"How is he getting along?" Willebrandt asked.

"Not so well." Rogers described the cell, the dearth of light and air, the torture of losing control. Every time he saw Remus there seemed to be less of him, mentally and physically, as though he were caving in on himself. Rogers recounted his odd interview with Dodge during the Jack Daniel's trial, when the ex-agent flexed his muscle and showed off a pair of pistols. Dodge had also mentioned Willebrandt's name, Rogers said, and read a letter in which she praised him for his excellent work with the Bureau of Investigation.

After a moment, Willebrandt told Rogers that she had written only one laudatory letter to Dodge back in 1923, during his fruitful investigation of Willie Harr and other bootleggers in Savannah. That was two years before he left the Bureau, and she had not written one since — especially not one that invited him to resume his job as a Prohibition agent. Considering the controversy surrounding Dodge and her department's ongoing quest for honest personnel, she would never have welcomed the disgraced agent to return.

When Rogers left, Willebrandt reviewed the department's intelligence on Dodge. There were developments she had not shared with the journalist, nor indeed with anyone. After La Guardia's speech on the House floor, Dodge circulated an eight-page response, mailing it to members of Congress and even to the White House; Everett Sanders, secretary to President Coolidge, had then sent a copy to Willebrandt. It was an odd document — dense paragraphs full of denials, obfuscations, references to scripture, and personal diatribes against Remus. "His egotism knows no bounds," Dodge wrote. "To satisfy his vanity he had a large tombstone erected upon his family lot in Chicago, and under his direction it was located at such a point upon the family lot that the coffin containing the body of his father had to be cut in two in the construction of its foundation, and it has been his boast that after his death he desires to have a tombstone placed over his body bearing the inscription, 'Here lies George Remus, the King of the Bootleggers.' "

La Guardia harangued the Department of Justice, demanding Dodge's file. Willebrandt's office refused, explaining that "reports of this character are of a confidential nature." Meanwhile J. Edgar Hoover launched a new investigation into Dodge, uncovering a variety of unscrupulous and possibly illegal behavior and bizarre proclamations. The ex-agent had threatened witnesses who had testified on behalf of Remus in his cross-petition for divorce. He had claimed to have evidence that would "crucify Hoover" and force his resignation — paperwork allegedly proving that the Justice Department had conspired to save a prominent Cleveland whiskey dealer from indictment. He had boasted that his information would "explode the country," although he'd try to protect Willebrandt in the process.

Dodge's strange accusations were the least of his transgressions. Hoover told Willebrandt that he'd obtained "positive documentary evidence" that Dodge had handled and sold whiskey certificates in Cleveland six months before he resigned his position. While working on the Atlanta penitentiary case, Dodge hosted "whiskey parties with women" and accepted $10,000 from bootlegger Willie Harr — an investment in a future business venture. Hoover enclosed a personal note along with his report.

"It is needless to say," the director wrote, "that I am astounded at some of the statements attributed to Dodge. He has either completely lost his mind or is endeavoring to rival Ananias' reputation" — a reference to a biblical figure who lied to the Holy Spirit and was struck dead on the spot. "However, there are certain allegations made in the attached affidavits which would indicate that Dodge has violated, or probably proposes to violate, certain Federal Statutes. I am, therefore, calling these to your attention and would appreciate receiving your instructions as to the action you think should be taken upon these matters."

Willebrandt was direct in her response. "I have read your memorandum," she wrote, "with enclosures concerning Franklin L. Dodge. I do not think there is anything here on which action can be taken or future investigation based. Sale of whiskey certificates is excepted from the National Prohibition Act. It is not unlawful and I see nothing else in this report on which we could base prosecution."

She never elaborated, or wrote of this incident to her parents, or commented on her own relationship with Dodge. For Willebrandt, the situation was more complex than it seemed. Prosecuting Dodge, or even publicly condemning his behavior, would highlight her own poor judgment in trusting him — a mistake for which she, as a woman, might not be forgiven. She risked ruining not only her own career but also the prospects of other women politicians for years to come.

As if to validate her decision, she scrawled a note to herself on Hoover's memo: "there is <u>nothing</u> else."

Hoover disagreed. He had pledged to target corrupt agents, regardless of their connections to powerful government officials. Even though Dodge was no longer with the Bureau, the director would continue the investigation on his own.

Alone in his cell, searching for fragments of stars through his slice of window, Remus became aware of a strange apparition, arising from his body but manifested by his mind. This "halo" hovered brightly just above his head, vanishing and appearing at whim — a more potent sensation than the brainstorms, which were wholly internal, invisible predators feasting on his thoughts. This halo felt like "electrical stars" aligning in his mind, wresting control, directing and guiding him in the outside world.

The halo "impelled" him to do things, speaking in a language only he understood. Or so he would claim.

TESTIMONY OF
IMOGENE REMUS

My name is Augusta Imogene Remus and I am more than twenty-one years of age. I was married to George Remus in Newport, Kentucky on June 25, 1920, and am still his wife although I have instituted suit for a divorce. . . . In discussing with me the question of his possible deportation, my husband, George Remus, stated at different times and places that he was not a citizen of the United States; that his father never became a naturalized citizen of the United States, but that when the case came to a final issue, he, George Remus, would testify that his father did become a naturalized citizen of the United States before he, George Remus, reached the age of 21 years, thereby conferring United States citizenship on him, the said George Remus; he also stated that he would testify that his father's naturalization papers "were lost in the shuffle" and that he could not produce them.

Don't Let Him Catch You Asleep

Remus's watchman, William Mueller, did not visit his boss in jail, but he did monitor the Price Hill mansion, seeing who came and went — including Imogene. She spoke freely in front of the watchman, and he made notes of their conversations. She once complained, he later alleged, that she'd lost a gun. "Never mind looking for it," she told Mueller. "I have plenty more of them."

She often brought a man to the house, whom Mueller recognized as Franklin Dodge. One afternoon he watched Imogene and Dodge carry every last plant from the home, reducing the lush, exotic atrium to a few stray twigs and leaves. They loaded the plants into Imogene's silver roadster, which, in homage to her husband, once had the initials "G.R." imprinted on each door. Mueller approached the car for a closer look: The original monogram had been removed and replaced with the letters "F.D.," in bright gilded lettering. When Dodge realized that he was being watched, he ran behind the machine, crouching low until Mueller retreated. On another occasion, Mueller spotted Dodge in the parlor window, staring down the driveway, where the stone lions still stood proud. At the sight of Mueller making his rounds, Dodge lowered the blinds.

After the couple stole the plants, they set about stripping the house, room by room, item by item. Imogene tried to enlist Mueller's help, asking him to remove a clock from the wall. When the watchman refused, she replied, "Why? Don't be afraid that Mr. Remus will ever come back here — we are going to have him deported. We have it all arranged. He will go back the same as he came, with his little bundle."

Mueller believed his boss would come home, and he planned to describe this scene and repeat those words when he did. He couldn't intervene — it was, after all, Imogene's home — but he recorded every item as it passed through the front door and was loaded into a caravan of trucks. When they finished their work even the lions were gone.

As the threat of deportation intensified, Remus scrambled to defend himself from behind bars. The immigration commissioner suddenly had a wealth of evidence listing Remus's birth year as 1876: insurance claims, documents relating to his pharmaceutical and legal careers, divorce records from his first wife and his marriage license to Imogene, his application to a Masonic organization in Chicago, and a copy of his original birth certificate announcing that Franz Emil Georg Remus was born on November 13 of that year. Remus claimed that the records were "erroneous." That birth certificate belonged not to him but to a deceased brother who happened to share a birthday; it was German custom to name the next child of the same sex after a sibling who had passed.

Various family members, well schooled in Remus's claims, came to his aid, traveling from around the country to Cincinnati to testify before the Immigration Commission. An uncle suggested that Remus had advanced his age by two years, from nineteen to twenty-one, in order to be eligible for a pharmacist's license. His sister Elizabeth spoke of him with affection and admiration: "George is a self-made man. . . . He made a lot of money practicing law in Chicago, and he had no reason to leave there. He made a mistake when he came to Cincinnati. George, at all times, was good to his mother and the rest of the family. He was always willing to help one in need." Accompanied by sheriffs, Remus was permitted to take a day trip to Cincinnati for an interview with an officer from the Immigration Commission, which devolved from assurances that he was a legal citizen into a rant against Imogene and Dodge.

"Do you know whether or not your wife has been instrumental in having these proceedings for deportation placed against you?" the officer asked.

"Yes," Remus said. "She and this other person, Franklin L. Dodge. . . . He was working in the Secret Service Department of the Department of Justice at Washington for years. . . . He has been to my home since I have been in jail in Troy."

After this interview, and unbeknownst to Remus, J. Edgar Hoover received a memo from an agent advising that the government drop the deportation proceedings, lest they renew negative scrutiny of Dodge. "The reason for this is that if these proceedings come up as scheduled," the memo said, "a lot of publicity to Mr. Dodge and others will undoubtedly come. . . . I deem it absolutely essential that this or anything else do not happen at this time to cause publicity in the Dodge matter."

Hoover forwarded the memo to Willebrandt, although he had no intention of halting his own investigation.

Still concerned for Remus's health, Conners took a train to Washington and met privately with Willebrandt.

"Remus is dying in the Troy jail," he told her. "He won't live his term out."

299

For once, she took pity on Remus. On March 24, she authorized and arranged for his transfer to the Scioto County Jail in Portsmouth, Ohio, about 130 miles southeast.

Soon after his arrival, the Portsmouth sheriff shared with Remus a letter he'd received:

Sheriff — Portsmouth, Ohio

Dear Sir,
Better keep your eye on that Bird Remus. He is trying to cause you trouble, same as he does wherever he goes . . . watch your step with this bird for he is a lying, squealing rat who will not hesitate to do anything. He has sent more people to the penitentiary than most judges. He sent thirteen people to the pen from St. Louis that were in the whiskey business there with him. He will squeal so watch your step. He has no principles and will do anything. . . .

He has committed everything from murder down, bribery, arson, highjack liquor, nothing he has missed; don't let him catch you asleep. Be wide awake with him because there is nothing he won't do.

a friend

Remus added the letter to his long list of

Dodge's and Imogene's transgressions.

Despite the letter's warnings, the sheriff at Portsmouth found Remus to be a model prisoner and even made him a trustee of the jail. He was permitted to venture outside without the supervision of a guard as long as the sheriff's son chauffeured him. He ran the kitchen, cooking three meals per day for sixty inmates. Using his own money, he shopped at grocery stores for ice cream and cake, buying enough for everyone to have seconds and thirds. He befriended an eleven-year-old boy prisoner suffering from a "mumpy neck"; Remus rubbed salve on the swollen area while sharing stories of gun battles with whiskey pirates. Once he even captured an escaped prisoner, sprinting down Market Street in hot pursuit until he tackled him. "Although Remus is short and stout he can run like a deer," the sheriff noted. On another occasion he rushed to assist a prisoner who had collapsed to the floor. As guards lifted his body to a mattress, Remus took charge.

"Get some camphor and some ammonia," he ordered, "as quick as you can get it." He gave a pocketful of change to a guard, who raced to the nearest drugstore. When he returned Remus dribbled a bit of each liquid into his hands and laid them on the prisoner, grazing his forehead, pummeling his chest, kneading his arms. Beads of sweat slid from his forehead and splashed on the sick man's face. He pounded and squeezed and rubbed, nearly in a trance, until the man at last sputtered and shook himself awake.

Even with his improved circumstances Remus wallowed in gloom and defeat. With each visit Conners brought another tale of treachery. A few weeks prior, Conners had gone out to the Price Hill mansion to check on a Pierce-Arrow he planned to repossess on Remus's behalf. While he stood on Hermosa Avenue, a car came careening around the corner and aimed itself straight at him, with clear intent and full speed. An odd coincidence, he believed, until he received a call at his home that evening.

"If you make another trip," Imogene said, "I will have you killed on the road."

At the conclusion of this story, Conners watched Remus go "from alarm into an uncontrollable rage," hurling himself at the windows and doors of the visiting room, pinballing back and forth. Conners managed to subdue him with soothing words and appeals to reason; Remus's time in jail was almost up, and then they could rebuild and repair what was left of his life.

"I have been informed," Remus confided, "that when I am released, Dodge will be there waiting for me."

■ ■ ■ ■

Late on Sunday, April 24, 1927, reporters arrived at the Portsmouth jail for Remus's final interview as a prisoner. He claimed that he was excited to return to his mansion for good and had no definite plans for the future. "I'm not ashamed to look any man in the eye and tell him I was a bootlegger," he said and lowered a chicken breast onto an inmate's dish. "I never harmed a man, woman or child. . . . They're a lot of hypocrites down there in Washington — they vote dry and drink hard liquor. Those Congressmen cry for Prohibition enforcement, and four times out of five their stomachs are glowing from a half dozen drinks . . . plenty of whiskey was drunk in that town — all with the compliments of George Remus."

When asked if he would consider returning to bootlegging, Remus lay down his serving spoon. Looking straight into the reporter's eyes, he asked, "Do you think I'm crazy?"

Testimony of George Conners

Q. Now any other incidents, Mr. Conners, that you think of?

A. I told Remus I went to talk to [Imogene's divorce attorney] Judge Dixon for possibly an hour with a view toward settling the case out of court. I laid my cards on the table, and I asked him what her assets were. He said, "I don't think she has got a dime" and I said, "I know better than that, Judge Dixon."

I told Remus that Judge Dixon and I discussed the matter for possibly over an hour, and that Judge Dixon told me he would get in touch with Mrs. Remus, who was in town at that time, and that he would let me know within a week and get in touch with me with a view of settling the matter up. I told him that I asked Judge Dixon if he thought she was sincere, and he said he thought she was.

In view of me telling Remus that, a couple of weeks later Remus asked if I had heard anything from Judge Dixon, and I told him I had not. Remus then flew into a rage and said, "I told you that they were not sincere in it, they never had any intention of doing it, all they are doing is to try to stall for time, stall around and delay the case hoping that I would be killed before the divorce case is set." He again flew into a violent rage for hours at a time for three days after discussing it. He said, "If they think they are going to rob and destroy me, they are mistaken."

Q. Now have you detailed all of the incidents you can think of?

A. Mr. Remus at that time, during his ravings, told me that he was in thirteen or fourteen prisons in the United States, and he named them to me, and he said, "In every one of them I was in they persecuted me and hounded me and tried to drive me out of the country," that there was a conspiracy to kill him, that there was a conspiracy to rob him, that there was a conspiracy to keep him in jail. His ravings lasted three days. . . .

And he not only told me that, but he told every person he would meet on the street, "What do you think of that?" And I would say to him, "Don't be talking with these people, they don't want to hear that," and then he would fly into a rage with me and say, "Why not? That is the truth, isn't it?"

No Quarter

At midnight the prison door swung closed behind him, a defiant and resounding bang. He hoped it was the last time he would ever hear such a sound. There was Conners, ever prompt and reliable, waiting by his Buick. The men embraced. At last it was over. No more arrests, trials, prosecutions. No more begging Mabel Walker Willebrandt to lower his bond or drop his charges or show him mercy. He had spoken the truth when he told reporters he had no definite plans, but certain ideas had begun to take hazy focus in his mind. In the long term, he would write a book about his prison experiences and accept nothing less than a $250,000 advance. Hollywood had already made inquiries about his story. He would go on a lecture tour titled "Does Crime Pay?" and confess that neither the challenge of bootlegging nor the money it yielded had been worth putting his life on pause. "I ask no quarter and I give no quarter," he would tell the crowds. "Rather than bend one iota I would much rather cease to exist."

The short-term plans were simpler. Go home to the mansion, sleep in his own bed. Dispossess Imogene of the premises if she still dared to occupy those rooms, no matter whose name was on the deed. Defeat the calls to deport him from the country. Spend most of his time and every dollar he had left reclaiming his fortune and making sure that she was left without a penny or an inch of land. Cooperate with the authorities to ensure she was harassed and taxed and possibly arrested. Never let her or her pimp get the best of him again.

It was a glorious night, fifty degrees and clear, the moon carving jagged light across the Ohio River. With Conners by his side, planning a celebratory breakfast with their friends, it felt almost like old times, the days ahead bulging with opportunity. For four hours there was no talk of Dodge, or Imogene's betrayal, or the divorce still wending its way through the courts. By the time Conners rounded the corner onto Hermosa Avenue, the sky was still black and freckled with stars. The mansion loomed like a mountain, its outline rising and dipping, majestic even in the dark. The car began to slow as it approached the driveway, when Remus noticed something out of place — or rather, two things *not* in place: the stone lions that

307

had stood guard at the entrance for seven years. They were gone, ripped from their bases, as though they'd never been there at all.

Remus leapt from the car and sprinted toward his front door. It was padlocked shut and studded with spikes. Sprinting around the perimeter of his mansion — past the caretaker's cottage, the tennis court, the baseball diamond built for the neighborhood kids — he found that every entrance had been permanently locked. He smashed a window and climbed through, heedless of its glass teeth.

Gone, all of it: the jungle of exotic plants; his signed portrait of George Washington; the matching sets of Follot chairs, their backs tufted and scalloped like seashells. Where were his gold piano and rare books? His sterling cutlery, each handle engraved with a baroque letter "R"? His fine bone china, under which he hid $1,000 bills for his guests? In the third floor ballroom, leather seats that had lined the walls had been pried from their hinges. Marble statues had been kidnapped from the fireplace mantels. Solid wood doors had cavities where once sparkled squares of stained glass. Crystal chandeliers the size of his limousine had been torn from the ceiling. The servants' clock would never summon anyone again. She hadn't even left behind a photograph of herself, a memento for him to worship or destroy.

He wandered from barren room to barren room and assessed what remained: a table and gas range in the kitchen. Sixty-three pairs of her shoes. An old cot and a pair of men's oxfords that weren't his size. And a few pieces of silverware, left behind for spite, from a set he'd never seen, each one etched with a "D" for Dodge.

He staggered toward the indoor pool. If he closed his eyes he could conjure the memory: December 31, 1921, when he and Imogene hosted revelers from across the country to celebrate the new year and unveil "The Imogene Baths." She had destroyed even this, the pool he'd built in her name and honor, stripping it of every last flourish: the pedestals deprived of their Grecian gods, the ground pockmarked from stolen urns, the walls scarred with the impressions of missing silver sconces. All that remained was the water, and he stood over it now, his rippled reflection gazing back, broadcasting his horror.

"Well, she left the water," he shouted. "I think I'll hop in and take a swim." In that moment it was the funniest sentence he'd ever heard. His laugh started low in his gut and hit the air as a shriek, sliding up the scales and back down again, deepening into a sob. He fell to his knees, tears dropping through his fingers, and lost all sense of himself.

■ ■ ■

Conners hoisted Remus from the floor and led him back to the car. He wanted to take his friend away from that skeleton of a home. The breakfast he'd planned would have to wait. Remus needed sleep and tranquillity, not company and questions. He pulled into his own driveway a few miles away, letting Remus scream and rave, his neck veins engorged and his pupils sliding out of sight. Once the brainstorm had passed, he guided Remus past the rooms where his wife and children slept and showed him to another, where he left him alone.

Conners invited Remus to stay for as long as necessary. He tried to reanimate him, restore order over his thoughts. He assisted him with logistical tasks: ordering replacement furniture for the mansion; inviting Remus's sister Anna and her husband, Gabriel Ryerson, to move in; summoning the watchman, Mueller, to resume his duties. He took Remus to movie palaces, an old favorite pastime made all the more thrilling by the recent debut of the Vitaphone, a system that electronically linked a record to the projector, synchronizing image with sound. These attempts often failed. Fifteen minutes after the curtain rose Conners would drag Remus from the theater in the throes of a brainstorm, his breath escaping in haggard gasps. Sometimes they visited three theaters in one afternoon without managing to view an entire film.

Remus's condition worsened after sundown. He awakened Conners nearly every night, appearing at his bedroom door and mumbling about Imogene and Dodge: "I see them right before me all the time." They were phantom figures dashing down the street, camouflaging themselves in shifting shadows. Every memory of Imogene became a ghost — and Conners knew well how terrified Remus was of ghosts — but he could not explain her away with reason or put her back in a box, far from Remus's subconscious. At the moment they had no idea where Imogene was, but she had never been more present, imprinting herself on all of Remus's thoughts.

Conners tried a new approach, producing a deck of cards, playing hand after hand with Remus until sunrise. Six weeks had passed since the breakdown at the mansion, and since then he estimated his friend had not slept more than two hours at a time. Around 3 A.M. Remus threw down his cards and insisted on taking a walk. For hours they stalked the streets of Cincinnati, strolling by the stately mansions of Price Hill and then driving downtown to walk some more, finding solace in the quiet clamor of dawn. A queue of taxis hummed at Government

Square. Patrons tumbled from a family-run speakeasy in Over-the-Rhine, where the ten-year-old son poured liquor through a tube from a bedroom on the third floor. Down the slope of the basin, the waterfront was crowded with rough wooden flats, and the air reeked of fish and factory smoke, so thick and unstirred they could taste it with each breath. They'd begun at the top of the city and ended at its bottom, with nowhere to go but back up.

By mid-June Conners lost his patience. He rented a suite for his friend at the Sinton Hotel, the same place where Remus and Imogene had stayed after their honeymoon, another reminder of all he had lost. Remus spent half of his time at the Sinton and the other half at his home, roving his expansive grounds, now a willful tangle of bare branches and dead blooms. He tried to sleep in his bedroom where, according to the house-keeper, Dodge had eaten breakfast every morning. Most nights he gave up and slept on the floor, covering himself with carpets. He surmised that over the previous two years he'd averaged only three hours of sleep per night. His sister Anna did her best to restore a sense of comfort and familiarity, making breakfast and setting out the papers for Remus to read.

Before dawn one morning, Remus called and pleaded for Conners to come. When he arrived he found Remus circling his yard, poking his walking cane at shrubs and shadows. Mueller stood helpless nearby.

At the sight of Conners, Remus sighed with relief. There was somebody "in the grounds with flashlights," he insisted, and now he was trying to find them. Discreetly, Conners pulled the watchman aside.

"Did you see them?" he asked.

Mueller shook his head. "No, I didn't see any."

Conners went home, only to be summoned again the following night. Now Remus insisted that a caravan of cars had crept up his driveway, slowing taking the circular bend across his yard and exiting as quietly as it came.

This vision the watchman confirmed.

Worried, Conners stayed for four nights at the mansion. Remus told him everything he'd learned from Mueller: the systematic dismantling of his home; Dodge hiding behind car doors; Imogene's desire to send him back to Germany. Over those four nights the strange automobiles did not reappear, but Remus's rhetoric intensified. He was tortured by the idea that Dodge had possession not only of his wife but also his clothes and jewels, all of the personal effects he'd so carefully acquired. "I have heard that Dodge was wearing my diamonds in Detroit," he said. "If I don't get ahold of them soon I know there will be trouble."

He hired private detectives and gave them two tasks: Find his money, and trail his wife and Dodge from city to city. If the detectives encountered them, they were to call Remus at once so that he could catch them together personally. One detective reported seeing Dodge and Imogene at the Roosevelt Hotel in New York City with $30,000 worth of Remus's securities. Within the hour Remus boarded a train, only to be told upon his arrival that the couple had just checked out. Another advised Remus to hustle to Canada; the couple had been spotted over the border with $100,000 worth of his securities. This time Remus missed them by a half hour. He took numerous trips himself — to New York, Washington, Detroit, St. Louis, Atlanta, and Chicago — but they were always one step ahead of him, robbing him of the chance to either gather evidence or crack a skull. "If I ever meet Dodge," he told Conners, "it will be 'goodbye Dodge.' "

His fury at failing to catch them together was exacerbated by the sight of Imogene alone, sitting across the table in her lawyer's office, her face composed into a smug and wretched smile. Their divorce hearings stretched over the summer and became progressively more absurd. Every week seemed to bring a new suit or countersuit or accusation of contempt. There were delays and continuances and endless depositions and affidavits against judges for "bias and prejudice." During one deposition Remus lifted Imogene's lawyer from his seat and attempted to hurl him out the window. Following that outburst Remus's lawyers quit, and he announced that from now on he would be representing himself.

At the end of August, Remus received a call from a Bureau of Investigation agent named Tom Wilcox, who explained — to Remus's delight — that he was investigating Dodge, per the orders of Director J. Edgar Hoover. From Remus's understanding of the conversation, Wilcox had verified several important facts concerning Dodge's behavior and had come to a conclusion: Dodge should be arrested and indicted for violating the National Prohibition Act; for "assisting, aiding and abetting in the pay of $15,000 so as to kill a government witness" — namely, Remus himself; for "not doing his legal duties" during his employment as a special agent; and finally, under the Mann Act, for his cross-country exploits with Imogene. Wilcox wired his conclusions to Hoover, but again Willebrandt refused to take action. While she admitted that Dodge was guilty of "inexcusable conduct" and "transactions of a questionable nature," she insisted that his actions did not warrant criminal prosecution.

Remus considered this news. He still suspected that Willebrandt had or was having "relations" with Dodge, a situation he called "the thing behind the thing." The agent had a tawdry and undue influence on the prosecutor, moving her to act against Remus for the previous two years. It was why, Remus believed, Willebrandt had set his bail higher than that of his co-defendants, why she forced only him to serve a year on the nuisance charge, and why she now still refused to prosecute Dodge.

Before hanging up, Wilcox shared one last piece of news: There was a new plot afoot, set in motion by Imogene and Dodge, to murder Remus before the divorce trial.

Remus immediately summoned Conners. "My god, she surely is desperate," he said. "Trying to kill me before the divorce case even takes place. You and I have got to watch ourselves, because sooner or later they are bound to get us."

Conners watched as he raved and tore around, pacing and rubbing his head and throwing his hands from side to side. Suddenly he stood still again, turned to Conners, and said, "They will never take me if I see them first."

Remus went straight to the butler's pantry, where he'd kept Imogene's pearl-handled revolver since Conners filched it from her purse. From that day forward, Remus carried the gun with him at all times.

Testimony of
William Hoefft

Q. What is your occupation, Mr. Hoefft?

A. I was manager of the Sinton cigar stand. . . . I was up in Mr. Remus's room and we were having a conversation, and he stood up in front of me and he said, "My God, Hoefft, I just had information that I was going to be killed" and I said to him "I wouldn't pay any attention to anything like that" and he said "You don't understand."

He turned away from me and went into the bathroom and he put his hands to his face, pulling his cheeks down and looking into the glass and he said, "How long is this going to last?" shaking from side to side. . . . I tried to talk to him but he just stood there with his head in his hands and he said, "I don't see how anybody could persecute another person in that manner for such a length of time." . . . His eyes were staring, they had a stary look, and he seemed to be looking through you and not at you.

Q. During the first part of the interview everything was lovely, perfectly lovely, everything was all right?

A. Yes, sir.

Q. Did it ever occur to you, Mr. Hoefft, that you were specially invited up to Remus's room, and that this thing was particularly staged for you?

A. No, sir.

THE HITMAN

On the afternoon of October 5, 1927, the day before his divorce trial, Remus opened the door of his suite at the Sinton Hotel only to find a strange young man: early twenties, with receding dark hair and thick, muscled shoulders that strained against his jacket. He introduced himself as Harry Truesdale and said it was imperative that they talk. He had been hired to kill Remus, he explained, but now he merely wished to deliver a warning: His wife wanted him dead.

The story began in August, at a dog racing track in Springdale, Ohio. Truesdale was watching the greyhounds gallop around the track when he felt a tap on his shoulder. He turned to face a stranger, whose smile revealed a mouthful of gold teeth. The man identified himself as "Jew John Marcus" — surely the name meant something to Remus, as Marcus was an old bootlegging associate, one embittered by Remus's testifying for the government in the Jack Daniel's trial.

"I know how you could make ten thousand dollars," Marcus told Truesdale. "If you would kill a man, you could get that much money."

Truesdale told him he was interested, and Marcus promised to make the necessary introductions.

Four days later, in Cincinnati, Marcus took Truesdale to the Hotel Alms, the site of Remus and Imogene's failed attempts to reach a divorce settlement. Marcus hesitated outside the closed door of Suite 708 and then gave it a solid rap.

Imogene Remus appeared. Marcus introduced Truesdale, explaining that he was the man for the job. Muted laughter and the clink of glasses drifted from another room in the suite, and the tilt of Imogene's body suggested that she wished to return there.

She appraised Truesdale slowly, from his flat cap to his oxfords, and ordered him to come back the following day.

He did, by himself, and this time Imogene was alone. Curtly she stated her business: Truesdale would receive $10,000 if he would kill George Remus — he would receive half of the amount from her and half from someone else.

"Who is this other party?" Truesdale asked.

"Franklin Dodge," she said and admitted that she felt "very bitter" toward her estranged husband, so much so that she "wished someone would beat his brains out, or anything."

"What good would it do you to have something like that happen?"

"A lot of good."

"Would it mean thousands?"

"Yes," she admitted. "It would mean more than that."

She advanced him $250 to cover expenses, and said he would get the rest when her husband was "bumped off."

Truesdale began tailing Remus, learning his schedule and habits, recording the moments when he was alone and vulnerable. Often he sat in a chair positioned by the left side of the elevator, which offered a clear view of Remus's suite. He watched visitors come and go and studied Remus's nervous movements, the way he sometimes walked to the elevator and back again, as though he feared someone were watching. Once, when Remus left his door open a crack — by error or design, Truesdale didn't know — he considered slipping into the suite and killing Remus on the spot.

He didn't, fearing that someone would discover him in the act.

After following Remus in this manner for two weeks, Truesdale called Imogene from a pay phone at the Dow Drug Store in Fountain Square. She advised him to hang up and instead come to see her at the Hotel Alms. When he arrived he found the door to her suite open. A valise was open on the bed, crammed with clothes and toiletries. "I'm going away," she explained. "I'm going to Michigan." She planned to be gone for at least a week, and it was imperative that Truesdale complete his assignment soon; he needed to kill Remus before the divorce trial started on October 6. He should call the Hotel Alms regularly to inquire if she was back, and they would meet again soon.

After this conversation, Truesdale returned to Hamilton, Ohio, where he knew Remus had some business. He watched Remus get into a limousine and head to the Grand Hotel, well known for providing bootleg liquor and subterranean rooms for clandestine deals.

He called the Alms Hotel and discovered that Imogene had returned. Wait there, she told Truesdale. She would meet him in Hamilton that evening in front of the Rentschler Building, at the corner of Second and High Streets. Midnight, sharp.

At the appointed hour, as Truesdale walked toward Imogene, he noticed a man across the street, tall and broad and backlit by the moon. "Is that man with you?" Truesdale asked.

"He is," Imogene said. "That's Franklin

Dodge. It's the same man who's to give you five thousand dollars."

Imogene and Truesdale entered the Grand Hotel to scan the register, checking for Remus's name or a name written in his handwriting. They found neither, so they decided to wait outside; hopefully they would catch him coming or going.

Within a moment a blue coupe pulled up next to Dodge, idling in the street. Imogene excused herself and walked over, poking her head into the car. When she returned to Truesdale she was carrying a pistol.

"If he should come up here," she said, "*I'll* shoot him."

They sat on a concrete block and talked for a while longer, looking up and down the street, monitoring everyone who approached the hotel. Truesdale had a sudden and disturbing thought: Imogene never intended to pay him. She had never mentioned any associates besides Franklin Dodge, and yet there was a carful of men across the street who were aware of their plans. In fact, at this point, it was fair to assume that Imogene was planning to double-cross him in some way, killing him to ensure his silence or turning him in to the police, anonymously, as a hired killer. He had failed to execute the plan on her schedule. He knew too much and had done too little.

As they talked, Truesdale watched her play

with the gun in her lap, turning it over, running a finger along the barrel. He felt a hot stab of fear.

"If I see him now," Imogene repeated, "I will kill him myself."

They sat and waited, to no avail. Imogene decided to return to Cincinnati with Dodge. Truesdale was to stay behind and keep watch, and come to the Hotel Alms the following day.

Instead, Truesdale went to the Hotel Sinton to tell Remus of his wife's plans.

When Truesdale finished telling his story, Remus jumped up from his chair. "He started raving," Truesdale later said, "and I didn't know what was the matter with the man. . . . I thought that the man would go crazy, he gripped his hands, the perspiration burst out of his forehead, his eyes bulged out, and he run across the room like he was going to jump out of the window."

In that moment Truesdale didn't know which Remus, Imogene or George, was more dangerous.

TESTIMONY OF
ETHEL BACHMAN

Q. Mrs. Bachman, I am going to call your attention to the 5th day of October. Where were you that day?

A. I was at the Hotel Alms.

Q. During the evening of October 5, did Mrs. Remus leave the rooms?

A. Yes, sir, she left the Hotel Alms around 7 o'clock.

Q. Did she make a statement of any kind?

A. When she left she made this remark — that she was going out on an errand and she would let me know the next day the outcome of that errand; it would be very valuable to her if it materialized.

Q. That closes your answer, doesn't it?

A. Yes, sir, that is all she said.

BLOOD ON THE PRIMROSE PATH

At 10 P.M., a few hours after Harry Truesdale left his suite at the Sinton, Remus called his driver, George Klug, for a ride back to the Price Hill mansion. Remus was quiet until they pulled up into the driveway, at which point he gave Klug an order: "Be here about seven o'clock. You will take me to the Alms Hotel. I want to see my wife and talk things over with her." It would be his last chance to do so before they met in court to finalize their divorce.

Klug nodded and shifted into reverse, disappearing around the corner of 8th Street.

Inside, Remus found his brother-in-law, Gabriel Ryerson, sitting at the kitchen table.

"Would you like some refreshments?" he asked.

Remus declined. "I'll be awfully busy tomorrow morning," he said. "I want to get up a little earlier than usual."

He turned in for the night.

■ ■ ■ ■

When Remus came downstairs in the morning, Anna, Ryerson, and Klug were already gathered in the kitchen. Each of his senses was amplified, its power sharpened: the sizzle of batter on a griddle; the scent of percolating coffee; his sister's odd behavior, her quick but stilted movements and the grim set of her lips. The newspapers were waiting for him. He scanned the front page headlines of the *Enquirer*. Babe Ruth and Lou Gehrig led the Yankees to a win over the Pirates in the first game of the World Series. A German "alien" was accused of having plotted to kill former President Woodrow Wilson during the World War. Luella Melius, a prima donna of the Chicago opera company, shared her dismay at the behavior of "bobbed-hair passengers" on an ocean liner: "I thought I knew something about the art of attracting men, but I am a novice."

Anna set a plate of pancakes in front of Remus.

"Good morning, Anna," Remus said. "How are you this morning?"

"Fine," she told him. "Well, this is going to be your big day."

"Yes, Anna."

They ate in silence, the only sound the scraping of forks and their dry, audible swallows. Anna looked only at her meal, as though the mere sight of her brother might burn her eyes. Her mind hummed with disquieting thoughts and fearful premonitions: She sensed that something was about to happen — either a violent act by her brother, or one against him.

Cincinnati was in the midst of an Indian summer, the sun asserting itself in a cloudless sky. Remus dressed in a chocolate brown silk suit and white shirt with a four-in-hand tie. He chose a fedora with the brim turned down instead of his usual bowler. No underwear, as always. The blue Buick was parked in the driveway. Remus was aware of his stout body folding itself, angling into the back seat. He felt himself being carried along a familiar route, from high atop the city into its heart.

By 7:30 A.M. they had arrived at the Hotel Alms and parked at the corner. It was rush hour, and a stream of pedestrians sluiced around the hotel, the ladies in cloche hats and the men in garish ties, all full of direction and purpose. Cars swerved and honked along Victory Parkway, Model Ts and Packards merging and accelerating. From the back seat of the Buick, Remus had a clear view of the entrance. If he did nothing, he would be divorced within ninety minutes.

"When she comes out," he told Klug, "you call her. I want to talk to her."

"Why don't you go into the hotel?" Klug asked.

Remus was insistent. "I want to talk to her on the outside."

It was about this time, he would say, that the halo appeared above his head, and shooting stars launched into an orbit around him, and his mind began speaking to him in that odd language, the words forming a directive he must obey.

And there she was, wearing a black silk dress and matching turban, although she did not mourn the demise of their marriage. A small purse dangled from her forearm. He clocked every movement of her swinging limbs, the way she drew the sun's spotlight. Ruth walked alongside her. Tomorrow would be his stepdaughter's twentieth birthday. A maddeningly exact replica of her mother in both appearance and temperament, she, too, wanted nothing to do with him. He was surprised to see Ruth; he had expected Dodge, and was disappointed by his absence.

Remus's eyes shifted back to Imogene, who was smiling and laughing. The halo sent a message: "That answers it."

Before Klug could jump from the Buick and call out to Imogene, she and Ruth disappeared inside a taxicab.

Remus said, "Catch that car."

■ ■ ■ ■

As they pulled out and approached the parkway, Imogene swiveled in the taxi and saw Remus behind her. "There is Remus," she said, nudging Ruth, and before she could whisper the second syllable of his name his car was next to theirs, door to door, nearly moving as one.

"Get ahead of it," Remus told Klug. "I want to talk to her." Klug stepped on the gas.

Imogene's driver was on the inside lane of the parkway, passing the bridge, when a blue Buick crept up alongside him, hovering on the left. From the back seat came a frantic command — "drive fast" — and he could not tell whether mother or daughter had given it. He obliged, cutting ahead, lunging and lurching, dodging roadsters and coupes, gaining speed.

Remus's car followed close behind, darting left. Through the cab's rear window he could trace the outline of Imogene's head, the curve of her shoulder. He imagined a revolver in her handbag, a bullet ready for him.
    His halo intensified; the stars shot faster and brighter, a fireworks display that only he could see.

■ ■ ■ ■

Imogene's driver tried again, speeding south, the women in the back seat now eerily silent. He pulled ahead, crossing McMillan Street and swerving into Eden Park, a meandering green ribbon overlooking the Ohio River Valley.

Remus was almost on her now, both cars hurtling toward Mirror Lake, and with one last push he passed her, taking in her face as he blurred by. His car swerved to a stop five feet in front of the cab, making a T and trapping her.

He watched as Imogene leapt from the cab, graceful even in terror. Ruth followed, exiting from the same door. Imogene pushed her back inside and confessed, "I am afraid."

Remus unlocked his own door and let himself out.

Imogene sprinted down the road toward the Spring House gazebo. A pink slip peeked out from beneath the hem of her dress. Remus walked after her, his steps quickening, the halo blazing. No matter how fast she ran, he would always catch up. He could hear her breath coming in stunted gasps. She was an arm's length away. He reached toward her and caught her by her lovely wrist. He held her tight as she twisted and turned; from a distance it might have looked as if they were dancing. She whirled back toward him and stayed still this time, raising her face to his, settling her gaze. Her breath came at him fast, tickling his chin. The smooth pearl handle felt cool against his palm.

"Daddy dear, I love you," his wife whispered. "Daddy dear, don't do it!"

In its strange new language his mind said, "She who dances down the primrose path must die on the primrose path."

From a distance he watched himself defy her, burrowing the barrel so deeply into her flesh that he barely heard the shot. A flock of birds launched themselves from the trees and scattered overhead. She fell against him and slid down, leaving a thin scarf of blood on his pants.

He felt a yanking at his elbow, the sleeve of his coat sliding up his arm, and heard a soft keening behind him. Turning halfway, he saw Ruth. Her face folded into exquisite origami, one of her mother's expressions. She grasped his lapel and screamed, "Do you know what you are doing?"

As Ruth tried to hold Remus still, her mother rose to her feet and began to run, hands atop her head, her wound exposed.

Remus broke free and started after her.

Testimony of
Ruth Remus

Q. Had your father made any threats against your mother?

A. He has in the past two years continually . . . he said he would follow her to the ends of the earth and see that she didn't have a dime or thread of reputation left.

Q. Did he ever threaten to kill her?

A. He often said he would get her.

Q. He never used the word "kill"?

A. No, sir.

Q. You weren't afraid at any time up to the 6th to leave the hotel because of any threat he had made?

A. The last two years he had been continually making threats and mother was always frightened about her life, both she and I. We were both terribly frightened but the last six months it sort of wore down and she got kind of used to it.

Q. When you got up Thursday morning was it your plan to go to Judge Dixon's office and then to the Court House for the divorce hearing?

A. Yes, sir.

Q. Did you see Remus with his car?

A. Just as we approached the bridge Mother said, "There is Remus." Her first instinct was pleasure; she was pleased to see him. . . . Her eyes sparkled. I think her impression was that he was coming to try to make up.

WHAT A BEAUTIFUL
MORNING IT IS

From the side of his cab Imogene's driver saw her coming down the hill, hands crowning her head, a ring of blood blooming across her abdomen. Remus followed, his steps long and deliberate, his gait steady. A bystander thought he looked "incredibly calm." His left hand still gripped the gun.

Ruth bolted around Remus, catching up to her mother. Imogene faced oncoming traffic and summoned the strength to scream. "My God, somebody help, this man is killing me!" She waved her arms. "I am shot, help me. I am shot, terrible bad."

A long queue of cars had stopped, their drivers immobile with curiosity and horror. No one moved to help her. No one said anything.

She yanked on the door of an idling car, but the driver refused to unlock it. She tried the next car. This time the driver flung his door open and said "Get in." She had just enough energy left to slump to the seat. Ruth slid in beside her and propped her mother up, cupping her under the shoulders. "Drive straight ahead," she pleaded to the driver, "and take her to a hospital."

The man hesitated. He had heard the gunshot and witnessed the man standing over her, revolver in hand. He knew the shooter was nearby and did not want to encounter him with the victim in his car.

"It is all right, go ahead," Ruth urged. She was crying and hyperventilating, half-screaming her words. "We know who shot her. It was Mr. Remus."

"I don't want to go ahead," the man explained. "The man who shot this woman has just gone around the curve there — no use going after him and possibly start an argument again."

He reversed the car and began speeding in the opposite direction. Ruth wrapped her arms around her mother and sobbed into her shoulder.

Remus looked down at his hand and realized that he was no longer holding the gun. His driver, Klug, was nowhere to be found. He strolled past the gazebo, where Imogene had fallen mere moments earlier, followed the bend in the reservoir, and found himself on Martin Drive. The sidewalk was lined with flowers in their final bloom and trees just beginning to brown. He quickened his pace to a near jog, veering crookedly along the path, as though he were both in a hurry and helplessly lost.

A passing driver noticed Remus, assumed he was running late, and guided his car to the path.

"Can I give you a lift?" he asked.

"Yes!" Remus said, and hurried over. "I got lost in the park." He settled into the back seat and said he'd like to go to the Pennsylvania Depot. "It's a beautiful morning."

"Yes," the man agreed.

"Where are you going?" Remus asked.

"Newport."

"Are you going to meet anybody?"

The driver, thinking this a strange question, ignored it. Peering into his rearview mirror, he noticed that his passenger was fidgeting and tugging around, struggling with something unseen. The driver made up his mind then that something was very wrong, that this man was "not natural."

"Thank you for the lift," Remus said. "What a beautiful morning it is."

During the drive to the hospital her mother grew heavier in her arms. The dress was scorched at the bullet's entry. Ruth tried not to look at the wound, but she would never unsee all that blood — rivulets streaming down her mother's steel gray stockings, seeping into her patent leather pumps. Ruth wanted her to speak — to say something, anything, just a small promise that there remained enough of her to save.

"I know I'm dying," Imogene said.

"Oh, Mother," Ruth replied, using a scolding voice. "No you are not."

"Yes I am," Imogene said, her words softer this time. "Isn't George terrible for doing this?"

Ruth grew hysterical again. She thought of the next day, her twentieth birthday, and the party her mother had planned for her.

"I'm dying," Imogene said again and shifted half-shut eyes to her daughter. "Be a good girl," she whispered.

At the Pennsylvania Depot, Remus finally exited the car but didn't walk into the station. Instead he stood by the driver's side door, peering down.

"You don't know who I am," he said to the driver.

"No," the driver said, genuinely confused.

"My name is George Remus."

Now the driver was stunned. "Are you the Remus of liquor fame?"

"Yes."

The driver shook his hand. "I often heard of you," he said, "and I'm glad I met you."

"I did some shooting in the park," Remus confessed.

The driver's mind clicked, putting the

pieces together. So this isn't *really* Remus, he thought, but an impostor who had "been ranting about the Remus case and got kind of unbalanced." He bid this strange man a good day and drove off, hoping that would be the last he heard of him.

The Ford carrying Imogene stopped at a light at the corner of Locust and Gilbert, where a police officer named William Knight stood on traffic duty. He heard a scream and saw a young woman leaning out her window, waving him over.

"My mother is shot!" she cried.

"Who is it?" Knight asked.

"This is Mrs. Remus," the girl said.

Knight saw an older woman half-reclining at the bottom of the machine, chin on the seat, legs folded on the floor, kneeling in a pool of blood.

"Who shot you?"

The woman mustered the energy to answer. "George Remus."

Knight knew the name. "Your husband from Price Hill?"

"Yes."

Knight let himself into the car, sitting next to the driver, and they were moving again. He rotated in his seat and continued talking to Imogene, hoping to keep her alert.

"Where did this happen?" he asked.

"In Eden Park."

"Why did he shoot you?"

She whispered, "He followed me from the Alms Hotel."

It was her last coherent answer.

They pulled into Bethesda Hospital. Knight checked his watch: 8:20 A.M. He lifted Imogene from the car, her bloody chest imprinting on his, and begged for a chair to transport her to the emergency room. Ruth scrambled from her seat, dashed into the hospital, and returned with a chair. The elevator operator brought them to the fifth floor. On the way Knight studied Imogene's wound, and saw the jagged hole in her dress, singed by gunpowder; she had been shot at point-blank range. At the commotion, Imogene stirred.

"Do you think I'm going to die?" she asked Knight.

"No," he assured her. "Not the way you look."

"Do something for me," she urged, adding the words "doctors" . . . "get" . . . "busy."

Imogene closed her eyes. Silently, Knight hoped that she could make a dying statement that could be used in court, but he did not use those words. He asked if she would like to make a "statement," but by this time the victim was unable to respond at all.

A fleet of nurses whisked her away. Ruth followed as far as they would allow. One nurse cut the clothes from her mother's body.

The pink slip was blackened and scorched. The wound itself was encircled by a dark ring of charred flesh. The door to the operating room closed and Ruth was left to wait in the hall.

The taxi driver who had picked up Imogene and Ruth that morning arrived at the hospital, carrying Imogene's purse. Officer Knight examined its contents: lipsticks, powder, money, two perfume samples, a book of coupons for $1 taxi rides. There was no gun.

From the Pennsylvania Depot, Remus called a cab and requested a ride to the Cincinnati Police Department's Central Station, where he arrived at 8:30 A.M. Officer Frank McNeal was on duty.

"I just shot my wife and I came to surrender," Remus announced. "My name is George Remus."

McNeal did not react to the name and began writing on a notepad.

"Where did this occur?"

"Somewhere on the driveway in Eden Park."

"What did you do with the gun?"

"I lost that in the scuffle."

Remus began to pace, walking to one end of the room, pivoting on a heel, and racing back. McNeal asked him to stand still and answer questions, but the pacing continued.

"How many times did you shoot?"

"I don't know," Remus said. "I think three times. The gun jammed on me."

"What became of her?" McNeal asked, scribbling on his pad.

Still pacing, Remus said, "This is the first peace I have had in two years and a half."

At 8:30 A.M., just as Remus turned himself in, Imogene lay flat on a table in the operating room, with Dr. Howard Fischbach poised above her. He removed the remainder of her dress and found a perforation through her corset. With her bare chest exposed to him, he followed the perforation to her abdomen, noting the bullet's point of entry. Her underwear was saturated with blood. He took her vitals and announced his observations: "Conscious but in a state of shock, pulse still fairly good, pale, highly nervous, suffering great pain." A nurse administered an anesthetic of nitrous oxide, ether, and chloroform, releasing the liquid with a dropper onto a sheet of gauze fixed by a wire mask.

The doctor opened Imogene's abdomen. He found a gunshot wound below the sternum, powder burns discoloring the bone. He probed further: perforation of the anterior and posterior walls of the stomach and through the left lobe of the liver; severe laceration of the spleen; a puncture through the lower portion of the lung, with the bullet lodged just under the skin in the back, between the seventh and eighth ribs. He extracted the bullet and placed it in a sterile bowl for safekeeping. Food escaped from the opening in her stomach; he could see every item she'd eaten for breakfast. He removed the spleen to stop the hemorrhaging, cleansed the abdomen of food, and inserted drainage tubes.

Seventy-five minutes after Imogene arrived in his room, he sewed her shut. At 10:50 A.M., he watched his patient die. He declared the official cause of death to be shock and hemorrhage from a gunshot wound to the abdomen.

Eager to safeguard the bullet, the doctor placed it in an envelope, labeled it, and turned it over to the Hamilton County coroner, along with Imogene's body. Hundreds of curious Cincinnatians surrounded the building, hoping in vain for a glimpse of the corpse.

As soon as she received the news Ruth made a long-distance phone call to Lansing, Michigan, to tell Franklin Dodge that her mother was dead. In a daze, she spoke to the reporters who had gathered in the hospital corridor. "She feared something like this would happen," Ruth said. "Remus appeared as a crazy man, cursing as he turned the gun on my mother in the park." She then returned to her mother's suite at the Hotel Alms, where she succumbed, according to one witness, to "a state of nervous collapse."

Lieutenant Frank McNeal approached Remus, now pacing in a cell at the station. One hand was curled into a tight fist, punching the palm of the other.

"Your wife just died," McNeal said.

Remus stood still. In a clear, calm voice, he said, "Very well, gentlemen. I thank you."

"What do you wish to say?" McNeal asked.

"What more is there to say?" Remus asked. After a moment he added, "It is the penalty that one pays for being contrary to the debt one owes society."

Within the hour Remus was sitting in a squad car with four officers, heading back toward Eden Park to examine the scene of the crime. The rush hour traffic had thinned, and the drive was quick: Ninth Street to Vine, Vine to Eighth, over Eighth and the viaduct to Gilbert, where they entered the park. They walked through its center, trying to retrace every step, when Remus told them he couldn't recall his route. "If you take me out to the hotel and come back," he offered, "I will have a different recollection of the thing." He was polite and solicitous, as though they were discussing business instead of murder.

The men piled back into the squad car, drove to the Alms Hotel and entered the park at McMillan Street, stopping fifty feet from the gazebo. They walked south, arriving at the curve of the reservoir. Remus gazed out toward a cluster of trees and said, "It is down this way a little farther." After another fifty feet, Remus stopped. "Here is where the scramble happened," he said. "Here is where we will find the gun." He separated clusters of bushes and crawled through grass and checked in the shadows of trees. Officer Charles Frick acknowledged that Remus helped in every way he could, but Imogene's revolver was nowhere to be found.

In Chicago, Remus's first wife, Lillian, responded to reporters' inquiries. Despite her own divorce petition, in which she accused her ex-husband of "pure malice" and various instances of physical abuse, she now offered a rousing defense. "She made his life so miserable that he was driven to it," Lillian said. "She made him a pauper. Again and again she threatened his life. Why, George Remus wouldn't hurt a fly."

■ ■ ■ ■

PART III
THE COLOSSAL
VITALITY OF HIS
ILLUSION

■ ■ ■ ■

THE SMILING CHARLIE TAFT

As Remus chased Imogene in Eden Park, Hamilton County prosecutor Charles P. Taft II — or Charlie, as he was known — said goodbye to his wife, Eleanor, and drove downtown to his office on the fourth floor of the courthouse. The couple had just spent a month at the family cottage in Murray Bay, Quebec, the Tafts' preferred vacation destination since the Gilded Age, in no small part because it was difficult to access, splayed along the north side of the St. Lawrence River, fifty miles north of the northern tip of Maine.

While there, they celebrated the seventieth birthday of Charlie's father, William Howard Taft, former president and current chief justice of the U.S. Supreme Court, with Charlie's mother, his two siblings and their spouses, and everyone's children. They spent languorous days swimming in the clear chilly water; the evenings brought genteel dances that ended promptly at midnight. Charlie hosted his annual High Tea, attended by sixty neighbors who feasted on sandwiches, tea, and coffee. "Hell, no white gloves," he insisted. "Summer clothes." That day, October 6, 1927, happened to be his tenth wedding anniversary, and the trip had been an idyllic celebration.

The grim expressions on his colleagues' faces yanked Taft from his reverie. There had been a brutal murder that morning, they told him. On the way to his divorce hearing the bootlegger George Remus had shot his wife in Eden Park and was now in custody at the Central Police Station.

Taft did not need to hear another word about the situation to recognize its significance: The Remus case would be the most important of his career.

Newly thirty, Charlie Taft had never lived outside of the public eye. He was two years old when his father, at the behest of President William McKinley, sailed with the family to Manila to organize a civilian government during the Philippine-American War. Eight years later, at age eleven, he moved into the White House, a place he already knew well through play dates with the children of his father's predecessor, Theodore Roosevelt. He and Quentin Roosevelt had organized a "White House gang," numbering seven in all, and drafted a manifesto: "to confound all rules of deportment, mingle in the lives of presidents and policemen, win victories, taste honor, and suffer punishment, while engaging in escapades that easily reached the pages of the national press."

One of their first missions involved lobbing spitballs at the portrait of Andrew Jackson, an offense that earned Charlie a week's banishment from the White House. "Just imagine how I would feel," a perturbed Teddy Roosevelt scolded, "if you rowdies, gangsters, villains threw spitballs at my portrait!" When the Taft family moved into the White House, Charlie earned a mention in the *New York Times* for organizing a game of tag on the roof. He earned another for being caught with a bag full of explosives he'd intended to set off on the Fourth of July, a cache that included two bundles of powder crackers and three boxes of "giant torpedos."

Charlie's sense of mischief was exceeded only by his charm. Even his father found it impossible to restrain him. "As to Charles," the president wrote to his wife, "he is so attractive even in his naughtiness that he will have to grow into a less attractive age before he can have the necessary discipline." She shared his sentiments, even as she found her son's boundless energy exhausting. "He is so restless as if he had quicksilver in his veins," she said. "It tires you to keep up with him." As he grew into adulthood this dynamism was amplified by his physical presence: six foot two and 190 pounds, a natural and gifted athlete, playing football, baseball, and basketball at Yale. Fishing became such a passion that he kept a canoe permanently tied to the roof of his car and even incorporated it into his tombstone — on the back was an image of a man with a fishing pole and the words "Gone fishing."

The former president worried about his son's reckless pace and whiplash mind, both of which tended to get in the way of focusing on a single goal at a time. In addition to a busy home life with Eleanor and their children, he formed the prestigious law firm of Taft, Stettinius & Hollister with his brother Robert, taught Sunday school at his Episcopal church, and served on the board of directors for numerous organizations: the Y.M.C.A., the Community Chest, the Cincinnati Children's Hospital, the Widows and Old Men's Home, and the Colored Industrial School. In 1924, concerned about Cincinnati's rampant and entrenched political corruption, he joined the fledgling Cincinnatus Association, whose goal was to change the current system, which relied on a mayor and a large city council, to a government headed by a city manager. He made the first speech on the Association's behalf. "There is no Republican way or no Democrat way to pave a street," he said. "There is only an honest and efficient way as compared with a dishonest and ineffectual way." The "Charter Party" won, and Charlie insisted on a new city council representative of Cincinnati's diverse population. It was, he pointed out, "the only way of assuring the appropriate number of minorities, such as blacks and women."

His father sent a letter urging him to slow his pace. Charlie responded by running for Hamilton County prosecutor. He won handily, taking office in November 1926; even his legal opponents were obliged to acknowledge his charisma. "He smiled me out of court," one attorney claimed. A longtime political adversary called him a "good guy and a straight shooter." Regardless of the circumstances, it was impossible not to like Charlie Taft. Self-deprecating, slow to anger, utterly without pretension, he was so immersed in his work of bettering the world that he often neglected himself. "He is generally neatly and well dressed," said one observer, "but in summer time he tackles the heat of court practice without the slightest thought that the linen coat he wore the day before and the day before that is by then all but shapeless."

In his brief time as prosecutor, Charlie had so far handled two major criminal cases. The first was a murder involving three defendants, all of whom were convicted and sentenced to life in prison. He was currently enmeshed in the second, a trial against influential Cincinnati bootlegger George "Fat" Wrassman, accused of killing a speakeasy proprietor. The defendant claimed self-defense, but Taft was hoping for a conviction of first degree murder and the death penalty, arguing that Wrassman had shot the proprietor in cold blood and then kicked his body down a flight of stairs.

So far the case had been difficult and tumultuous, owing in no small part to the skill of Wrassman's defense attorney, thirty-six-year-old Charles Elston. Once a prosecutor himself, Elston anticipated Taft's strategies and arguments before he made them and was not averse to bold and risky tactics. In one recent murder trial, he had represented a young man charged with firing two shots into a police officer's chest. Elston argued that the defendant had been "weak mentally from boyhood" and was insane at the time he committed murder.

Which brought Taft's mind back to the case at hand: He had to prepare for the possibility of George Remus pleading insanity.

At 2 P.M. that afternoon, Remus received a visitor to his cell. The man introduced himself as Dr. W. C. Kendig, the county alienist — a term likely derived from the French adjective *aliéné,* meaning "insane," which led to the noun *aliéniste,* a doctor who treated mental alienation.

"Mr. Remus," he began, "I have been sent over here by the prosecutor's office to make an examination of you."

"Very well, Doctor," Remus said. "Go ahead and just go as far as you'd like. . . . I am perfectly normal in every respect."

The doctor kept his tone even. "Your plea will not be insanity?"

"Emphatically no, it will not."

Dr. Kendig inquired about Remus's history and marriage. Every time the conversation called for the word *wife*, Remus substituted it with the phrase "the decomposed mass of clay." She was not an educated woman "but a very shrewd and attractive woman." They had plans to retire to some secluded spot and live happily, but while he was confined in Atlanta "this decomposed mass of clay and her pimp . . . broke up my home, robbed me of my fortune and double-crossed the federal government." This pimp and the decomposed mass of clay had taken everything from his house, save the pearl-handled revolver with which she met her death. And now he'd transitioned from "George Remus the millionaire, to George Remus the murderer."

He spoke this monologue, noted a police officer, with "repressed excitement."

"Are you insane?" Dr. Kendig asked.

"Positively no," Remus assured him, but then offered an addendum. "No man could be perfectly sane and commit the crime that

355

I've done."

In her office at the Department of Justice, Mabel Walker Willebrandt stayed long after her colleagues had quit for the day, hunched over a pile of newspapers, scissors in hand.

It had been a hectic summer. She was in the running for a federal judgeship in California, but President Coolidge so far had withheld his support. "He's <u>abstract</u> in his thought of women unattached to some man," she wrote, and wondered how she might "humanize" herself to him. She'd successfully argued before the Supreme Court, in the case of *United States v. Sullivan,* that the Fifth Amendment did not protect bootleggers from filing income tax returns, setting the stage for tax evasion cases against the country's most notorious gangsters, including Al Capone. Another case bound for the Supreme Court would determine the legality of wiretapping private telephone conversations; given her own feelings about the need for privacy, Willebrandt planned to recuse herself.

In addition, she'd committed to a rigorous schedule of public speaking and magazine writing. An upcoming article for *The Smart Set,* titled "Give Women a Fighting Chance," compared the world's treatment of boys and girls:

A boy must do the job well, and develop

personality.

A girl must do the job well and develop personality. PLUS —

Break down skepticism about her ability.

Walk the tight-rope of sexlessness without loss of her essential charm.

Keep up an impersonal fight against constant efforts to sidetrack her.

Devote extra work and thought to making an opportunity out of every little opening.

Make the hard choice between giving up children and home life in order to advance, or having them in the face of increased prejudice.

And lastly, maintain a cheerful and normal outlook on life and its adjustments in spite of her handicaps.

But on this night she disregarded everything else on her calendar, at work and at home. Instead she read article after article about what George Remus had done. The shooting was the denouement of what she'd put into motion by sending Dodge into the bootlegger's life, initiating an unpredictable chain of events. Now a woman was dead, and an innocent girl motherless.

Each headline and quote was more disturbing than the last: REMUS KILLS SPOUSE; SAYS HE'S GLAD. WIFE'S ALLEGED AFFAIR WITH FORMER DEPARTMENT OF JUSTICE AGENT BLAMED FOR

357

SLAYING. RUTH REMUS, WHO FOUGHT TO SAVE MOTHER, ASSERTS STEPFATHER ACTED AS IF DEMENTED. "The shooting was no surprise to me," admitted a Remus associate. "I expected one of the couple to be shot sooner or later." One article, titled "The Women in Remus's Life," named seven women who had affected the bootlegger: ex-wife Lillian, mother Marie, accountant Blanche Watson, Ruth, Romola, Imogene, and Willebrandt herself. "Mrs. Willebrandt is a very able woman and I certainly ought to know," Remus said. "Certainly the outcome of the prosecution she conducted with such success has profoundly influenced my life."

Willebrandt clipped them all and pasted them into Remus's file, which now filled three thick binders. She knew the substantial list of grievances Remus held against her and suspected that her name would come up during the trial. If prosecutor Charlie Taft desired her help, she would gladly take his call.

REMUS'S BRAIN EXPLODED

Remus occupied private quarters on the top floor of the Hamilton County jail, away from the other prisoners. The five-room suite had a bedroom, a personal bathroom, a law library, and an office with ample space for books, a desk, a table, and a typewriter. He was permitted to receive visitors, with no restrictions.

Hours after the murder, as the evening editions broke the news, Chauffeur George Klug arrived at the station and claimed he'd had no idea what Remus had intended. George Conners came next, armed with necessary provisions: twenty suits, a silk robe, three topcoats, and various documents — legal papers, photostatic copies of letters, handwritten notes — collected from Remus's library. Remus discarded his brown suit, still stained with Imogene's blood, and changed into a gray jacket, silk shirt, and black tie. He stored the documents inside a small metal trunk, which he called his "liberty box."

Romola took a train from Chicago, arriving the morning after the murder. She had forgiven her father for abandoning her all those years ago, preferring to focus instead on his occasional gestures of kindness. When she was a child he'd bought her a revolver, a weapon she'd later use to scare away an intruder. He was always generous with money. And he had supported her dreams of an acting career, which began when she was ten and portrayed Dorothy Gale in *The Wizard of Oz* — the first person to play the role on film, cast by L. Frank Baum himself.

Rushing to her father's cell, Romola embraced him and kissed his cheek. "I love my father more than anything in the world," she told reporters, "and I'll stand by him to the end. He needs the love and tender care of a woman and I am going to give it to him."

Remus also addressed the crowd. "I see the press is here in all its grandeur," he said, welcoming them with a sweep of his arm. "No doubt you want to see Exhibit A. Well here it is." At that, he leapt a foot off the ground and clicked his heels.

His demeanor, observed one reporter, was more akin to that of a "statesman discussing a topic of general interest rather than a man charged with a capital offense." He appeared poised, unruffled, and eager to answer any question, no matter how personal. His wife — "that piece of degenerated clay," he clarified cheerfully — had sought to injure him by every means. Dodge and his wife "broke him." He was justified in doing what he did; in fact, he "owed this to society."

One reporter waved a piece of paper; it was a statement from Franklin Dodge, in which the former agent claimed Remus had paid a man $8,000 in the hope of killing him. Remus laughed, a prolonged shriek, and asked a question in response: "Why should I spend $8,000 to have any man killed when I could buy a bullet for a few cents and do it myself?"

Another reporter raised a hand. "No doubt you had this all planned," he said. "It seems to me that you also would have planned your getaway."

That was the lone question that provoked Remus, stripping away his sheen of urbanity and calm.

"Your youth excuses you for the question you have asked," he replied, each word imbued with anger. "Why should I go about the country as a fugitive from justice — a man with a price on his head? If you have a clear conscience you have nothing to fear, and consequently why should I run away? A man who feels that he has performed a duty to society and that he has committed no moral wrong does not run away from the consequences of his act, but would do just as I have done, give himself up."

Remus maintained that position the following day, when he appeared in municipal court. His gregarious mood had returned, and he shook hands with reporters and gadflies before a police court judge called his name.

"Here," Remus said, stepping forward.

"You are charged with murder," the judge said. "What is your plea?"

Remus didn't hesitate: "Not guilty."

"Are you ready for trial?"

"I am."

On his way from the courtroom Remus stopped to speak with reporters, who asked if he'd hired a lawyer to assist with his case. With a flourish, he produced two telegrams from his pocket: one from W. W. O'Brien, Clarence Darrow's law partner; and the other from Hugh J. Daily, a former assistant federal prosecutor in Chicago, both offering their services to defend him. Remus said he'd declined. "George Remus will defend George Remus," he explained. "I am now George Remus the lawyer, not George Remus the bootlegger." Privately, Remus had been following the case of George "Fat" Wrassman, which was nearing its end. If Wrassman's attorney, Charles Elston, emerged victorious over Taft, Remus planned to hire him as cocounsel.

In the corridor, Remus scoffed at Taft for anticipating an insanity defense. "Do I look like an insane man?" he asked. "Anyone who thinks I am insane needs to have his own mentality examined." He paused a moment, reviewing his words, and laughed. "That does sound crazy, doesn't it?" he added. "The insane always think that everybody else is crazy."

Remus spent the weekend entertaining more visitors at his jail suite. Blanche Watson came to say that she had told his sister and brother-in-law the news. John Rogers, his reporter friend from the *St. Louis Post-Dispatch,* also paid a visit and was shocked by Remus's demeanor. "I never saw him so tranquil in my life as when I saw him three days after the murder," Rogers reported. "He appears to be an entirely different man." If Remus had been insane, as Rogers once believed, his mind had been swiftly and miraculously restored.

On Monday, October 10, 1927, it took a jury just ninety minutes to acquit Wrassman, and Remus asked Elston to assist with his defense. In addition to murder cases, Elston special-ized in acrimonious divorces, once winning $100,000 in alimony for a woman — twice the amount specified in her post-nuptial agreement (among her husband's offenses: insisting that the servants dine at their table and then directing all of his conversation toward them). "At the earnest solicitation of my friends, I have decided to have Attorney Elston associated with me in my trial," Remus announced. "Remus will handle his own defense, but Mr. Elston will be associated with him."

Together they began debating strategy. The first order of business: entering a plea — "not guilty" by reason of . . . what? One option was "justifiable homicide."

They could catalogue Imogene's undeniable offenses — her theft of his money and assets, her betrayal with Dodge — and argue that her deplorable behavior warranted his own. More than that, her behavior *begat* his own, an initial spark of violence that spread and set their lives ablaze. She was an immoral woman, and therefore Remus was morally right to kill her. Theirs would be history's oldest and most common defense.

The second option: temporary insanity, or, in legal parlance, "transitory insanity." The scaffolding would be the same, using Imogene's own perfidy to explain what precipitated her death. Had she remained faithful, Remus never would have suffered brainstorms, those momentary lapses in consciousness that obliterated all rational thought. Transitory insanity would explain the shooting stars and the gleaming halo that followed him, whispering murderous commands.

Remus knew well the legal precedence for

the transitory insanity defense. It was first used successfully in the United States in the case of Daniel Sickles, a future Civil War general who murdered Philip Barton Key II, son of "The Star-Spangled Banner" author Francis Scott Key and the district attorney of Washington, D.C. In the winter of 1859, Sickles received an anonymous letter claiming that his much younger wife, Teresa, was having an affair with Key. When confronted, Teresa composed and signed a confession, admitting her indiscretion with typical Victorian verbosity: "I did what is usual for a wicked woman to do." The following morning Sickles, armed with three handguns, fired three shots at Key, the last one at point-blank range.

Sickles's defense team included Edwin Stanton, a nationally renowned attorney and the future secretary of war under Abraham Lincoln. During the trial Stanton crafted a motive previously untested in American jurisprudence: Sickles's mind had been "affected" by his wife's betrayal, and he shot Key not in cold blood but in a fleeting "transport of frenzy." It took a jury only one hour to deliberate and return a verdict of not guilty. At the news, Stanton giddily danced a jig.

More recently, in 1907, eccentric Pittsburgh millionaire Harry K. Thaw stood trial for the murder of famed New York City architect

365

Stanford White. Thaw had long resented White, convinced that he'd conspired to exclude Thaw from prestigious Manhattan men's clubs, and a strange love triangle only intensified his antipathy. Stanford White, an unabashed libertine, had pursued fifteen-year-old model and showgirl Evelyn Nesbit; during one encounter, he reportedly plied her with champagne and raped her. After forgiving her "benevolent vampire," she continued their relationship.

But Nesbit had another ardent admirer in Thaw, who attended all of her performances, sent her gifts, and whisked her away on an extended vacation in Europe. In a Paris hotel suite, Nesbit confided the rape to Thaw. "[White] became blacker and blacker with everything she told me all that long night," Thaw later wrote, "and for days afterwards, and for month after month." Even after marrying Nesbit, Thaw nurtured his hatred for White. During a musical playing at Madison Square Garden's rooftop theater, Thaw ambushed White and shot him three times, exclaiming, "I did it because he ruined my wife!"

Thaw's defense attorney announced that his client had suffered from brainstorms — the first major murder trial to employ the term — and argued that Thaw had "for three years been suffering from a disease of the brain which culminated in the killing." The prosecutor scoffed at this reasoning and posed a question to the jury: "If the only thing that lies between a citizen and his enemy is a brainstorm, then let every man pack a gun." Thaw's first jury was deadlocked, but a second concluded that he was "not guilty on the ground of insanity at the time of the commission of his act."

But Sickles and Thaw weren't at the front of Remus's mind. As a lawyer in Chicago, Remus had himself used a "transitory insanity" defense for a client, and now he recalled the details of that case with extra clarity.

On the night of October 16, 1913, the concierge at the Sherman House in Chicago received a complaint about a disturbance in Room 1105. A detective found the door unlocked. The floor and walls were awash in blood. A man, later identified as William Cheney Ellis, stood by the bathroom. On the bed lay a woman, her face partially obscured by a handkerchief. Her throat had been carved, a jagged smile stretching from ear to ear. Further inspection revealed gunshot wounds through the brain and heart. The man in the bathroom wore a woman's kimono and had a cigar clamped between his teeth.

Ellis, a wealthy leather merchant in Cincinnati, was married to Eleanor, a prominent socialite. She had traveled to Chicago to visit family, and Ellis, who suspected her of an affair, followed her to the city. At a Chicago police station, he made a detailed confession:

> I shot her as she lay in bed. She was
> awake, but did not see my revolver. The first
> shot hit her in the breast. The blood spurted
> out and seemed to madden me. She half
> rose and pleaded with me to spare her life.
> I became a furious beast and fired again
> and again. She sank down and lay still. I
> screamed at her, and in my frenzy hacked
> at her round white throat with a knife pen.
> Suddenly I knew what I had done. I wanted
> to die. I shot myself and tried to cut my
> throat. When I thought I had ended it all I
> lay down beside her and kissed her stiffen-
> ing lips as life ebbed from her.

When Ellis hired Remus to defend him, the attorney was already well versed in the science and psychology of insanity. He read widely and greedily, devouring any book that probed the intersection of medicine and law, and grew particularly enthralled with the work of Richard von Krafft-Ebing, an internationally acclaimed Austro-German psychiatrist. In 1879 he published his *Text-Book of Insanity,* which was translated into English and quickly recognized as a seminal text by American medical and legal authorities. Krafft-Ebing devoted a section to "transitory insanity," outlining symptoms and expressions of the condition, all of which Remus studied intently:

- "The rapid attainment of the height of the disease, with only slight variations of intensity, and the sudden and critical end of the attack, with the immediate restoration of the former mental state. . . ."
- "The forms of disturbance of consciousness in transitory insanity may be states of somnolence, sopor, stupor, and semi-consciousness."
- "The whole condition presents the features of an intense cerebral irritation . . . the patient becomes delirious and raving . . . any reflex in the nervous paths of speech finds expression in inarticulate howling and shrieking; only now and then in the incoherent flight of ideas are disconnected words and sentences to be distinguished."

In March 1914, after a two-week trial, Remus delivered a five-hour closing argument detailing how Ellis had been temporarily insane when he shot his wife. "Gentlemen of the jury," he concluded, "the best that is in me is none too good for this poor unfortunate victim of circumstance. . . . If I thought that poor Ellis murdered his wife — that beautiful loving mother and wife of his children — if I thought that this man that you see before you

369

knew what he was doing when he killed that woman, I would say to you, hang him — yes, tear him from limb to limb. But if you do not believe that he was in his right mind — if you believe, as the evidence of the defense has clearly shown, that he was insane — then do your duty as citizens and acquit him."

The prosecutor sought to discredit the "transitory insanity" defense. He declared that Remus could have persuaded alienists "to swear that Brutus had a 'brainstorm' just before he dug his assassin's dirk under the seventh rib of his old friend Julius Caesar. . . . Has it come to pass that a man can kill his wife in a rage and then have twelve good men say, 'Why, sure, poor fellow, you were working under a storm. The storm is over. The sky is clear; and let the crime be committed?' I don't think so."

The jury returned with a guilty verdict, but one tempered by compromise. Ellis would not be sent to die in the electric chair, as the prosecution had wished. He would not even spend the rest of his life in jail, but merely serve a sentence of fifteen years. As Remus boasted to the press, this meant that Ellis would serve only eight and a half years, with time deducted for good behavior. Remus considered it a win.

Now, with his own life on the line, he intended to improve upon that outcome. "What! Remus insane?" he joked to Elston, but it was decided: He would plead transitory insanity. He would take all of the symptoms he'd exhibited over the past two years — the raving, the violent fits, the catatonic spells — and create a narrative of madness, inviting jurors to experience the downfall of his mind.

Accordingly, Remus changed his language when he spoke to the press. He shed his defiance, and the murder became, in a sense, something that had happened to him as much as to Imogene.

He summarized his defense in just three words: "Remus's brain exploded."

As Remus conferred with Elston, Taft chose two assistant prosecutors. Carl Basler, thirty-eight, was a fellow scion of Cincinnati society who'd ably assisted Taft during the "Fat" Wrassman trial. Walter K. Sibbald, thirty-five, had known Remus for years and had even represented him in insolvency court after Remus's client William Cheney Ellis refused to pay his legal bills.

The three prosecutors assessed their knowledge of the case and the defendant, searching for proof of premeditation. Through interviews with Remus's longtime nemeses they discovered a dark and compelling piece of evidence: Remus had allegedly killed an Indiana sheriff in 1923 while running whiskey from St. Louis to Cincinnati. Imogene Remus

371

had intended to relate the details of the slaying in divorce court on the morning she was murdered.

Another discovery was equally damning. Imogene's lawyer revealed that his client had refused to sign a divorce settlement because she knew the full extent of Remus's assets — he was even a part-owner of the Cincinnati Reds — information she'd also planned to reveal. Remus hadn't even bothered to prepare a defense for court that day, presumably because he knew a divorce would never come to pass; he would kill her instead.

Even so, the prosecutors anticipated a difficult case, with many intangibles. Foremost among them was Remus's status as a folk hero. The jury pool would likely be made up of people, some fellow German immigrants among them, who abhorred Prohibition and drank Remus's liquor. Their friends and family might be among the thousands formerly employed by Remus. Their children might have played baseball on the grounds of Remus's mansion or gone swimming in his pool or gathered outside the gates of his estate, waiting for him to pull up in his touring car and flip a quarter into their outstretched hands.

Then there was the matter of the victim herself. Prohibition was on trial, but so too was the status of women. Many men still bristled at the idea that their wives and mothers and daughters now had the vote. Fearing that the flappers' brazen style made men appear more effeminate, the male students of Syracuse University organized a club to protest "smoking among women, women who wear flopping galoshes, and the intrusion of women into realms heretofore restricted to men." Even those who embraced "modern girls" might find Imogene's behavior disturbing — proving, as it did, that women were as capable of betrayal as men, and even had the gall to hope to get away with it.

As the lawyers strategized, Conners continued the search for Remus's fortune, placing an advertisement in newspapers across the country and in Canada:

TO BANKS, DEPOSITARIES, SAFETY DEPOSIT VAULTS, SECURITY AND INVESTIMENT BROKERS

Any one of the above institutions throughout the United States and Canada, particularly Ontario, Winnipeg and Manitoba provinces, having any knowledge of Augusta Imogene Remus or under the assumed names of Augusta Imogene Holmes, Augusta Imogene Brown, Augusta Imogene Grey, Augusta Imogene Campbell, Ruth Holmes and Ruth Remus, renting safety deposit boxes, having bank accounts, investment securities or collateral pledged, please notify George Remus, Hamilton county jail, Cincinnati, Ohio.

After a trip to Lansing, Michigan, Conners rushed to visit Remus with some triumphant news: He'd discovered that Imogene had rented a safety deposit box in an American State Savings Bank in that city. A certain "A. H. Holmes" had opened the box in September 1926 and had last visited on August 13 of the current year. This woman had twice visited the bank with Franklin Dodge, whose face was recognizable to everyone in Lansing, his hometown. The manager showed Conners a picture of Imogene Remus, and he confirmed that Imogene and A. H. Holmes were one and the same.

Elston wasted no time in securing a court order to have the box opened. The State of Michigan, hoping for a sizable inheritance tax from Remus's long-lost fortune, sent representatives to oversee the proceedings. Dodge issued a statement insisting that if Imogene had opened a safety deposit box in Lansing he knew nothing about it, and that he had only ever seen her in the company of others — never alone. On October 26, Dodge drove from Detroit to Lansing, arriving the same time as Elston and the bank officials, but fled to his home after being accosted by the press. Remus commented from jail, claiming that the box should contain $1.8 million worth of stocks, bonds, and warehouse certificates, "but only Dodge knows how much is left."

In the presence of Elston, numerous members of the press, state officials, and a city commissioner, the bank manager produced the key for the box, holding it aloft for everyone to see. The government officials nodded their consent. Elston craned his neck. The journalists hovered their pens over notebooks. Slowly, the bank manager inserted the key in the lock and turned. She tunneled her hand into the box, one foot wide and two feet long, and moved it left to right, back and forth.

When she retracted her hand, it was empty.

THE LOOSEST KIND
OF A TONGUE

In the days leading up to the trial, both the prosecution and the defense scrambled to finalize their cases. At a meeting in Washington attended by Elston and Basler, Elston requested that the Department of Justice "produce records in the department said to bear upon the alleged relations between Dodge and Mrs. Remus." Specifically, Elston wanted the files of Thomas Wilcox, the special agent who had been investigating Dodge and who'd recently alerted Remus to another plot against his life. Willebrandt declined but offered a compromise: the names and addresses of "persons who might be in possession of information of interest to both the state and the defense."

After the meeting Basler wrote to J. Edgar Hoover with a more complicated request. If the Department planned to prosecute Dodge, he hoped that they would wait until after the murder trial. "Naturally we would make every effort, as we think you would," Basler wrote, "not to embarrass a prosecution if subsequent action against a person involved could be taken as well later as at the present time."

Hoover was coy in his response — not because he wished to mislead Basler but because he himself didn't know if Willebrandt would ever prosecute Dodge. "We are both engaged in investigating and prosecuting crime," he wrote, "and I am certain that you know that our attitude here has been to cooperate as far as it is possible for us to do so."

Determined to find a prosecutable offense, Hoover continued to investigate Dodge. He instructed Agent Wilcox to "pursue this investigative inquiry and to the exclusion of all other matters" and requested the names of all informants regarding Dodge and "The Remus Matter." He did not share his activities with Willebrandt, nor did he forward an intriguing bit of correspondence from another special agent based in Chicago. "I understand from fairly reliable sources," the agent wrote, "that certain newspaper reporters, especially those representing Chicago interests, are endeavoring to secure some expression, possibly from George Remus, upon which they could base any sort of a story connecting former Agent Dodge with Mrs. Willebrandt."

This, too, went into Hoover's private file on Dodge, marked as classified.

■ ■ ■

Reporters visiting Remus's jail suite — his "suite de luxe," as it became known — were greeted with a question. "What'll it be?" the prisoner asked. "Scotch, rye, bourbon or beer?" He stocked all of them in abundance, although he himself continued to abstain. While they sipped he launched into a rambling monologue, suggesting that Prohibition, too, was on trial and that jurors should be aware of the hypocrisy of the very men who were prosecuting him:

George Remus has more at stake than anybody else in this case. George Remus is preparing himself both physically and mentally for this case. George Remus is no longer the bootlegger. It is George Remus the lawyer who will appear in court. George Remus knows law. . . . Some very high reputations will be damaged when George Remus tells his story. . . . George Remus's mouth was closed. It was closed on things that came from the very steps of the White House. Now George Remus can talk.

He paced from wall to wall, his face flushed, sweat dappled across his pate.

"What would you say if I told you that" — and here Remus referenced an Ohio senator, a man the reporters all knew but wouldn't name — "drank some of George Remus's liquor? Another got Remus to supply him liquor for his family when they needed it for medicine. George Remus probably could have had high political office for himself for George Remus had much to do with politics. If George Remus loses his case, George Remus will go down to dust. He will not flinch. If George Remus wins, prison walls never will know him again."

When reporters inquired as to the composition of his ideal jury, he surprised them with his response: "I would be happiest if I could have twelve women judge me. . . . No more bitter and stern judge was ever in the world than one woman sitting in judgment on another who has betrayed her mate."

Taft, also pursued by the press, impulsively disregarded his father's advice and offered a comment, sharing his theory about Remus's motive: Imogene knew of his involvement in the murder of an Indiana sheriff, and he needed to prevent her from making it public. From his cell Remus called the allegation "ridiculous," a characterization supported by an Indiana prosecutor who said he was unaware of any connection between Remus and the murdered sheriff. In fact, two bank robbers had confessed to killing the sheriff and were now serving twenty-year terms in the Ohio penitentiary at Columbus.

Taft, realizing that his underworld source had set him up, decided not to mention the incident at trial. He still believed that they had plenty of evidence to prove conspiracy and premeditation. And as his father pointed out, Remus's defense would consist solely of an emotional appeal, certain to collapse under the weight of facts.

"He talks so much that he may prove himself to be suffering from mental aberration," the elder Taft mused, "but I should think he was suffering only from the poisoned atmosphere of this bootlegging, divorce making, sensational press publicity, and that he is normal in the view of this who enjoy nothing else. You are going to have difficulty in preventing him from lying with the facility of the loosest kind of a tongue about what he believed and had reason to believe as to the schemes of his wife and her alleged paramour . . . it is a real opportunity for usefulness and for added experience. Remus is bound to advertise you in the course of advertising himself."

Journalists across the country prepared for the Remus trial, certain to be unlike any they'd ever seen. Will Rogers, beloved vaudeville star, actor, and humorist, commented on the case in his famous "Daily Telegrams" column, syndicated in five hundred newspapers to an audience of forty million readers.

"I think this fellow Remus, who is on trial, should be a hero to us men," he wrote. "He is the only man in our time that has had the foresight to shoot his wife first."

High-Class Gentlemen

On Monday, November 14, 1927, Remus prepared to make legal history, becoming the first person to act as his own attorney after pleading insanity, an absurdity that prompted questions and theories from opinion writers across the country. If George Remus, the accused, is insane, then why isn't the attorney George Remus insane? If George Remus, the accused, is insane, was he in a fit condition to employ George Remus as attorney? Furthermore, if George Remus the attorney is insane, does he not disqualify himself from representing George Remus the accused? Is George Remus the attorney setting up an inevitable mistrial for George Remus the accused on the grounds of improper assistance of counsel — and might this have been the plan of both George Remuses all along? As for the claim of temporary insanity, was it truly possible for George Remus to be cured the very instant he fired a fatal shot?

Escorted by a bailiff, Remus arrived at the

Hamilton County Common Pleas Court attired in a blue suit, a crisply starched cream shirt, a black tie adorned with a pearl, black shoes and socks, and tortoise-shell eyeglasses, clearly playing the part of seasoned attorney rather than deranged defendant. It was the day after his fifty-first birthday. In one arm he carried two books, *Paterson's Complete Ohio Criminal Code* and *Wharton and Stille's Medical Jurisprudence;* in the other, his "liberty box" full of legal briefs and a card from Romola that read, "To Daddy; I hope your next birthday will be much happier."

Smiling, he paused to greet spectators — housewives, doctors, businessmen, laborers — all of whom had lined up at sunrise to vie for one of 110 seats in the courtroom. "I'm sorry to meet you under such circumstances," he told them, offering his hand. Deputy sheriffs turned nine hundred hopefuls away, making exceptions for curious off-duty judges and lawyers eager to watch one of their own, sane or otherwise, defend himself on a murder charge. "It is a most remarkable spectacle," wrote the *Cincinnati Enquirer,* "and scores of attorneys, who under no circumstances could be induced to spend time in a courtroom where they were not personally interested, have come to see and hear this stockily built man, with the shiny bald head, as he appears in his dual role of lawyer and defendant."

A special section housed reporters from every major newspaper in the country, as well as representatives from several German-language newspapers eager to glimpse the famous "König der Bootlegger" (King of the Bootleggers). Fearing that the intense media scrutiny would affect the proceedings, Judge Chester R. Shook banned telegraph equipment, typewriters, tripod cameras, and flash photography from the courtroom. Judge Shook, forty-three, had been elected to the court only a year earlier, his first public office, and had done so with the full support and endorsement of Cincinnati's legal community. The *Enquirer* called him "a climber who could not be discouraged by adversity," and he was determined to conduct this trial, destined to be the most high-profile of his career, with dignity and decorum.

Remus took his place beside co-counsel Elston, set down his books and steel box, and rubbed his hands to restore circulation. At the table to his right sat Taft, Basler, and Sibbald, the very caliber of men Remus once hoped would attend his parties; now, at last, he had their attention. Behind Judge Shook, on a raised platform, sat three court-appointed alienists who would determine whether Remus was indeed insane at the time of the murder, and assess his current mental state as well.

On nearby Sycamore Street a repaving project was underway, filling the courtroom with the clang of metal and crunch of gravel. One hundred ten spectators leaned forward, fearing they might miss the opening words.

"Call the jury," Judge Shook directed.

One by one the prosecution and the defense evaluated prospective jurors from a pool of seventy-five men and women. Ohio law granted the State four peremptory challenges and the defense sixteen, a clear advantage for Remus. Twelve jurors and an alternate would be selected to serve. Both sides dismissed some contenders without debate. One man had served on a jury within the past year. Another was deemed too old. Several women explained that they had small children or sick family members to care for. Others escaped by virtue of clerical errors on their summonses. Once Judge Shook cleared these names from the list, the true interrogations began.

Basler stood, facing a farmer named John Trautman. He wished to determine what the juror knew about Remus's bootlegging past and associates, including George Conners, who was expected to testify on his friend's behalf.

"Do you know this man Conners, called Remus's lieutenant?"

Remus leapt from his seat. "He's not my

385

lieutenant, he's my secretary!"

Judge Shook sustained the objection.

"With all due respect to Your Honor," Basler said, "we will not refer to this man Conners as Remus's secretary."

Remus tore his glasses from his face and pointed at Basler. "I object to Mr. Conners being referred to as 'that man Conners,' " he shouted. "He is fully as high-class a gentleman as Mr. Basler."

Unconvinced, Basler rephrased the question: "Do you know this man Conners, who served time in Atlanta at the same time Remus did?"

Remus circled his left arm at Basler as though drawing a target. "There can be no reason for asking that question except to prejudice the jury," he said.

Judge Shook sustained the objection. Trautman answered anyway, stating that he had never heard of Conners. Basler, deeming the juror acceptable, turned him over to the defense.

Remus was still on his feet. "Would the fact that I am charged here with murder," he asked Trautman, "and the fact that I am participating in the presentation of my own defense, prejudice you against me, the defendant?"

Now Basler objected. "It is ridiculous to think that an insane man should question and examine jurors."

"The claim of the defense," Elston clarified, "is that the defendant was insane at the time the crime was committed."

"Does the defense say that the defendant is insane now?" asked Judge Shook.

Elston took a step toward the bench and raised his voice. "The defense says that Remus was insane at the time; his condition now is a question to be decided through the evidence in this case at the trial."

"How can the Court pass upon the matter unless advised by the defense as to its claim?" Shook countered. "It is necessary for the Court to know at this time."

"I don't think the Court has the right to ask that or to ask me to answer it," Elston said. Remus scribbled his co-counsel's words on a notepad. "Our defense is insanity at the time the act was committed, and the jury is not concerned with his sanity or insanity at any other time."

Shook agreed with Elston and overruled the objection.

Remus stood and continued questioning John Trautman. Would the fact that his name had appeared frequently in the newspapers prejudice him? Remus asked.

The farmer looked at him, confused.

"In other words," Remus said, "you are not going to hold it against the defendant, are you, Mr. Trautman? Your family affairs are such that marital difficulties of others would not prejudice you?"

Trautman said no, they would not.

Remus accepted him, satisfied with the sequence of events. Should the jury find him insane, any sanity hearing in the future would have to recognize that the Court had determined him mentally competent to question his own jurors.

Every morning, rain or shine, the queue outside the courthouse grew. Reporters profiled the most dedicated attendees: a weathered, pock-marked man who muttered, "Gee whiz, that man Remus sure is holding down the state stage." A large woman dressed in black, chewing her left forefinger until its skin turned raw and white. An old man who cupped his hand behind his ear. Remus, aware of his growing caucus of fans, spoke with exaggerated affect, as though teaching a group of restless pupils: "dee-fen-dant"; "vi-o-lay-shun"; and "Dan-ee-ells," in reference to the Jack Daniel's case.

With each successive juror the questions grew sharper, designed to extract every last bias. Taft immediately dismissed anyone opposed to capital punishment. He inquired as to whether a juror might be influenced by a plea that a man, by necessity, had taken the law into his own hands. He excused one when he admitted, "I've been in the same kind of trouble. I had a wife who ran away with my money too." A female chicken farmer seemed a good prospect until asked if Remus's background as a bootlegger would prejudice her against him. "I do not believe in the business and am against anyone in it," she insisted, "but I could forgive him."

To another Taft explained the proper procedure for determining a person's sanity, outlining three criteria: "Was the accused a free agent in forming the purpose to kill? Was he at the time capable of judging whether the act was right or wrong? Did he know at the time that it was an offense against the laws of God and man?"

Remus stood to object. There were more than two hundred tests for insanity, he said, and these three alone were far from sufficient. Should the Court desire, he would be happy to explain sixty such tests he used in defending his client William Cheney Ellis in Chicago.

Judge Shook overruled. A point for Taft.

By Thursday night twelve jurors had been accepted: ten men and two women with varying backgrounds and occupations — a cigar maker, a baker, a painter, a produce dealer, a food salesman, a retired liquor dealer, two farmers, two machinists, and two housewives. They were to be sequestered at the Hotel Metropole for the duration of the trial and would be permitted access to newspapers,

389

but only after bailiffs had cut out all mentions of Remus. On Friday, the final day of jury selection, both sides were poised to question the remaining pool in order to select an alternative.

Judge Shook called order, and Remus stood to address the juror.

"The fact that I have been disbarred as a practicing lawyer in Illinois as a result of my conviction under the violation of the National Prohibition Act," he began, "is that point to prejudice you against me if I take the witness stand?"

"No, sir," the juror replied.

Basler objected. Judge Shook ordered the jury to leave the room so that the prosecutor could elaborate. They had evidence, Basler claimed, that the Chicago Bar Association had been eager to disbar Remus for ten years and merely used the conviction as a convenient excuse.

"I object, if the Court please," Remus said.

"Well, the jury is not here," Shook pointed out.

Remus punched the air with his left fist, a gesture that had become familiar over the course of the week.

"Oh, Your Honor, no," he said. "Will you give me a chance to be heard on that? The press is here. Every word uttered by the prosecutor's office and by this defendant goes throughout the country and this civilized land, if the Court please."

Now Shook was annoyed. "So far as I know, the case is not being tried in the press." Turning to Taft, he asked the prosecutor to explain the objection. Taft repeated Basler's assertion that the Grievance Committee had tried to disbar Remus for years.

For Remus, for whatever reason, the words coming a second time — and from Taft's mouth — were an insult he could not mitigate with a smile or bow or sardonic retort. His skin reddened by degrees: starting at the tip of his collar, coasting over the knob of his throat, encroaching upon his cheeks, and washing over the smooth expanse of his pate, until the whole of his head looked like a rose in furious bloom.

"A nice statement to be made by the son of the Chief Justice!" he shrieked, his left arm spinning, propelling him to turn as he spoke: toward Taft, toward the spectators, toward the press, toward Judge Shook, back to Taft. "He knows that the defendant is charged with murder and he makes these statements for no other purpose than to cause prejudice as a result of these newspaper men that are here."

The newspaper men scratched at their pads, noting every aspect of Remus's demeanor: "His face livid, his words darting forth like rapier thrusts . . . an enraged Remus, a temporarily uncontrollable Remus. . . ."

Remus's arm swung wider and faster. Tears streaked down his face. His voice veered into a high falsetto. "He knows that in no Court of Justice that kind of statement would be taken for granted." He whirled back to face Taft. "It has been the pleasure of this defendant to appear before that High Chief Justice" — a reference to Taft's father — "but the specimen as given by the offshoot of that great, renowned character is pitiful."

He rotated and flailed. The tears flew from his skin with each spin of his head, the same trajectory of a boxer's sweat after taking a hit. His voice swelled and broke under the weight of its fury. "Five hundred judges and members of the Chicago bar have volunteered to come down here as character witnesses."

He lumbered toward Taft, arm whirling, a gesture meant to convey his fearsome strength and what he intended to do with it.

"A blind rage," the reporters noted, "completely out of control of himself" . . . "his thick neck and stout body quivered. . . ."

The table was the only thing between them. He raised and lowered his arm like a hammer, cracking his fist against the wood. "Man," he boomed, "if I had you in the corridor I would wreck you physically!"

Taft, his face inscrutable, stood quiet and still.

Basler reared up on his feet. "Get back

there or I'll punch you!" he screamed at Remus.

"Bah!" Remus said, and took a step closer to Basler. "You are no better than the rest. You have drunk my liquor not in pints, but in barrels."

Several bailiffs inserted themselves between the two sides, creating a barrier.

"Mr. Remus," Judge Shook said. "I have warned you twice before. I will warn you again now that if this occurs again I will take action that will prevent you from serving as your own lawyer."

"Yes, thank you, Your Honor," Remus said, and turned to the press table. "How was that?" he asked, wiping his brow. "Did I make an impression?"

After the alternate juror was accepted, the jury performed its first official duty, herding into a bus to visit two relevant sites, Remus's mansion and Eden Park. Reporters tagged along, following in a caravan of roadsters and sedans, making the steep trek up to the top of the city. They parked along Hermosa Avenue and found the main entrance, the black iron gates cracked open. The grand rooms, now oppressive in their emptiness, betrayed no hint of a festive past.

Instead they found Marie Remus, the defendant's mother, a tiny, white-haired woman who spoke in broken English and beckoned the crowd to follow her. "Mr. Remus needs me now," she said, never once referring to her son as "George." She led them through the card room, the ballroom, the dining room, the bedroom of "Mr. Remus" (furnished only with a single bed and a framed picture of mother and son), through the doorways stripped of their glass transoms and, finally, into the billiard room, where a mahogany pool table was the solitary adornment. "That was too heavy for her to move," she said, tapping the wood, "or it wouldn't be here."

Bailiffs ended the tour, escorting the jurors out. Mother Remus followed. That evening, as was her custom, she would bring him a bowl of Hasenpfeffer, the traditional German rabbit stew. "Such a good boy until he married that woman," she said. "Poor boy, he always wanted a home, and all he got was this place."

The jurors drove on to Eden Park, taking the winding road to the Spring House Gazebo, where city firemen had long since flushed away the blood.

ALIENIST NO. 1

In addition to observing the trial, the three alienists were obliged to conduct physical and psychological examinations of Remus. The first, Dr. David Wolfstein, had an impressive résumé: 1889 graduate of the Medical College of Ohio; director of mental diseases at the Cincinnati General Hospital; professor of mental diseases at the University of Cincinnati; a member of the American Neurological Association; a three-year stint of studying nervous and mental diseases in Europe.

Before Dr. Wolfstein met with Remus at the Hamilton County Jail, he outlined the parameters for their interview. He planned to investigate Remus's family history, his state of mind prior to and following the murder, his ability to reason and to show will, his attitude toward the law, his conception of right and wrong. The doctor believed that "transitory, maniacal insanity" — a term that recently had fallen out of favor — was more accurately described as delirium, usually following scarlet fever or pneumonia. During such a state, a person might act in ways resembling temporary insanity, followed by excitement and loss of memory.

His first impression of Remus was that he was a prosperous businessman, careful with his attire and appearance and "scrupulously" clean. Remus greeted Wolfstein as if the doctor were visiting his home, showing him around the five rooms of his prison suite, pointing out the library and stash of liquor, the space where he shadow-boxed in the middle of the night. After that he gave the doctor a tour of his life, starting with his German immigrant parents, the pressure to help support the family, the nights spent on the floor of his uncle's pharmacy, the father who drank too much. In elementary school, he learned well and kept up with his classes. While studying pharmacology, he led a student walkout on an examination he'd deemed overly "severe." In the case of his first marriage, he contended that his wife was "in the right" to seek a divorce. He spoke fondly of Clarence Darrow as a mentor when he was a young Chicago lawyer. He had been the head of the Chicago Athletic Club's water polo team and an avid member of the Anti–Capital Punishment Society. But law was a "great strain," which was part of the reason he ventured into bootlegging.

"Don't you think," the doctor asked, "that

going into a business like the bootlegging business was a great strain, and a great hazard?"

"Well," Remus admitted, "it was, but it was no such strain as that of the criminal law cases."

Leaning forward in his chair, the doctor next inquired about the defendant's sexual life.

"Oh," Remus said, somewhat surprised by the question. "I have been like every man, but not nearly as bad as most. I could have had every opportunity but I did not take advantage of it. I could have had all kinds of women at my feet if I had wanted them, but I did not take advantage of that."

The doctor noted that Remus appeared to possess no sexual abnormalities or perversions. Nevertheless, he would order a Wassermann test to determine if Remus had any mental disease resulting from syphilis. He found Remus's method of communication "harmonious"; the defendant laughed and joked and employed sarcasm at appropriate moments. The doctor noted that although Remus was said to react "in an insane manner" at the mention of Franklin Dodge or Imogene Remus, he heard these names dozens of times with no effect at all. So far the doctor believed Remus to possess "a good mind, a clear mind and a logical mind."

"About what time," he asked, "did you

begin to entertain the idea of killing Mrs. Remus?"

For a moment Remus pondered the question. "It began with rumors of disloyal conduct on her part shortly before I left the penitentiary in Atlanta."

If the doctor was surprised at this admission of premeditation, he did not betray it. "When did you first make threats against Mrs. Remus?"

When he returned to his home in Price Hill, Remus said, and discovered what she had done to it. He threatened her over the telephone and recalled precisely what he said: "I will get you if I have to follow you to China."

The doctor took notes on Remus's "symptoms of insanity or oncoming insanity" — the recurring halo, the shooting stars. "When did you make up your mind to kill Mrs. Remus?" he asked.

When he learned that she planned to kill him first, Remus said, "I heard she had sluggers in front of the Sinton Hotel." Exhibiting none of the memory loss associated with transitory insanity, Remus vividly recounted the morning of October 6. He remembered the weight of the gun in his hand and the lifting of that weight after he fired the shot and tossed it away. He would never forget the startled look of the man who drove him to the station.

"Did you know you would have to account for this?" the doctor asked. It was a deliberate question, carefully worded, as Remus had stated that he'd been "uncontrollably insane" at the time of the murder.

"I knew I would have to account for this act legally," Remus said.

The doctor nodded; here was more evidence of premeditation. "When do you think you were sane again?"

"Six or eight or twelve hours after the thing was over. I felt free, I felt perfectly free."

"Why did you kill her?"

"From principle, I killed her from principle. Mrs. Remus was the style of woman who should be removed for the betterment of the community."

In the next breath, Remus, appearing to realize the direction of the doctor's inquiry, threw his thoughts into reverse. He'd only decided to kill Imogene when he saw her "laughing and joking" as she left the Alms Hotel. He cited the work of Cesare Lombroso, an Italian criminologist and authority on the science of crime.

"Psychologists," Remus said, "generally recognize that every man who commits a crime is insane." He denied that he had committed the murder with any premeditation.

The doctor noted Remus's sudden shift in tone. Perhaps that, too, was part of his act.

"My defense is going to be temporary

maniacal insanity," Remus reminded the doctor. "I got Mr. Ellis off on that plea."

CONSPIRACIES

On the first official day of the trial the spectators arrived earlier than usual, heaving as one toward the courthouse doors. An entrepreneurial huckster waved tickets bearing the words REMUS TRIAL ADMISSION: HAMILTON COUNTY COURTROOM, $1.25. A sheriff shooed him away. There was a mad and violent scramble for seats, all of them filled within minutes, and those left standing pressed themselves against every available wall. Those shut out of the courtroom entirely formed a queue in the hallway, hoping that someone inside might leave and relinquish a spot. It was the largest crowd so far, with many prominent lawyers in attendance, eager to hear Remus deliver his own opening argument. Five extra deputies stood on duty, two each behind the prosecution and defense tables and one circulating the room. Remus entered clutching his steel box under his arm, which he allowed the deputies to search. They found only a sheaf of papers and a lemon sliced in two.

Judge Shook called order. "Each side will be limited to two hours," he announced. "Each side will make a plain statement of its case. There will be no emotion and no argument. There will be simple statement of the facts that the evidence will bring out."

Remus stood and pointed a thick finger at his throat. "Your Honor," he said, voice breaking, "I have a very bad —"

Before he could finish the sentence, Shook ordered him to be seated. The defendant retrieved a notepad and pen and began sucking audibly on the lemon.

Sibbald pushed back his chair and rose, facing the jury.

"We're here to try the charge of murder — and no other charge," he began. "Remus had the assistance and encouragement of others of the Remus gang."

At the word *murder* Elston objected. "It is conceded that there was a killing, but not a murder. 'Murder' presupposes the existence of certain elements which the state has to prove."

Judge Shook overruled the objection but granted Elston another point: He would allow evidence for a scope of two years, from 1925 until the day of Imogene's death.

Sibbald continued. During his allotted two hours he built the foundation for a conspiracy, suggesting that Remus had long planned the murder and anticipated his defense. His accomplices, most notably his accountant, Blanche Watson, engaged in an elaborate cover-up to make it seem that only Remus was responsible for the crime. "After we have shown to you," Sibbald said, taking one last stroll before the jury, "that this defendant in a cold-blooded manner deliberately, purposely, intentionally and maliciously shot and killed this defenseless woman, we feel we will be justified in asking you to return a verdict that will carry with it the extreme penalty."

As Sibbald took his seat, Elston meandered toward the jury.

"The defendant in this case had expected to make his opening statement," he explained, "but because of the fact that his voice is somewhat seriously affected he has asked me to make his statement for him."

A chorus of disappointed murmurs arose from the crowd.

"We expect to show you, ladies and gentlemen of the jury, that at the time George Remus fired the shot that took the life of Imogene Remus, he was not a free agent, and was not a sane and normal man, and was not capable of entertaining premeditation, deliberation, malice and purpose and intent to kill."

He paused. Remus slurped on his lemon.

Elston went on: "The evidence will disclose

403

that prior to the time he was sentenced to Atlanta he lived with his wife Imogene Remus; that the relations between them were of a most affectionate nature; that after he was sentenced to Atlanta those relations continued to such an extent that Mrs. Remus came to Atlanta to live a part of that time there and be near him. The evidence will disclose that the affection was so great between them that on her bended knees she scrubbed his cell."

A courtroom illustrator sketched a portrait of Remus and his lemon, capturing the soft bend in his nose, the angle of his lips. Elston introduced his story's villain, Franklin L. Dodge, and a conspiracy of his own — one between this agent of the Department of Justice and Imogene, which brought about the "very mental condition" Remus suffered for two years until the day he fired that shot. This conspiracy, born in Atlanta when Remus was behind bars, included tips to immigration enforcement, the theft of money and valuables ("even chandeliers and seats that had been built into walls"), and various plots to murder him. "I couldn't begin to mention all the details of this conspiracy," Elston said. "I can only mention to you the highlights. Mr. Remus has called my attention to certain facts."

Remus stood for the first time that morning. The deputies tensed, anticipating an attack.

"Pardon me," he said, the words scratchy and subdued. "Does the record show I have lost my voice?"

"The reporter is taking everything you say, Mr. Remus," Judge Shook answered.

"Mrs. Remus made the statement to several that she intended to marry Dodge when she got her divorce," Elston continued. "These things the defendant turned over in his mind a thousand times a day. . . . The more he thought about them the more they preyed on his mind and tortured him."

Nearing the end of his two hours, Elston told the jury he was confident that they would find the defendant not guilty of the charges contained in the indictment. "I thank you," he said, taking his seat.

The back door creaked open, letting in a thin wedge of sunlight. Ruth Remus entered, dressed entirely in black, the click of her heels the only sound in the room. She held a handkerchief to her face, covering half of it, and kept her composure until she saw Remus. At the sight of her stepfather she began to cry. Remus blinked and reached for his handkerchief, but his own tears never came.

ALIENIST No. 2

Earl Armitage Baber, the superintendent of the Longview State Hospital in Cincinnati, specialized in the care of the "mentally diseased." In addition to observing Remus at the trial, he interviewed him on four separate occasions at the Hamilton County Jail. While he respected the work of Krafft-Ebing, the psychiatrist whose writings had influenced Remus, Baber considered that doctor's definition of insanity to be obsolete. Baber personally defined the condition as "a prolonged departure from a normal individual's method of thinking, acting and feeling." He recognized, however, that more had been written on the subject of insanity than on any other subject in modern medicine, making it impossible to distill the condition into a few short words. In polling twenty-five fellow physicians on their definitions of insanity, not one of them was the same.

"Don't you know it is wrong to take human life?" the doctor asked Remus.

"Absolutely."

"Would it be wrong to kill Dodge, in your estimation?"

"Morally, no," Remus said. "But legally, yes."

"How do you reconcile it?" the doctor asked.

"Why, most assuredly, the enemies that man has are by the score. He has betrayed every man he has ever been associated with, this person Franklin L. Dodge."

The doctor asked if Remus had considered the ramifications of killing his wife.

Remus stopped, looked at the doctor squarely, and said, "I do not care whether or not I go to dust."

A Blank About Everything That Happened

To make their case for a conspiracy, the state called Edward T. Dixon, Imogene's divorce attorney, who testified that she had come to his office the night before her murder.

"I will ask if you had your witnesses ready to go into court the next day?" Sibbald asked.

"I did."

"Did you appear that morning in court at all?"

"I did not," Dixon said, adding that he had gone to the hospital when he learned of the shooting.

Sibbald considered his next question carefully. He needed to emphasize that Remus hadn't issued any subpoenas for his divorce hearing, which meant that he hadn't planned to call even one witness — because he knew all along that there would be no divorce. "I will ask you if you know of your own knowledge whether the defendant, George Remus, had subpoenaed —"

"We object," Elston said.

Judge Shook overruled and turned to Dixon, reiterating the question: "Do you know of your own knowledge whether the defendant had subpoenaed any witnesses? Do you know that of your own knowledge?"

"I do," Dixon replied.

Sibbald took over. "Did he issue any subpoenas?"

"May I be heard," Remus said, "before the answer is given?" His sore throat healed, he had traded the lemon for chewing gum.

Shook overruled but Remus ignored him. "There were many depositions filed there, Your Honor, many depositions."

"May it please the Court," Sibbald said. "We submit that we are not referring to depositions in that question. We are referring to subpoenas." The distinction mattered; Remus's depositions were taken in early 1926 (before, presumably, he'd decided to kill Imogene), while subpoenas were relevant to the actual court date — the date of Imogene's murder.

"Your Honor," Remus countered, "the record shows the depositions were taken pursuant to the subpoenas."

Sibbald was perturbed. Despite Remus's attempt to confuse the jury by conflating depositions and subpoenas, the truth stood: He hadn't prepared for his divorce case because he'd been planning to kill his wife. "Will Your Honor caution the jury to disregard that statement?" the prosecutor asked.

Judge Shook complied. But the damage had been done, and Sibbald turned his witness over for cross-examination.

The prosecution's greatest hope for proving a conspiracy involved a significant risk: calling Remus's chauffeur, George Klug, who was being held on $10,000 bond for his role in the murder. They hoped to prove that after the shooting, Klug fled to Covington, Kentucky, to confer with Blanche Watson.

"How long have you known the defendant, George Remus?" Sibbald asked.

"Since about 1919 or 1920."

"How long have you known George Conners?"

"All my life."

Sibbald took a step closer to the witness stand, knowing exactly where he wanted to take the questioning. "What time did you get up the day before this killing?" he asked.

"It was around five o'clock that evening," Klug said. He'd slept most of that day because he had worked late the previous night, parking cars for a gambling club just outside the city. When he awakened, he went to a local café where he received a phone call from Conners, who told him to meet Remus in his room at the Sinton Hotel.

Sibbald held up a hand, interrupting him.

"Don't you recall," he said, "that two weeks

ago in the prosecutor's office you told us you met Remus in the lobby with him and got into the machine?"

"No, I don't," Klug said.

Sibbald glanced back at Taft and Basler, a silent but furious exchange.

"Didn't you make that statement to me?" Basler asked, his voice raised.

Klug spoke with perfect calm. "I don't think I did."

"Don't you recall telling me you also saw Conners and got the keys to the machine from him?" Sibbald insisted.

Klug shrugged. "I am not positive I seen him there. I recall telling you that, yes."

"And do you recall telling me at that time that you didn't go up to Remus's room?"

At this, Elston stood and objected to the prosecution's cross-examination of its own witness.

"We are taken by surprise," Sibbald admitted.

"All right," Judge Shook said. "You may proceed under that theory."

Sibbald tried again, asking how long Klug had stayed in Remus's hotel room that evening.

"Between five and ten minutes," Klug said. "I didn't see anyone in there outside of Mr. Remus."

Sibbald struggled to contain his anger. The prosecution contended that the murder was planned in the room at that time with four people present: Remus, Conners, Watson, and Klug himself. "Now do you recall, Mr. Klug, when you were up in the prosecutor's office the other evening, that you said there were several people in those rooms?"

"I did no such thing."

Sibbald sighed. "Who have you been talking to about this case since you talked to me?" he asked.

"I have not been talking to anyone about this case."

Sibbald shouted his next question: "Do I understand you to say, Mr. Klug, that your mind is a blank about everything that happened before seven o'clock that evening?"

Remus stood. "We object to the form of the question, Your Honor."

Sibbald couldn't bring himself to look at Remus. "I submit to Your Honor that we haven't got anything out of this witness but suppositions and guesses."

Elston chimed in, clearly enjoying himself. "We object to that statement," he said. "That is absolutely wrong."

"And we move, Your Honor," Remus added, "that that statement be stricken out."

Klug's testimony lasted for five more hours, bleeding into the next day. He maintained his impressive obfuscation. When Sibbald read part of Klug's grand jury testimony aloud,

412

Klug appeared flummoxed and shook his head, insisting that he didn't remember making any of the quoted statements. He didn't recall telling the prosecution about specific conversations he'd had with Remus. He insisted that he hadn't looked in the rearview mirror to watch Remus shoot Imogene. In fact, as far as he knew, there'd been no revolver in the car on that day.

Sibbald next focused on Klug's behavior after the shooting. "Before you went to Price Hill in that automobile, and before you passed George Conners's house, where did you go?"

"I went over to Blanche Watson's."

Sibbald was shocked by this response — in all of their interrogations, Klug had never mentioned this — and asked the next question quickly, hoping to build momentum.

"Who went over with you?"

Elston raised a hand. "Now we object to that, if Your Honor please, unless the prosecutor is claiming that George Remus went there with him."

"Now, Your Honor," Sibbald said. "We are getting right into the fact of the covering up of the connections of others in this case."

"May I answer that, if the Court please?" Remus asked.

"I want to hear from you," Judge Shook said.

"The specific charge that the defendant is

413

here charged with is the willful, malicious and wanton killing of the deceased," Remus began. Nothing in his voice suggested he was speaking of himself. "And that is the only proposition before this court and jury to determine. It does not say in the indictment that a body of people confederated and conspired to commit this act. The only specific allegation, as I remember it as read by the prosecutor's office, is that on October 6, 1927, the said George Remus did willfully, maliciously and wantonly kill the deceased."

Remus's voice cinched in his throat, and his next words rang bell-like, high and clear.

"Is George Remus, the defendant, charged with murder, responsible for the activities of witnesses that appear in this court of justice, activities after the completion of the alleged offense?" he asked. "Never in all my life, if the Court pleases, have I heard of the absurdity of a legal prosecution as made by this prosecutor. I respectfully submit that the evidence is wholly immaterial, incompetent and inconsequential as to the activities of the defendant charged with this crime."

Judge Shook made a surprising ruling: Throughout the trial, the state must show not only a conspiracy to commit a murder, but also to conceal any fact connected with the murder. It was another blow to the prosecution; so far their evidence had failed to show either.

Remus stood and boomed, "Thank you, Your Honor."

Judge Shook ordered him to sit. Remus obeyed, laughing hysterically.

Remus received no visitors in his quarters that evening but issued a statement for Thanksgiving Eve: "Thankful! Yes a million times thankful for the peace of mind, soul and being that no verdict can rob me of, and which now on this day of thanks is my solace."

ALIENIST NO. 3

All told, Dr. Charles E. Kiely, a consultant in psychiatry at six hospitals in the Greater Cincinnati area, observed Remus in court and in jail for thirty-six days. During his first examination, Remus confessed that he would "kill Dodge if I ever got the chance." In Kiely's opinion, he displayed strong criminal tendencies and criminal sympathies. To wit: Remus's claim that, as an attorney, he would never represent the prosecution and would only work on behalf of the accused. He knew he could, through political influence, have held elective office as a prosecutor, but the possibility never appealed.

Like his colleagues, Kiely asked Remus to specify the moment when he decided to kill his wife. On the first occasion, Remus responded that the idea struck before he left the Atlanta prison and had suspected improper relations between Imogene and Dodge. On the second, he said he made up his mind when he heard she'd hired gunmen to stalk and kill him. And on the third, Remus said that the decision was final when she got into her taxicab smiling and laughing as though she hadn't a care in the world — in effect, the same pattern of answers he'd given to Dr. David Wolfstein.

Kiely continued this line of questioning, asking if he'd left his home that morning with the intention of killing anyone.

"My mind was not definitely made up that morning," Remus insisted. "Some individuals I couldn't identify came to my house about half past six that morning in a machine and asked for me, but by the time I got dressed and came downstairs they were gone. But I knew they would be at the Alms Hotel."

"Who do you mean by 'they'?" the doctor asked.

Dodge and his wife, he answered. He understood that Dodge had been at the Alms Hotel two or three mornings previously with her and had eaten breakfast there. He went out to the Alms without any intention to kill Dodge, although he had "some such notion in my mind."

Kiely nodded, taking notes, noticing the contradictions and discrepancies. George Remus possessed "egotism" and a "violent temper" and was "a very dangerous individual to be at liberty."

None of which meant that George Remus was, in Kiely's belief, insane.

THE ARCH-CONSPIRATOR OF ALL AGES

In the interest of expediting the trial, the prosecution and defense agreed to a session on Saturday, November 26. With the jury absent, Judge Shook announced that the court had received the alienists' report, which he would now read aloud for the record.

"Basing our conclusion upon conversations with and examinations of the said George Remus," Shook read, "including our observations of him in the court room during the progress of the trial thus far, we are of the opinion that the same George Remus is now sane and was on October 6, 1927, sane. This present opinion, however, is provisional and subject to modification depending upon further developments in the trial."

Taft, gleeful, suggested that the report go to the jury.

"Absolutely not," Elston said.

Shook assured him that it would not be sent to the jury and told a bailiff to call them in.

Remus rose from his seat and approached

the bench. "Your Honor," he said, voice quavering, "may I just, if the Court please . . . I do sure, from my heart, appreciate the kindness the Court has established here, and the report of the alienists as well." He dabbed at his tears, the first he'd shed since the trial began.

But Elston wasn't finished. Hoping to advance the notion that Remus was now sane — sane enough, at least, to conduct his own defense — he requested that the three alienists be removed from the judicial dais.

"I have advised with them from time to time," Shook said. "But if either side objects to their presence here, of course I shall request them to take seats elsewhere."

Elston began to respond but Remus held up a hand and spoke over him. He asked that Shook disregard Elston's request and permit "these honored alienists" to sit exactly where they were. Elston appeared annoyed but withdrew his request in deference to his client.

Remus's face, noted one observer, was now "wreathed in smiles."

The defense began its case, calling to the stand A. Lee Beaty, a former federal prosecutor — in fact, the first black man to hold that position. During his tenure he specialized in cases involving corrupt dry agents, winning convictions in all but one.

419

"When did you first become acquainted with Mr. Remus?" Elston asked.

It was the latter part of 1924, Beaty said, when Remus left for Atlanta. The following year, when Remus was charged with conspiracy in the Jack Daniel's case, Beaty supervised the "removal proceedings" — transporting Remus from Atlanta to St. Louis so that he could serve as a government witness. He saw Remus about six times during the Jack Daniel's trial.

"Mr. Beaty, from what you saw of Mr. Remus, and from your conversations with him, have you reached an opinion as to his sanity or insanity?" Elston asked.

"I have," he said, adding that he believed that Remus was insane at that time.

"Will you tell us what conduct or statements or acts of this defendant caused you to reach that conclusion?"

"He came into my office," Beaty recalled, "and he made accusations there that I knew were untrue. He talked incoherently. He raved in there."

"Just what did he say about it?"

"He said that the government . . . was conspiring with members of some gang to take his life."

"Were the officers high in the government or not?" Elston asked.

"One of them was very high in the service of the Department of Justice."

Relishing the exchange, Elston took his time. "You are not referring to Franklin L. Dodge, are you?"

"I am not. When I say one very high in the service of the Department of Justice, Franklin L. Dodge was also involved in that same charge."

Taft raised his hand. "May it please the Court," he said, "we think that if there is going to be any reference to government officials, the names should certainly be in the record."

Beaty frowned and shifted, turning to face Judge Shook. "Judge, I decline to give the name because that official, I know who it is, and it is a person whom I have absolute confidence in and I don't think that person's name should be brought into the case."

"Now Mr. Beaty," the judge said, "the Court is going to order you to answer that question."

Beaty spoke softly. "Mrs. Mabel Walker Willebrandt."

The defense called Richard E. Simmons Jr., an attorney for the Ohio and Kentucky Distilling Company, of which Remus had owned 53 percent. During the course of his interactions with Remus he had reached a conclusion on Remus's mental health. When certain subjects were raised, he explained, the defendant's "muscles became bound and

421

his arms sideways, and his voice raised and a perspiration on his forehead, and his gesticulation with his hands."

He recalled one incident in particular from the summer of this year, his very last meeting with Remus. The defendant had wished to create a trust for his daughter, Romola, so Simmons prepared a trust agreement, took the portion of the money that Imogene Remus was not claiming as hers, bought bonds with the money, and put them in a safety deposit box. He requested that Remus, Blanche Watson, and Romola visit his office to sign a receipt verifying that this money had been received.

"Are you twenty-one years of age?" Simmons asked Romola as a formality.

"Yes," she said.

As he handed her a pen Remus stood and roared, "That beautiful little daughter of innocence shall never sign her name upon a paper which bears the name of George Remus, declared by everybody to be the arch-conspirator of all ages!"

At that, Simmons watched Remus pound himself on his chest with such force that it sounded "like a man hitting a boiler, like he had some metal or some plate there," a motion he repeated again and again, a strange harsh clang of knuckles on flesh. As he beat his chest he called out his alleged sins: He was accused of being a gunman — and yet had never held a gun in his hand. He had been accused of being a drunkard — and yet had never taken a drink. All the while he rapped on his body as though it were a door or window, some barrier keeping him from the other side.

"Did you at any time discuss the subject of his wife and Franklin Dodge?" Elston asked.

Yes, Simmons said. On the day before they gathered to create Romola's trust, Remus had seemed perfectly rational. But just prior to the signing, Simmons told Remus that Imogene recently had come to his office. She knew that the federal government was suing the distilling company for $200,000 in back taxes, and she informed Simmons that she and Dodge had gone to the Department of Internal Revenue in Washington and had asked them to file a lien on all of its profits. She then visited the Court of Domestic Relations in Cincinnati and secured an injunction preventing anyone from collecting money from Remus's interests other than herself.

At this Taft jumped to his feet. "Wait a minute," he said. "We ask to strike from the record all of the testimony that has to do with the conversation with Mrs. Remus or the acts and conduct of anyone except George Remus."

Judge Shook dismissed the jury to issue his ruling: Since the defense had introduced sufficient evidence that George Remus was suffering from a "diseased mind," they may therefore proceed to show the cause of that condition. Any information conveyed to Remus that could have contributed to this diseased mind would be admissible, even if it weren't true.

Taft sank down in his seat. Now nothing was off-limits in terms of Imogene's behavior. In the eyes of the jury, she would transform from victim to defendant, with no way to answer the charges leveled against her.

Unbeknownst to Taft, his father was growing increasingly concerned about the tone and direction of the trial. "I am very much interested in Charlie's fight against Remus," he wrote to a friend. "Remus is a disreputable and lawless kind of man, who is conceited about his knowledge of law. . . . I hope his conceit may betray him into a revelation of his real character, and that the jury will not be wheedled into any belief that he is insane."

DÉJÀ VU IN PRICE HILL

On the same day Willebrandt's name was mentioned in court, she received a wire from prosecutor Charlie Taft requesting her assistance. "Remus has a witness here," Taft wrote, "a man named Marshall, who seems to be connected with the District Attorney's office in Alaska. We have assumed that this was the same man who prosecuted the Jack Daniel's case in Indianapolis. In any event, we should like to have a copy of the letter that Marshall wrote to you, recommending the parole of Remus."

She filed Taft's letter with her clippings on the Remus case, a collection that grew thicker by the day. Many of her old colleagues were in the headlines: John Marshall, her partner on the Jack Daniel's case, had traveled four thousand miles on behalf of a murderer; Remus was threatening to "parade" the names of long-dead Jess Smith and Warren Harding; and Franklin Dodge had been subpoenaed by the defense to produce any records taken from Remus's home. She'd discovered that J. Edgar Hoover was still investigating Dodge and ordered a halt on his activities; he could resume, if he so desired, after the trial's conclusion. And another former assistant district attorney, Allen Curry of St. Louis, was scheduled to take the stand that morning to tell tales of Remus's alleged insanity.

She would respond to Taft's request, but there was something else she wished to do first.

"My name is Allen Curry," the witness said. He'd served as Assistant United States Attorney for the Eastern District of Missouri for four years.

"Do you know the defendant in this case, George Remus?" Elston asked.

"I seen him one time," Curry said. "Just previous to the finding of the indictment at Indianapolis in the Jack Daniel's distilling case." At his behest, Remus had come to his office in the federal building to prepare for an interview with the grand jury, but began acting violently as soon as he heard the name Franklin Dodge.

While Elston continued his questioning, a bailiff approached the prosecution's table and tapped Taft on the shoulder. His secretary had come to the courtroom with word of an important phone call. Taft excused himself

426

and headed to his office on the fourth floor, where he discovered that Willebrandt was on the line. She'd hoped to speak with Taft before Curry took the stand.

"Do you know Curry?" Taft asked.

Willebrandt didn't hesitate. "I know plenty."

Taft returned to the courtroom as Elston was finishing his questioning.

"What opinion did you form?" Elston asked. "That he was sane or insane?"

"My opinion was that he was wholly insane."

Elston yielded the floor to the prosecution. Quickly, Taft leaned close to Basler and whispered a summary of Willebrandt's call.

Basler stood. "Will you tell us why you sent for him?" he asked Curry.

"I sent for him because at the time I was expected to present the case anew to the grand jury, and Willebrandt, who is in the attorney general's office, had decided —"

"You mean Mrs. Willebrandt?" Basler asked.

"Mrs. Willebrandt from the Attorney General's office was deciding differently," Curry explained; she wanted the case to be tried in Indianapolis instead of St. Louis.

"Now Mr. Curry," Basler said, stepping closer to the witness. "Would you mind explaining to this Court and jury the occasion of your leaving the service of the United States government? Was your resignation by request?"

"No, sir, it was not."

"Was your resignation," Basler said slowly, "required by Mrs. Willebrandt, whom you referred to as Willebrandt a few minutes ago?"

"No sir," Curry said. "Mrs. Willebrandt had —"

"Because you were involved in a White Slave case out there and discharged —"

"No sir."

"— for malfeasance of duty in office as United States Attorney?"

"No sir."

Elston objected, but Basler had managed to discredit the witness.

One after another, defense witnesses took the stand to describe Remus's odd behavior, and a pattern began to emerge. His breakdown at the sight of his empty mansion in April, after being released from serving his final sentence, had not been the first such incident.

George Conners recounted an episode from 1925, soon after Remus was released from the Atlanta penitentiary. Imogene had gotten an injunction preventing Remus from entering his mansion. Remus had asked Conners to drive him by just for a glimpse, and on the way over he had a brainstorm in the car.

"He grabbed me while I was driving, from

the rear," Conners said, "and I had to pull directly to the curb and stop." He remembered Remus's precise words: "My god! How can she lock me out of my house? . . . I know they cannot issue an injunction restraining a man from entering his own home, and that is my home and I am going into it right now."

Remus had leapt from the car and sprinted across the street. Conners followed, the outline of his friend's stout form vanishing and reappearing as he scuttled across the grounds. Using both force and reason, he led Remus back to the car and drove to a hotel. "I stayed with him all night that night," the witness testified, "and he got very insane that night in the hotel."

When the injunction was dissolved, Conners continued, he took Remus back to the mansion. "We tried to get in and all the doors were locked and the windows barred, and we asked the watchman for the key and he said he did not have any. Mr. Remus broke a window and I crawled through the window, opened the door and let him in, and when he saw sight of the house —"

Sibbald, conferring with Taft and Basler, stood and asked, "May we have the time of this?"

"Give the dates, Mr. Conners," Judge Shook said.

"Possibly between the 17th and 22nd," Conners answered and confirmed that the year was 1925.

He resumed his story: "A lot of the furniture was crated, and paintings, etcetera, were crated, and everything was taken out of the house except some pieces of furniture he had in the Remus Building moved for him." They had gone upstairs to Remus's bedroom, only to find that it had also been stripped; only a cot remained, with no pillow or blanket. Remus stood there, staring at the empty and desolate space, and fainted, falling stiffly onto the hardwood floor. Conners dropped to his knees and slapped at his cheeks, rousing him.

"I wanted to get a doctor," Conners testified, "but Mr. Remus came to very quickly and he got up, and we called the watchman in, and he got into a violent argument with the watchman as to why he permitted her to do it. He said he could not help it."

At this, Conners recalled, Remus reared up on his feet and leaned into the watchman. "The hell you could not!" he screamed, hurling himself against the watchman's chest. Conners wedged himself between the two men and Remus relented, letting his body fall limp as they dragged him to the cot.

"He was in the same condition," Conners said. "He was starry. I did not know what he was staring at. He did not even know me at that time when I came into the room." Remus had looked at him with unseeing eyes and asked, "What do you want?"

"I am Conners," the witness remembered saying. "Don't you know me?"

"Oh," Remus responded. Then he lay back down, keeping his starry eyes open.

An hour later, still on the stand, Conners spoke of a similar incident that had occurred two years later, in April 1927, when he picked Remus up at midnight from the Portsmouth jail.

"We got into Cincinnati about four o'clock in the morning," he testified, "and he wanted to go out to his home first. When we got out there we couldn't get in, the doors were all locked and the windows were barred and so forth . . . all the doors had long spikes in them; the house was completely stripped of everything at this time. The fine furniture had been taken and the book cases had been removed from the walls with his books . . . the only thing that was in the house, I believe, was a bed and a pair of shoes that didn't fit Remus. Mr. Remus at that time lost all control of himself . . . he was delirious a couple of days. He was uncontrollable, he would burst out into frequent rages."

"Mr. Conners," Elston said, "from all of these incidents which you have related to us, did you reach an opinion as to the sanity or insanity of the defendant George Remus?"

"Yes sir," Conners said. "I reached the opinion that he was insane at times."

Judge Shook wasn't satisfied. "The question asked was whether or not Mr. Remus was sane or insane, that is the question, and you may answer it yes or no. Was he sane or insane?"

Conners relented. "Insane."

Taft consulted his notes. Remus's watchman, William Mueller, had testified previously for the defense about his boss's return from prison. Now he was taking the stand again. Mueller's earlier testimony had mostly matched Conners's, but with one significant discrepancy: Conners had said that Remus argued with Mueller about the state of the mansion in 1925, while Mueller insisted that it was 1927. This was Taft's chance to highlight the inconsistencies, and suggest that these narratives were at best unreliable and at worst fabricated.

"When was it that Remus got into the house by breaking one of the back windows?" Taft asked.

"The latter part of April, in 1926."

Already the watchman was confusing his story. "You mean last April," Taft clarified. "That is '27, isn't it?"

" '27, yes sir," Mueller agreed.

Taft hoped to confuse him further. "And didn't he get into the house in September 1925 by breaking in one of the back windows?"

"I didn't know he broke any window."

"You were not there at the time?" Taft asked, setting the trap for him to contradict Conners.

"Yes, sir," Mueller said, indicating he had been there.

"And you know all the furnishings in that house had been moved out at the time except for a few things that were not, don't you?"

"Yes, sir," Mueller said. Another contradiction: his earlier testimony had Imogene and Dodge ransacking the house in 1926, when Remus was serving his sentence in Troy. He had recalled detailed scenes of Dodge hiding behind cars and lowering blinds.

"And Remus went all through the house at that time, didn't he? And he saw the house vacated as it was, then, back in September 1925?" Taft asked.

"Yes, sir."

"Were there any outbursts as he went through the house?"

"No, sir."

"None at all? No explosions of rage, or outbursts?"

"No, sir."

Taft was satisfied. He hoped that jurors would question Conners's and Mueller's stories, and maintain that skepticism for the testimony to come.

Remus's divorce lawyer Benton Oppenheimer

took the stand.

"When did you first become acquainted with George Remus?" Elston asked.

"In the early part of September 1925," Oppenheimer said, and recalled a visit to Remus's home shortly after his release from the Atlanta penitentiary. "When we got out there," he testified, "we found the house practically stripped of all of its furniture and furnishings and Mr. Remus's clothes had been placed on the back porch . . . he acted like a man who had lost control of himself. He went around the house from room to room, wrung his hands, uttering expressions of amazement, surprise, that he had been treated in that manner, that his personal belongings had been removed, that his furniture had been removed. Went around and looked into the various closets . . . his appearance was that of a man who was in a complete state of physical collapse."

Elston nodded. "From all that you observed of the defendant during all of the period of time that you saw him, state whether or not you reached the conclusion that he was sane or insane."

"I reached the conclusion that he was insane."

Professional bondsman Clarence L. Owens took the stand. In September 1925, he had signed Remus's $50,000 bond in St. Louis.

"I got him out," Owens testified, "so he told me to come to Cincinnati and he would pay me, so about two days after that I came to Cincinnati and I met him in the Sinton Hotel, so I asked him about the money and he started raving about his wife running away with all of his money."

Owens returned to St. Louis, and two days later Remus wired him to come back.

"So I came and met him at the Sinton Hotel and he had taken me out to his house," Owens recalled. "At the time he told me he didn't have any money and he would show me the reason why, so we went out to his house and it was empty, and he started raving . . . he went on through the house, an empty house there, talking to himself."

"Now," Elston said, "what conclusion did you reach from the things you saw him do, that he was sane or insane?"

"I reached the conclusion that he was insane."

Paul Y. Anderson, the Washington correspondent for the *St. Louis Post-Dispatch,* took the stand. In 1925 he had been working with John Rogers on the series about Remus's bootlegging empire. They had interviewed Remus in December, during the Jack Daniel's trial in Indianapolis.

"During the time you were writing these articles, how often would you see Mr.

Remus?" Elston asked.

"I met him at George Conners's house in the morning and drove to his house and had lunch there and spent the afternoon there," Anderson said. "Rogers was with me. When we came in the place was very barren, the floors were bare and there wasn't much furniture in the place. And Remus said, 'I must apologize for bringing you into a place like this, but my wife has stripped the house of all the furniture.'"

Remus had given the reporters a tour, guiding them from room to room. "Anderson," he said, "I lavished all of the money I could get together to make this a beautiful place. . . . When I was not present, she had charge of all of my affairs and all of my furniture. She has moved it out and she has gone around over the country with this parasite and living in expensive hotels and sleeping with this pimp and spending my money."

Anderson recalled what Remus had done next: "He began raving and he stamped up and down the front room and he pulled at his head and he said, 'This is driving me mad. No man ever had to bear what I have had to bear.' . . . Sometimes he would walk a little while and he would be as solemn and sonorous as an archbishop. Then he would jump like a man with a hornet in his pants and tear around the room."

"From what you saw and what you observed, you reached what conclusion?" Elston asked.

"Well," Anderson said, "I reached the conclusion that he was exceptionally intelligent and sane and bright and shrewd about everything except that one subject. On that subject he was crazy as a bedbug."

Manuel Rosenberg took the stand. A newspaper artist with the *Cincinnati Post,* he had covered "every angle" of George Remus for six years.

"Were you ever out at the house?" Elston asked.

"The day he came back from Portsmouth," Rosenberg recalled. "I was there the day after. . . . He came up to the office with Conners, and he asked me to come take a look at the condition of the house."

"Now I wish you would describe for the benefit of the court and jury just what Mr. Remus's condition was when he went out to the house with you on that occasion?" Elston asked.

"Well, he was quite wild," the witness replied. "I would say, trying to get into the house, he couldn't get in, the door was locked, the windows were all locked. He was kind of fuming around, the watchman came along, the three of us, and we boosted him up to the window. He had some kind of instrument in his hand and he pried open the window and shoved him in and he managed to get the door open on the inside and he let us in. . . . Every time he would come to an empty room, he would start singing in a peculiar way, he would holler and shout and sing in a very peculiar manner."

"Did you reach any conclusion in your mind as to his sanity or insanity?" Elston asked.

"I didn't give it much of a thought at the time, but I know I thought on the subject of Mrs. Remus and Franklin Dodge he was quite off. He would go wild every time you mentioned it."

The prosecutors tallied up this *déjà vu* testimony, so similar in tone and theme it seemed that the witnesses had followed a script: Five tours of the empty mansion in 1925 and three in 1927, all of them — save for Mueller's version of 1925 — featuring "brainstorms" complete with ferocious rampages, pacing, hair pulling, hand wringing, glassy eyes, reddened flesh, and cascades of incoherent blather. Some of these tours had occurred on adjacent days, requiring Remus to stage his home as though it were the first time he'd seen it: relocking windows and doors that had already been opened; hiring a locksmith to participate in his charade; feigning surprise and despair at each ransacked room. If the witnesses were following a script, it was one that Remus himself had written. This was evidence, was it not, of premeditation? Every time Remus invited someone to witness one of these tours, did he anticipate that they would later recall his "insane" behavior in a court of law?

Together Taft, Basler, and Sibbald cross-examined these witnesses, giving their questions a tone of incredulity. Didn't Conners know that Remus had arranged for furniture to be removed in 1924, before he went to Atlanta? That some pieces were put in storage and others sold to pay off bills? Hadn't Conners seen the 1924 newspaper advertisements of an auction at the Remus mansion? Didn't Anderson think it odd that Remus had this extreme reaction nearly four months after his release from Atlanta? Moreover, did anyone find it improbable that Remus knew that his mansion had been emptied for two years and yet was still having violent outbursts in 1927? Didn't Rosenberg see that this tour was staged for the benefit of the press? Didn't Remus tell Oppenheimer that he had already been to the house and was well aware of its condition?

"I did not know that he had been out there since his return," Oppenheimer said.

"Well," Basler countered, "didn't Remus tell you that in the presence of newspaper men and the newspaper artist and some others he had gone through that house, having

439

forced an entrance through a window previous to your visit there?"

"Now we object, if the Court please," Elston said. "That is not the testimony. The testimony as to that is the second return from the Portsmouth jail. Mr. Basler is all mixed up."

Basler watched Elston. He was flustered, floundering. The defense attorney knew full well that Oppenheimer was speaking of a visit in 1925, not 1927. Oppenheimer had said so himself.

"I think I am not mixed," Basler said, his words laced with fury.

It didn't matter. The witnesses didn't know, couldn't remember, or would never have thought that Remus's disturbing behavior — in their view, evidence as clear as anything that the man had been cruelly wronged — might instead be merely a performance he gave whenever it happened to suit him.

At each prosecutor's query Remus "snorted derisively," in the words of one reporter, causing such a disturbance that Judge Shook issued a warning.

As she had since the trial's beginning, Ruth Remus sat among the other spectators. She had a clear view of the evidence table, which lacked the missing pearl-handled revolver but displayed her mother's outfit from that morning, the black dress and pink slip and suede shoes, piled in a crumbled heap and still dappled with blood. Every day she avoided looking at it, letting her eyes flit instead to the prosecution team or the alienists or to her stepfather. She looked at Remus now, and after his final derisive snort she laughed even louder.

A few days later, on December 3, Ruth released a statement. "In the court room daily he smiles at his well-trained witnesses," it began. "Many people are already saying, 'Remus can get away with murder.' He often told Mother and I that he could get away with anything."

SUN IN SCORPIO

The witness gave his name: "Harry Truesdale."

"Do you know George Remus, the defendant in this case?" asked Elston. Jurors assessed the man on the stand — early thirties, pink-cheeked, pudgy — and anticipated another tale of Remus touring his empty mansion. Instead, in a quiet and emotionless voice, Truesdale began the story of how Imogene Remus had offered him $10,000 to kill her husband. "One time I thought of killing him in his room," he said, "but there was too many people went in and out of there, he always had a lot of men callers coming in and out. . . ."

Truesdale paused, and Remus filled that space with a deep and resonant sob. His voice was a bass guitar, the note strumming low and persistent, overtaking the room. Hundreds of heads swiveled in his direction, and the sob stretched itself into words. "Will you adjourn Court for a minute, Your Honor?"

Remus asked.

With haste Judge Shook excused the jury. Remus slumped back into his chair and fell forward, pressing his head against his arms. His shoulders shook. The low, strumming sob began anew. The jurors began filing from the courtroom, glancing at Remus as they passed, many crying or wiping tears. Romola, sitting by her father's side, wrapped her arms around his neck and joined in his sobs. Several deputies rushed to Remus, creating a barrier around him. Together they hoisted him to his feet. Shuffling past the bench, Remus turned to Judge Shook. "Excuse me, Your Honor," he said, his voice trembling. "I couldn't help it."

He took one step, then another, the bailiffs propping him up, when, as one reporter described, "there burst from his throat an eerie yell, a half-strangled wail with a peculiar nasal intonation, that swept through the courtroom and electrified the audience, already in a state of emotional suspense." The half-strangled wail continued as Remus disappeared through the door leading to the judge's office. Romola followed, still sobbing, and behind her came the three alienists and court attachés and newspaper men, none of them willing to miss a second of the spectacle.

Even with the door closed, Remus's strange warbling keen traveled to the courtroom. His daughter's own cries persisted with similar volume and a deeper pitch, and Remus's sister, sitting among the spectators, added her own prolonged screech, their three voices together forming a brash and unsettling tune. "It was evident to the spectators," noted one observer, "that a drama of life, one of an intensity seldom witnessed in a courtroom, was happening before their very eyes."

In Judge Shook's anteroom, Remus flailed and thrashed on a couch. Bailiffs hovered over him, pinning his limbs. The piercing wails persisted, unabated and unabashed. Romola, having regained her composure, petted and shushed him. A court attaché caught her arm and led her to a corridor outside the anteroom. Remus broke from the bailiffs' grip and pitched forward on the couch, tucking his knees under his chin and hugging his calves to his chest, rocking back and forth and crying, "Will this never end? Oh, will it never end?"

The bailiffs tried again, reaching for his arms, but Remus jerked himself loose with sufficient force to rip his sleeves from his cuff links. Refolding into the fetal position, he screamed one word: "Persecution!" He remained in this state for fifteen minutes; the jurors, in the jury room, were a short distance away and heard it all.

At the alienists' request, bailiffs escorted Remus to his quarters and laid him down on his cot. The doctors stayed, observing him and asking questions: Did he know his name? Where he was? What was happening around him? After fifteen minutes, they decided that Remus was not fit to return to the courtroom, and Judge Shook ordered an adjournment until the afternoon. A nurse stripped him of his clothes, applying ice packs to his head and bags of hot water to his feet. He was left to rest.

At 2 P.M., Elston and an alienist checked on Remus. He was still in a highly nervous state, they determined. His features twitched. The only coherent word he uttered was "persecution." Elston returned to the courtroom and said that Remus was in no condition to resume the trial. Judge Shook found the jurors, still sequestered, and told them that "the defendant is unable to appear in Court."

A half hour later, after another visit to Remus, the alienists released a signed statement: "We find that Mr. George Remus has recovered from his emotional attack of this morning and at 3 P.M. was calm and resting very comfortably."

As Remus recovered, all those who witnessed the episode debated its authenticity. Elston, naturally, contended that Remus had suffered a true brainstorm — if he had been planning a scene, why would he have asked the Court to declare a recess? Wasn't it true that he did not break down completely until reaching the anteroom, out of sight (if not earshot) of the jurors? And did anyone notice that Remus, during his outburst in the anteroom, refused to permit a photographer to take a photo of him and in fact begged the photographer to leave him be? Did that sound like a man courting publicity? Furthermore, Elston said, Harry Truesdale had told the truth about Imogene hiring him as a hitman; even if he hadn't, it mattered only that Remus believed his story.

Taft pointed out that Remus had a long history of dramatic behavior in the courtroom — after all, his nickname in Chicago was "the weeping, crying, Remus" — and argued that this scene was as carefully planned as everything else in his life. In fact, the defense had brought Truesdale to Cincinnati, where the witness had calmly conferred with Remus in his quarters. The defendant and his daughter Romola (an aspiring actress, it should be noted) knew exactly what Truesdale planned to say on the stand. The scene had clearly been faked.

Speculation about Remus's fate had become the latest national pastime, and the chatter only intensified with the news of his courtroom breakdown. Around dinner tables, at racetracks, over tea in the serene parlors of women's clubs, and behind the camouflaged doors of speakeasies, everyone posed questions and predicted the final denouement. Although the three alienists initially concluded that Remus was sane, both at the time of the murder and at present, were they likely to reverse that decision? Should this happen, Judge Shook could discontinue the trial and send Remus to the Probate Court, where the defendant might transform his demeanor once again into one of rational thought and perfect calm — thereby convincing the judges of his sanity. Owing to double jeopardy, Remus could never again be tried for murdering his wife. He would reenter the world as a free man, resuming his life as though Imogene Remus had never been a part of it.

In New York City, members of the Astrologers Guild convened at the Hotel McAlpin hoping to divine Remus's future. After studying the placements of planets and stars, they concluded that Remus would not be sentenced to die for his crime but neither would he go free; instead, he would be incarcerated in a prison or asylum. His horoscope further revealed that he would die by his own hand, using either poison or gas as his weapon of choice. Although the group expressed confidence in their skills and predictions, they issued one caveat: They were equipped only with the date of Remus's birth and not the hour, and an error of even a few minutes could render the entire reading useless.

VERY EMOTIONAL, SOMEWHAT UNSTABLE

On the morning after his outburst, Remus's final witnesses arrived from Chicago, among them attorney and businessman Harry Pritzker — whose family was on its way to becoming a politically powerful dynasty — and Remus's old partner Clarence Darrow, now internationally famous for his work in the Scopes "Monkey Trial" and the case of child killers Nathan Leopold and Richard Loeb. Darrow visited Remus privately in his cell, telling reporters that he had come not to assist with Remus's defense but to testify to his good character. Remus wept at the sight of Darrow and engulfed him in ursine arms. "My friend, this is wonderful of you, wonderful!" Remus said. "I can never repay."

At Remus's request the bailiffs escorted him to the courtroom a few minutes early. As Judge Shook entered and ascended his dais, Remus jumped to his feet. "Your Honor," he said, "I want to apologize to you and the jury" — here he turned to the jurors, hand on his heart — "for my unmanly conduct of yesterday."

Shook ignored him. He was tired of all of it: the squabbling among the lawyers, Remus's antics, the circus of spectators and press. A few days earlier he'd invaded a huddle of journalists, turned to a representative of the *Cincinnati Post,* and said, "I'd sell you my job right now for a dime."

As Clarence Darrow took the stand, courtroom illustrators commenced their sketches, capturing his bowed shoulders and soiled suspenders, the greasy wedge of hair that dipped over his brow, the cheekbones that peaked sharply beneath leathered skin.

"Where do you reside, Mr. Darrow?" Elston asked.

"Chicago." He spoke in a soft, tumbling baritone.

"How long have you been a lawyer?"

"For fifty years next April," Darrow said, adding that he first met Remus when he, too, was a practicing lawyer in Chicago. He had not seen Remus for some time, maybe ten or twelve years.

"Do you have the means of knowing what his reputation for peace and quiet was during the time that you knew him?" Elston asked.

"I think so, yes."

"What was that reputation?"

"It was good."

Taft stood abruptly. "We object," he said. "This witness's knowledge, the nearest point of which is ten years ago, has no relevancy in this case of the shooting in Eden Park."

Judge Shook overruled and let Darrow's answer stand.

Emboldened, Elston continued this same line of questioning. "Did you have the means of knowing what his reputation was during the time you knew him for being a law-abiding citizen?"

"I never heard it questioned," Darrow said. "I will say it was good."

"Did you have the means of knowing what his reputation was during the time you knew him as a practicing lawyer?"

Darrow folded his arms. "I never heard it questioned."

"We object, Your Honor," Taft said. "We fail to see what the reputation as a lawyer has to do with the shooting in Eden Park on that date."

Remus raised his hand, in which he held a white handkerchief. "May I be heard?" he asked, a slight tremor in his voice.

"Proceed," said Judge Shook.

"Your Honor," Remus began, "in the opening statement of the prosecution, they had contended Remus was a man of mediocre abilities as a lawyer. They took that stand in the opening statement, and we have, if the Court please, witnesses that have known the said defendant for years, a lifetime. His life is at stake, if the Court please, the defendant's life. Now, then, in view of the fact that Mr. Darrow has many momentous matters throughout this civilized world. . . ."

Taft objected; Shook overruled.

Remus appeared on the verge of another brainstorm. With one hand he rubbed his eyes; with the other, he punched his handkerchief at the air. "Mr. Darrow," he croaked, "surely, I thank you, the sage of the Twentieth Century, proud as I am to know that so great a humanitarian has given up his time to come before this Court and jury." He let his eyes flit from Darrow to the judge to the jury, taking the time to exchange a glance with each of the people who would decide his fate.

It was Taft's turn.

"Did you ever hear him argue a case to the jury?" the prosecutor asked, tilting his head at Remus.

"I never heard him," Darrow said. He leaned forward in his chair and began rubbing the surrounding railing, as though clearing it of dust.

"Don't you know," Taft continued, adopting an accusatory tone, "he was known as 'the weeping and crying Remus'?"

Darrow's fingers traced the railing, back and forth. "I knew he was a very emotional fellow, somewhat unstable."

"Well, now, you have stated that Mr.

Remus's reputation and standing as a lawyer was good?"

"Yes."

"When you said that, did you know that beginning with 1912 and lasting until 1919, Mr. Remus was called before the Grievance Committee, repeatedly, of the Chicago Bar Association?"

"I didn't know that."

"Don't you know," Taft said, increasing his volume, "that in 1920 Remus was indicted in Chicago for conspiracy to violate the Prohibition law and that the indictment is pending?" He was referring to a raid that occurred shortly before Remus and Imogene moved to Cincinnati. Agents had discovered that fifteen barrels of whiskey had been withdrawn on false permits from the Sibley Warehouse and Storage Company and traced them back to Remus. Federal authorities declined to pursue Remus after he skipped his hearing and left the city.

"I would not regard an indictment as affecting 'peace and quiet,' " Darrow replied.

"And would you still regard him as a law abiding citizen?" Taft pushed. Darrow's eyes strayed toward the window. From Main Street came the muted sounds of guttural engines and Klaxon horns. After a moment he turned back to Taft and quietly said, "I know a good many law abiding citizens who buy it."

■ ■ ■

Six weeks into the trial, after witness testimony that tallied more than five thousand
typed pages, both sides were prepared to
deliver their closing arguments. Before they
could do so Judge Shook made an announcement: The alienists had issued their final
report. He ruled that the jury would be
permitted to read only a brief excerpt, which
explained that the alienists had made a "very
exhaustive" study of Remus and "unanimously found him sane at the time of the
murder." Remus's erratic courtroom behavior
had failed to persuade them.

Over Elston's objections, Taft was permitted to question the alienists in front of the
jury, thereby introducing more of the report
into the court record. Although Remus was
supposed to react "in an insane manner" at
the mere mention of Franklin Dodge and
Imogene, the doctors noted that both names
were repeated at least one hundred times with
no effect on Remus whatsoever. While it was
true that, on several occasions, "Mr. Remus's
face was red, his head was red, his movements accelerated and his remarks indicated
anger," these reactions were appropriate with
the subject being discussed. As for the most
recent incident, it was the doctors' collective
opinion that it was not in any way "allied with

an insane state of mind."

During their testimony Remus faced the jurors wearing a grand and effusive smile; many of them smiled back. He rose to cross-examine Dr. Baber, reveling in the absurdity: A man claiming that he was insane up until very recently was cross-examining an expert on the subject of insanity.

"Would the firing of a shot killing a human being be a mental aberration?" he asked.

"That would all depend on the circumstances," the alienist answered. "The aberration present at that time would be a departure from normal."

"Julius Caesar was considered a lunatic?" asked Remus.

Taft objected, pointing out that there was no such term as *lunatic* in ancient Rome.

Remus rephrased the question. "Was Nero considered a lunatic, Doctor? Wasn't it a fact that when Nero burned Rome, the Romans rose in arms and called him a lunatic?"

The doctor shook his head. "I don't remember any such event."

The prosecution and the defense rested. Each side would have four hours to present closing arguments, but since there were only two and a half hours remaining in the day's session, Judge Shook decided to split the time; Taft and Elston could speak first, and Remus would address the jury on Monday morning.

Taft spoke in calm and dulcet tones, neutralizing the severity of his words. "There is only one way that the community is safe with a man like Remus around," he began, "and that is when Remus is dead." If they failed to sentence Remus to the electric chair, he would be "back on the street to kill again." The facts of the case were clear. Remus killed his wife in cold blood on the morning of October 6 for one reason: Imogene Remus had known too much about where George Remus had been and what he had done. In divorce court that morning, she had planned to disclose the extent and location of all of his assets, enabling the federal government to put liens on his properties and collect income tax. "Finally," Taft said, "George Remus was facing a showdown, and rather than face it he killed her . . . he shut her mouth in the only way he knew how."

He pivoted to the subject of Franklin Dodge, currently sequestered in an unnamed Cincinnati hotel, waiting to be called to testify. "Well, poor fellow," he continued, "he's the most famous co-respondent in the United States, perhaps in the world. Remus, the publicity hound, certainly gave him a ride. And wasn't he a fine publicity hound, this Remus? Is there a better story than the wife of the king of the bootleggers linked up with the ace of the Prohibition department?"

Taft threw up his hands, as if to indicate he

couldn't imagine one.

"He didn't dare take the stand," he taunted, smirking at Remus. "He was afraid of what the State would do to him. Oh, he'll address you. He may throw a fit for you. He'll get down on his knees, probably. I know he'll weep. But he didn't dare to take the stand."

Taft walked the length of the jury, letting them ponder his words. "George Remus had the big head. He couldn't believe for a long time his wife had the nerve to refuse to do his bidding. But she rebelled at his cruelty, at being forced to live the life of a felon's wife. She wanted to get away from it. . . . Remus had to seal her lips. He killed her."

As soon as Taft returned to his table, Elston took the floor. His address was short and to the point, an opening act to the speech Remus would deliver Monday. "Mr. Taft has told you considerable about what Remus did and how Mrs. Remus was finally trying to get away from him because of the life he led," Elston said. "Well, ladies and gentlemen of the jury, do not forget that when Remus came to Cincinnati to become a bootlegger, his wife came with him, and that she shared in all the benefits he got out of it."

He paused, taking his time to make eye contact with each juror and point a finger at his client.

"There is a claim — and it is admitted — that he told her he would follow her to China,

456

if she didn't return to him what was his," he said. "Well, ladies and gentlemen, if Imogene Remus did to George Remus what we all know she did, China was not far enough to follow her to."

Outside the Hamilton County Courthouse, observers of the Remus trial — in Cincinnati and elsewhere — prepared for the holiday season and the coming new year. Romola Remus bought a miniature pine tree, which she would decorate and place next to her father's table in the courtroom. Ruth Remus traveled to Milwaukee for the funeral of her biological father, a victim of tertiary syphilis.

Franklin Dodge, still sequestered in his hotel, planned a trip home to Michigan and released a statement to the press. "I have been under subpoena for nineteen days," it read. "The subpoena was issued by the defense. Why they have failed to call me, in view of all their repeated assertions about my conduct, about which they knew that I would have no hesitancy in speaking the truth to anyone, anywhere and any time, I fail utterly to understand." With Remus in mind, Willebrandt lobbied for a strengthening of the Volstead Act, arguing that "big bootleggers" should be sentenced to a maximum fine of $10,000, five years imprisonment, or both. She would spend Christmas at home in Los Angeles, escaping rumors in Washington that she was planning to resign.

On Saturday night, December 17, Remus invited one of his favorite reporters, James Kilgallen of the International News Service, for a private interview in his quarters. He wanted the newspaper man's advice on an effective closing argument. At the appointed hour the intercom buzzed.

"Come right up," Remus said through a speaking tube.

Kilgallen complied and found his host in an unusually serious mood.

"In the courtroom I'm a dual personality," Remus told him. "In defending myself, I forget there is a physical George Remus. I feel detached from him." He told Kilgallen that he planned to deliver his own closing argument and asked for a "good lead" to start his speech.

Kilgallen thought for a moment. Wear a gray suit instead of a dark one, he advised. And since he'd be facing a "Christmas jury," why not stick a sprig of holly in his lapel? As for a dramatic opening, he suggested the following: "Ladies and gentlemen: Before you stands Remus the lawyer," and then point dramatically to his chair and add: "And there, in that empty chair sits Remus, the defendant." Underscore the idea that there were several different Remuses: Remus, the savvy and successful businessman; Remus, the betrayed husband; Remus, the lawyer;

Remus, the man in a fight for his life.

"Great!" Remus said.

Kilgallen turned to go but was stopped by a hand on his shoulder.

"Fancy yourself in prison," Remus said, "locked behind bars and for months and months knowing that the woman to whom you had given everything in your life, your very soul, was in the arms of another man. Wouldn't it drive you to madness? Wouldn't it?"

William Howard Taft followed the trial obsessively and with increasing frustration. "I think Charlie has a pretty hard fight," he confided to his son Robert, "and I shall not be disappointed if he loses, but I am glad he is making the fight, for if there ever was a case that impeached the decency and proper self-respect of the Cincinnati public, in reference to the liquor traffic, this case is it. Remus seems to get sympathy because he is a bootlegger in that wet community. I judge he is a very bad man, utterly unscrupulous, audacious and a bluffer . . . and then to cap it all, to put that criminal Clarence Darrow on the stand to testify to anybody's character is a joke."

But the former president also had more ominous concerns. A friend had telephoned with word "from one of the underworld in

St. Louis" that Remus was planning to kill his son.

"I am afraid about Charlie," he confessed in a letter to his daughter Helen. "I wrote Charlie and warned him and told him to have the men whom he has about him, the bailiffs and others, see to it that Remus is not permitted to get hold of a weapon. He is a very bad man and care should be taken in dealing with him. I haven't said anything to your mother about it, because I don't want her to worry, but in these days apparently the killing of a man does not seem to be of a great deal of importance."

AMERICAN JUSTICE

On Monday, December 19, it was at last Remus's turn. He believed that he was ready. He knew that the unusual spectacle of a murder defendant, particularly one of his theatrical prowess, pleading for his own life, would draw international attention and that hundreds were clamoring to hear him, lined up on Main Street in the cold. They were expecting a dazzling and virtuosic display, a rigorous legal argument etched with pathos and grace. Sheriffs flourished clubs to force them away from the doors.

Remus had taken Kilgallen's advice and dressed in a light gray jacket with a sprig of holly jutting from his lapel. The courtroom was unbearably hot: all these people in wool hats and coats and gloves, pressed shoulder to shoulder and front to back, mouths open, breathing in his direction. His performance would be athletic, by accident or design, and he would only get hotter, the sweat darkening his Christmas suit. The clock struck noon

461

and it was time. He recalled Kilgallen's second bit of advice, about his opening words and actions, and let himself begin.

"Here before you stands Remus the Lawyer," he announced, swinging his arm as if he were a game show prize. "In the chair there" — and now he gestured to the chair he'd used throughout the trial — "sits Remus, the defendant, charged with murder." The drama of the moment was somewhat diminished by the presence of the 250-pound deputy who had planted himself in that same chair.

Remus pressed on. "May it please the Court, and ladies and gentlemen of this jury. This is the sixth week in which we have all sat here, in which we have all partaken in the trial of a case in which the civilized nation and, if you please, the civilized world's eyes are upon the same. . . . I, as the defendant's lawyer, desire to thank you, Your Honor, for the fairness and the squareness in which you have administered justice in the functioning of your judicial duties; and to you ladies and men of this jury, who have been away from your home and those people who are dear and sweet to you." He nodded in the direction of the prosecutors' table and delivered his insult politely: "I want to compliment you for the fairness and the consideration that you have shown in listening to Mr. Taft's harangue, and to Mr. Basler's harangue, and to Sibbald's if you please . . . and may it please you folks, if I am a little enthusiastic you must forgive me."

He skulked along the jury box, moving as close as he could to the twelve people sitting inside it. He had so much to cram into his allotted time. The list of points to make and questions to raise all jostled for attention in his mind. "What is the meaning of insanity?" he asked. "You simply use your common sense . . . as you have gone through life since the age of an infant, and when there are the emotions that are registered in the cranium, in the brain cells of the individual, all those emotions cause an abnormal condition of the mind. Now, then, when a crime is committed under those circumstances, the person is, of necessity, abnormal."

Taft objected; Judge Shook sustained.

A moment or two was lost with their legalese. Remus spoke faster.

Newspaper men who had known Remus for years were shocked at his obvious unease, the desperation lurking beneath the surface of each word. His mind meandered from path to rhetorical path. He referred to "the unfortunate death of the deceased." If there was a conspiracy to murder the deceased, then it was an "embryonical condition" on the night before the murder. On to Dodge: "Is there any question in your minds, folks, but the fact that this human parasite, using the powers of the United States which he was involved with for years, being the hypocrite that he was, the ace of the Prohibition Department, the deuce of aces was in it? And when you think, folks, that the Honorable Charles P. Taft 2nd, the son of a former president of this wonderful country of ours, the son of the Chief Justice of this wonderful Supreme Court . . . here we have it in the record that the son of the Chief Justice was going around the country with this social leper, this social parasite, this ace of the Prohibition Department —"

Another objection from Taft, sustained.

"This social leper among men —"

Another objection from Taft, sustained, and an ensuing discussion that would total seven pages in the official record. More time lost, attention further diverted, momentum stalled. Remus returned to the notion of a conspiracy, recalling an associate's wife who had testified for the defense, and somehow drifted into the virtues of womanhood: "And when I see beautiful Mrs. Bruck on the witness stand, and she tells her story in that sweet manner, so beautiful in all her simplicity of womankind . . . and I say, if the Court pleases, I tell you when womankind is beautiful, and sweet and noble and queenly, is there anything more beautiful in life than good womankind? I say not."

His words came in a rush, accompanied by frantic movements and fluctuations in mood.

"He shouted and he talked softly," one reporter observed. "He bounced and he stalked up and down in front of the jury box. He slapped his thighs and he shot his upraised left hand high into the air. He pleaded, his hands outflung in beseeching gestures, and he gesticulated wildly. He leaped and he paraded. At times he bowed himself almost double."

Another stroll before the jury and Remus seemed to right himself, remembering his purpose, and spoke of Imogene's sale of the Fleischmann distillery while he was in prison. "Some of the things that the unfortunate deceased, in her zeal to obtain possession of with this horrible human parasite, that has squirmed his horridness into our very midst here, I tell you that the money, the Fleischmann money was used to make the payment on the income taxes —"

The prosecution team had been holding its objections while Remus rambled and flailed; now they pounced. Sustained.

Remus tried again. "After years of incarceration, after years of hardship, never in the annals of criminology has the defendant for the violation of one law has been in nine different penal institutions and jails. . . ."

He swirled to face the prosecutors' table, a striking hue of red creeping up the length of his neck, matching the sprig of holly. "And then the high-handed methods of the prosecutors' office has the temerity to tell you ladies and men of this jury that the said defendant is a rat. Have you ever heard of anything that is more absurd than that. Look at the profile of Mr. Basler, scan it, if you will, and see which face, which physiognomy, which expression has that of sincerity and that of hypocrisy, if you please. Remus has been convicted of the charge of selling good liquor —"

Objection; sustained.

During the pause Remus remembered that he was defending himself at his own murder trial. "Do you folks think for one moment that if the defendant had contemplated this act on October 6, 1927, he would have taken George Klug with him to drive that car? Never in the world, and why does the defendant so say? Because the evidence shows conclusively that when the said defendant got out of that car George Klug continued to go on and left the defendant alone in the public highway. As to how the act was committed, how the thing happened, how the homicide was committed he doesn't know, and never will know of his own five senses."

He faced the jury again, the redness receding from his skin, and pivoted to the subject of his childhood. "The defendant started his life for five dollars a month in the drugstore, and he built his way up, although he may have contaminated his neighbors, we cannot all be born with a golden spoon in our mouth" — here he turned back to the prosecutors' table and hurled his words — "Mr. Charles P. Taft the Second —"

Taft objected; sustained.

Remus glanced at the clock and realized he had only twenty-eight minutes left. In his remaining time he strove to corral his argument. His mind was a conveyor belt, thoughts roving past at quickening speed, the relevant ones always just out of reach. He mentioned the witnesses who had traveled from all over this "civilized country" on his behalf ("what everlasting gratitude on my bended knees I should give"); the reporters representing publications "to the tune of three thousand throughout the world"; a defense of his bootlegging past ("if the said defendant goes down to oblivion, he goes down as a martyr to the cause of an inherent right to you"); the conspiracy between his wife and Franklin Dodge ("the deceased, with this moral pervert, with that human parasite, was floating around the country with the automobiles that were bought by the defendant's money"). . . .

Judge Shook interrupted. "Your time is up now, Mr. Remus, but I am going to give you until 3:30."

"Thank you, Your Honor," Remus said, but still he struggled for coherence. Imogene's entire extended family got "into the good graces of the defendant" so that they could

467

plunder his money. He himself, the defendant George Remus, had in his lifetime both sacrificed principles for mercenary benefits and sacrificed those mercenary benefits for principles. Perhaps recalling his grand New Year's Eve party of 1921, a night he spent waiting for Cincinnati's social elite to arrive, he faced Taft again: "That is the principle upon which the defendant has gone through life, and, Charles Taft the Second, I want you to understand that if the defendant were your neighbor he would not be a discredit to the State Prosecutor."

"You have five minutes left," Judge Shook warned.

He spun back to the jury and delivered his final plea, addressing the twelve men and women as if they were the only people in the room. "Let every one of you go home and be content. I the defendant do not desire any sympathy, in any way, shape or form or manner; if you folks feel that under your sworn duty, as ladies and men of this jury, you that have a higher power than the president of the United States as to the guilt or innocence of this defendant, if you feel that he should be electrocuted, do your duty, don't flinch; the defendant won't flinch."

He took slow steps, meeting each juror's gaze. There was a good chance that, in the heyday of the Circle, friends and relatives and neighbors of those jurors had themselves

468

been employed and paid generously by Remus. They knew the German brewers who were forced to shut down and witnessed the harassment of German citizens. They understood Remus, and he them, in a language Charlie Taft would never speak.

"The defendant stands before you defending his honor and the sanctity of his home," he continued. "The defendant is on trial for that, and if that is murder, punish him. . . . This has smashed hardships upon most of us, and as you retire into the consideration of your verdict, bear in mind that that which is most sacred, most beautiful, most glorious to all of us is our family, our offspring, our home. I thank you, and a Merry Christmas to you."

With a bow, he returned to his table. A collective sense of disappointment fell upon the room. Spectators exchanged perplexed glances. Where was the weeping, crying Remus they had so eagerly anticipated? The physical threats against Taft, the intervening sheriffs? The shrieking and fainting and brainstorms so dramatic that they had to shut down the proceedings? Remus had cast himself in a dual role that, in the end, he was unable to fulfill. "It was only right at the end of a plea of nearly two hours," wrote one, "that the shouting, leaping, parading, gesticulating Remus hung his sentences together in continuity of expressed thought." The correspondent from the *Cincinnati Enquirer* concluded, simply, that Remus "failed to click."

Despite Remus's disappointing performance, Taft went on the defensive, requesting that Judge Shook decline to offer a straight "not guilty" verdict, which would allow Remus to avoid both jail and the insane asylum. Since Remus had admitted killing his wife and had pleaded insanity, Taft argued, it followed that he must be found insane *or* be given a heavier sentence. Judge Shook agreed, ruling that Remus could be found not guilty only by reason of insanity.

On December 20, Shook presented the charges to the jury and offered five possible verdicts: First Degree Murder without mercy (electric chair); First Degree Murder with mercy (life imprisonment, without hope of pardon); Second Degree Murder (life sentence, but with hope of pardon); Manslaughter (penitentiary sentence of one to twenty years); and Not Guilty by reason of insanity. On that final possibility, Shook issued instructions that carried a hint of warning.

"In support of this defense of insanity," he said, "the Court has permitted a great deal of evidence to be introduced with reference to communications made to defendant, George Remus, whether true or untrue, and regardless of their source, solely for the purpose of proving their effect upon his mind. . . . In this case there was no excuse or justification for the shooting and killing of Imogene Remus by the defendant, George Remus, no matter how many wrongs, if any, had been perpetrated upon him either by the deceased or any other person, unless the communications of such wrong conduct resulted in the condition of the mind constituting insanity, which is alleged to have existed on October 6, 1927. Furthermore, the law does not justify one person in taking the life of another because the latter may be of bad moral character."

He gave the case to the jury at 12:59 P.M. If they hadn't reached a verdict by 1:15, they were to break for lunch and return at 2:45 for further deliberations. The lawyers, press, and spectators also adjourned for lunch. Remus, accompanied by Romola, returned to his quarters.

The ten men and two women filed into the jury room. One juror, Robert E. Hosford, carried five verdict ballots. The ballot he wanted was on the bottom of the pile, and he pulled it to the top for his fellow jurors to see.

Within ten minutes they decided to break for lunch, even though they had already reached a decision.

At 2:54 P.M., nineteen minutes after they

471

returned, the foreman rapped on the jury room door. As no one had expected such a speedy verdict, the courtroom was still empty, and sheriffs spent the next hour searching the streets for the lawyers and fetching Remus from his quarters. Anxious spectators shoved their way through a rear door until they filled every seat and lined the walls, rows deep, ignoring the maximum capacity. Judge Shook ascended his dais. Romola huddled close to her father.

"Have you agreed upon a verdict?" Judge Shook asked.

"We have, Your Honor," said the foreman.

Remus lifted a pair of horn-rimmed glasses to his lips. His skin was pale, and he withheld all expression.

"You will give your verdict to the Clerk of the Court," Shook ordered.

The foreman rose and handed the sealed envelope to the clerk, who opened it with a vigorous rip and unfolded its contents. The audience in the courtroom leaned forward as he read: "We, the jury, on the issue joined, find the defendant not guilty of murder, as he stands charged in the indictment, on the sole ground of insanity."

A moment's hush and then chaos, shouts and whistles and a thunder of applause. Deputies shouted in husky voices: "Keep quiet! Keep quiet!" The crowd rushed toward Remus with outstretched hands, all wanting a piece of his infamy, drawn to his grotesque and cagey charm. He rose unsteadily, as though being face-to-face with the verdict — although it was one he desired — vexed him in some private way.

"This is American justice," he managed. Deputies encircled him, gripping his arms, leading him through the throng. "Thank you, thank you!" Remus shouted over his shoulder. His fans attempted to follow. Romola's Christmas tree toppled and fell to the floor. "Sit down, sit down!" called the bailiffs and deputies, clearing a path. As Remus passed from the courtroom into the corridor a strange sound, a kind of keening laughter, rose above the mayhem:

"Ha, ha, ha, he, he, he."
"Ha, ha, ha, he, he, he."
"Ha, ha, ha, he, he, he."

It was Remus's voice, whipped into its highest octave and teetering on hysteria. In the corridor five hundred admirers — many of them women — closed in on him, shouting congratulations into his ears and launching into a chorus. "Not guilty — hooray! Not guilty — hooray!" Remus began to weep, booming, brazen wails accompanied by fat tears. "Not guilty — hooray!" The chant spilled back into the courtroom. Judge Shook abandoned the bench for his conference room. Spectators tripped trying to reach Elston, the next best thing to Remus. Without warning, a pretty young girl approached and kissed him. "And I don't have the least idea who it was," Elston confessed. Remus's sister Anna Ryerson bounded toward the lawyer. "Thank God!" she said, pumping his hand. Taft crept away unnoticed, retreating to his office upstairs. When reporters tracked him down, he called the verdict a "gross miscarriage of justice."

William Howard Taft quickly shared the news with his younger brother, Horace. "I see that that which we expected happened in the Remus case," he wrote, and despaired for his son. "Poor fellow, he has had a hard fight, and to struggle against such obstacles must have been disheartening. He will now have to try to keep Remus in the insane asylum, as I hope he may, though I don't think you can be confident of anything that happens in such a mess."

Across the country, in Los Angeles, Willebrandt prepared to gather a fresh batch of clippings for her Remus file.

Fifty people, among them members of the jury and a number of young girls, followed Remus to his jail quarters. Juror Robert Hosford addressed the crowd, confessing that they would've given Remus a straight acquittal had it been an option. "Do you know what we termed it in the jury room?" he asked. "Let's go out and give Remus a Christmas present. Let's make him happy one Christmas; he wasn't last Christmas." Juror Ruth Cross stepped forward, gazing at Remus as she spoke. "As the evidence unfolded, I began to pity Remus and hate the prosecutor's assistants. I thought Remus must have been insane when he killed her. Anyway, I believe Remus was justified in what he did."

"Why did you decide the way you did?" a reporter asked.

"We felt that Remus had been greatly wronged, that he had suffered almost beyond human endurance," Hosford explained. "One of the factors that decided us was that Remus already had served in nine jails for the violation of the Prohibition law — all for the same offense."

After apologizing to Elston for being a "most unruly client," Remus dispensed a statement to the assembled newspaper men, hastily written but far more lucid than his closing plea.

"Thank God for a verdict that lifts the greatest burden man must ever stand," it read. "To the jury, to the Court, to the Prosecutors, to the office of the Sheriff and the jailer I extend my deepest appreciations for all that they have done. God alone knows the thing that is within my heart at this moment. The rest of my life I will dedicate to stifle the insult that is upon our statutes, known as the National Prohibition Act. Had there been no Prohibition law to fill the coffers of a class that seeks only and practices only venality, there could have been no act for which a jury of my peers would have to acquit me." Dudley Nichols, famed reporter for the *New York World,* compared the scene to the finale of the new play *Chicago,* in which the two murderesses thank the American people for their support — earned not by virtue of their innocence but by their ability to entertain.

Remus posed for pictures, adopting the grandstanding, cheerful demeanor of a politician on the stump. There he shook hands with Hosford, with pretty, dark-eyed Ruth Cross squeezed between them, her face tilted up toward Remus. They stood side by side and intertwined their arms as the cameras flashed. Romola jumped in, hugging the jurors as though they were old friends. Remus decided that pictures weren't enough; the jurors would each receive an autographed copy of one of Romola's songs. And since they were so kind to acquit him, perhaps they would also enjoy a drink or two from his private stash? "The damnedest thing I ever saw," said one out-of-town newspaper man, a veteran who'd covered numerous trials across the country. "Is that the way they always do things down here?"

■ ■ ■ ■

Inspired to continue advocating for Remus, the jury filed a formal petition with Judge Shook requesting that Remus be "immediately freed" so that he might spend Christmas with his mother and family. Shook allowed himself to express the full measure of his disgust. "This petition is the most intolerable, outrageous, insulting and audacious thing ever given a court of justice," he said. He demanded and received an apology from each juror.

Although the Remus jury failed to impress Judge Shook, the manager of a Cincinnati burlesque house decided that its members would be brilliant behind the footlights. He reached out to each of them, offering "Broadway salaries" for a week's appearance, and even planned to approach Remus himself; the bootlegger could earn $2,500 per week for the "merest little appearance between the ingénue and the soubrette."

The prospective title of his production: "Twelve Good Men and True in the Transitory Insanities of 1927."

Probate Court Testimony of George Remus

Q. Got any feeling about your dead wife, having killed her?

A. None in the slightest.

Q. No remorse?

A. Oh, I feel sorry to think she was unfortunate, that she would be tied up with that kind of human parasite.

Q. Do you believe in eternal life?

A. I believe in a system of evolution.

Q. Do you believe in the continuance of the soul after death and the presence of a condition of rewards and punishments for what you do in this life?

A. That depends upon what you call the soul. I think there are ethereal waves and electrons in the ether, and what we call God is very much of a disputed matter.

Q. We want to go more on the question of reward and punishment and the future life. You know there are a whole lot of fellows in this world who get nothing out of this world at all, and if there is a system of

478

absolute justice they have all reason for getting their reward in the next life. Do you believe in that at all?

A. Yes, I like that theory very much.

Q. Now, Mrs. Remus left this world rather unprepared for the next world, didn't she? And she certainly had no chance of squaring her accounts after you had shot her, because she was unconscious after you shot her?

A. Yes, that is my understanding.

Q. Has anything ever entered your mind about what the state of her soul is — if you believe there is a state of soul hereafter — of whether she is in heaven?

A. My answer is that a woman — I mustn't use the word "woman" — a person who is so depraved, so degenerated as to lose all person of womankind the way she did, that whatever is in the future, in the hereafter, so far as she is concerned, can not be bad enough or good enough. Do you see what I mean?

Q. You loved her at one time, didn't you?

A. Yes, there was no question about it.

THE UNFORTUNATE WOMAN

On December 28, after Remus's testimony before the Probate Court, five psychiatrists — including two who had observed the murder trial — declared him to be sane but a threat to society. In their opinion, Remus was "histrionic, an actor, and a bad actor at that," who could stage anything he wanted by using the gestures and emotions appropriate for that moment. He was "a very dangerous man to be at liberty," owing to his egotism, violent temper, and penchant for spinning conspiracy theories. He was "a psychopath . . . unmoral, lacking a sense of ethics, emotionally unstable, being subject to unrestrained outbursts of temper and rage and egocentric to a pathological degree."

Nevertheless, Judge William Lueders agreed with only half of their findings, determining that while Remus was indeed a dangerous person to be at large, he was also insane. He committed Remus to the Lima State Hospital for the Criminally Insane "until such time when he has been restored to reason." He added that the burden of proof rested upon Remus; in order for him to be released, he would have to satisfy the court that he was no longer insane at some future date.

Reporters found Remus in his jail quarters, eating lunch. A representative from the *New York Times* handed him typewritten copies of the judge's decision and the alienists' report. Remus glanced at them briefly before taking another bite of food and a sip of coffee. "Well, what about it, eh?" he asked. "Oh, we'll appeal it, of course. It's the most humorous decision I've ever known in my whole life — a humorous joke, a farce."

The reporters bent their heads, scribbling frantically.

"The alienists had better have their minds examined," he continued. "This shows that they are self-confessed perjurers. They say something in one court and a few days later they come into another court and say something different. This opinion is so ridiculous, so ludicrous, that it strikes me as being one of the nine wonders of the world."

While Elston began filing appeals, newspapers across the country pondered the decision. "Remus elected to profit by the insanity plea," opined the *Indianapolis Star,* "and should be required to take the consequences." The *Ohio State Journal* agreed: "When a man of violent and vindictive nature deliberately

481

plans and executes a murder, pleads demoniacal insanity and is held not responsible for the act on that ground, it seems only the part of common sense and ordinary prudence to take the jury's word for his mental condition and shut him up." The Cincinnati-based *Labor Advocate* impugned the integrity of the psychiatrists: "The most disgusting thing connected with the Remus farce were the 'alienists' for the state. Their testimony goes to prove that alienists always testify for the side that pays them. These three 'Docs' swore that Remus was sane a few days ago; but now, in order to help the state out, they add 'but dangerous.' If all the sane but dangerous people were put in the asylum we would have to build many more institutions to hold them."

Taking a different angle altogether, the *Chicago Tribune* posed a question: "Now how about Dodge? Mrs. George Remus is dead. George Remus, who shot her, has been sentenced to the insane asylum. . . . Two sides of this triangle have been disposed of, one by a crime and another by the law. Does nothing attach to Dodge, no degree of legal responsibility, and is it because he is a Federal Prohibition agent?"

J. Edgar Hoover still wished to answer that question. Bypassing Willebrandt, Hoover tried her colleague, Assistant Attorney General O. R. Luhring. "Now that the Remus trial has been concluded," he wrote, "I would appreciate being advised as to whether it is your wish that the Bureau proceed further in the investigation of Dodge." Luhring responded, outlining three possible avenues by which the Department of Justice might pursue Dodge: his alleged violation of the Mann Act; his selling of Remus's liquor certificates; and his involvement in the purported conspiracy to kill Remus.

Luhring addressed each scenario one by one: "As to the first lead, it seems to me that any further investigation from this standpoint is hardly advisable in view of the fact that the alleged victim, Mrs. Remus, is dead. As to the second, relative to the certificates, it appears that this matter was considered by Assistant Attorney General Willebrandt and that the conclusion was reached that there was no violation of the National Prohibition Act." But the third lead, Luhring wrote, seemed viable: Threatening government witnesses was a federal crime, and since Remus was cooperating on the Jack Daniel's case at the time that Dodge conspired to kill him, the Department of Justice would have grounds to pursue the case. "However, as the case involved a violation of the National Prohibition Act," Luhring concluded, "it would seem to me that the question as to any further investigation in this matter should be determined by Assistant Attorney General Wille-brandt's division."

Resigned, Hoover sent a memorandum to Willebrandt, conveying that she alone could decide to prosecute Dodge for conspiracy to murder a government witness.

Willebrandt stood firm, even on this serious charge. If she prosecuted her disgraced "ace of detectives," she would, in effect, be putting herself on trial. On the matter of whether she issued an official response, history is silent. But Hoover's memo shows a scrawled note: "No need."

On January 6, 1928, exactly three months after Remus killed Imogene in Eden Park, Elston and two deputy sheriffs arrived at his jail quarters to transport him to Lima State Hospital. Placed under observation, Remus would be permitted some freedom to come and go from his cell. On his first Sunday at the asylum, Remus joined the church choir. A new set of alienists — three of whom were hired and paid by Remus — conducted lengthy interviews probing every facet of the patient's psyche.

During the final week of February, at the Court of Appeals in Lima, Remus and Sibbald met for the first time since the murder trial. "I am surprised at your stand," Remus told the prosecutor. "For forty-two wearisome days you contended in my homicide trial at Cincinnati that I was sane. Twenty-four hours after the jury filed out with the verdict you so well remember, you appeared before the Probate Court and insisted I was insane. Here you are again fighting my plea of sanity."

One by one, Remus's hired alienists reported favorable observations. The halo Remus spoke of was possibly "confusion of mentality from worry" rather than a hallucination or illusion. He wasn't insane but merely affected by "fury and violence" from extreme circumstances. Although phrenology — the practice of discerning one's character through the shape of one's head and features — was on the decline, the doctors took and interpreted Remus's measurements. He seemed logical and coherent and "sane beyond a doubt." Nothing in the contours of his skull indicated any mental deficiency. His prominent forehead, receding quickly from the eyebrows at a sharp angle, indicated great intelligence. He possessed the "head of a powerful mind."

The doctors drew their own conclusions about the circumstances surrounding Imogene's death. Any man in a similar situation, facing such betrayal and loss, would be capable of murder. It was shocking, the way that a sudden and drastic change could cause a normal mind to "deviate." For women, pregnancy or menopause could be dangerously unbalancing; for men, it was injury, disease, and crisis — especially one so lengthy and severe as what Remus had endured.

Even so, Remus had "learned a good deal in the last few years," and he "probably would think it over more" if he again experienced a reason and urge to kill. For the first time, Remus conceded that murdering Imogene was "morally and legally wrong," although he expressed this regret in a "very cheerful" manner. He'd even cultivated a sanguine attitude toward Franklin Dodge. "I am fifty years old," Remus told the alienists. "My life expectancy is twelve years. I have some litigation to do after I get out of here and I want peace. So far as Mr. Dodge, or anyone else, is concerned, bygones are bygones." Besides, he was certain that the United States government would "take care of Dodge" and save him the trouble.

Dr. Kenneth L. Weber, an alienist who was not on Remus's payroll, formed a more discriminating — and disturbing — opinion. He believed that Remus was hyperactive and euphoric, with a paranoid bent and an affinity for "grandiose ideas." Everything about him was "big": his body, his intellect, his plans, his ego, his lies, his inventiveness, his imagination, his speech. When asked a question that could be answered in a few words, Remus often took a half hour to finish his response.

He had an abundance of eccentricities, including his aversion to underwear. "That in itself doesn't mean so much," Weber testified, "but added to other things it has some slight significance." Remus was emotionally unstable, devoid of normal emotional reaction, and incapable of displaying typical sorrow or remorse. He had lived unethically and immorally. He did not "react unpleasantly" to crime. The doctor concluded that Remus was insane and dangerous, with homicidal tendencies, and should remain at the hospital for further study.

On March 20, after listening to the alienists' testimony, the Allen County District Court of Appeals found that the petitioner was not insane and ordered his discharge from Lima State Hospital. When told of the verdict, Remus wept and grasped his attorney in his arms. "It's wonderful," he said. "I knew they would believe me." Charlie Taft, still enraged by his own courtroom defeat, insisted that "the fight to keep Remus behind bars will go on." He beseeched the Lima authorities to deny Remus bail, while the Allen County prosecutor appealed to the Ohio Supreme Court.

The fight fizzled quickly. Two of the three appeals judges defended their decision and denounced the initial trial verdict for creating this legal showdown. "It may be," they announced, "that the verdict in the trial at Cincinnati, which verdict acquitted the petitioner on the sole ground of insanity at the time he committed the homicide, was a miscarriage of justice. We frankly say that if his mental condition was, at the time he committed the homicide, as it was shown to be at the time of the trial before us, the verdict was a most flagrant and reprehensible outrage of judicial administration, which cannot be too strongly condemned."

On June 28, the Ohio Supreme Court upheld the decision of the Court of Appeals by a four to three margin and ordered that Remus be released. Upon hearing the news, Remus, grateful for his ex-wife's kind words to the press, sent a telegram to Romola in Chicago: "I am leaving for Cincinati to be with my friends. . . . Get in touch with your mother and tell her I will see her in a few days. Say I am feeling splendid. With love, Father."

Cincinnati reporters were waiting to meet him at 7:35 P.M., when his train arrived at Central Union Station. "I am very, very happy to return home, where I have thousands of friends," Remus announced. "I shall open my home here and remain in the city where people have been so kind to me." Conners and Elston drove him to his mansion at 825 Hermosa Avenue, the first time he'd been there since the morning he killed his wife.

Remus wandered nervously through all thirty-one rooms, a spirit haunting its ruins. Neither the emperor nor his castle, both constructed with such fervor and conviction, had endured. The ceilings still gaped where the chandeliers had been torn out; his priceless memento of George Washington was still missing; his library pillaged and useless; his baroque furniture still scattered across the country, repurposed for other people's lives. He would never again parade visitors through his house as he had before the murder, ranting and raving and yanking his hair as he tallied the sins against him. Until the mansion was torn down in 1934, he invited friends to visit very infrequently. But when he did, he always ended his tour by the pool.

It cost $175,000 to build back in 1920, he'd tell them, far more money than he possessed now, and was designed with Imogene in mind. "The unfortunate woman used to test the water of the pool with her pretty toes here," Remus would say, looking over the edge. "Then she used to dive and splash . . . she would be like a mermaid. . . ." The thought died, only halfway complete, and for the first time in his life Remus failed to find the words.

A HAMMER TO THE ANGELS

In April 1930, during the annual Easter egg hunt in Eden Park, a young boy searching near the greenhouses spotted a strange object in a thicket: a rusty pearl-handled .32-caliber revolver. The hunt's organizers turned it over to Captain John McNamara, chief of the Park Police, who believed it to be the gun George Remus used to murder his wife on a fall morning in 1927. Remus could not be found for comment.

The federal government did take care of Franklin Dodge, but not in the way Remus had anticipated. In November 1930, Dodge was indicted by a federal grand jury in Savannah, Georgia, on seven counts of perjury, stemming from testimony he'd given in the trial of a local bootlegger. The indictment charged that Dodge's testimony contradicted reports he'd submitted to Willebrandt while investigating the bootlegger seven years earlier.

490

Dodge pleaded guilty to all seven counts and was sentenced to thirty months in prison. He did his time in the Atlanta Federal Penitentiary, the same institution where he'd first met George and Imogene Remus. After his release in the spring of 1933, Dodge went home to Lansing, Michigan, and was appointed the chief disbursement clerk in the auditor's department. The press noted a curious connection: The auditor general who had offered Dodge the position currently occupied the vast and magnificent Dodge family estate. Dodge's appointment, wrote one Michigan newspaper, was "highly disturbing" and "set the public literally aghast." His boss told the press that Dodge was perfect for the job because he had no friends.

Dodge lived the remainder of his life in Michigan and out of the public eye, quietly marrying a woman named Ruth Randall in 1950. He died on November 26, 1968, at the age of seventy-seven.

For the rest of her career with the Department of Justice, Mabel Walker Willebrandt endured frequent reminders of her association with Remus and Dodge. An attorney in Philadelphia wished to know why Dodge was "gagged, muzzled and prevented" from testifying at Remus's trial. A politician from Mobile, Alabama, called Remus the "human filth of rubbish in America" and hoped that he might still be deported to Germany. An anonymous woman from Price Hill, Cincinnati, reported an exchange she'd overheard between two lawyers: "Well, you know Remus got away with murder, and don't you forget it! The government cannot deport him either, not that bird — he's too foxy." The letter writer also heard that Remus had returned to bootlegging. "Mrs. Willebrandt," she pleaded, "if there is such a thing as a really trustworthy man, one that cannot be reached with money, you could send him to investigate these rumors . . . you could put Remus either behind the bars again or better still put him out of this country altogether. It would be a wonderful thing for you, a woman, to accomplish."

Instead Willebrandt planned a series of spectacular raids on New York City nightclubs and speakeasies, to be executed in greatest secrecy. One hundred fifty agents from across the country convened in New York, visiting establishments undercover to gather evidence in preparation. On June 29, 1928, the evening before the first raid, the Mabelmen gathered at the local Prohibition headquarters at One Park Avenue. Their wardrobes were carefully chosen — savvy New Yorkers knew that the most shabbily dressed man in any nightclub was usually a federal agent. Willebrandt took every precaution to prevent nightclub owners from learning of her plans. The agents were locked inside and would not be informed of their destinations until the very last minute. Willebrandt even ordered that the telephone wires be disconnected. Just after midnight, the raids began. They resulted in 108 indictments of speakeasy proprietors, including Texas Guinan, famous for her trademark greeting: "Hello, suckers!"

The timing of the raids coincided with the Democratic National Party's nomination of Al Smith as their presidential candidate for the 1928 election. Democrats accused Willebrandt, who had promised to campaign for Republican nominee Herbert Hoover, of using her office for political gain. Rattled by the charges and worried that the negative headlines would affect the outcome of the indictments, she nevertheless kept her word, stumping for Hoover across the country and courting women's groups and the devout with warnings of what might become of America if it elected Smith.

At a church convention in Nashville, Tennessee, she was introduced as "the most outraged and cruelly treated woman in America." She urged her Methodist audience to vote against Smith, not because he was a Catholic but because he was a threat to Prohibition. "Governor Smith's prohibition plan," she charged, "would put white aprons on the states and make them serve as bartenders."

Willebrandt never mentioned, let alone impugned, Smith's religion, but the candidate viewed the speech as a personal attack — part of a "whispering campaign" that suggested he planned to take orders from Rome. He gave Willebrandt a nickname she immediately loathed, "Prohibition Portia," and aired his sentiments to great public sympathy. *Time* magazine leapt to his defense, claiming that Willebrandt "laid herself open to Democratic charges of religious incendiarism."

Newspapers resurrected news of her 1924 divorce, prompting Smith's outraged supporters to write to the Department of Justice. A letter from a New York businessman landed on her desk: "To judge the story of your life as given in the press, you seem to be one of those women with a heart like a stock ticker that does not beat over anything except money and publicity." Similarly scathing missives followed, all of them questioning her morals and character and suggesting that she was destined for hell. Declaring the attention "just too much," Willebrandt spent a night driving through the streets of Washington with a friend, doubled over in the passenger seat, sobbing. When Hoover won, the press had kinder words; a reporter for *Collier's* declared that "no other woman has ever had so much influence upon a presidential campaign as this one."

Willebrandt denied rumors of her impending resignation, secretly hoping that Hoover might reward her loyalty by promoting her to attorney general. One evening in February 1929, he called her at home.

"Anyone on the line?" Hoover asked by way of introduction. He apologized for not visiting in person and then got to the point. "I just wanted to tell you that the new Attorney General is a friend of yours," he said and revealed that his choice was Solicitor General William D. Mitchell, who was neutral on Prohibition. "I say that because maybe when you see him you might not think so, but he is and we want you to stay on . . . at least for a while. It will be best for you."

Willebrandt was shocked. She shared the insult with her parents: "I was intensely *hurt* that he asked me that way . . . the courteous thing would have been for him to ask me to come to his house to talk to me face to face. I think it goes to prove the thing I have feared, and my instinct has told me long ago — that fundamentally he doesn't feel on a level with women nor deal with them as men."

She resigned from the Department of Justice on June 15, 1929, proud of her record. From 1922 to 1928 more than 160,000 Prohibition-related cases had landed on her desk. She had presented 278 cases before the Supreme Court, the fourth-highest number among members of the bar; "her graceful tailored figure," wrote the *American Mercury,* had been "a regular adornment" there. The following month she published a book, *The Inside of Prohibition,* which detailed the successes and, more abundant, the failures of the nation's most unpopular law. "No political, economic or moral issue has so engrossed and divided all the people of America as the prohibition problem," she wrote in the opening chapter, "except the issue of slavery." Interspersing policy analysis with personal anecdotes, her prose was tinged with a palpable anger.

She wrote of "repulsive facts" about alcohol permits, the "psychological damage" wrought by incompetent politicians, the "bad odor" of corrupt agents, and the "folly" of denying that the wets were winning the war. The last subject in particular was a painful and personal defeat — not because she believed in the law but because she so hated to lose. If Prohibition was to succeed, she concluded, it would need a smarter and more inclusive selection of agents and officials, especially women, working to enforce it.

She opened a private practice, with offices in Washington and Los Angeles, partnering with her old beau Fred Horowitz (whose Chateau Marmont finally opened that year, with Willebrandt choosing all of the furniture and fabrics). One of her first clients was Fruit Industries, Ltd., an association of California grape growers that utilized a loophole in the Volstead Act allowing for the private production of table wine. She fought to expand their market and was criticized as a traitor by her old Prohibition allies. "I do not conduct my private practice in the newspapers," she told an inquiring reporter. She worried not about the press but about Al Capone, who was seeking to cut a deal with a rival outfit of grape growers and create a market in Chicago and Brooklyn.

Her practice thrived. She represented the Aviation Corporation and won two landmark cases in the nascent field of aeronautical law. While promoting commercial air travel, she got her pilot's license and befriended aviators Amelia Earhart and Jacqueline Cochran. Her work caught the attention of movie mogul Louis B. Mayer, who hired her to handle federal regulation and tax matters for Metro-Goldwyn-Mayer. Star clients followed, among them Jean Harlow and Clark Gable and director Frank Capra. When various celebrities were accused of Communist sympathies by the House Un-American Activities Committee, Willebrandt drafted a letter on behalf of the Screen Directors Guild that began: "Official investigations into the political beliefs held by individuals are *in violation of a sacred privilege guaranteed* the citizen in this free Democracy."

Willebrandt couldn't entirely resist the lure

of politics, campaigning for Dwight D. Eisenhower in 1952, but her loyalty to the Republican Party was tested in 1960 with the nomination of Richard Nixon. "You know my affinity for the underdog," she wrote to a friend, "and I, tho a life time Republican, find myself more and more secretly rooting in my heart for Kennedy. As I think you know, I do not like Nixon; I do not trust him. I think he just plays his luck for Nixon." In that year her health and hearing worsened. She cast a glance back at her life and decisions and sent sorrowful letters to her daughter, Dorothy. "I realized how many times how grievously I failed you. . . . I want you to know that every memory you have given me throughout all of your life is precious — rewarding and cherished as the golden threads throughout the years too wasted on law and other things that tarnish." She argued her final case in 1962, involving a $22 million St. Louis estate. She confided to a friend that the judge was "pretty cute."

Her hearing, always poor, worsened still. An operation that had failed to restore it also affected her balance. Her wobbly gait caused frequent falls. At cocktail parties, clutching a friend's arm, she was mortified by chatter that she was drunk. One evening, she fell into a bush outside the home of a film director. Another time, a gusty wind toppled her so badly she fractured her wrist. At home, struggling to take off a dress, she lost her balance and "flew like the man on the trapeze feet in the air, my feet hitting several things enroute and kerplump!" A week passed before she realized she'd cracked six vertebrae.

In 1962, after being diagnosed with emphysema, she reduced her cigarette habit to a "reasonably moderate rate," closed her office, sold her West Hollywood home, and moved into a small apartment. For once, at age seventy-two, she luxuriated in having nothing at all to do, confessing to a friend that she just didn't "care any more. I'm mentally a perfect beach comber, dozing in the sunlight, interested only in not being bothered and in no one cutting off my sunlite!!!"

She died in April 1963, having pre-wrapped and pre-addressed gifts to friends and family. In all of the tributes celebrating her achievements, one friend, future federal Judge John J. Sirica — who a decade later would preside over the Watergate case — speculated about what might have been: "If Mabel had worn trousers, she could have been president."

After his defeat in the Remus trial, Charlie Taft penned a cathartic article for *The World's Work* titled "So This Is Justice!" in which he blamed the verdict on two factors: the public's tendency to favor the unwritten law, and the German-American citizens of Cincinnati. "They have in their hearts a resentment against Prohibition that is a condition, not a theory," he wrote. "For this group Remus appears as a genial individual of their own race, who generously supplied them with good whiskey." Trying for optimism, he expressed the hope "that the case is bound to produce some good if the lessons taught by it are thoroughly absorbed by the public and by our lawmakers."

In this realm, at least, Taft was vindicated. In response to the Remus verdict the National Crime Commission, chaired by former secretary of war Newton D. Baker, convened a special committee to study the issue of juries and the insanity defense. The committee, led by Ethel Roosevelt Derby, daughter of former president Theodore Roosevelt, issued a report that was highly critical of current practices: "The utter absurdity of entrusting the difficult determination of the mental responsibility of an accused person for his acts to twelve laymen, admittedly unable to pass on the question from their own knowledge or training, has been made so manifest in the recent trial of George Remus in Cincinnati." The committee recommended that disinterested medical experts, and not juries, should determine a defendant's sanity.

Taft lost his bid for nomination for a second term for district attorney. For the next decade he refrained from politics but was then elected to the Cincinnati City Council, where he served three nonconsecutive terms. During meetings he listened to Cincinnati Reds games on the radio, an earbud tucked discreetly beneath his hair. From 1955 to 1957 he served as the city's mayor, becoming so beloved a leader that he earned the sobriquet "Mr. Cincinnati."

He died on June 24, 1983, at the age of eighty-five. In a retrospective about Taft and the Remus case, the *Cincinnati Enquirer* wrote that Taft had not underestimated Remus back in 1927, as so many had thought, because Remus hadn't been on trial. "It was," the paper wrote, "Prohibition that was on trial."

In August 1929, Ruth Remus filed a petition in probate court seeking annulment of her adoption and restoration of her former name, Ruth Holmes. In her application, she referred to her mother's murder in oblique legalese: "your petitioner further represents to this Court that by reason of the circumstances surrounding the death of said Augusta Imogene Remus she believes it will be to her best interest to have the said adoption set aside and held for naught." She added a pointed comment about Remus: "neither the petitioner nor the said George Remus have acknowledged the existence of the adoption of this petitioner nor in any way observed the status of parent and child." Her petition was granted in October 1929, two years after her mother's death.

A photo of Ruth from around this time shows her sitting on a lush patch of grass, holding a dog, flanked by two half brothers from her father's second marriage. Buoyant coils of brown hair slope over her right eye. On this day, at least, she was smiling.

Ruth married in 1930 and within ten years had two sons of her own. In 1947, she checked into Columbia Hospital in Milwaukee for a hysterectomy. Afterward she was given a blood transfusion intended for a different patient with the same name, in what proved to be a fatal error. She died that evening at the age of thirty-nine.

Romola Remus continued to pursue her acting and singing career, benefiting from the notoriety of her father's crimes. Packard, the motor car company, used her name in newspaper ads, boasting, "This well known musician is accustomed to the best of all lines." The Oriole Terrace, a cabaret in Detroit, billed her as "The Girl Who Stood By Her Dad." By the fall of 1928 she had tired of questions about her father, telling reporters and fans alike that she was trying to forget the past.

In her later years she shared stories of her childhood in Chicago but never mentioned her father's name. In one column penned for the *Tribune,* she recalled a memory from when she was twelve years old. She was walking down Michigan Avenue on a sunny spring afternoon with her father, "a prominent criminal lawyer," who was never too busy to take his "best girl" out for a matinee. She'd inherited his love of reading, and together they had read aloud numerous biographies of Abraham Lincoln. On this afternoon, they had encountered a tall and serious gentleman who stopped to greet her father. "Meet my little girl, Mr. Lincoln," Remus said. "She has always been an admirer of your father, Abraham Lincoln." And Robert Todd Lincoln shook her hand.

She used her married name, Romola Dunlap, as her byline.

When she died in February 1987, she was remembered mostly for being the first to play Dorothy in *The Wizard of Oz* in a movie and for singing in her church choir. She had lived in the Uptown neighborhood of Chicago with a cat, a turtle, a parakeet, and dozens of books stuffed with her clippings. She had no immediate survivors and specified in her will that her age not be disclosed.

Remus continued trying to recoup the money and property he'd lost, seeking fragments of his old life. The efforts filled his days. He filed a motion in probate court in Chicago to claim Imogene's entire estate, which amounted to $1,589.46 in credit with a

Pierce-Arrow automobile agency on a car she'd traded in. The traded automobile had been his, Remus insisted, and so the credit also belonged to him. In 1929, he arranged for the managers of two Chicago banks to open safety deposit boxes reportedly belonging to Imogene, which he hoped contained $1.8 million in cash and diamonds she'd stolen while he was imprisoned. One contained fifteen bottles of liquor; the other, six bottles.

He became a frequent presence at the Hamilton County Common Pleas Court, filing lawsuits against former bootlegging associates. The amounts varied widely and were sometimes to the penny. In October 1931 alone he appeared in court three times, seeking sums of $3,000, $150,000, and $245,918.40. Several years later he was still at it, filing a claim of $196,700 against the estate of a racetrack magnate who, for being allied with Al Capone, had been executed on a busy Chicago street. In September 1934 he sold his mansion to one Miss Alice Delehanty, who deemed the house uninhabitable and had it razed. The property carried a government lien of $34,000 and was assessed at $60,000, a mere 8 percent of his renovation costs back in 1920. His lone success was in recovering valuables he claimed were hidden by Imogene's family, including his treasured signature of George Washington.

Although the federal government dropped deportation proceedings against Remus, he remained in their sights for some time. Owing to *United States vs. Sullivan,* the case successfully argued by Willebrandt before the Supreme Court in 1927, income gained from bootlegging was subject to income tax. One week before Al Capone was convicted of tax evasion, Assistant Attorney General Haveth Mau brought proceedings against Remus in federal court, seeking to collect the $10,000 fine the bootlegger never paid after his 1922 conviction as well as $158,255 in unpaid taxes from liquor sales. Remus claimed that he had no such fortune; meanwhile, his former accountant, Blanche Watson, helped him hide whatever money he did have.

He married Watson in 1941, and they moved to 1810 Greenup Street in Covington, Kentucky, just across the river from Cincinnati, where Remus lived in quiet and deliberate obscurity. He traveled occasionally, spotted by reporters at racetracks and by old contacts in various cities where he once closed deals and paid bribes. "Tell no one I am here," he pleaded. "Tell nobody you have seen me. I want to get out of the spotlight, you see." One afternoon in Washington, D.C., a friend noticed a paunchy man with a briefcase wandering the corridors of the House Office Building.

"George," the friend called. "Wait a minute. . . . George, come back!"

But Remus hurried away, without once looking back.

In August 1950, he suffered a stroke while exercising at the Cincinnati Gym. When he died from a cerebral hemorrhage two years later, at the age of seventy-nine, he was living in a boardinghouse under the care of a nurse. The headline of his obituary in the *Cincinnati Times-Star* read: "Another Gatsby Passes."

He was buried in Watson's family plot in Riverside Cemetery in Falmouth, Kentucky, in a grave distinguished from all the others nearby. A sculpture of a woman perched on the shoulders of two angels looms over him — a sculpture rumored to have been one of the few pieces left from the mansion. One morning soon after Remus's death, the cemetery caretaker discovered that the angels had been vandalized, their wings struck from their shoulders and reduced to cement crumbles at the base of the tombstone.

As the legend has it, someone had written a letter to Watson arguing that given the events of Remus's life, he was not fit to be guarded by angels. For reasons known only to her, Watson set out to the cemetery, hammer in hand, and with a few hard blows demolished their wings.

Legend also has it that Imogene Remus haunts Eden Park, wandering along the bank

506

of Mirror Lake, always pausing by the Spring House Gazebo, where, on a fall morning in a different, distant time, she realized that she was about to die. She wears the same black Parisian hat and sleek silk dress, now clean of dirt and blood. Most of the time she's silent, gazing into the reflecting pool, content to let the world rush around her. On other nights — and it is always at night — she runs, wild and sobbing, as though she still hears his footsteps behind her, and feels the heat of him closing in.

ACKNOWLEDGMENTS

My first instinct when I finish a book is to dance on my desk and have a cocktail (usually not at the same time) and then to thank everyone who put up with me and/or helped along the way. Writing history is the next best thing to time travel, and I could not have made this strange and fascinating journey back to the 1920s without the generous patience and assistance of numerous people.

Chief among them is my editor, Emma Berry, who inherited this book but quickly and enthusiastically made it her own. Her keen eye and thoughtful suggestions improved the book (including its title) immeasurably, and I am lucky to have benefited from her intelligence, dedication, humor, Scorpionic energy, and excellent conversation over tapas and wine (cheers to our next book)!

I'm incredibly fortunate to have a mighty and talented team of advocates at Crown: David Drake, Gillian Blake, Annsley Rosner,

509

Elena Giavaldi, Caroline Cunningham, Steve Messina, and the dedicated sales reps who would brave a gun battle with whiskey pirates to help my work find its readership. And I am eternally grateful to my extraordinary publicists, Dyana Messina, Lisa Erickson, and Rachel Aldrich, who worked tirelessly to strategize, schedule, and spread the word, all the while bringing a welcome sense of calm to the process — no easy feat. The bourbon (and bourbon cakes) will always be on me. A special thanks also to Domenica Alioto, who first recognized the potential of this story and remained a staunch friend and champion throughout.

I am hugely indebted to every single bookseller and librarian who has said a kind word about *The Ghosts of Eden Park* and pressed copies into readers' hands. Without them I wouldn't have a job.

For thirteen years, Simon Lipskar has been a fierce and fearless agent, a loyal confidant, an invaluable partner, an ass-kicker, a truth-teller, and a terribly sore winner of bets (I'll *definitely* get him on the next round). I am lucky to have him on my side.

There were a great many people who helped make my years of research both enjoyable and fruitful. Alan March of the Delhi Historical Society shared his encyclopedic knowledge of Cincinnati and treated me to the best chili I've ever had. Diane Gehrum Osbourne

510

told marvelous tales of her ancestor Johnny Gehrum, one of George Remus's "boys." Joyce Meyer of the Price Hill Historical Society & Museum let me sift through numerous volumes of Remus clippings and memorabilia. Sharon Calder spoke about her relatives Augusta Imogene Brown and Ruth Redell Holmes Williams, and their lives with Remus. Once again Karen Needles was my National Archives Sherpa, helping me find a hefty cache of relevant files. James Dailey shared his incredible collection of Remus photos. Mike Welt pointed me in the right direction for additional photos. Michael Vander-Heijden of Yale University's law library set me up at an enormous, gorgeous overhead scanner. For an entire week, from opening till closing, I copied all 5,500 pages of a murder trial transcript and relished every moment. Katie Ranum tracked down countless obscure journals, articles, and deeds. Richard Thomas introduced me to some fine Cincinnati people and the finer points of whiskey. Matthew J. Boylan of the New York Public Library is a research god and general godsend.

I wouldn't survive this business without my community of writers, readers, and friends who unfailingly offer advice, support, and a seat next to them at the bar. An incomplete list, in alphabetical order: Brooke Berry, Tony Biancosino, Diane Bierman, Corey Bishoff,

Vicki Bishoff, Susannah Cahalan, Ada Calhoun, Susan Ciccarone, Dan Conaway, Joseph D'Agnese, Jennifer Fales, Beth France, Emma Garman, Christine Gleason, Matthew Goodman, Sara Gruen, Thomas Hess, Meredith Hindley, Kevin Hogan, Joshilyn Jackson, Denise Kiernan, Gilbert King, Rick Kogan, Gary Krist, Erik Larson, Alison Law, Elisa Ludwig, Kate Murray, Kim Michelle Richardson, Renée Rosen, John and Eileen Sabatina, Mark Sabatina, Anna Schachner, Rachel Shteir, Amy Sohn, Margaret Talbot, the exceptional women of Sob Sisters (too many to name here), and my invaluable No-Town Escape Crew: Jason, Laura, Mary, and Melisa. Thanks, also, to the wonderful and incredibly generous Sandy Kahler.

Chuck Kahler has always supported my expeditions into the past, and has long been my best companion in travel of all kinds.

Most of all, thank you for reading.

BIBLIOGRAPHY

ARCHIVAL SOURCES

The State of Ohio vs. George Remus: Records and Arguments. Yale University Law Library, New Haven, Connecticut.

George Remus Collection. Delhi Historical Society, Cincinnati, Ohio.

George Remus Collection. Price Hill Historical Society & Museum, Cincinnati, Ohio.

Investigation of Hon. Harry M. Daugherty, Formerly Attorney General of the United States, Hearings before the Select Committee on Investigation of the Attorney General. United States Senate, 68th Congress, 1924.

Memorial Tributes to J. Edgar Hoover in the Congress of the United States. 93rd Congress, 2nd Session, Washington, D.C.: U.S. Government Printing Office, 1974.

Taft, William Howard. Papers, 1915–1953 (WHTP). Manuscript Division, Library of Congress, Washington, D.C.

Willebrandt, Mabel Walker. Papers

(MWWP). Manuscript Division, Library of Congress, Washington, D.C.

Department of Justice, Mail and Files Division, 23-1907. National Archives and Records Administration (NARA), College Park, Maryland.

Department of Justice, Mail and Files Division, 226220–226225. NARA, College Park, Maryland.

Department of Justice, Mail and Files Division, 29-1220. NARA, College Park, Maryland.

Department of Justice, Division of Records, 23-42-28. NARA, College Park, Maryland.

Department of Justice, Tax Division, file 5-645 to 5-647. NARA, College Park, Maryland.

Department of Justice, Federal Bureau of Investigation/Department of Justice file on Franklin Dodge. FOI/PA# 1346338, NARA, College Park, Maryland.

Records of the Immigration and Naturalization Service, Subject and Policy Files, 1893–1957, RG 85, file 55438-947 to 55438-968. NARA, College Park, Maryland.

BOOKS, PERIODICALS, AND DISSERTATIONS

Ackerman, Kenneth. *Young J. Edgar: Hoover, the Red Scare, and the Assault on Civil Liber-*

ties. Cambridge, MA: Da Capo Press, 2008.

Allen, Frederick Lewis. *Only Yesterday: An Informal History of the 1920s.* New York and London: Harper and Brothers, 1931.

Anthony, Carl Sferrazza. *Florence Harding: The First Lady, the Jazz Age, and the Death of America's Most Scandalous President.* New York: William Morrow, 1999.

————. *Nellie Taft: The Unconventional First Lady of the Ragtime Era.* New York: William Morrow, 2005.

Asbury, Herbert. *The Great Illusion: An Informal History of Prohibition.* New York: Dover Publications, 2018.

Blocker, Jack S., Jr. "Did Prohibition Really Work? Alcohol Prohibition as a Public Health Innovation." *American Journal of Public Health,* vol. 96, no. 2, February 2006.

Brown, Dorothy M. *Mabel Walker Willebrandt: A Story of Power, Loyalty, and the Law.* Knoxville: University of Tennessee Press, 1984.

Caraway, Robin. *Newport: The Sin City Years.* Charleston, SC: Arcadia Publishing, 2010.

Coe, Alexis. "By Reason of Insanity." *Lapham's Quarterly,* May 21, 2015.

Cook, Philip J. *Paying the Tab.* Princeton, NJ: Princeton University Press, 2011.

Cook, William A. *King of the Bootleggers: A Biography of George Remus.* Jefferson, NC:

McFarland & Co., 2008.

Daugherty, Harry M., and Thomas Dixon. *The Inside Story of the Harding Tragedy.* New York: Churchill, 1932.

Drowne, Kathleen Morgan, and Patrick Huber. *The 1920s.* Westport, CT: Greenwood Press, 2004.

Gentry, Curt. *J. Edgar Hoover: The Man and the Secrets.* New York: W. W. Norton & Company, 2001.

Grace, Kevin. *Cincinnati Revealed.* Charleston, SC: Arcadia Publishing, 2002.

Hanson, Neil. *Monk Eastman: The Gangster Who Became a War Hero.* New York: Alfred A. Knopf, 2010.

Hartog, Hendrik. *Man and Wife in America: A History.* Cambridge, MA: Harvard University Press, 2002.

Haynes, Roy Asa. *Prohibition Inside Out.* New York: Doubleday, 1923.

Hotchkiss, Julie, and Joyce Meyer. *Remembering Remus in Price Hill.* Cincinnati, OH: Edgecliff Press in partnership with the Price Hill Historical Society and Museum, 2011.

Keeling, Arlene. *Nursing and the Privilege of Prescription: 1893–2000.* Columbus: Ohio State University Press, 2007.

Keyes, Frances Parkinson. "Homes of Outstanding American Women." *Better Homes and Gardens,* March 1928.

Kobler, John. *Ardent Spirits: The Rise and Fall*

of Prohibition. New York: Da Capo Press, 1993.

Krafft-Ebing, Richard von. *Text-Book of In-sanity.* Philadelphia: F. A. Davis, 1905.

Lerner, Michael A. *Dry Manhattan: Prohibition in New York City.* Cambridge, MA: Harvard University Press, 2008.

Long, Lois. "And Those Were Tables for Two." *New Yorker,* February 17, 1940.

Martin, John S. "Mrs. Firebrand." *New Yorker,* February 16, 1929.

McCartney, Laton. *The Teapot Dome Scandal.* New York: Random House Trade Paperbacks, 2009.

McCullough, David. *John Adams.* New York: Simon & Schuster, 2008.

McGirr, Lisa. *The War on Alcohol: Prohibition and the Rise of the American State.* New York: W. W. Norton & Company, 2016.

McKay, Bob. "The Bootlegger." *Cincinnati Magazine,* December 1978.

McKay, Milton. "Insanity: Another Legal Fiction." *The Outlook,* February 6, 1929.

Means, Gaston, and Max Dixon Thacker. *The Strange Death of President Harding.* New York: Gold Label Books, 1930.

Mee, Charles L., Jr. *The Ohio Gang: The World of Warren G. Harding.* New York: M. Evans & Company, 2014.

Mellin, William, and Meyer Berger. "I Was a Wire Tapper." *Saturday Evening Post,* September 10, 1949.

Mencken, H. L. "Five Years of Prohibition." *American Mercury,* December 1924.

Metcalfe, Philip. *Whispering Wires: The Tragic Tale of an American Bootlegger.* Portland, OR: Inkwater Press, 2007.

Miller, Nathan. *New World Coming.* Cambridge, MA: Da Capo Press, 2004.

Miller, Zane L., and Edward Bruce Tucker. *Changing Plans for America's Cities: Cincinnati's Over-the-Rhine and Twentieth Century Urbanism.* Columbus: Ohio State University Press, 1998.

Murphy, Walter F. *Wiretapping on Trial: A Case Study in the Judicial Process.* New York: Random House, 1967.

Nesbit, Evelyn, and Deborah Dorian Paul. *Tragic Beauty: The Lost 1914 Memoirs of Evelyn Nesbit.* Morrisville, NC: Lulu, 2006.

Okrent, Daniel. *Last Call: The Rise and Fall of Prohibition.* New York: Scribner, 2010.

Peretti, Burton William. *Nightclub City: Politics and Amusement in Manhattan.* Philadelphia: University of Pennsylvania Press, 2007.

Potter, Gary W., and Thomas Barker. *Wicked Newport: Kentucky's Sin City.* Charleston, SC: History Press, 2008.

Rogers, Will. *Daily Telegrams, Vol. 1: The Coolidge Years, 1926–1929.* Stillwater: Oklahoma State University Press, 1978.

Rolfes, Steven J., and Kent Jones. *Historic

Downtown Cincinnati. Charleston, SC: Arcadia Publishing, 2001.

Rosenberg, Albert, and Cindy Armstrong. *The American Gladiators: Taft Versus Remus.* Hemet, CA: Aimwell Press, 1995.

Ross, Ishbel. *An American Family: The Tafts, 1678–1964.* Cleveland: World Publishing Co., 1964.

Scott, Harry Fletcher. *Language and Its Growth.* Chicago: Scott, Foresman and Co., 1935.

Sexton, Robert Fenimore. "Kentucky Politics and Society: 1919–1932." PhD dissertation, University of Washington, 1970.

Sinclair, Andrew. *The Era of Excess.* New York: Faber & Faber, 1962.

Singer, Allen J. *Stepping Out in Cincinnati.* Mount Pleasant, SC: Arcadia Publishing, 2005.

Smith, Ron, and Mary O. Boyle. *Prohibition in Atlanta.* Charleston, SC: American Palate, 2015.

Solberg, Carl. *Riding High: America in the Cold War.* New York: Mason & Lipscomb, 1973.

Spinelli, Lawrence. *Dry Diplomacy: The United States, Great Britain, and Prohibition.* Lanham, MD: Rowman & Littlefield, 2008.

Stone, John K. "George Remus: King of the Bootleggers." Master's thesis, Xavier University, April 1989.

Suess, Jeff. *Lost Cincinnati.* Mount Pleasant,

SC: Arcadia Publishing, 2015.

Taft, Charles P. II. "So This Is Justice." *World Work,* May 1928.

Wead, Doug. *All the Presidents' Children: Triumph and Tragedy in the Lives of America's First Families.* New York: Atria Books, 2004.

Weekley, Ernest. *More Words Ancient and Modern.* Freeport, NY: Books for Libraries Press, 1971.

Weiner, Tim. *Enemies: A History of the FBI.* New York: Random House, 2012.

Willebrandt, Mabel Walker. *The Inside of Prohibition.* Indianapolis: Bobbs-Merrill Co., 1929.

———. "First Impressions." *Good Housekeeping,* May 1928.

———. "Give Women a Fighting Chance!" *Smart Set,* February 1930.

Williams, David. "The Bureau of Investigation and Its Critics, 1919–1921: The Origins of Federal Political Surveillance." *Journal of American History,* vol. 68, December 1981.

Willis, James A. *The Big Book of Ohio Ghost Stories.* Mechanicsburg, PA: Stackpole Books, 2013.

Zeitz, Joshua. *Flapper: A Madcap Story of Sex, Style, Celebrity and the Women Who Made America Modern.* New York: Three Rivers Press, 2006.

Zimmerman, Elena Irish. *Atlanta in Vintage*

Postcards: Volume 1. Mount Pleasant, SC: Arcadia Publishing, 1999.

NOTES

Prologue: Reckoning, 1927

An hour ago he was eating breakfast: *The State of Ohio v. George Remus* (hereafter *Ohio v. Remus*), testimony of Anna Ryerson, 457.

The sun, strong for the season: The October 6, 1927, edition of the *Cincinnati Enquirer* mentioned "mild Indian summer weather."

His brain had wandered to a shadowy land: *Ohio v. Remus,* statement by George Remus, 372.

He spoke of a halo: Ibid., testimony of Dr. David Wolfstein, 2942.

He described shooting stars: Ibid.

He embarked on nationwide searches: Ibid., testimony of Robert L. Dunning, 2451.

He announced, with unwavering conviction: Ibid., testimony of A. Lee Beaty, 626.

His Little Imo: Ibid., testimony of Ruth

523

Remus, 2666.

his truest and sweetest: Ibid., testimony of Dr. Shelby Mumaugh, 92.

his Prime Minister: *New York Evening World,* June 7, 1922.

his centipede, his monkey, his gem: *Ohio v. Remus,* letter from Remus to Imgene read during the testimony of Dr. E. D. Sinks, 295.

He just wished to talk to her: Ibid., testimony of George Klug, 99.

black silk dress: *Cincinnati Enquirer,* January 22, 1925.

pearl-handled revolver: *Ohio v. Remus,* testimony of George Conners, 1364.

PART I: THE PURSUED AND THE PURSUING

All the Rope He Wants

where Prohibition forced breweries: Suess, 58.

"dream palace": *The Evening Review* (East Liverpool, Ohio), November 29, 1927.

a heated pool: *Ohio v. Remus,* probate testimony of George Remus, 728.

George Remus would be forty-four: There has been much debate about Remus's true birth date. In April 12, 1927, A. W. Kliefoth, the American Consul General in

Berlin, obtained a copy of Remus's birth certificate, which specifies the date as November 13, 1876. Records of the Immigration and Naturalization Service, Subject and Policy Files, 1893–1957, RG 85, file 55438-947, National Archives and Records Administration, College Park, Maryland (hereafter NARA).

Imogene, as she preferred, was thirty-five: Birth certificate of Augusta Brown, September 30, 1884.

"dust girl": *Ohio v. Remus,* testimony of Emmett Kirgin, 7.

she and her husband separated ten times: *Chicago Tribune,* November 23, 1916.

"cruelty": *The Day Book* (Chicago, Illinois), March 6, 1915.

"pure malice": *Rockford Republic* (Illinois), March 8, 1915.

"coming home early in the morning": Ibid.

she couldn't recall the names: District Director Thomas Thomas to the commissioner general of immigration, February 15, 1927, RG 85, file 55438-947, NARA.

mean and abusive alcoholic: *Ohio v. Remus,* testimony of Dr. Kenneth L. Weber, 808.

Remus quit the eighth grade: Examination of George Remus, RG 85, file 55438-947, NARA.

the city's West Side: *Chicago Inter Ocean,*

March 24, 1894.

earning $5 per week: *Battle Creek Enquirer* (Michigan), November 23, 1927.

sleeping on a cot in the stockroom: *Ohio v. Remus,* testimony of Dr. David Wolfstein, 2929.

"druggist's devil boy": *Battle Creek Enquirer* (Michigan), November 23, 1927.

for the charitable price of $10: *Ohio v. Remus,* probate testimony of George Remus, 4.

Remus's Cathartic Compound: Ibid., 5.

Remus's Cathartic Pills: Ibid.

"complexion remedy": *Chicago Tribune,* July 22, 1902.

Remus's Lydia Pinkham Compound: *Ohio v. Remus,* testimony of Dr. Shelby Mumaugh, 25.

Remus's Nerve Tonic: Ibid., probate testimony of George Remus, 2.

consisting of fluid extract of celery: Ibid., 4.

"Doctor Remus": Ibid., testimony of Dr. W. H. Vorbau, 931.

Abraham Lincoln's stint as a bartender: *The Advance,* September 11, 1913.

"The Weeping, Crying Remus": *Ohio v. Remus,* testimony of Clarence Darrow, 1840.

"the Napoleon of the Chicago Bar": Ibid., probate testimony of George Remus, 386.

"There has been a lot of talk" to **"Look!":** *New York Times,* December 19, 1927.

he had first ingested an elixir: Ibid.

He would give Imogene allowance money: *Buffalo Times,* March 2, 1919.

"the gutter"; "make a lady out of her": *Ohio v. Remus,* testimony of George Conners, 1336.

her eleven-year-old daughter, Ruth: 1920 census.

wanting a $15 reward for its return: *Chicago Tribune,* February 4, 1919.

Imogene thought that $5 would suffice: Ibid.

five foot six and 205 pounds: Application for the Fidelity Mutual Life Insurance Company, policy no. 241449, RG 85, file 55438-947, NARA.

spending nearly six hours: *Cincinnati Post,* January 2, 1922.

Remus dragged the man outside: *Ohio v. Remus,* testimony of Dr. W. H. Vorbau, 932.

"poisonous potions": *Chicago Tribune,* February 8, 1901.

doused them with ammonia: Ibid.

throwing punches over witness testimony: *News Journal* (Mansfield, Ohio), March 4, 1913.

wearing slippers: *Chicago Tribune,* February 6, 1919.

punched him in the eye, revamped his

nose: *Brooklyn Daily Eagle,* December 4, 1927.

knocked out a tooth: *Chicago Tribune,* February 16, 1919.

"I acted in self-defense" to "legal writ of ejectment": Ibid.

After five minutes of deliberation: Ibid.

beat, punched, struck, choked, and kicked: Ibid., March 8, 1919.

lump sum of $50,000, $25 per week in alimony, and $30,000 in a trust: Ibid.

"He is a perfect gentleman" to "never hang himself": *Kansas City Star,* February 10, 1919.

She claimed to the press: *Cincinnati Enquirer,* October 7, 1927.

unreasonable and nearly impossible to enforce: *St. Louis Post-Dispatch,* January 3, 1926.

"petty, hip-pocket bootlegging": Ibid.

"so-called best people": Ibid.

"men without any brains at all": *Cincinnati Enquirer,* January 21, 1952.

"a chance to clean up": Ibid.

"the greatest comedy": Investigation of Hon. Harry M. Daugherty, Formerly Attorney General of the United States, 68th Congress, 2400.

he craved the thrill: *Louisville Courier-Journal,* March 10, 1926.

80 percent of the country's pre-

Prohibition bonded whiskey: Bob Mc-
Kay, "The Bootlegger," *Cincinnati Magazine,*
December 1978.

always listing someone else as the owner:
St. Louis Post-Dispatch, January 3, 1926.

Bribe state Prohibition directors: Ibid.

Organize a transportation company:
Ibid., January 7, 1926.

arrange for his own employees to hijack:
Robert Fenimore Sexton, "Kentucky Politics and Society: 1919–1932," PhD dissertation, University of Washington, 1970.

"the Circle": *Louisville Courier-Journal,*
March 1, 1926.

Remus had always been terrified: *Ohio v.
Remus,* probate testimony of George
Remus, 548.

died in an insane asylum: Ibid., probate
testimony of George Remus, 2935.

strange story behind his father's death:
Letter from Peter Gross to the Commissioner of Immigration, June 19, 1927, RG
85, file 55438-947, NARA.

Remus locked her in the attic: Ibid.

June 25, 1920: Testimony of Imogene Remus
to the Immigration Commission, RG 85,
file 55438-947, NARA.

**a writing room, and a Louis XVI candy
shop:** "Buildings Main," available at http://
www.cincinnativiews.net/buildings_main
.htm.

"We must buy the Lackman place": *At-*

lanta Constitution, October 30, 1927.

a record for a residential sale: *Cincinnati Enquirer,* November 18, 1919.

put the deed in Imogene's name: Ibid.

Testimony of Marie Remus: Testimony of Marie Remus to the Immigration Commission, RG 85, file 55438-947, NARA.

The Circle

"John P. Alexander": *Cincinnati Enquirer,* May 14, 1922.

$50,000 worth of drugs: *St. Louis Post-Dispatch,* January 4, 1926.

an expenditure of ten dollars: Ibid., January 3, 1926.

"confidential men": Ibid., January 10, 1926.

"traffic man": *Louisville Courier-Journal,* March 2, 1926.

"the man, Friday": Ibid.

"all-around man": Ibid.

"Prime Minister": *New York Evening World,* June 7, 1922.

"partner in everything": *St. Louis Post-Dispatch,* January 12, 1926.

invest personal funds: Ibid.

There was nobody in the world: Ibid.

Remus would own 35 percent: *Ohio v. Remus,* testimony of Dr. Albert Pfeiffer, 880.

binding and gagging the watchmen, cut-

ting telephone wires: *Pittsburgh Daily Post,* September 17, 1923.

"Stick 'em up high!": *St. Louis Post-Dispatch,* January 6, 1926.

"Pull your triggers!"; "Shoot, you cowards": Ibid.

He catapulted himself: Ibid.

"You have more guts": *Press Courier* (Oxnard, California), January 9, 1928.

hired a few of the leader's men: Ibid.

devoted husband and the father of a baby girl: *St. Louis Post-Dispatch,* January 4, 1926.

son of poor Irish immigrants, Conners had worked: Ibid.

that narrowed as they approached: *Louisville Courier-Journal,* March 4, 1926.

small business growing grapes: *St. Louis Post-Dispatch,* January 4, 1926.

He had one condition: Ibid.

Remus offered $100 per week: Ibid.

His hired hand, Johnny Gehrum: Ibid.

"We're all going to get pinched": Ibid.

hopping from foot to foot: Ibid.

"Get out of the way and shut up": Ibid.

they could see anyone: *Louisville Courier-Journal,* March 4, 1926.

stashed at strategic points: Ibid.

old voting booth was repurposed: *St. Louis Post-Dispatch,* January 4, 1926.

connected by an electric buzzer: Ibid.

dimmed their headlights three times: Ibid.

bold globe of a floodlight: Ibid.

"Death Valley Farm": *Cincinnati Enquirer,* April 16, 1922.

"There go the whiskey trucks!": *St. Louis Post-Dispatch,* January 6, 1926.

Remus welcomed three thousand men: *Atlanta Constitution,* July 15, 1928.

spent $74,000 in renovations: *St. Louis Post-Dispatch,* January 7, 1926.

wove the name "Remus": Ibid.

"I must corral myself together": *The Tennessean,* November 27, 1927.

"the egregious and excruciating principle at stake": Ibid.

"from the teeming fullness of my grateful heart": Ibid.

"if you please": *St. Louis Post-Dispatch,* January 3, 1926.

"if I may": Ibid.

"will you pardon my saying": Ibid.

"may I observe here": Ibid.

certain words tinged: William A. Cook, 5.

fastidiousness that bordered on phobia: *Ohio v. Remus,* testimony of Dr. K. L. Weber, 790.

the only material touching his skin: Ibid., testimony of Dr. A. C. Adams, 1069.

could not tolerate the feel of a button: Ibid., testimony of Dr. Albert Pfeiffer, 882.

He never wore underwear: Ibid., testimony of Dr. Albert Pfeiffer, 790.

"Remus was in the whiskey business"; "Cincinnati was the American mecca": *St. Louis Post-Dispatch,* January 7, 1926.

Treasury Department contacted William Mellin: William J. Mellin as told to Meyer Berger, "I Was a Wire Tapper," *Saturday Evening Post,* September 10, 1949.

"Here's the dope on Remus"; "What do I do now?": Ibid.

"My boy, come back tomorrow": Ibid.

"Son, where is your home office?": Ibid.

Mellin told him: Ibid.

"Son" to "forget about it": Ibid.

It never came: Ibid.

Life Has Few Petted Darlings

Remus received a call: *St. Louis Post-Dispatch,* January 8, 1926.

for the paltry investment of $1.48: Ibid., January 5, 1926.

white marble pillars and cascading ferns: *Brooklyn Daily Eagle,* February 6, 1919.

dressed with monochromatic precision: Means, 86–87.

diamond and ruby ring: Ibid., 86.

soft hush of a nearby fountain: *Brooklyn Daily Eagle,* February 6, 1919.

"reasonably large operator": Investigation of Hon. Harry M. Daugherty, 2402.

"consideration": Ibid.

one permit allowed for the withdrawal: Ibid., 2405.

would pay Smith $1.50 to $2.50: Ibid., 2406.

first permit would name the Central Drug Company: Ibid.

"showdown": *Louisville Courier-Journal,* March 1, 1926.

a *deus ex machina* in the form of a pardon: Ibid., March 2, 1926.

produced $50,000, all in $1,000 bills: Investigation of Hon. Harry M. Daugherty, 2408.

"For all of my life": Willebrandt to her parents, Christmas 1923, Mabel Walker Willebrandt Papers (hereafter MWWP), Library of Congress, Washington, D.C.

call from an old law professor: Brown, 45.

flash flood rampaging through their tent: Ibid., 10.

"acting like a child": Willebrandt, "First Impressions," *Good Housekeeping,* May 1928.

she bit a pet cat's ear: Brown, 11.

"Look above and beyond the immediate task": *Brooklyn Daily Eagle,* June 22, 1924.

milked the cow on their Kansas farm: Ibid.

"Life has few petted darlings": Brown, 128.

After challenging a principal: Ibid., 15.

nearly unfathomable range of expertise: Ibid., 28.

discipline one boy with a rod: Ibid., 16.

"enthusiastic licking": Ibid.

she utilized a procedure: Ibid., 36.

"going straight": Ibid., 37.

bank account was so depleted: Ibid., 48.

her daily ice-cold bath: Frances Parkinson Keyes, "Homes of Outstanding American Women," *Better Homes and Gardens,* March 1928.

painstakingly styled her hair: Brown, 122.

"being on the other side": Willebrandt to her father, undated, MWWP.

"tall, benevolent, interested, and gracious": Willebrandt to her parents, January 6, 1924, MWWP.

"irrepressible friendliness": Ibid.

sensed that he preferred privacy: Ibid.

would not deter her from ruthlessly enforcing it: *Baltimore Sun,* September 16, 1928.

smuggled gallons of liquor: *Arizona Daily Star,* April 10, 1921.

New York garbage scows: Hanson, 282.

liquor-filled torpedoes landing on Long Island: *Popular Science,* November 1929.

bottle-shaped buoys: Ibid.

dummy smokestacks: Ibid.

"liquor submarines": Ibid.

seagoing tugs with compartments: Ibid.

annual output of 286 million gallons: Willebrandt, *The Inside of Prohibition,* 27.

more than 1,200 breweries had produced: Ibid.

The term *bootlegger:* Weekley, 22.

Amputees hid booze in their hollowed wooden legs: *Arizona Daily Star,* April 10, 1921.

Women tied pints to each string: Ibid.

Barbershops stocked whiskey in tonic bottles: Ibid.

squirt guns with a two-drink capacity: Ibid.

goat barns, cowsheds, and cesspools: Ibid.

worried about a glut in the market: Ibid.

four agents were shot within a week: Ibid.

whiskey pirates preyed upon the bootleggers: Ibid.

Laughing, she assured him: Brown, 47.

California clarets she so loved: John S. Martin, "Mrs. Firebrand," *New Yorker,* February 16, 1929.

"There has been an old complaint": Brown, 38.

personal staff of six: *San Francisco Chronicle,* August 30, 1921.

"The Queen": Martin, "Mrs. Firebrand."

Her salary was $7,500 per year: *Richmond*

Palladium (Indiana), September 2, 1921.

paid to members of Congress: *Baltimore Sun,* April 1, 1923.

"pretty and young" lawyer: Ibid.

"the age-old adage": Ibid.

women should not be appointed: *Akron Beacon Journal,* August 30, 1921.

"At the same time": Ibid.

$1,800 worth of liquor: Okrent, 129.

purchasing the Old Overholt rye distillery: Ibid., 134.

Wells Fargo wagons: William A. Cook, 45.

"a politician in sheep's clothing": Brown, 53.

arthritis treatment: Means, 125.

"kind of half servant and half glorified valet": Investigation of Hon. Harry Daugherty, 3237.

"Oh, don't pay any attention to Jess" to **"I will reach you":** Ibid., 3235.

"almost unbelievable condition": James R. Clark to Harry Daugherty, August 17, 1921, Department of Justice, Mail and Files Division, Willebrandt file on George Remus, 23-1907, NARA.

"one of such magnitude and so far-reaching": Ibid.

"stamp out in this community": Ibid.

She would soon scrawl: Ibid.

Testimony of A. W. Brockway: *Ohio v. Remus,* 279–280.

engraved with the initials "G.R.": Ibid., testimony of Orin Weber, 1122.

a pair of stone lions: *New York Evening World,* June 7, 1922.

gave a number multiple times: Ibid.

a $100,000 diamond winking from her hand: Ibid.

blithely wrote a check for $4,000: Ibid.

enrolled the thirteen-year-old in the Sacred Heart Academy: *Cincinnati Enquirer,* February 22, 1970.

diamond-studded gold and platinum figurines: *New York Evening World,* June 7, 1922.

Remus called her "Princess": *Cincinnati Enquirer,* January 4, 1922.

"little honey bunch"; "bunch of sugar": *Ohio v. Remus,* testimony of John Snook, 1960.

"apple of his eye — not one, but both": Ibid., letter from Remus to Imogene, read during the testimony of Dr. Shelby Mumaugh, April 26, 1924, 92.

simply, "Gene": Ibid.

just one nickname for him: Ibid., testimony of John Snook, 9.

self-proclaimed photographic memory: Ibid., probate testimony of George Remus, 15.

back and forth to Chicago, New York, Washington: Ibid., 657.

even he found the magnitude: *St. Louis Post-Dispatch,* January 7, 1926.

stretched across nine states: Ibid., May 25, 1924.

from New York to Kansas: Ibid., January 9, 1926.

clients included the head of the Chicago mob: William A. Cook, 50.

Deposits that averaged $50,000 a day: *Springfield News Leader* (Missouri), April 6, 1924.

average salary was $1,400 per year: "Facts & Figures: Income and Prices 1900–1999," available at https://usa.usembassy.de/etexts/his/e_prices1.htm.

$2.8 million deposit: *St. Louis Post-Dispatch,* May 25, 1924; Investigation of Hon. Harry M. Daugherty, 2426.

yearly gross of eighty million, a net of thirty: *Ohio v. Remus,* probate testimony of George Remus, 459–460.

took Conners four hours to count: Ibid.

forcing him to carry as much as $100,000: *Springfield News Leader* (Missouri), April 6, 1924.

he considered opening his own bank: *Cincinnati Times-Star,* January 21, 1952.

paying twenty to thirty thousand dollars at a time: *St. Louis Post-Dispatch,* January

8, 1926.

Edgewood distillery in Cincinnati for $220,000: Ibid., January 9, 1926.

and within five days removed: Ibid.

the Squibb Distillery in Lawrenceburg: Ibid.

from the Fleischmann in Cincinnati: Ibid.

He and Conners landed upon a solution: Ibid.

noted the variety of license plates: *Cincinnati Enquirer,* May 11, 1922.

the runners soon upgraded: *St. Louis Post-Dispatch,* January 7, 1926.

they equipped their roadsters: Ibid.

extra supplies of gas, oil, and water: Ibid.

To ensure that his runners remained loyal: Ibid., January 9, 1926.

especially good customers: Ibid.

From the day Death Valley opened: Ibid.

conducted practice drills: Ibid.

One afternoon, without advance warning: Ibid.

"What do you want?": Ibid.

"There must be some mistake"; "Wait while I call up": Ibid.

"What does this mean?": Ibid.

"I'm surprised they're there" to "have they?": Ibid.

"No, but if they start"; "What are you going to do": Ibid.

"I think you can handle them"; "Go back and see": Ibid.
"Now listen" to "What do you say?": Ibid.
"It's all right with me"; "See what he says": Ibid.
"Well, I don't like to see"; "Still, I sure would like": Ibid.
"All right" to "I need one myself": Ibid.
"good fellow": Ibid.
Conners assembled parting gifts: Ibid.

Mabelmen

employed about five hundred agents: Memorial tributes to J. Edgar Hoover in the Congress of the United States, 93rd Congress, 2nd Session, Washington, D.C.: U.S. Government Printing Office, 1974, 86.
issues other than Prohibition: David Williams, "The Bureau of Investigation and Its Critics, 1919–1921: The Origins of Federal Political Surveillance," *Journal of American History,* vol. 68, December 1981.
1,500 field agents: McGirr, 69.
"Mabelmen": Martin, "Mrs. Firebrand."
ex-policemen, bailiffs, deputy sheriffs: *The Literary Digest,* August 1, 1925.
$1,200 per year: Allen, 249.
"in the nigger part of town": Okrent, 137.
the pseudonymous "Stewart McMullin": Ibid.
"The dominant reality": Willebrandt, *The*

Inside of Prohibition, 195.

Franklin L. Dodge Sr.: *Lansing State Journal* (Michigan), December 24, 1999.

entertained Supreme Court justices: "Mrs. Frank L. Dodge," available at https://www.lansingmi.gov/977/Mrs-Frank-L-Dodge.

once played host to perennial presidential hopeful: Ibid.

as deputy factory inspector: *Lansing State Journal* (Michigan), September 18, 1913.

fire escapes: Ibid.

the cleanliness of towels: Ibid., June 5, 1914.

an arrest for speeding: Ibid., April 22, 1915.

a special deputy for the U.S. Marshal Service: Ibid., June 25, 1917.

a census of Lansing's "alien enemies": Ibid.

considered a rising star: *Cincinnati Enquirer,* March 20, 1925.

His most recent triumph: *Battle Creek Enquirer* (Michigan), June 30, 1920.

strange Prohibition agent: *St. Louis Post-Dispatch,* January 10, 1926.

"There's not a drop in the place": Ibid.

the track at Churchill Downs was "fast": *Louisville Courier-Journal,* October 22, 1921.

Belle of Elizabethtown, Twinkle Blue, and Colonel Taylor: Ibid.

The following morning, Conners went to church: *St. Louis Post-Dispatch,* January 10, 1926.

unoccupied at the moment: Ibid.

"Do you want anything?": Ibid.

"Any what?": Ibid.

"Why, any liquor": Ibid.

"We aren't looking": Ibid.

pretending to be drunk: Ibid.

"Well, have you got any": Ibid.

"We're not in the liquor business": Ibid.

"We're Prohibition officers": Ibid.

"Then we haven't got any business"; "Come on, Johnny": Ibid.

"biggest boner" of his life: Ibid.

"Oh" to "search of your premises": Ibid.

"like a race horse at the barrier": Ibid.

doing forty-five in second gear: Ibid.

The agents shunted Gehrum: Ibid.

tossing an automatic pistol: Ibid.

Mary Hubbard watched: *Louisville Courier-Journal,* March 4, 1926.

She'd had enough: Ibid.

A servant ushered: *The Daily Republican* (Rushville, Indiana), November 28, 1927.

2,800 legal tomes: *Ohio v. Remus,* testimony of Dr. David Wolfstein, 2984.

Remus couldn't believe it: *St. Louis Post-Dispatch,* January 10, 1926.

He'd been warned the previous day: Ibid.

"madder than a hyena with a split lip": Ibid.

their day off: Ibid.

"All right, Conners"; "You and I will take it": Ibid.

"Don't go, Daddy!": Ibid.

"blubbered and pawed around": Ibid.

"That's what happens": Ibid.

fruits of their search: John K. Stone, "George Remus: King of the Bootleggers," Master's thesis, Xavier University, April 1989, 10.

dozens of sacks containing assorted brands: *Louisville Courier-Journal,* March 7, 1926.

record books containing information: *Cincinnati Enquirer,* October 30, 1921.

Seven showed up in person: William A. Cook, 52.

where a thousand spectators: Stone, 12.

five of Remus's associates: *Cincinnati Enquirer,* October 30, 1921.

the office closed and the lights darkened: Stone, 13.

Her husband was out of town: Ibid.

"This is an outrage"; "They better not come": *Atlanta Constitution,* October 30, 1927.

As she spoke she fingered: Ibid.

"Devout lager pontoons satyr": James Clark to the office of Attorney General Harry Daugherty, October 26, 1921, Willebrandt file on George Remus, 23-1907, NARA.

For translation, she passed: Ibid. "Mr. Hoover for translation" is scrawled on the top.

Testimony of Carlos Clapper: *Ohio v. Remus,* 283.

A Man's Home Is His Castle

"Your Honor" to "such a heavy bond": *Cincinnati Enquirer,* November 2, 1921.

As a finishing touch: Ibid.

$15,000 bond for Brown: Ibid.

$50,000 for Remus: *Cincinnati Enquirer,* November 5, 1921.

Imogene offered to sign the bonds: Ibid.

an $80 case of whiskey now sold for $110: William A. Cook, 53.

the Hotel Washington in D.C., at the Plaza in New York, and at the Claypool in Indianapolis: Investigation of Hon. Harry M. Daugherty, 2403.

domed concourse at Union Station: Ibid., 2410.

one brown and one blue: McCartney, 9.

"a first-class revolt": Allen, 88.

"But I look so fat": *Cincinnati Enquirer,* November 20, 1921.

preacher was arrested and fined $600: *Akron Beacon Journal,* December 29, 1921.

"She smokes, drinks, and 'damns' ": *Min-*

545

neapolis Tribune, December 4, 1921.

totaling $750,000: *St. Louis Post-Dispatch,* January 12, 1926.

"A man's home is his castle": *Washington Post,* April 28, 1938.

poker hands: *Battle Creek Enquirer* (Michigan), November 21, 1927.

The pool table in the billiard room: Ibid.

Plush leather seats lined the periphery: Ibid.

solid gold piano: McKay, "The Bootlegger," *Cincinnati Magazine,* December 1978.

worth more than $50,000: *Ohio v. Remus,* testimony of Dr. David Wolfstein, 2982.

Outside, five full-time gardeners: *Battle Creek Enquirer* (Michigan), November 21, 1927.

the brother of President Harding's Airedale terrier: *Cincinnati Enquirer,* June 29, 1924.

A baseball field beckoned: Ibid., August 1, 2011.

built and perfected for $175,000: *Ohio v. Remus,* testimony of Dr. David Wolfstein, 2938.

Scalloped silver sconces: *Cincinnati Post,* January 2, 1922.

a variety of Turkish and Swedish needle baths: Ibid.

even electric baths: *Aurora News* (Kansas), July 6, 1893.

"frisky": Ibid.

statues depicting ancient Greek swimmers: *Cincinnati Post,* January 2, 1922.

terra-cotta circles and pearl-hued squares: George Remus collection, Price Hill Historical Society.

"the Imogene Baths": *Cincinnati Post,* January 2, 1922.

"a snappy woman": *Battle Creek Enquirer* (Michigan), November 23, 1927.

"turn the trick": Ibid.

"The kind of woman" to "feline in her every movement": *Atlanta Constitution,* October 30, 1927.

"middle-aged flapper": *New York Times,* April 16, 1922.

"Not life but movement": Ibid.

Printed on tea-colored paper: George Remus papers, Delhi Historical Society, Cincinnati, Ohio.

"Mrs. Geo. E. Remus" and "Mr. Geo. E. Remus": Ibid.

Six maids addressed: *Lansing State Journal* (Michigan), November 18, 1927.

"Cin-cin-nasty": Sferrazza Anthony, 5.

more than one hundred in all: *Cincinnati Enquirer,* January 1, 1922.

"Jazz suits": *The Haberdasher,* vol. 76, July 1922, 64.

The honeyed notes of a string orchestra: Ibid.

Models attired in Grecian gowns: Ibid.

A representative from the *Cincinnati Times-Star:* *Cincinnati Times-Star,* January 1, 1922.

"He's in a side room": *Atlanta Constitution,* October 30, 1927.

"And I've got Imogene": Ibid.

Remus lit guests' cigars with $100 bills: *Washington Post,* April 28, 1938.

$1,000 bill tucked beneath his plate: McKay, "The Bootlegger," *Cincinnati Magazine,* December 1978.

stickpin topped by a knob of diamonds: Suess, 138; *Cincinnati Enquirer,* December 4, 1983; Hotchkiss and Meyer, 11.

watch engraved with the letter "R": George Remus papers, Delhi Historical Society, Cincinnati, Ohio.

a chain of brand-new 1922 sedans: Hotchkiss and Meyer, 11; McKay, "The Bootlegger," *Cincinnati Magazine,* December 1978.

"Swimming is my hobby"; "I have dreamed of having my own pool": *Cincinnati Post,* January 2, 1922.

might fill the pool with whiskey: Hotchkiss and Meyer, 19.

Gus Schmidt's Band: Ibid., 7.

"spirit of the new year": *Cincinnati Times-Star,* January 2, 1922.

"A Happy New Year!": Ibid.

"Take a swim": Hotchkiss and Meyer, 7.

Remus followed, wearing his tuxedo:

McKay, "The Bootlegger," *Cincinnati Magazine,* December 1978.

He announced his intention to swim: *Cincinnati Post,* January 2, 1922.

make a wager: Ibid.

a biography of Abraham Lincoln: William A. Cook, 55.

his customary post-swim snack: *Washington Post,* April 28, 1938.

and a bowl of ice cream: *Davenport Democrat and Leader* (Iowa), August 24, 1926.

Tear the Heart Out of Washington

"It is inconceivable": William Harrison to Harry Daugherty, January 5, 1922, Willebrandt file on George Remus, 23-1907, NARA.

requesting Remus's tax returns: Willebrandt to David H. Blair, commissioner of internal revenue, April 25, 1922, Willebrandt file on George Remus, 23-1907, NARA.

"Appreciation is extended by this Department": Willebrandt to William Harrison, January 20, 1922, Willebrandt file on George Remus, 23-1907, NARA.

an update about the investigation: Memo for Willebrandt, undated (circa February 1922), Willebrandt file on George Remus, 23-1907, NARA.

"appears recently to have deceased": Ibid.

Agent Dodge had spoken to Hubbard's wife: *Chicago Tribune,* October 8, 1927.

"knowing too much": *St. Louis Post-Dispatch,* October 8, 1927.

to visit Cincinnati herself: Investigation of Hon. Harry M. Daugherty, 3331.

"Old Mother Hubbard": *St. Louis Post-Dispatch,* January 10, 1926.

"She seemed to me": *Cincinnati Post,* May 10, 1922.

Rumors abounded: *Cincinnati Enquirer,* May 11, 1922; Willebrandt memo (undated), Willebrandt file on George Remus, 23-1907, NARA.

Day and night, Dodge parked his sedan: *Ohio v. Remus,* probate testimony of George Remus, 522.

"everyone and his brother": Memo to Roy Haynes (passed to Willebrandt), February 3, 1922, Willebrandt file on George Remus, 23-1907, NARA.

"water under the dam"; "take care of itself": *St. Louis Post-Dispatch,* January 10, 1926.

"red-penciled": Memo to Willebrandt from Roy Haynes, 23-1907, NARA.

"crowded too far"; "tear the heart out of Washington": Ibid.

soft-skinned and pink-nailed: *Louisville*

Courier-Journal, February 24, 1952.

"a ravishing vision of a silken-clad ankle": *Chicago Tribune,* February 16, 1919.

Judge John Peck had ordered the jury: *Cincinnati Post,* May 8, 1922.

a diverse group: Ibid.

"big gentleman"; "leading spirit": *Cincinnati Post,* May 9, 1922.

sums were paid to "G.R." and "Mrs. G.R.": Ibid.

"was there but didn't do any hard work": *Cincinnati Enquirer,* May 11, 1922.

had not been manufactured in twenty-five years: *St. Louis Post-Dispatch,* January 10, 1926.

Remus got a break: *Cincinnati Post,* May 22, 1922.

"Whatever else we think": Ibid.

sat in silence: *Cincinnati Enquirer,* May 17, 1922.

"George Remus — guilty": Ibid.

"George Remus, have you anything to say?": Ibid.

"I have nothing": Ibid.

"The very air seemed a little dryer"; "The way of the transgressor": *Cincinnati Commercial Tribune,* May 17, 1922.

"Congratulations on the splendid manner": Willebrandt to Thomas Morrow, May 17, 1922, Willebrandt file on George

Remus, 23-1907, NARA.

a separate letter to Morrow: Willebrandt to Morrow, May 9, 1922, Willebrandt file on George Remus, 23-1907, NARA.

wearing a bold red dress: William A. Cook, 68.

accented with a leather money belt: *The Morning News* (Wilmington, Delaware), March 15, 1924.

"not a bit of sentiment": Investigation of Hon. Harry M. Daugherty, 2412.

"The conviction is there": Ibid.; *St. Louis Post-Dispatch,* January 8, 1926.

"It doesn't make any difference": Investigation of Hon. Harry M. Daugherty, 2414.

"Not one of the boys" to **"not guilty by the jury":** Ibid.

"The court of appeals will undoubtedly": Ibid.

"How do you know that?": Ibid.

"On account of my friendship": Ibid.

more money than the nearly $300,000: *New York Times,* May 17, 1924.

counted off twenty $1,000 bills: Investigation of Hon. Harry M. Daugherty, 2414.

a large glass fishbowl: Means, 205.

"tipsters of the underworld": Ibid.

averaged $60,000 per day: Ibid., 206.

had met a few times before: Investigation of Hon. Harry M. Daugherty, 2906.

"almost a nervous wreck": Ibid.

a modest one-time payment: Ibid.

Testimony of Emanuel Kessler: *Ohio v. Remus,* 93.

A Terrible, Terrible Scream

which made Imogene nervous: *Ohio v. Remus,* testimony of Ruth Remus, 2648.

"not very nice": Ibid.

"Stop the car": Ibid.

"Get out": Ibid.

against the brake, stripping the gears: Ibid.

"Why, George, aren't you ashamed": Ibid., 2469.

Remus reached for the first weapon: Ibid.

wanted to be the official owner of their home: Ibid., 2651.

"a terrible, terrible scream": Ibid., 2653.

"I'm sorry for scaring you": Untitled clipping, George Remus papers, Delhi Historical Society, Cincinnati, Ohio.

"It was more an order": Ibid.

"When my friend and I crossed": Ibid.

"Remus was a poor boy": Ibid.

"Remus has always been a good student": Ibid.

Remus was disbarred: *Cincinnati Enquirer,* October 7, 1922.

"Remus sold good liquor": *Coshocton Democrat* (Ohio), November 15, 1927.

one Naseem Shammas: *Indianapolis News,*

July 20, 1923.

a crook with a bad reputation: *Ohio v. Remus,* testimony of Dr. Kenneth L. Weber, 820.

peddled shoddy rugs and draperies: Ibid.

Remus had forbidden Imogene: Ibid.

"What do you mean by taking my wife?": Ibid., probate testimony of George Remus, 328.

"What do you mean?": Ibid.

wedged a foot against the door: Ibid.

"What do you mean by taking": Ibid.

"Well, we have some business matters": Ibid.

"You know that isn't the manly thing to do": Ibid.

"Well, I meant no wrong by it": Ibid.

"Well, you have no business to": Ibid.

Remus struck him again: Ibid.

Testimony of Emmett Kirgin: Ibid., 1.

A Middle Finger of Unusual Prominence

On the morning of November 29, 1922: Willebrandt diary, entry for November 29, 1922, MWWP.

"wide, earnest, truthful [and] brown": Quoted in Okrent, 139.

"invariable costume during the day": Ibid.

"dainty and exquisite dresses": Ibid.

"essentially feminine"; "she dislikes to

think so": Martin, "Mrs. Firebrand."

"exactly pretty"; "too large and too serious for that": *Brooklyn Daily Eagle,* June 22, 1924.

"intelligent": Ibid.

"medium-sized"; "a suggestion of plumpness": Ibid.

"beautiful picture"; "a black spangled gown": Brown, 142.

a little man came rushing up: Ibid.

"girlie girlie stuff": Ibid.

"Why the devil": Ibid.

"I try not to think of myself"; "By this I do not mean": *Evening Star* (Washington, D.C.), April 28, 1922.

"one of those militant anti-Suffragettes": Willebrandt to her parents, 1923, MWWP.

"anti-everything that is so progressive": Ibid.

"It was a stag party": Ibid.

tailored suit and loose blouse: Brown, 60.

arranged her hair over her hearing aid: Ibid.

"The dread shadow of deafness": Willebrandt to parents, Christmas 1922, MWWP.

"highly important in the enforcement": *New York Times,* November 30, 1922.

"giving its stamp of approval": *Burlington Free Press,* November 30, 1922.

Certain revenue statutes: *San Francisco*

Chronicle, January 3, 1923.

Offenses falling under these statutes: Ibid.

"whom I love dearly, from afar": Willebrandt to parents, January 2, 1923, MWWP.

"Since everyone was convinced": Ibid.

"Admiral of the Bootleggers": *Ohio v. Remus,* testimony of Willie Harr, 1166.

liquor from Scotland, France, and Nassau: *New York Times,* August 17, 1923.

inside man-made cement caves: Brown, 57.

"fruit" or "potatoes": Ibid.

"Bootlegger Team": Ibid.

"worse than useless": *Minneapolis Tribune,* December 18, 1923.

"absolutely crooked": Ibid.

"After a few days in the city": Ibid.

fifteen Bureau of Investigation agents: "Can This Woman Make America Dry?" *Collier's,* August 9, 1924.

operating under a pseudonym: Willebrandt file on Willie Harr, 5-647, NARA.

"ace of investigators": *St. Louis Post-Dispatch,* March 24, 1926.

onslaught of accusations: Brown, 102.

"He is really in a much": Willebrandt to parents, March 28, 1923, MWWP.

"Isn't he a peach?": Willebrandt to parents, May 18, 1923, MWWP.

"the finest woman assistant": Willebrandt diary, entry for October 7, 1922, MWWP.

"having the devil of a good time": Ibid.

adept at palmistry: *New Castle News* (Pennsylvania), October 14, 1926.

"low set thumb": *Atlanta Journal,* June 23, 1925.

"middle finger of unusual prominence": Ibid.

"strong and elastic": Ibid.

"If you want to lean back"; "Never have we seen": Ibid.

too afraid to tell him: *Brooklyn Daily Eagle,* June 22, 1924.

"Jew John" Marcus: *St. Louis Post-Dispatch,* January 11, 1926.

one of the first whiskey runners: Ibid.

Formerly a pickpocket and gambler: *Hamilton Evening Journal,* February 4, 1931.

"put many a rival on the spot": Ibid.

reserved exclusively for men: *Cincinnati Enquirer,* August 22, 1905.

trays heavy with larded beef sirloin: Ibid., January 11, 1926.

"the problem of Prohibition is almost solved": Brent Coleman, "Prohibition's Anniversary a Reminder of Time Cincinnati's Beer Business Was Crippled," January 17, 2017, available at https://www.wcpo.com/news/insider/prohibitions-anniversary-a-reminder-of-time-cincinnatis-beer-business-was-crippled.

"I'm not interested" to **"ones I already own"**: *St. Louis Post-Dispatch,* January 11, 1926.

"Well, this is one distillery": Ibid.

"the biggest Republican politician": Ibid.

"Are you sure he can be trusted?": Ibid.

"Absolutely": Ibid.

"All right": Ibid.

amateurish and unbusinesslike: Ibid.

"closed incident": *Ohio v. Remus,* testimony of Dr. Kenneth L. Weber, 816.

"personal investment": *St. Louis Post-Dispatch,* January 11, 1926.

install a buzzer system: Ibid., December 14, 1925.

one buzz would signal: Ibid.

"all velvet": Ibid., January 11, 1926.

"One must be patient in these matters": Ibid.

check in with Jess Smith: Investigation of Hon. Harry M. Daugherty, 2417.

whose vagina Harding christened "Mrs. Pouterson": *New York Times,* July 12, 2014.

head buried in the trashcan: Miller, 110.

Dynamite

"personal matter": *The Times* (Shreveport, Louisiana), November 18, 1928.

"love-nest hidden away somewhere": Ibid.

had felt like Joan of Arc: Brown, 19.

"necessary adjustments": Willebrandt, "Give Women a Fighting Chance!" *Smart Set,* February 1930.

"preservation of *her* freedom": Ibid.

"feel very much more comfortable": Willebrandt to her parents, June 19, 1923, MWWP.

"the shock of suicide": *Ithaca Journal* (New York), June 1, 1923.

"You have done very wonderful work": Willebrandt to her parents, June 19, 1923, MWWP.

upheld Remus's conviction: *Cincinnati Enquirer,* July 1, 1923.

"his ace in the hole": *St. Louis Post-Dispatch,* January 11, 1926.

"George Remus has always met": *Pittsburgh Press,* November 15, 1927.

"It's dynamite" to "break into the penitentiary": *St. Louis Post-Dispatch,* January 11, 1926.

"a few drops of croton oil": Sferrazza Anthony, 472.

A Sacramento woman took credit: Ibid.

The Ku Klux Klan cited a papist plot: Ibid.

others blamed the Klan: Ibid.

twenty-odd murders: *St. Louis Post-Dispatch,* April 24, 1955.

a constant and menacing presence: Ibid.,

January 11, 1926.

"Tell them to be careful"; "We could all get ten years": Ibid.

"could only sit tight": Ibid.

boldly announce an order of whiskey: Ibid.

His partners now owed him: Ibid.

U.S. Supreme Court followed suit: *Cincinnati Enquirer,* January 8, 1924.

"up along the line": Investigation of Hon. Harry M. Daugherty, 3234.

I am of the emphatic opinion: Ibid.

as complicit as Daugherty: Willebrandt to her parents, February 19, 1924, MWWP.

"yellow-livered, dishonorable craven": Ibid.

President Coolidge made the honorable decision: Investigation of Hon. Harry M. Daugherty, 3234.

"a puny, little toothless sort of thing": Brown, 56.

dispatched another team of agents: *Ohio v. Remus,* testimony of Allen Curry, 911.

Testimony of Henry Spilker: Ibid., 119.

The Brainstorms

the humiliation of arrest: *St. Louis Post-Dispatch,* January 12, 1926.

"took her from a hovel": *Ohio v. Remus,* testimony of George Conners, 1335.

"Never mind"; "When this is all over":

Louisville Courier-Journal, March 14, 1926.

long trip around the world: *St. Louis Post-Dispatch,* January 12, 1926.

"live a life of peace": *Ohio v. Remus,* probate testimony of George Remus, 703.

"faithfully look after it": *St. Louis Post-Dispatch,* January 12, 1926.

prepared a power of attorney: William A. Cook, 79.

$1 million worth of whiskey certificates: *Louisville Courier-Journal,* March 14, 1926.

he wrote a check for $115,000: *St. Louis Post-Dispatch,* January 12, 1926.

He also set up a trust for Romola: *Ohio v. Remus,* testimony of Richard E. Simmons, 723.

"kill Remus": *Chicago Tribune,* October 27, 1927.

selected a pearl gray silk suit: *Indianapolis Star,* January 26, 1924.

his favorite bowler hat: Ibid.

diamond stickpin resembling those: Ibid.

as usual, no underwear: *Ohio v. Remus,* testimony of Dr. Albert Pfeiffer, 790.

prepare a chicken supper: *Cincinnati Enquirer,* January 25, 1924.

George Conners wept openly: William A. Cook, 80.

in good spirits: *Cincinnati Enquirer,* January 25, 1924.

for his "boys": Ibid.

"regretted sincerely that no action": Ibid.

"great solace"; "cheerfulness": Ibid.

"The way the courts have handled": William A. Cook, 80.

"Do you have anything": Ibid.

"I have never tasted liquor in my life": Ibid.

a public car on the same train: *Cincinnati Enquirer*, January 25, 1924.

"kept up": *Philadelphia Inquirer*, January 26, 1924.

"sparkle the same as ever": Ibid.

"reduce": *Gaffney Ledger* (South Carolina), January 29, 1924.

chided an associate for being even stouter: Ibid.

"protracted vacation": Ibid.

"Oh well": Ibid.

his copy of *Dante's Inferno*: *Philadelphia Inquirer*, January 26, 1924.

"finest institution of its kind": *Brooklyn Daily Eagle*, July 9, 1902.

every modern convenience: Ibid.

Arms protruded between them: *Cincinnati Enquirer*, January 24, 1926.

She began to cry: *Asheville Citizen-Times*, January 26, 1924.

one large collective breath: *Cincinnati Enquirer*, January 26, 1924.

requiring inmates to wear white cloths: *Brooklyn Daily Eagle*, July 9, 1902.

produced better results: Ibid.

"If there is a surviving spark": Ibid.

"Millionaire's Row": *Asheville Citizen-Times,* January 26, 1924.

If the bootlegger paid $10,500: *Wisconsin State Journal,* February 10, 1925.

"judicious presents": *St. Louis Post-Dispatch,* January 12, 1926.

"habitable": Ibid.

high-limit poker: *Louisville Courier-Journal,* February 14, 1925.

little to assuage his humiliation: *St. Louis Post-Dispatch,* January 12, 1926.

"Remus, who paid millions to buy his way": Ibid.

"brainstorms": *Ohio v. Remus,* testimony of George Conners, 1007.

flowers or a bit of roast chicken or cake: *The Tennessean,* November 27, 1927.

"little bunch of sweetness"; "little bunch of nerves": *Ohio v. Remus,* testimony of Willie Harr, 1157.

she was permitted to cook for him: *Belevedere Daily Republican* (Illinois), October 10, 1927.

on her hands and knees: *Ohio v. Remus,* testimony of Willie Harr, 1172.

calling him "Daddy": *The Tennessean,* November 27, 1927.

"How she loves to show off": Ibid.

"the angel of the pen": Ibid.

choosing to play in a baseball game: *Ohio v. Remus,* testimony of Ruth Remus, 2641.

"unkindly remarks"; "fussing"; "abuse": Ibid., testimony of Willie Harr, 1177–1179.

"Why does my sister cry"; "Why is she unable to sleep?": Ibid., testimony of Grace Campbell, 2476.

"Because she doesn't understand me": Ibid.

a variation of this conversation: Ibid.

To the only true and sweetest little girl: *Ohio v. Remus,* letter from Remus to Imogene, read during the testimony of Dr. Shelby Mumaugh, 92.

Testimony of George L. Winkler: Ibid., 316.

The Wielders of the Soap

a rumpled linen suit and customary bow tie: *Brooklyn Daily Eagle,* March 15, 1924.

"somewhat ghoulish smile": Ibid.

"They knew the game": Ibid.

"I would like to ask one question": Investigation of Hon. Harry M. Daugherty, 123.

"Oh, I don't know"; "I guess the largest sum": Ibid.

"John Adams": *Buffalo Enquirer,* August 29, 1924.

a tankard of hard cider: McCullough, 36.

"In the most pathetic way": Willebrandt to her parents, April 20, 1924, MWWP.

"The Republican Party has no apology"; "His policy was vigorously": *Cincinnati Enquirer,* April 22, 1924.

"Corruption in high places"; "Women always are the wielders": *Louisville Courier-Journal,* April 25, 1924.

At noon on May 15: *Cincinnati Enquirer,* May 16, 1924.

permitted to exchange his prison grays: *Chicago Tribune,* May 17, 1924.

testified that Remus had a deal: Investigation of Hon. Harry M. Daugherty, 1482.

"with an intense and trembling earnestness": *Chicago Tribune,* May 17, 1924.

"mind had not been normal": Ibid.

"sacred and holy": Ibid.

"Every person who has one ounce": Ibid.

marking them with "J.S." in the corner: Ibid.

Remus would not be molested: Ibid.

"the general" would intervene: Ibid.

"You never had any doubt?": *St. Louis Post-Dispatch,* May 25, 1924.

"There was none from my viewpoint": Ibid.

"And you have been double-crossed?": Ibid.

"I don't know": Ibid.

"good secluded spots": Ibid.

"not favorable to letting him": Willebrandt to Harlan Stone, September 26,

1924, 23-1907, NARA.

She pleaded with the marshals: *Cincinnati Enquirer,* May 23, 1924.

"nothing or very little": *Palladium-Item* (Richmond, Indiana), May 27, 1924.

I had nothing to do with the alleged conspiracy: *Cincinnati Enquirer,* May 23, 1924.

two inmates managed a sensational escape: *Atlanta Constitution,* April 5, 1923.

"Several men are in the same cell" to **"is no less than criminal":** Willebrandt to her parents, April 15, 1923, MWWP.

"appeared half drunk, and talked most uncouthly": Brown, 92.

The Ace of Investigators

He felt depressed: *Ohio v. Remus,* testimony of Dr. Shelby Mumaugh, 40.

Remus prepared a signed affidavit: *Chicago Tribune,* August 29, 1924.

"not disposed to do anything for Remus": *St. Louis Post-Dispatch,* January 12, 1926.

Harr had recognized the ruse: *Ohio v. Remus,* testimony of Willie Harr, 1159.

Remus could provide Dodge: Rosenberg and Armstrong, 40–41.

"Play up to him": *Akron Beacon Journal,* October 10, 1927.

Testimony of Frieda Schneider: *Ohio v. Remus,* 178.

"told me that he secured": Rosenberg and Armstrong, 41.

"honest and informed": Ackerman, 376.

"Everyone says he's too young": Gentry, 125.

"Every effort will be made": Ibid., 128.

enough to indict eleven men: Rosenberg and Armstrong, 41.

"fascinating prettiness": *Atlanta Journal,* June 23, 1925.

"Much has been written": Ibid.

"Dear Mrs. Willebrandt, I am enclosing": Dodge to Willebrandt, General Correspondence, A-I, MWWP.

"done it all"; "Firing the men": Willebrandt to her parents, Christmas 1924, MWWP.

"clearing out the politicians": Ibid.

private two-room suite: *St. Louis Post-Dispatch,* January 12, 1926.

more, reportedly, than any person or institution: *Burlington Free Press,* May 20, 1925.

his own radio set: Ibid., May 25, 1925.

President Coolidge's inaugural address: *Pittsburgh Post-Gazette,* May 19, 1925.

"bachelor's apartment"; "take life languidly": *Palladium-Item* (Richmond, Indiana), June 4, 1925.

"cultivating" Dodge: *Times Herald* (Olean,

New York), October 10, 1927.

"Well, Daddy": *Ohio v. Remus,* testimony of George Conners, 1568.

I again sit down to write: Remus to Imogene, read during the probate testimony of George Remus, 364–365.

"misconduct": *Ohio v. Remus,* testimony of Willie Harr, 1183.

"insincere": Ibid., testimony of Emanuel Kessler, 99.

"He doesn't *want* to believe me": Ibid., testimony of Willie Harr, 1183.

A crimson flush spread: Ibid., 1175.

"Your visitor has contaminated": Ibid., testimony of Emanuel Kessler, 112.

"I will crack a skull": Ibid., testimony of Grace Campbell, 2505.

guards pried him from Harr: Ibid., testimony of Willie Harr, 1158.

Remus had apologized: Ibid., 1176.

Remus, Harr, and three others who had testified: Ibid., 1160.

offered circulating ice water: Zimmerman, 71.

Imogene took a room: *Ohio v. Remus,* testimony of Willie Harr, 1173.

Willebrandt had ordered three deputy sheriffs: Ibid., 1159.

special nights for white audiences: Smith and Boyle, 139.

even their "bottled in bond" whiskey:

Atlanta Constitution, October 4, 1922.
"Are you going out at night?": *Ohio v. Remus,* testimony of Willie Harr, 1175.
"Yes": Ibid.
"I don't understand why": Ibid.
after deliberating for sixteen hours: *Hamilton Evening Journal,* February 20, 1925.
My only wife: *Ohio v. Remus,* letter read during testimony of Dr. E. D. Sinks, 295.
often in Dodge's company: Ibid., testimony of Emanuel Kessler, 95.
"I don't think my wife is treating me right": Ibid., testimony of Willie Harr, 1183.
Testimony of Olive Weber Long: Ibid., 195.

A Disturbance in Room 902

"disregarding the solemnity": Brown, 168.
"Mr. Mabel Willebrandt": *Montana Standard* (wire service): November 11, 1928.
"She has managed things so expertly"; "Ask her about it": Ibid.
"Her features reveal"; "Her whole career": Ibid.
"a private affair": Willebrandt to her parents, December 1926, MWWP.
Fred's perplexing and irksome habits: Willebrandt diary entry for December 16, 1922, MWWP.

"I've been going to orphanages": Willebrandt to her mother, October 1, 1924, MWWP.

"I hope we *can* make some money": Willebrandt to her mother, March 22, 1923, MWWP.

"Dodge is said to be": *Cincinnati Enquirer,* March 20, 1925.

calling the agent her "confidant": *Detroit Free Press,* August 6, 1933.

violating the National Motor Vehicle Theft Act: FBI/DOJ file on Franklin Dodge, FOI/PA# 1346338, NARA.

Sweeney revealed that Dodge often took: Statement of E. J. Sweeney, FBI/DOJ file on Franklin Dodge, FOI/PA# 1346338, NARA.

"conferences with reference to Mr. Remus": Ibid.

"Frank, you are getting yourself"; "If George ever finds out": Ibid.

Dodge laughed: Ibid.

"Old kid": Ibid.

Sweeney dropped into the party: Ibid.

"What do you want the drawing room for?": Ibid.

Dodge smirked: Ibid.

"Frank, is she going with you?": Ibid.

"Well, I'm not going alone": Ibid.

"Frank, this woman is a scheming woman": Ibid.

Dodge laughed: Ibid.

He had heard a lady's voice: Statement of Carlos Clapper, FBI/DOJ file on Franklin Dodge, FOI/PA# 1346338, NARA.

pressed his ear against the door: Ibid.

A "Miss Conan": Ibid.

"Who is it?": Ibid.

"Mr. Dodge had his trousers on": Ibid.

"What are you doing in this room?": Ibid.

"I'm in there with my fiancée. She's sick": Ibid.

"Why didn't you notify"; "I'll get a doctor": Ibid.

"She doesn't need"; "She just has": Ibid.

"Because she has a headache": Ibid.

"all ruffled up": Ibid.

"Why did you allow this man": Ibid.

her "fellow": Ibid.

paying the bill for both rooms: Ibid.

Catalyst

"Bet you $200 to $100": Untitled clipping, Willebrandt file on George Remus, 23-1907, NARA.

"You're on": Ibid.

"hawk-eyed men": Lois Long, "And Those Were Tables for Two," *New Yorker,* February 17, 1940.

**"might just as well be called *Ten Nights on Long Island":* St. Louis Post-Dispatch,* April 25, 1925.

Dear Madam. As the date of my release: Remus to Willebrandt, August 6, 1925, Willebrandt file on George Remus, 23-1907, NARA.

"Sir"; "You can readily understand": Willebrandt to Remus, August 10, 1925, Willebrandt file on George Remus, 23-1907, NARA.

"the St. Louis crowd": *St. Louis Post-Dispatch,* Janaury 12, 1926.

"so considerate, so devoted, so faithful": *Minneapolis Tribune,* March 28, 1926.

ten and twelve at a time: *Ohio v. Remus,* testimony of George Conners, 1335.

first, second, third: Ibid.

"When you return": Ibid., read during the testimony of Ruth Remus, 2745.

"As we used to be": Ibid., closing argument of George Remus, 11.

Federal officials in Cincinnati: *Chicago Tribune,* August 1, 1925.

Dodge had accepted: FBI/DOJ file on Franklin Dodge, FOI/PA# 1346338, NARA.

introduced him to "Mr. Dodge": Ibid., statement of Will Schneider.

"Mr. Remus's goods": Ibid.

After they finished: Ibid.

"misunderstand": Ibid.

"doing business": Ibid.

"He is a very nice"; "I think he can be": Ibid.

Publicly, Dodge said: Dodge to Fiorello La Guardia, April 8, 1926, Willebrandt file on George Remus, 23-1907, NARA.

occasionally called "Mabel Jr.": Brown, 126.

Dorothy's honorary "aunts": Ibid.

"the dearest, wisest little two year old I ever saw": Willebrandt to parents, August 2, 1925, MWWP.

The girl already dressed herself: Brown, 124.

"an unusual find": Ibid., 126.

Willebrandt forced her daughter: Ibid., 128.

ten days before the expiration: *Ohio v. Remus,* testimony of John Snook, 1957.

caught giving "tips": Ibid., 1965.

"No," he said: Ibid., 1958.

"Why haven't you been staying"; "I had telegraphed": Ibid., 1959.

gone to Michigan "with others": Ibid.

"This is important business" to "handle by business": Ibid.

"I am afraid of him": Ibid., 1960.

"What are you afraid of?": Ibid.

"He threatened to strike me": Ibid.

"of such a character"; "traveling around with Dodge": Ibid., 1975–1976.

"affect his peace of mind": Ibid., 1976.

"a man of violent temper": Ibid.

"No, he is not going to strike": Ibid., 1960.

"I won't strike you": Ibid.

"little honey bunch"; "little bunch of sugar": Ibid.

"Just go over there"; "Sit down and finish": Ibid.

a small diamond ring: Ibid., 1961.

"I think it would be better": Ibid., 1964.

George, After our conversation today: *Danville Bee* (Virginia), November 16, 1927.

"although she has conducted herself" to **"enter suit for divorce"**: *Cincinnati Enquirer,* September 1, 1925.

She wished to reclaim: Ibid.

"represents that she is in great fear": Ibid.

"a very surprised man": *Ohio v. Remus,* testimony of John Snook, 1962.

Dear Imo, I was more than amazed at the abruptness: *Danville Bee* (Virginia), November 16, 1927.

the onset of his "diseased mind": *Ohio v. Remus,* testimony of Leo Burke, 600.

Testimony of Oscar Ernie Melvin: Ibid., 212.

PART II: CARELESS PEOPLE

A Bolt from the Blue

lost fifty-three pounds: Ibid., probate testimony of George Remus, 707.

"a Jewish comedian's": Ibid., testimony of John Theobald, 2130.

sent him a meager $100: Ibid., testimony of George Conners, 1499.

"Being in jail"; "I have not been able": *Miami News,* September 6, 1925.

"with the enthusiasm of any doughboy": Ibid.

"In prison here" to **"before my release":** Ibid.

Tears veiled his eyes: Ibid.

"I can't understand how anyone": *Cincinnati Enquirer,* September 3, 1925.

His voice broke: Ibid.

"She has been a real wife"; "Her action in bringing suit": Ibid.

"All right, George": *Ohio v. Remus,* testimony of John Theobald, 2130.

Remus arranged for groceries: Ibid.

"We're sorry you got" to **"you will be all right":** Ibid.

"No," Remus said quickly: Ibid.

"I don't know what to make of it": Ibid.

"Your bond in St. Louis": Ibid., testimony of George Conners, 1327.

Remus looked startled: Ibid.

"I had an inkling of it": Ibid.

He asked Conners why his bond: Ibid.

Mabel Walker Willebrandt was behind: Ibid., 1328.

"My God!" to "would do it": Ibid.

"I know it to be a fact": Ibid.

Remus started breathing heavily: Ibid.

He tried to calm him: Ibid.

She still loved him: Ibid., 1519.

"I understand that if they get me"; "Had you heard?": Ibid., 1332.

"I had," Conners said: Ibid.

"Were you surprised at Mrs. Remus": Ibid.

"I was not": Ibid.

"Why?": Ibid.

"Didn't you know about it?": Ibid., 1332–1333.

"No": Ibid., 1333.

"I know she had approached": Ibid.

"justified": Ibid.

"I know that little woman"; "There were some other": Ibid.

"My God" to "from Cincinnati": Ibid.

"She used to write ten or twelve"; "Sometimes in your home": Ibid., 1335.

"By God, Conners"; "I picked her up": Ibid., 1336.

gripped his old friend: Ibid.

"Control yourself!"; "The situation will work": Ibid.

"Maybe you are right": Ibid.

"When she wrote the note": Ibid., 1525.

Remus found a bondsman: *St. Louis Post-Dispatch,* January 12, 1926.

"What has become of my wife?": Ibid.

"She has gone away with Dodge": Ibid.

"With Dodge!": Ibid.

"Remus has been betrayed": Ibid.

"The Remus case is not in good shape": J. C. Dyott to Willebrandt, April 6, 1925, Willebrandt file on George Remus, 23-1907, NARA.

"at or near the town of Bedford, Ohio": Ibid.

"the notorious king of the bootleggers": *St. Louis Post-Dispatch,* August 6, 1929.

"the gentleman Remus": Ibid.

"the moving spirit": Ibid.

"Take me before a grand jury"; "I'll tell them all": Ibid., January 12, 1926.

He added that he was making: *Ohio v. Remus,* testimony of August Steinbach, 2261.

"I am George Remus": Ibid., testimony of Allen Curry, 878.

"Mr. Remus," Curry began: Ibid.

"Yes, that is what I came for": Ibid., 879.

"Now, Mr. Remus": Ibid.

"Curry" to "ruined my life forever": Ibid.

"He walked the floor": Ibid.

"Mr. Remus, sit down": Ibid.

"I want to know"; "I wasn't talking": Ibid., 879–880.

"I know that, Curry"; "I know that": Ibid., 880.

it could be mistaken for a child's: *Lansing State Journal* (Michigan), November 14, 1927.

"Oh": *Ohio v. Remus,* testimony of Allen Curry, 880.

"face was drawn": Ibid.

"He has taken my wife": Ibid.

"I am being watched by detectives"; "They have hired gangsters": Ibid.

Testimony of Orin Weber: Ibid., 1122.

Not Mrs. Remus Any Longer

"dealt in millions of dollars": *Ohio v. Remus,* probate testimony of George Remus, 15.

"a woman who is neither young nor pretty": *Brooklyn Daily Eagle,* January 1, 1928.

"She liked to have money": Ibid.

"not to squander": Ibid.

"broken, and in no condition": Ibid.

"mastermind": Ibid.

secured a change of venue: *Richmond Item,* November 7, 1925.

He now believed that Dodge: *Ohio v. Remus,* probate testimony of George Remus, 552.

eating at his table and sleeping in his bed: Ibid., testimony of William Mueller, 1411.

"in a compromising position": Ibid., probate testimony of George Remus, 552.

"dear"; "honey": William A. Cook, 104.

$150 to $200 per barrel: *Ohio v. Remus,* testimony of George Conners, 1351.

"It looks like now"; "I know she has pawned": Ibid.

"starry": Ibid., 1345.

His pupils disappeared: Ibid., 1336.

"It would be an angel of mercy": Ibid., 1411.

silent for ten minutes: Ibid., 1337.

He sensed that Remus: Ibid.

Finally Remus rose: Ibid., 1338.

his face twitched: Ibid.

Conners was so overwhelmed: Ibid.

"My God, just think of that": Ibid.

Conners counted twenty-five repetitions: Ibid.

"Did you ever think": Ibid.

He'd always thought she would: Ibid.

"I must have been blind": Ibid.

"Hello, this is Mrs. Remus talking": Ibid., 1350.

"Oh no" to **"what belongs to me":** Ibid.

"improper relations": *Marion Star* (Ohio), October 8, 1925.

She and Dodge had conspired: Ibid.

"squandered and dissipated": *St. Louis Post-Dispatch,* October 31, 1925.

"humiliation, mental anguish or embarrassment": *Cincinnati Enquirer,* October 8, 1925.

"absolutely absurd and false"; "very honorable woman"; "above reproach": Ibid., October 9, 1925.

"life and activities"; "mentally responsible": Ibid.

a suite at the Claypool Hotel: *Indianapolis Star,* October 28, 1925.

"I would be very reluctant" to "grants him any immunity": Willebrandt to John Marshall, October 23, 1925, Willebrandt file on George Remus, 23-42-28, NARA.

"It is of course realized"; "It is my opinion": Memo from John Marshall to Willebrandt, November 1, 1925, Willebrandt file on George Remus, 23-42-28, NARA.

"I must say to you": John Marshall to Willebrandt, undated, Willebrandt file on George Remus, 23-42-28, NARA.

"Mrs. Imogene A. Remus, 40 years": Report of Special Agent in Charge Eckart, November 16, 1925, Willebrandt file on George Remus, 23-42-28, NARA.

Detroit, Mich. — McLaughlin: J. Edgar Hoover memo to Willebrandt, November 27, 1925, Willebrandt file on George Remus, 23-42-28, NARA.

"Mr. and Mrs. E. J. Ward": Report of Agent R. P. Burhuss, November 20, 1925, Willebrandt file on George Remus, 23-42-

28, NARA.

"Have you seen either your wife"; "Have you in any manner": Ibid.

"I have not": Ibid.

"catch them together"; "nab": Ibid.

"I will get the house detective"; "I can hardly keep": Ibid.

The agent told Remus: Ibid.

"He was in a great agonized state" to **"puffing like a bull":** *Ohio v. Remus,* testimony of John Rogers, 1009.

city's first earthquake-proof building: *Los Angeles Times,* December 29, 1996.

"those delicious lazy Sundays": Willebrandt diary, entry for December 17, 1922, MWWP.

"never really belonged to anyone": Quoted in Brown, 136.

Dearest, The year is up: Letter to Fred Horowitz from Willebrandt, undated (circa December 1925), MWWP.

That Social Pervert, That Social Leper, That Social Parasite

final week of November: *Ohio v. Remus,* testimony of John Rogers, 297.

while investigating the Ku Klux Klan: *St. Louis Post-Dispatch,* March 4, 1937.

corrupt activities of a federal judge: Ibid.

"Unusual things in usual number": Ibid.

"the greatest correspondent in the

world": *Ohio v. Remus,* testimony of George Conners, 135.

the voice, low and gruff: Ibid., testimony of John Rogers, 298.

"Who is this?": Ibid.

"That doesn't make any difference": Ibid.

"How do you know": Ibid.

"Because Mrs. Remus and Dodge": Ibid.

"Paid what?"; "Fifteen thousand dollars": Ibid.

"To whom?"; "That is all": Ibid.

"Remus is here": Ibid.

"We will look out"; "We don't pay much attention": Ibid.

"There is evidently something": Ibid.

Imogene and Dodge had recruited: Ibid., testimony of John Marshall, 284.

"czarina of Prohibition matters": Ibid., probate testimony of George Remus, 552.

"has been intimate": Ibid., 37.

"Now listen"; "You are not going to leave": Ibid., 700.

rented a private apartment: Ibid., testimony of John Marshall, 974.

Secret Service men: Ibid., probate testimony of George Remus, 701.

Colt .45 revolver and some bullets: Ibid., testimony of Russell Moritz, 1991.

"full authority of the government": Ibid., probate testimony of George Remus, 701.

"I am his master"; "Physically": Ibid., 54.

"If there has ever": *St. Louis Post-Dispatch,* January 3, 1926.

"When I returned": Ibid.

That pimp Dodge"; "That social pervert, that social leper, that social parasite": *Ohio v. Remus,* probate testimony of George Remus, 39.

"mash"; "flat as a pancake, absolutely": Ibid., 758.

"cracked": Ibid., testimony of Paul Anderson, 1290.

"swelled like a cobra's": Ibid., 1288.

"If I could get": Ibid., testimony of John Rogers, 305.

"crack a skull": Ibid.

"Don't attempt anything like that"; "Don't resort to violence": Ibid.

"Don't talk to me of violence!": Ibid.

he had traveled to Atlanta: Ibid., 306.

Rogers called to make an appointment: Ibid., 289.

An article in that day's *Indianapolis Star*: *Indianapolis Star,* December 7, 1925.

Dodge opened the door: *Ohio v. Remus,* testimony of John Rogers, 289.

"I have got"; "You were present": Ibid., 290.

"You're misinformed" to "Union Station": Ibid.

"Well, we will": Ibid.

"In view of all the charges": Ibid.

"That's nobody's business": Ibid., 290–291.

"George Remus looks upon you": Ibid., 291.

"Well, if you want to know": Ibid.

"There naturally must be"; "More bad feeling": Ibid.

"Feel this muscle": Ibid.

"I have got this for Remus"; "I could crush him": Ibid.

"You are a large man": Ibid.

"Yes, I weigh": Ibid.

"Are you still": Ibid.

"No, I am not": Ibid.

"As a matter of fact": Ibid.

emerged with a letter: Ibid.

where two pistols lay: Ibid., 292.

"That is for Remus"; "That is all I have to say": Ibid.

twelve-by-fifteen-foot space: *Indianapolis News,* March 27, 1915.

gauger at the Jack Daniel's distillery: *Logansport Pharos-Tribune* (Indiana), December 15, 1925.

detailed the milking itself: *Sheboygan Press* (Wisconsin), December 15, 1925.

"bung starter": *St. Louis Star and Times,* December 15, 1925.

electric buzzer: *Noblesville Ledger* (Indiana), December 15, 1925.

"She had made rum-running": *Louisville*

Courier-Journal, December 17, 1925.

After breakfast at the Claypool: *Ohio v. Remus,* testimony of John Rogers, 288.

"Daddy, don't kill me!": Ibid., testimony of Paul Anderson, 1286.

Rogers gauged Remus's reaction: Ibid., testimony of John Rogers, 289.

"Look what a spectacle": Ibid.

"disappointed at efforts": *Indianapolis Star,* December 16, 1925.

tried to assassinate: *Ohio v. Remus,* testimony of John Rogers, 289.

Rogers was the lone reporter: Ibid.

"That's what I get": *St. Louis Post-Dispatch,* December 2, 1927.

Remus was remarkably calm: *Ohio v. Remus,* testimony of John Rogers, 1023.

"It takes two good men": Ibid.

The bootlegger lashed: Ibid.

Imogene made a prediction: *Louisville Courier-Journal,* December 17, 1925.

"We object": *Cincinnati Enquirer,* December 17, 1925.

"We feel": Ibid.

"It has appeared in the newspapers" to **"it failed utterly":** Ibid.

"If Mrs. Remus has": Ibid.

"This is going to be": *St. Louis Post-Dispatch,* December 2, 1927.

Testimony of John S. Berger: *Ohio v. Remus,* 1199.

"Looks like Dry New Year": *Santa Cruz Evening News* (wire service), January 2, 1926.

drinking levels plummeted: Okrent, 249.

Cirrhosis rates, fatalities from alcohol, and arrests: Jack S. Blocker Jr., "Did Prohibition Really Work? Alcohol Prohibition as a Public Health Innovation," *American Journal of Public Health,* vol. 96, no. 2, February 2006, 233–243; Okrent, 249; (Philip J.) Cook, 25.

"offenses against chastity"; "foul language": Okrent, 248.

"Sad Decline of Swearing Lamented": *New York Times,* September 14, 1924.

"the biggest joke": *St. Louis Star and Times,* November 4, 1926.

consuming more than ever before: Okrent, 249.

ten thousand new ones: Ibid., 257.

employing fifty thousand people: Ibid., 256.

one for about every 215 New Yorkers: *New York Times,* April 29, 2007.

"There is not less drunkenness": H. L. Mencken, "Five Years of Prohibition," *American Mercury,* December 1924.

Thirty-nine percent: Zeitz, 21.

**"embalmer"; "petting party"; "dropping the pilot"; "given the air"; "thrown

down": *The Flapper,* July 1922.

"When I was a girl"; "Now this so-called flapper": *St. Louis Star and Times,* April 23, 1925.

"a seething mob": Okrent, 254.

relied on liquor sale taxes: Ken Burns and Lynn Novick, *Prohibition,* documentary series, 2011.

enforcement of fishing and hunting laws: Okrent, 256.

a loss of $11 billion: Ken Burns and Lynn Novick, *Prohibition,* documentary series, 2011.

agents under the civil service: *Literary Digest,* March 19, 1927.

"I refuse to believe": Willebrandt, *The Inside of Prohibition,* 121.

"My dear Mrs. Willebrandt": Marshall to Willebrandt, January 20, 1926, Willebrandt file on George Remus, 23-1907, NARA.

"If anybody has any notion": Willebrandt memo to Howard Jones, Willebrandt file on George Remus, 23-1907, NARA.

"After what my wife has done": Clipping, untitled and undated, Willebrandt file on George Remus, 23-1907, NARA.

"He's from New York": Lerner, 238.

given to him privately: *Ohio v. Remus,* testimony of George Conners, 1372.

"Mr. Chairman and gentlemen": *Congressional Record* — House, March 24,

1926, 6174.

fearing he was not skilled: Ibid.

"When a United States official": Ibid.

"The gentleman has made a statement": Ibid.

"I will come to that"; "I will give his name": Ibid.

"In the early part of 1922": Ibid.

"Mr. Chairman, will the gentleman yield?": Ibid.

"I will yield later"; "The gentleman from Texas": Ibid.

"became very friendly": Ibid.

"keep Remus in jail": Ibid.

"persecution": Ibid., 6175.

"I think," he concluded: Ibid.

"I wish to ask the gentleman": Ibid., 6176.

"They are not unfortunate criticisms"; "Would not the gentleman": Ibid.

"No," Edwards said: Ibid.

"Ought we not to hold": Ibid.

"What do you want" to **"I would put him in jail":** Ibid.

"It is the liquor interests": Ibid.

"Surely the gentleman": Ibid.

"No," Blanton said: Ibid.

"I do condemn them"; "I had this knowledge": Ibid.

his colleagues gave him: Ibid.

fine silk suit and matching bowler: *Chicago Tribune,* March 25, 1926.

visit his daughter, Romola, and to save

1,550 cases: Ibid.

"He had three or four grievances": Ibid.

"They are getting wise" to **"no mistake in investigating Dodge":** Ibid.

"had remained true blue": Ibid.

"easy street": Ibid.

"I'm going to stay in Chicago"; "Real estate is going to be": Ibid.

A Pearl-Handled Revolver

"life of hell": *Ohio v. Remus,* testimony of Robert L. Dunning, 2454.

Remus had lost his mind: Ibid., testimony of John Rogers, 1016.

Raised veins laid tracks: Ibid., 1065.

"have wild drinking parties": Ibid.

without any connection between the two: Ibid., 1014.

made a pact: Ibid., 1049.

filed a lawsuit: *Louisville Courier-Journal,* May 24, 1926.

Organizing a fleet of trucks: *Star Press* (Muncie, Indiana), April 2, 1926.

"Imogene is in town": *Ohio v. Remus,* testimony of John Rogers, 292.

"Where is she?": Ibid.

"At the Alms Hotel": Ibid.

a box of candy: Ibid., testimony of Julia Brown, 2801.

Victory Parkway and Locust Street: Locust Street is now William Howard Taft

Road. Email from Alan March, January 28, 2019.

special entrance through the hotel garage: *Cincinnati Enquirer,* November 8, 1925.

"Here," he said: *Ohio v. Remus,* testimony of Julia Brown, 2802.

grabbing the lapels of his coat: Ibid.

"Daddy, I am so glad": Ibid., testimony of John Rogers, 293.

at the final second Remus turned: Ibid., testimony of John Conners, 1461.

"whiskey certificates": Ibid., testimony of John Rogers, 1033.

"I am glad to see Remus" to "a friendly settlement": Ibid., 293.

"Everything would be all right": Ibid.

"What is the matter with me?" to "cruel to you": Ibid., 294.

"friendly way": Ibid.

"Well," Imogene said: Ibid.

"All right, tell it" to "Go ahead and tell it": Ibid.

"Do you mean about Romola?": Ibid.

"Yes," she said: Ibid.

"Well, Romola is my daughter"; "You certainly don't object": Ibid.

"Well, that is it": Ibid.

"Is that all"; "Is that the only incident": Ibid.

"That is enough, isn't it?": Ibid.

"Well," he said: Ibid.

"a genteel lady of advanced years": Ibid., 1032.

"Mr. Rogers," she said: Ibid., 295.

"I will do all I can": Ibid.

"Well, you will be doing us": Ibid.

Mrs. Brown waved a hand: Ibid., 1038.

heading for the bathroom: Ibid., 295.

"I am awfully glad, Mr. Rogers"; "I understand he listens to you": Ibid., 295.

"I think a disinterested person" to "previous association": Ibid., 295–296.

"I fear the whole thing": Ibid., 296.

"What do you mean by that?": Ibid.

"I am afraid": Ibid.

"Oh," she said: Ibid.

"It should be obvious"; "He is the man": Ibid.

"Well, never mind"; "Mr. Dodge is our friend": Ibid.

"I was just telling Mrs. Remus": Ibid.

"Precisely," Remus said: Ibid.

"What are you people doing here?" to "right to be here": Ibid., testimony of George Conners, 1363–1364.

"Of course you have" to "go to a hotel": Ibid., 1364.

"for the purpose of trying": Ibid.

"I will settle this myself": Ibid.

Conners leapt from his seat: Ibid.

"That man cannot": Ibid.

"If you would be reasonable"; "fooling

around": Ibid.
he slipped the revolver: Ibid.
Testimony of Julia F. Brown: Ibid., 2787.

A Ghost at the Door

out with a cold: *Baltimore Sun,* June 8, 1926.
to be stored in Romola's apartment: *Ohio v. Remus,* testimony of George Conners, 1603.
nowhere to be found: Ibid., 1748.
"My god," he inevitably: Ibid., testimony of William Mueller, 676.
"red and bloated": Ibid.
Remus surrendered fifteen minutes early: *Cincinnati Enquirer,* July 2, 1926.
There were rumors he and Mrs. Remus: Ibid.
warned that no special courtesies: Ibid.
cell 13: Ibid.
"Hello, George! Remember me?" to "renew acquaintance": Ibid.
measured four by eight feet: *Ohio v. Remus,* testimony of John Theobald, 2162.
"the heavenly bodies above": Ibid., probate testimony of George Remus, 38.
wide, unbarred windows: Ibid., testimony of George Conners, 1394.
"I am sick just being": Ibid., 1387.
steam filled his stomach: Ibid., probate testimony of George Remus, 29.
"idiotic"; "This was started"; "I have

been": *Cincinnati Enquirer,* August 22, 1926.

a full transcript: *Ohio v. Remus,* testimony of George Conners, 1373.

"This was the first time the government": Ibid.

photostatic copies: Ibid., 1379.

various brokers arguing: Ibid., 1388.

"Where am I going to get lawyers": Ibid.

One anonymous letter: Ibid., 1397.

while running Jack Daniel's whiskey: *Cincinnati Enquirer,* October 29, 1927.

"a coward, and yellow"; "put a ghost at Remus's cell door": *Ohio v. Remus,* testimony of George Conners, 1397.

"That is Dodge's work" to "persecuting me in jail": Ibid.

"Does he always act this way?": Ibid.

his newspaper's recent photograph: *St. Louis Post-Dispatch,* October 10, 1926.

"infinite capacity for naughtiness": Brown, 129.

"marvelous": Ibid., 130.

"How is he getting along?": *Ohio v. Remus,* testimony of John Rogers, 300.

"Not so well": Ibid.

Willebrandt told Rogers: Ibid.

"His egotism knows no bounds" to "King of the Bootleggers": Dodge to Fiorello La Guardia, April 8, 1926, Willebrandt file on George Remus, 23-1907, NARA.

"reports of this character": Attorney General John Sargent to Fiorello La Guardia, June 8, 1926, Willebrandt file on George Remus, 23-1907, NARA.

ex-agent had threatened: Sweeney to Hoover, December, 22, 1926, FBI/DOJ file on Franklin Dodge, FOI/PA# 1346338, NARA.

"crucify Hoover": Ibid.

"explode the country": Ibid.

"positive documentary evidence": Hoover to Willebrandt, FBI/DOJ file on Franklin Dodge, FOI/PA# 1346338, NARA.

"whiskey parties with women": Wilcox to Hoover, FBI/DOJ file on Franklin Dodge, FOI/PA# 1346338, NARA.

"It is needless to say" to **"upon these matters"**: J. Edgar Hoover to Willebrandt, December 30, 1926, FBI/DOJ file on Franklin Dodge, FOI/PA# 1346338, NARA.

"I have read" to **"base prosecution"**: Willebrandt to Hoover, January 26, 1927, FBI/DOJ file on Franklin Dodge, FOI/PA# 1346338, NARA.

"there is nothing else": Ibid.

vanishing and appearing at whim: *Ohio v. Remus,* testimony of Dr. David Wolfstein, 2942.

"electrical stars": Ibid., testimony of Dr. Thomas A. Ratliff, 582.

"impelled": Ibid., testimony of Dr. K. L.

Weber, 798.

Testimony of Imogene Remus: Records of the Immigration and Naturalization Service, Subject and Policy Files, 1893–1957, RG 85, file 55438-947, NARA.

Don't Let Him Catch You Asleep

"Never mind looking for it"; "I have plenty more": *Ohio v. Remus,* testimony of William Mueller, 816.

carry every last plant: Ibid., 765.

replaced with the letters "F.D.": Ibid., testimony of Orin Weber, 1151.

ran behind the machine: Ibid., testimony of William Mueller, 766.

asking him to remove a clock: Ibid., 810.

"Why?" to "his little bundle": Ibid., 814.

even the lions were gone: *News Review* (Roseburg, Oregon), November 26, 1927.

"erroneous": George Remus memo, June 10, 1927, RG 85, file 55438-947, NARA.

uncle suggested that Remus: testimony of George Karg, RG 85, file 55438-947, NARA.

"George is a self-made man" to "help one in need": *Cincinnati Times-Star,* February 3, 1927.

"Do you know whether": RG 85, File 55438-947, NARA.

"Yes," Remus said: Ibid.

"The reason for this": Hoover to Wille-

595

brandt, January 29, 1927, Willebrandt file on George Remus, 23-1907, NARA.

"Remus is dying"; "He won't live his term out": *Ohio v. Remus,* testimony of George Conners, 1985.

she authorized and arranged: March 24, 1927, Willebrandt to Haveth Mau, Willebrandt file on George Remus, 23-1907, NARA.

Sheriff — Portsmouth, Ohio: *Ohio v. Remus,* probate testimony of George Remus, 548.

model prisoner: Ibid., testimony of Elza Canter, 2395.

trustee of the jail: Ibid.

He ran the kitchen: cooking three meals per day: Ibid., 2398.

he shopped at grocery stores: Ibid.

"mumpy neck": *Pittsburgh Daily Post,* April 24, 1927.

"Although Remus is short and stout": *Portsmouth Daily Times,* April 8, 1927.

"Get some camphor": *Ohio v. Remus,* testimony of Charles Hinea, 2238.

laid them on the prisoner: Ibid.

"If you make another trip": Ibid., testimony of George Conners, 1393.

"from alarm into an uncontrollable rage": Ibid., 1394.

"I have been informed": Ibid.

"I'm not ashamed" to **"compliments of George Remus":** *Portsmouth Daily Times,*

April 25, 1927.

"Do you think I'm crazy?": Ibid.

Testimony of George Conners: *Ohio v. Remus,* testimony of George Conners, 1421.

No Quarter

$250,000 advance: *Indianapolis News,* November 25, 1927.

Hollywood had already: *Cincinnati Enquirer,* April 26, 1927.

"Does Crime Pay?": *Cincinnati Enquirer,* September 3, 1925.

"I ask no quarter"; "Rather than bend one iota": Ibid.

a glorious night: Ibid., April 27, 1927.

padlocked shut: *Ohio v. Remus,* testimony of George Conners, 824.

third floor ballroom: *Escanaba Daily Press* (Michigan), December 3, 1927.

Marble statues had been kidnapped: Ibid.

Crystal chandeliers the size of his limousine: *Ohio v. Remus,* testimony of Dr. David Wolfstein, 2982.

The servants' clock: Ibid.

Sixty-three pairs of her shoes: Ibid., testimony of Benton Oppenheimer, 832–833.

An old cot and a pair of men's oxfords: Ibid., 833.

a "D" for Dodge: Ibid.

"Well, she left the water"; "I think I'll hop in": Ibid.

Anna and her husband, Gabriel Ryerson: Ibid., testimony of George Conners, 1400.

Fifteen minutes after the curtain rose: Ibid.

Sometimes they visited three theaters: Ibid.

"I see them right before me": Ibid.

the ten-year-old son poured liquor: Singer, 40.

a willful tangle of bare branches: *Daily Republican* (Rushville, Indiana), November 28, 1927.

Dodge had eaten breakfast: *Ohio v. Remus,* testimony of George Conners, 1411.

covering himself with carpets: Ibid., 1604–1605.

three hours of sleep per night: Ibid., probate testimony of George Remus, 942.

"in the grounds with flashlights": Ibid., testimony of George Conners, 1401.

"Did you see them?": Ibid.

"No, I didn't see any": Ibid., 1402.

caravan of cars: Ibid.

the watchman confirmed: Ibid.

"I have heard that Dodge"; "If I don't get ahold": Ibid.

catch them together personally: *Cincinnati Enquirer,* October 7, 1927.

numerous trips: *Ohio v. Remus,* probate

testimony of George Remus, 35.

"If I ever meet Dodge": Ibid., testimony of George Conners, 1411–1412.

"bias and prejudice": *Cincinnati Enquirer,* September 20, 1927.

hurl him out the window: Cook, 117.

he would be representing himself: *Cincinnati Enquirer,* September 20, 1927.

Tom Wilcox: *Ohio v. Remus,* probate testimony of George Remus, 60.

"assisting, aiding and abetting": Ibid., 208.

"not doing his legal duties": Ibid.

"inexcusable conduct"; "transactions of a questionable nature": Memo from Willebrandt to Howard Jones, March 15, 1927, Willebrandt file on George Remus, 23-1907, NARA.

"relations"; "the thing behind the thing": *Ohio v. Remus,* probate testimony of George Remus, 553.

It was why, Remus believed: Ibid.

new plot afoot: Ibid., 60.

"My god, she surely is" to "bound to get us": Ibid., testimony of George Conners, 1417.

raved and tore around: Ibid.

"They will never take me": Ibid.

Testimony of William Hoefft: Ibid., 753.

"I know how you could make"; "If you would kill a man": Ibid., testimony of Harry Truesdale, 1761–1762.

Marcus introduced Truesdale: Ibid., 1763.

half of the amount: Ibid., 1764.

"Who is this other party?": Ibid.

"Franklin Dodge": Ibid.

"very bitter"; "wished someone would beat": Ibid.

"What good would it do": Ibid.

"A lot of good": Ibid.

"Would it mean thousands?": Ibid.

"Yes," she admitted: Ibid.

"bumped off": Ibid.; *Journal Gazette* (Mattoon, Illinois), December 8, 1927.

Truesdale called Imogene: *Ohio v. Remus,* testimony of Harry Truesdale, 1766.

"I'm going away"; "I'm going to Michigan": Ibid.

bootleg liquor and subterranean rooms: *Journal News* (Hamilton, Ohio), June 3, 2005.

"Is that man with you": *Ohio v. Remus,* testimony of Harry Truesdale, 1774.

"He is" to "five thousand dollars": Ibid.

"If he should come up here": Ibid.

planning to double-cross him: Ibid., 1778.

hot stab of fear: Ibid.

"If I see him now": Ibid.

"He started raving" to "jump out of the

window": Ibid.
In that moment Truesdale didn't know: Ibid., 1779.
Testimony of Ethel Bachman: Ibid., 64.

Blood on the Primrose Path

"Be here about seven o'clock" to "over with her": Ibid., testimony of George Klug, 97–98.
"Would you like some refreshments?": Ibid., testimony of Gabriel Ryerson, 73.
"I'll be awfully busy"; "I want to get up": Ibid., testimony of Anna Ryerson, 84.
front page headlines: *Cincinnati Enquirer,* October 6, 1927.
"bobbed-hair passengers"; "I thought I knew something": Ibid.
Anna set a plate of pancakes: *Ohio v. Remus,* testimony of Anna Ryerson, 83.
"Good morning, Anna"; "How are you this morning?": Ibid., 457.
"Fine"; "Well, this is going to be": Ibid.
"Yes, Anna": Ibid.
She sensed that something: Ibid., 87.
Indian summer: *Cincinnati Enquirer,* October 6, 1927.
chocolate brown silk suit: *Ohio v. Remus,* testimony of Louis Schulze, 70.
fedora with the brim turned down: Ibid.
"When she comes out": Ibid., testimony of George Klug, 99.

601

"Why don't you go": Ibid.

"I want to talk to her": Ibid.

halo appeared above his head: Ibid., probate testimony of George Remus, 611.

black silk dress: Ibid., testimony of William C. Knight, 15.

"That answers it": Ibid., probate testimony of George Remus, 765.

"Catch that car": *Cincinnati Enquirer,* October 7, 1927.

"There is Remus": *Ohio v. Remus,* testimony of Ruth Remus, 27.

"Get ahead of it"; "I want to talk to her": Ibid., testimony of George Klug, 99.

"drive fast": Ibid., testimony of Charles Stevens, 44.

making a T and trapping her: Ibid., testimony of Ruth Remus, 29.

"I am afraid": Ibid., 28.

"Daddy dear, I love you"; "Daddy dear, don't do it!": Ibid., 506.

"She who dances": Ibid., testimony of Emmett Kirgin, 1.

"Do you know": Ibid., testimony of Ruth Remus, 507; *St. Louis Post-Dispatch,* November 25, 1927.

hands atop her head: *Ohio v. Remus,* testimony of Ruth Remus, 33.

Testimony of Ruth Remus: Ibid., 24.

"incredibly calm": Ibid., testimony of William Smith, 131.

"My God, somebody help": Ibid., testimony of Charles Stevens, 47.

"I am shot, help me": Ibid., testimony of William Smith, 131.

"Get in": Ibid., testimony of Evander Raulston, 111.

"Drive straight ahead": Ibid.

He heard the gunshot: Ibid.

"It is all right, go ahead" to **"It was Mr. Remus"**: Ibid.

"I don't want to go ahead"; **"The man who shot this woman"**: Ibid.

Ruth wrapped her arms: Ibid., testimony of Katherine Schulze, 112.

"Can I give you a lift?": Ibid., testimony of William Rulvershorn, 288.

"Yes!" Remus said: Ibid.

he'd like to go to the Pennsylvania Depot: *Cincinnati Enquirer,* October 7, 1927.

"Yes," the man agreed: *Ohio v. Remus,* testimony of William Rulvershorn, 288.

"Where are you going?": Ibid.

"Newport": Ibid.

"Are you going to meet anybody?": Ibid.

fidgeting and tugging around: Ibid., 288–289.

"not natural": Ibid., 292.

"Thank you for the lift"; **"What a beauti-**

ful morning it is": Ibid., 289.

steel gray stockings: *Cincinnati Enquirer,* October 7, 1927.

"I know I'm dying": *Ohio v. Remus,* testimony of Ruth Remus, 34.

"Oh, Mother": Ibid.

a scolding voice: Ibid.

"Yes I am"; "Isn't George terrible": Ibid., 35.

her twentieth birthday: Ibid., 34.

"I'm dying"; "Be a good girl": Ibid., testimony of Evander Raulston, 113.

"You don't know who I am": Ibid., testimony of William Hulvershorn, 575.

"No": Ibid.

"My name is George Remus": Ibid.

"Are you the Remus of liquor fame?": Ibid.

"Yes": Ibid.

The driver shook his hand: Ibid.

"I often heard of you": Ibid., 12.

"I did some shooting": Ibid.

"been ranting about the Remus case": Ibid.

"My mother is shot!": Ibid., testimony of William Knight, 14.

"Who is it?": Ibid.

"This is Mrs. Remus": Ibid.

"Who shot you?": Ibid.

"George Remus": Ibid.

"Your husband from Price Hill?": Ibid.

"Yes": Ibid.

He rotated in his seat: Ibid.

"Where did this happen?": Ibid.

"In Eden Park": Ibid.

"Why did he shoot you?": Ibid.

"He followed me from the Alms Hotel": Ibid.

The elevator operator brought them to the fifth floor: Ibid., testimony of Dr. Howard P. Fischbach, 171.

"Do you think I'm going to die?": Ibid., testimony of William Knight, 15.

"No," he assured her: Ibid.

"Do something for me": Ibid.

"doctors" . . . "get" . . . "busy": Ibid.

"statement": Ibid., 17.

pink slip was blackened: Ibid., 15.

Officer Knight examined its contents: Ibid., 16.

where he arrived at 8: 30 A.M.: Ibid., testimony of Emmett Kirgin, 1.

"I just shot my wife"; "My name is George Remus": Ibid., testimony of Frank McNeal, 10.

"Where did this occur?": Ibid., 11.

"Somewhere on the driveway": Ibid.

"What did you do with the gun?": Ibid.

"I lost that in the scuffle": Ibid.

Remus began to pace: Ibid.

"How many times did you shoot?": Ibid.

"I don't know" to "The gun jammed on me": Ibid.

"What became of her?" Ibid.

"This is the first peace": Ibid.

"Conscious but in a state of shock": Ibid., testimony of Dr. Howard Fischbach, 171.

A nurse administered an anesthetic: Keeling, 44.

the opening in her stomach: *Ohio v. Remus,* testimony of Dr. Howard Fischbach, 173.

safeguard the bullet: Ibid., 176.

a glimpse of the corpse: Rosenberg and Armstrong, 105.

to tell Franklin Dodge: Ibid., 104.

"She feared something like this"; "Remus appeared": *Akron Beacon Journal,* October 6, 1927.

"a state of nervous collapse": *Detroit Free Press,* October 9, 1927.

curled into a tight fist: *St. Louis Post-Dispatch,* October 6, 1927.

"Your wife just died": Rosenberg and Armstrong, 104; *Cincinnati Enquirer,* October 7, 1927.

"Very well, gentlemen": Ibid.

"What do you wish to say?": Ibid.

"What more is there to say?"; "It is the penalty": Ibid.

Ninth Street to Vine, Vine to Eighth: *Ohio v. Remus,* testimony of Edward Schwable, 408. In 1927, Ninth, Eighth, and Vine Streets were all one-way roadways (email from Alan March, January 28, 2019).

"If you take me out": Ibid.

"It is down this way": Ibid.

"Here is where the scramble happened": Ibid.

"Here is where we will find the gun": Ibid.

Remus helped in every way he could: Ibid., testimony of Charles Frick, 406.

"pure malice": *Rockford Republic* (Illinois), March 8, 1915.

"She made his life so miserable" to **"hurt a fly":** *Cincinnati Enquirer,* October 7, 1927.

PART III: THE COLOSSAL VITALITY OF HIS ILLUSION

The Smiling Charlie Taft

fourth floor of the courthouse: the 1927–1928 Williams Cincinnati City Directory.

genteel dances that ended promptly: "Mr. Taft's Murray Bay," *New Yorker,* September 4, 1926.

"Hell, no white gloves"; "Summer clothes": *Cincinnati Magazine,* August 1979.

"to confound all rules of deportment": Rosenberg and Armstrong, 76.

"Just imagine how I would feel": *Decatur Herald* (Illinois), May 6, 1930.

game of tag on the roof: *New York Times,* April 3, 1909.

"giant torpedos": Ibid., July 3, 1908.

"As to Charles": Ross, 147.

"He is so restless"; "It tires you to keep up with him": Rosenberg and Armstrong, 70.

"Gone fishing": *Cincinnati Enquirer,* June 29, 1983.

"There is no Republican way or no Democrat way": Rosenberg and Armstrong, 98.

"There is only an honest and efficient": Ibid.

"the only way of assuring": Ibid.

His father sent a letter: Wead, 213.

"He smiled me out of court": Solberg, 46.

"good guy and a straight shooter": *Nebraska State Journal,* June 27, 1937.

"He is generally neatly and well dressed": Ibid.

George **"Fat" Wrassman:** *Cincinnati Enquirer,* October 8, 1927.

Taft was hoping for a conviction: William A. Cook, 140.

Once a prosecutor himself: *Cincinnati Enquirer,* March 27, 1920.

"weak mentally from boyhood": Ibid., November 25, 1925.

aliéné: Fletcher, 262.

"Mr. Remus," he began: *Ohio v. Remus,* testimony of Robert L. Dunning, 2447.

"Very well, Doctor" to **"in every re-**

spect": Ibid.

"Your plea will not be insanity?": Ibid.

"Emphatically no": Ibid.

"the decomposed mass of clay": Ibid., testimony of Emmett Kirgin, 7.

"but a very shrewd": Ibid.

"this decomposed mass of clay and her pimp": Ibid.

"George Remus the millionaire": Ibid., 10.

"repressed excitement": *Sheboygan Press,* October 6, 1927.

"Are you insane?": *Ohio v. Remus,* testimony of Robert L. Dunning, 2448.

"Positively no": Ibid.

"No man could be perfectly sane": Ibid., testimony of Emmett Kirgin, 10.

"He's <u>abstract</u> in his thought"; "humanize": Brown, 116.

Willebrandt planned to recuse herself: Ibid., 77.

"Give Women a Fighting Chance": Willebrandt, *Smart Set,* February 1930.

REMUS KILLS SPOUSE: Willebrandt file on George Remus, 23-1907, NARA.

"The shooting was no surprise"; "I expected one of the couple": Untitled clipping, Willebrandt file on George Remus, 23-1907, NARA

"The Women in Remus's Life": *New York Daily News,* December 25, 1927.

"Mrs. Willebrandt is a very able woman";

"Certainly the outcome": Ibid.

Remus's Brain Exploded

The five-room suite: *St. Louis Post-Dispatch*, November 30, 1927.

permitted to receive visitors: *Indiana Gazette*, October 11, 1927.

changed into a gray jacket: Rosenberg and Armstrong, 105.

"liberty box": *Indiana Gazette*, October 11, 1927.

he'd bought her a revolver: *Chicago Tribune*, February 23, 1915.

cast by L. Frank Baum himself: *Los Angeles Times*, February 21, 1987.

"I love my father"; "He needs the love": Rosenberg and Armstrong, 105.

"I see the press is here" to "Well here it is": Cook, 121.

leapt a foot off the ground: Ibid.

"statesman discussing a topic": *Cincinnati Enquirer*, October 7, 1927.

"that piece of degenerated clay": Ibid.

"broke him": Ibid.

"owed this to society": Ibid.

"Why should I spend $8,000": *Detroit Free Press*, October 9, 1927.

"No doubt you had this all"; "It seems to me": *Cincinnati Enquirer*, October 7, 1927.

"Your youth excuses you" to "give himself up": Ibid.

"Here," Remus said: *St. Louis Post-Dispatch,* October 8, 1927.

"You are charged"; "What is your plea?": Ibid.

"Not guilty": Ibid.

"Are you ready": Ibid.

"I am": Ibid.

one from W. W. O'Brien: *Portsmouth Daily Times,* October 7, 1927.

"George Remus will defend"; "I am now George Remus": *Daily Republican* (Belvedere, Illinois), October 11, 1927.

Remus planned to hire him: *Cincinnati Enquirer,* February 10, 1952.

Remus scoffed at Taft: *St. Louis Post-Dispatch,* October 8, 1927.

"Do I look like" to "everybody else is crazy": *Cincinnati Enquirer,* October 8, 1927.

"I never saw him"; "He appears to be": *Ohio v. Remus,* testimony of John Rogers, 1057.

among her husband's offenses: *Cincinnati Enquirer,* September 16, 1925.

"At the earnest solicitation"; "Remus will handle": Ibid., October 14, 1927.

"I did what is usual": Hartog, 220.

"transport of frenzy": Alexis Coe, "By Reason of Insanity," *Lapham's Quarterly,* May 21, 2015.

Stanton giddily danced: *Washington Post,*

July 24, 1994.

"benevolent vampire": Paul, 31.

"[White] became blacker and blacker": *San Francisco Examiner,* May 18, 1947.

"I did it because he ruined": *Evening Star* (Washington, D.C.), March 4, 1907.

"for three years been suffering": *New York Times,* February 7, 1907.

"If the only thing that lies": *Lincoln Star,* April 11, 1907.

"not guilty on the ground of insanity": *New York Times,* January 22, 1910.

I shot her as she lay in bed: *Cincinnati Enquirer,* October 18, 1913.

"The rapid attainment": Krafft-Ebing, 206.

"The forms of disturbance": Ibid., 207.

"The whole condition presents": Ibid., 206.

"Gentlemen of the jury" to **"acquit him":** *Chicago Tribune,* March 5, 1914.

"to swear that Brutus" to **"I don't think so":** *Chicago Inter Ocean,* March 5, 1914.

"What! Remus insane?": *Cincinnati Enquirer,* February 10, 1952.

"Remus's brain exploded": *Lincoln Star,* November 14, 1927.

a fellow scion of Cincinnati society: *Cincinnati Enquirer,* February 6, 1927.

assisted Taft: Ibid., August 25, 1927.

Remus had allegedly killed: *Palladium-Item*

(Richmond, Indiana), October 28, 1927.

refused to sign a divorce settlement: Rosenberg and Armstrong, 172

part-owner of the Cincinnati Reds: Ibid.

Remus hadn't even bothered to prepare: *St. Louis Post-Dispatch,* November 22, 1927.

flip a quarter into their outstretched hands: Hotchkiss and Meyer, 28.

"smoking among women": *Baltimore Sun,* March 26, 1922.

TO BANKS, DEPOSITARIES: *Post Crescent* (Appleton, Wisconsin), October 12, 1927.

A certain "A. H. Holmes": *Ohio v. Remus,* testimony of Frieda Schneider, 178.

The manager showed Conners a picture: Rosenberg and Armstrong, 109.

knew nothing about it: *Cincinnati Enquirer,* October 26, 1927.

Dodge drove from Detroit to Lansing: Ibid.

"but only Dodge knows": *News Journal* (Mansfield, Ohio), October 11, 1927.

one foot wide and two feet long: *Ohio v. Remus,* testimony of Frieda Schneider, 186.

The Loosest Kind of a Tongue

"produce records in the department": *Cincinnati Enquirer,* October 21, 1927.

"persons who might be in possession":

Undated clipping, FBI/DOJ file on Franklin Dodge, FOI/PA# 1346338, NARA.

"Naturally we would make every effort": Basler to Hoover, October 27, 1927, FBI/DOJ file on Franklin Dodge, FOI/PA# 1346338, NARA.

"We are both engaged in investigating": Hoover to Basler, October 31, 1927, FBI/DOJ file on Franklin Dodge, FOI/PA# 1346338, NARA.

"pursue this investigative inquiry": Hoover to Wilcox, July 1, 1927, FBI/DOJ file on Franklin Dodge, FOI/PA# 1346338, NARA.

"The Remus Matter": Ibid.

"I understand from fairly reliable sources": L. C. Schilder to Hoover, October 31, 1927, FBI/DOJ file on Franklin Dodge, FOI/PA# 1346338, NARA.

"suite de luxe": *St. Louis Post-Dispatch,* November 30, 1927.

"What'll it be?": *Boston Record American,* September 25, 1971.

"Scotch, rye, bourbon or beer?": Ibid.

George Remus has more at stake: *Pittsburgh Press,* November 4, 1927.

"What would you say if" to **"will know him again":** Ibid.

"I would be happiest": *Tampa Times* (wire service report), October 12, 1927.

"ridiculous": *Indianapolis Star,* October 29, 1927.

two bank robbers had confessed: Ibid.

"He talks so much": Quoted in Rosenberg and Armstrong, 110–111.

"I think this fellow Remus"; "He is the only man": Rogers, 149.

High-Class Gentlemen

an absurdity that prompted questions: *Pittsburgh Press,* November 15, 1927.

was it truly possible: *Evening Journal* (Wilmington, Delaware), November 14, 1927.

attired in a blue suit: Ibid.

Paterson's Complete Ohio Criminal Code : William A. Cook, 127.

"liberty box": *Indiana Gazette,* October 11, 1927.

"To Daddy": *Evening Sun* (Baltimore, Maryland), November 14, 1927; *Cincinnati Commercial Tribune,* November 15, 1927.

"I'm sorry to meet you": *Evening Journal* (Wilmington, Delaware), November 14, 1927.

Deputy sheriffs turned: *Indianapolis News,* November 14, 1927.

"It is a most remarkable spectacle": *Cincinnati Enquirer,* November 18, 1927.

"König der Bootlegger": *New Yorker Volkszeitung,* October 22, 1927.

"a climber who could not": *Cincinnati En-*

quirer, October 31, 1927.

rubbed his hands to restore circulation: *Indianapolis News,* November 14, 1927.

to his right sat Taft: *Cincinnati Enquirer,* November 14, 1927.

On nearby Sycamore Street: Cook, 127.

"Call the jury": *Indianapolis News,* November 14, 1927.

seventy-five men and women: *Hutchinson News* (Kansas), November 16, 1927.

four peremptory challenges: Rosenberg and Armstrong, 116.

One man had served on a jury: *Cincinnati Enquirer,* November 15, 1927.

Another was deemed too old: Ibid.

Several women explained: Ibid.

"Do you know this man Conners": Rosenberg and Armstrong, 117.

"He's not my lieutenant": Ibid.

"With all due respect": Ibid.

Remus tore his glasses: William A. Cook, 131–132.

"I object to Mr. Conners"; "He is fully as high-class": *Cincinnati Enquirer,* November 16, 1927.

"Do you know this man Conners": *Lansing State Journal* (Michigan), November 15, 1927.

Remus circled his left arm: Ibid.

"There can be no reason": Ibid.

"Would the fact that I am charged": *Cin-*

cinnati *Enquirer,* November 16, 1927.

"It is ridiculous to think": Ibid.

"The claim of the defense": Ibid.

"Does the defense say": Ibid.

"The defense says that Remus": Ibid.

"How can the Court pass"; "It is necessary": Ibid.

"I don't think the Court"; "Our defense is insanity": Ibid.

"In other words"; "Your family affairs": Ibid.

"Gee whiz, that man Remus": *Lansing State Journal* (Michigan), November 16, 1927.

large woman dressed in black: Ibid.

old man who cupped his hand: Ibid.

"dee-fen-dant"; "vi-o-lay-shun": Ibid.

"I've been in the same kind of trouble": Rosenberg and Armstrong, 116.

"I do not believe in the business": *Cincinnati Enquirer,* November 16, 1927.

"Was the accused a free agent": Ibid.

more than two hundred tests: *Pittsburgh Press,* November 17, 1927.

a cigar maker, a baker, a painter, a produce dealer: Rosenberg and Armstrong, 122.

sequestered at the Hotel Metropole: Cook, 128.

but only after bailiffs: *Ohio v. Remus,* statement of Judge Shook, 557.

"The fact that I have": *Cincinnati Enquirer,* November 19, 1927.

"No, sir": Ibid.

"I object, if the Court please": Ibid.

"Well, the jury is not here": Ibid.

Remus punched the air: Rosenberg and Armstrong, 121.

"Oh, Your Honor, no" to "if the Court please": *Cincinnati Enquirer,* November 19, 1927.

"So far as I know": Ibid.

skin reddened by degrees: Ibid.

"A nice statement to be made"; "He knows that the defendant": *Tampa Times,* November 19, 1927.

his left arm spinning: Ibid.

"His face livid": *Cincinnati Enquirer,* November 19, 1927.

Tears streaked down: Ibid.

"He knows that in no Court of Justice"; "It has been the pleasure": Ibid.

He rotated and flailed: Ibid.

"Five hundred judges and members": Ibid.

He lumbered toward Taft: Ibid.

"A blind rage"; "completely out of control"; "his thick neck and stout body": Ibid.

He raised and lowered his arm: Ibid.

"Man," he boomed: *Tampa Tribune,* November 19, 1927.

"Get back there or I'll punch you!": *At-*

lanta Constitution, November 19, 1927.
"Bah!"; "You are no better": *Arizona Republic,* November 19, 1927.
Several bailiffs inserted themselves: Ibid.
"Mr. Remus," Judge Shook said: Ibid.
"Yes, thank you"; "How was that?"; "Did I make an impression?": *Lansing State Journal* (Michigan), November 19, 1927.
"Mr. Remus needs me now": Ibid., November 18, 1927.
"That was too heavy": *Danville Bee* (Virginia), November 14, 1927.
a bowl of Hasenpfeffer: *Lansing State Journal* (Michigan), November 18, 1927.
"Such a good boy"; "Poor boy": Ibid.
city firemen had long since: Email from Alan March, October 24, 2017.

Alienist No. 1

had an impressive résumé: *Ohio v. Remus,* testimony of Dr. David Wolfstein, 2910.
"transitory, maniacal insanity": Ibid.
"scrupulously" clean: Ibid.
where he shadow-boxed at 3 A.M.: *The Tennessean,* November 27, 1927.
"severe": *Ohio v. Remus,* testimony of Dr. David Wolfstein, 2929.
"in the right": Ibid., 2931.
"great strain": Ibid., 2933.
"Don't you think": Ibid.
"Well," Remus admitted: Ibid.

"Oh," Remus said: Ibid.

"harmonious": Ibid., 2940.

"in an insane manner": Ibid.

"a good mind": Ibid.

"About what time": Ibid.

"It began with rumors": Ibid.

"When did you first make threats": Ibid.

"I will get you": Ibid., 2941.

"symptoms of insanity": Ibid.

"When did you make up": Ibid.

"I heard she had sluggers": Ibid., 2942.

the weight of the gun in his hand: Ibid.

"Did you know you would": Ibid., 2943.

"uncontrollably insane": Ibid., 2944.

"I knew I would have to account": Ibid., 2943.

"When do you think you were sane": Ibid.

"Six or eight or twelve": Ibid.

"Why did you kill her?": Ibid.

"From principle": Ibid.

"laughing and joking": Ibid.

"Psychologists," Remus said: Ibid., 2944.

"My defense is going to be"; "I got Mr. Ellis off": Ibid., 2945.

Conspiracies

REMUS TRIAL ADMISSION: *Cincinnati Enquirer,* November 22, 1927.

sheaf of papers and a lemon sliced in two: Ibid.

"Each side will be" to "evidence will

bring out": *St. Louis Post-Dispatch,* November 21, 1927.

"Your Honor," he said: Ibid.

sucking audibly on the lemon: *Cincinnati Enquirer,* November 22, 1927.

"We're here to try the charge"; "Remus had the assistance": Ibid.

"It is conceded": *Ohio v. Remus,* general proceedings, opening statement of the prosecution, 24.

allow evidence for a scope of two years: *Cincinnati Enquirer,* November 22, 1927.

"After we have shown to you": *Ohio v. Remus,* general proceedings, opening statement of the prosecution, 41.

"The defendant in this case had expected": General proceedings, opening statement of the defense, 42.

"We expect to show you": Ibid.

"The evidence will disclose": Ibid., 44.

"very mental condition": Ibid., 48.

"even chandeliers and seats": Ibid., 52.

"I couldn't begin to mention" to **"attention to certain facts":** Ibid., 55.

"Pardon me"; "Does the record show": Ibid., 57.

"The reporter is taking everything": Ibid.

"Mrs. Remus made the statement" to **"tortured him":** Ibid., 58.

his own tears never came: *St. Louis Post-Dispatch,* November 21, 1927.

Alienist No. 2

"**mentally diseased**": *Ohio v. Remus,* testimony of Dr. Earl Armitage Baber, 2998.
"**a prolonged departure**": Ibid., 215.
"**Don't you know it is wrong**": Ibid., 207.
"**Absolutely**": Ibid.
"**Would it be wrong to kill Dodge**": Ibid.
"**Morally, no,**" **Remus said:** Ibid.
"**How do you reconcile it?**": Ibid., 205.
"**Why, most assuredly**": Ibid., 204.
"**I do not care**": *Cincinnati Enquirer,* December 16, 1927.

A Blank About Everything That Happened

"**I will ask if you**": *Ohio v. Remus,* testimony of Edward T. Dixon, 105.
"**I did**": Ibid.
"**Did you appear that morning**": Ibid.
"**I did not**": Ibid.
"**I will ask you if you know**": Ibid., 106.
"**We object**": Ibid.
"**Do you know of your own knowledge**": Ibid.
"**I do**": Ibid., 107.
"**Did he issue any subpoenas?**": Ibid.
"**May I be heard**": Ibid.
lemon for chewing gum: Rosenberg and Armstrong, 128.
"**There were many depositions**": *Ohio v. Remus,* testimony of Edward T. Dixon, 107.

"May it please the Court" to "referring to subpoenas": Ibid.

"Your Honor," Remus countered: Ibid., 108.

"Will Your Honor caution the jury": Ibid.

"How long have you known the defendant": Ibid., testimony of George Klug, 222.

"Since about 1919 or 1920": Ibid.

"How long have you known George Conners?": Ibid.

"All my life": Ibid.

"What time did you get up": Ibid., 225.

"It was around five o'clock that evening": Ibid.

"Don't you recall," he said: Quoted in Rosenberg and Armstrong, 130.

"No, I don't": Ibid.

"Didn't you make that statement to me?": Ibid.

"I don't think I did": Ibid.

"Don't you recall telling me you also saw": Ibid.

"I am not positive I seen": *Ohio v. Remus*, testimony of George Klug, 229.

"And do you recall telling me": Ibid.

"We are taken by surprise": Ibid.

"All right," Judge Shook said: Ibid.

"Between five and ten minutes"; "I didn't see anyone": Ibid., 231.

"Now do you recall, Mr. Klug": Ibid., 232.

"I did no such thing": Ibid.

"Who have you been talking to": Ibid.

"I have not been talking": Ibid.

"Do I understand you to say": Ibid., 233.

"We object to the form": Ibid.

"I submit to Your Honor": Ibid.

"We object"; "That is absolutely wrong": Ibid.

"And we move, Your Honor": Ibid.

"Before you went to Price Hill": Ibid., 308.

"I went over to Blanche Watson's": Ibid.

"Who went over with you?": Ibid., 309.

"Now we object to that": Ibid.

"Now, Your Honor"; "We are getting": Ibid.

"May I answer that": Ibid., 311.

"I want to hear from you": Ibid.

"The specific charge" to "wantonly killing the deceased": Ibid., 311–312.

"Is George Remus, the defendant" to "charged with this crime": Ibid., 312.

Judge Shook made a surprising ruling: Ibid., 334.

"Thank you, Your Honor": Rosenberg and Armstrong, 135.

Remus obeyed, laughing hysterically: *New York Times,* November 24, 1927.

"Thankful! Yes a million times": *Cincinnati Enquirer,* November 24, 1927.

Alienist No. 3

a consultant in psychiatry: *Cincinnati Enquirer,* December 31, 1948.

observed Remus in court: *Ohio v. Remus,* testimony of Dr. Charles E. Kiely, 182.

"kill Dodge if I ever got the chance": Ibid., 184.

"My mind was not definitely" to "the Alms Hotel": Ibid., 186.

"Who do you mean by 'they'?": Ibid.

Dodge and his wife, he answered: Ibid.

"some such notion in my mind": Ibid., 187.

"egotism"; "violent temper"; "a very dangerous individual": Ibid., 183.

The Arch-Conspirator of All Ages

In the interest of expediting the trial: *Ohio v. Remus,* general proceedings, 493.

"Basing our conclusion upon": Ibid., 565.

Taft, gleeful, suggested: Ibid.

"Absolutely not": Ibid.

"Your Honor," he said, voice quavering: Ibid., 567–568.

He dabbed at his tears: *Cincinnati Enquirer,* November 29, 1927.

"I have advised with them"; "But if either side": *St. Louis Post-Dispatch,* November 26, 1927.

"these honored alienists": Ibid.

625

"**wreathed in smiles**": Milton McKay, "Insanity: Another Legal Fiction," *The Outlook,* February 6, 1929.

winning convictions in all but one: *Cincinnati Enquirer,* January 10, 1926.

"**When did you first become**": *Ohio v. Remus,* testimony of A. Lee Beaty, 615.

"**removal proceedings**": Ibid., 616.

"**Mr. Beaty, from what you saw**": Ibid., 617.

"**I have**": Ibid.

"**Will you tell us what conduct**": Ibid.

"**He came into my office**": Ibid., 617.

"**Just what did he say about it?**": Ibid., 626.

"**He said that the government**": Ibid.

"**Were the officers high**": Ibid., 699.

"**One of them was very high**": Ibid.

"**You are not referring to**": Ibid.

"**I am not**": Ibid.

"**May it please the Court**": Ibid., 700.

"**Judge, I decline**": Ibid., 700.

"**Now Mr. Beaty**": Ibid., 701.

"**Mrs. Mabel Walker Willebrandt**": Ibid.

"**muscles became bound**": Ibid., testimony of Richard E. Simmons Jr., 722.

"**Are you twenty-one years**": Ibid., 724.

"**Yes**": Ibid.

"**That beautiful little daughter of innocence**": Ibid.

"**like a man hitting a boiler**": Ibid.

He had been accused of being a drunk-ard: Ibid.

"Did you at any time": Ibid.

Yes, Simmons said: Ibid., 725.

"Wait a minute," he said: Ibid., 728.

"diseased mind": Ibid., testimony of Leo Burke, 600.

"I am very much interested" to "he is insane": Taft to Dr. Henry Coe, November 25, 1927, William Howard Taft papers, Library of Congress, Washington, D.C.

Déjà Vu in Price Hill

"Remus has a witness here": Taft to Willebrandt, November 26, 1927, Willebrandt file on George Remus, 23-1907, NARA.

"parade": *Palm Beach Post,* November 25, 1927.

Franklin Dodge had been subpoenaed: *Arizona Republic,* November 29, 1927.

She'd discovered that J. Edgar Hoover: FBI/DOJ file on Franklin Dodge, FOI/PA# 1346338, NARA.

ordered a halt on his activities: Hoover to Luhring, December 28, 1927, FBI/DOJ file on Franklin Dodge, FOI/PA# 1346338, NARA.

"My name is Allen Curry": *Ohio v. Remus,* testimony of Allen Curry, 877.

"Do you know the defendant": Ibid.

"I seen him one time"; "Just previous to

the finding": Ibid.

While Elston continued his questioning: *St. Louis Post-Dispatch,* November 29, 1927.

"Do you know Curry?": Ibid.

"I know plenty": Ibid.

"What opinion did you form"; "That he was sane or insane?": *Ohio v. Remus,* testimony of Allen Curry, 880.

"My opinion was that": Ibid.

"Will you tell us why you sent for him?": Ibid., 890.

"I sent for him because at the time": Ibid.

"You mean Mrs. Willebrandt?": Ibid.

"Mrs. Willebrandt from the Attorney General's": Ibid.

"Now Mr. Curry" to "resignation by request?": Ibid., 905.

"No, sir, it was not": Ibid.

"Was your resignation," Basler said slowly: Ibid.

"No sir," Curry said: Ibid., 906.

"Because you were involved": Ibid.

"No sir": Ibid.

"for malefeasance of duty": Ibid.

"No sir": Ibid.

a brainstorm in the car: Ibid., testimony of George Conners, 1342.

"He grabbed me" to "into it right now": Ibid., 1342–1343.

"I stayed with him all night": Ibid., 1343.

"We tried to get in"; "Mr. Remus broke

a window": Ibid., 1343–1344.

"May we have the time": Ibid., 1344.

"Give the dates": Ibid.

"Possibly between the 17th and 22nd": Ibid.

"A lot of the furniture was crated": Ibid.

fainted, falling stiffly: Ibid., 1345.

"I wanted to get a doctor": Ibid.

"The hell you could not!": Ibid.

"He was in the same condition" to "What do you want?": Ibid.

"I am Conners"; "Don't you know me?": Ibid.

"Oh": Ibid.

"We got into Cincinnati" to "frequent rages": Ibid., 1399.

"Mr. Conners," Elston said: Ibid., 1428.

"Yes sir"; "I reached the opinion": Ibid.

"The question asked was": Ibid.

"Insane": Ibid.

"When was it that Remus got": Ibid., testimony of William Mueller, 931.

"The latter part of April, in 1926": Ibid.

"You mean last April"; "That is '27": Ibid.

" '27, yes sir": Ibid.

"And didn't he get into the house": Ibid.

"I didn't know he broke": Ibid.

"You were not there": Ibid., 932.

"Yes, sir": Ibid.

"And you know all the furnishings": Ibid.

"Yes, sir": Ibid.

"And Remus went all through the house": Ibid.

"Yes, sir": Ibid.

"Were there any outbursts": Ibid., 933.

"No, sir": Ibid.

"None at all?": Ibid.

"No, sir": Ibid.

"When did you first become acquainted": Ibid., testimony of Benton Oppenheimer, 828.

"In the early part": Ibid.

"When we got out there": Ibid., 831.

"From all that you observed": Ibid., 847.

"I reached the conclusion": Ibid.

"I got him out": Ibid., testimony of Clarence Owens, 1304.

"So I came and met him" to **"talking to himself"**: Ibid., 1304–1305.

"Now," Elston said: Ibid., 1309.

"I reached the conclusion": Ibid.

"During the time": Ibid., testimony of Paul Y. Anderson, 1285.

"I met him at George Conners's house" to **"all the furniture"**: Ibid., 1289.

"Anderson," he said: Ibid.

"He began raving": Ibid., 1290.

"From what you saw": Ibid.

"Well," Anderson said: Ibid.

"every angle": Ibid., testimony of Manuel Rosenberg, 706.

"Were you ever out": Ibid., 707.

"The day he came back" to **"condition of**

the house": Ibid.

"Now I wish you would describe": Ibid., 708.

"Well, he was quite wild" to "a very peculiar manner": Ibid., 708–709.

"Did you reach any conclusion": Ibid., 713.

"I didn't give it": Ibid.

1924 newspaper advertisements: *Cincinnati Enquirer,* June 29, 1924.

"I did not know that he had been out there": *Ohio v. Remus,* testimony of Benton Oppenheimer, 855.

"Well," Basler countered: Ibid.

"Now we object" to "all mixed up": Ibid.

"I think I am not mixed": Ibid.

"snorted derisively": *New York Daily News,* November 26, 1927.

the black dress: Ibid.

she laughed even louder: Ibid.

"In the court room daily he smiles" to "get away with anything": *News Journal* (Mansfield, Ohio), December 4, 1927.

Sun in Scorpio

"Harry Truesdale": *Ohio v. Remus,* testimony of Harry Truesdale, 1759.

"Do you know George Remus": Ibid.

"One time I thought": Ibid., 1766.

a deep and resonant sob: *Cincinnati Enquirer,* December 8, 1927.

"Will you adjourn Court": Ibid.

sitting by her father's side: Ibid.

"Excuse me, Your Honor"; "I couldn't help it": Ibid.

"there burst from his throat": Ibid.

"It was evident to the spectators": Ibid.

Bailiffs hovered over him: Ibid.

"Will this never end?": Ibid.

"Persecution!": Ibid.

"the defendant is unable": Ibid.

"We find that Mr. George Remus": Ibid.

"the weeping, crying, Remus": *Ohio v. Remus,* testimony of Clarence Darrow, 1840.

calmly conferred with Remus: *St. Louis Post-Dispatch,* December 8, 1927.

members of the Astrologers Guild: *Cincinnati Enquirer,* December 6, 1927.

Very Emotional, Somewhat Unstable

Remus wept at the sight: *The Bee* (Danville, Virginia), December 8, 1927.

My friend, this is wonderful"; "I can never repay": Ibid.

"Your Honor," he said: Ibid.

"I'd sell you my job": Cook, 151.

"Where do you reside": *Ohio v. Remus,* testimony of Clarence Darrow, 1821.

"Chicago": Ibid.

soft, tumbling baritone: *Lansing State Journal* (Michigan), December 8, 1927.

"How long have you been a lawyer?":
Ohio v. Remus, testimony of Clarence
Darrow, 1821.

"Do you have the means": Ibid., 1822.

"I think so, yes": Ibid.

"What was that reputation?": Ibid.

"It was good": Ibid., 1823.

"We object"; "This witness's knowledge": Ibid.

"Did you have the means of knowing":
Ibid., 1825.

"I never heard it questioned"; "I will say
it was good": Ibid.

"Did you have the means of knowing":
Ibid.

Darrow folded his arms: *Journal and Courier* (Lafayette, Indiana), December 8,
1927.

"I never heard it questioned": *Ohio v.
Remus,* testimony of Clarence Darrow,
1826.

"We object, Your Honor"; "We fail to
see": Ibid., 1828.

"May I be heard?": Ibid., 1829.

"Proceed": Ibid.

"Your Honor," Remus began: Ibid.

punched his handkerchief: *Cincinnati Enquirer,* December 9, 1927.

"Mr. Darrow," he croaked: *Ohio v. Remus,*
general proceedings, 1832.

"Did you ever hear him argue a case":

Ibid., 1840.

"I never heard him": Ibid.

He leaned forward in his chair: *Cincinnati Enquirer,* December 9, 1927.

"Don't you know," Taft continued: *Ohio v. Remus,* testimony of Clarence Darrow, 1840.

Darrow's fingers traced the railing: *Cincinnati Enquirer,* December 9, 1927.

"I knew he was a very emotional fellow": *Ohio v. Remus,* testimony of Clarence Darrow, 1840.

"Well, now, you have stated": Ibid., 1842.

"Yes": Ibid.

"When you said that": Ibid.

"I didn't know that": Ibid.

"Don't you know," Taft said: Ibid., 1846.

Agents had discovered that fifteen barrels: Cook, 27.

"I would not regard an indictment as affecting": *Ohio v. Remus,* testimony of Clarence Darrow, 1846.

"And would you still regard him": Ibid.

Darrow's eyes strayed: *Chicago Tribune,* December 9, 1927.

"I know a good many": Ibid.

"very exhaustive": *Cincinnati Enquirer,* December 16, 1927.

"unanimously found him sane": *News Messenger* (Fremont, Ohio), December 16, 1927.

"in an insane manner": Rosenberg and Armstrong, 212.

repeated at least one hundred times: Ibid.

"Mr. Remus's face was red": Ibid., 213.

these reactions were appropriate: *Detroit Free Press,* December 17, 1927.

"allied with an insane state of mind": Ibid.

a grand and effusive smile: Rosenberg and Armstrong, 214.

"Would the firing of a shot": *Detroit Free Press,* December 18, 1927.

"That would all depend"; "The aberration present at that time": Ibid.

"Julius Caesar was considered a lunatic?": *Ohio v. Remus,* testimony of Dr. E. A. Baber, 3021.

no such term as *lunatic:* Ibid., 3022.

"Was Nero considered": Ibid.

"I don't remember any such event": Ibid., 3023.

"There is only one way": *Chicago Tribune,* December 18, 1927.

"back on the street": Ibid.

"Finally," Taft said: Ibid.

"Well, poor fellow" to "ace of the Prohibition department?": Ibid.

"He didn't dare take the stand": *St. Louis Post-Dispatch,* December 17, 1927.

smirking at Remus: Ibid.

"He was afraid" to "take the stand": Ibid.

635

"George Remus had the big head" to "He killed her": Ibid.

"Mr. Taft has told you considerable" to "he got out of it": *Chicago Tribune,* December 18, 1927.

"There is a claim" to "follow her to": Ibid.

a miniature pine tree: *Cincinnati Enquirer,* December 21, 1927.

a victim of tertiary syphilis: Email from Sharon Calder, November 9, 2016.

"I have been under subpoena" to "I fail utterly to understand": *Cincinnati Enquirer,* December 18, 1927.

"big bootleggers": *Austin American,* January 21, 1928.

escaping rumors in Washington: Brown, 173.

"Come right up": *Troy Record* (New York), November 19, 1954.

"In the courtroom" to

"good lead": Ibid.

a gray suit: Ibid.

"Christmas jury": Ibid.

sprig of holly: Ibid.

"Ladies and gentlemen"; "And there, in that empty chair": Ibid.

"Great!": Ibid.

"Fancy yourself in prison" to "Wouldn't it?": Ibid.

"I think Charlie has a pretty hard fight": William Howard Taft to Robert Taft, De-

cember 11, 1927, William Howard Taft
papers, Library of Congress, Washington,
D.C.
**"from one of the underworld in St.
Louis":** William Howard Taft to Helen,
December 11, 1927, William Howard Taft
papers, Library of Congress, Washington,
D.C.
"I am afraid about Charlie": Ibid.

American Justice

Sheriffs flourished clubs: *Cincinnati Enquirer,* December 20, 1927.
"Here before you stands": Ibid.
swinging his arm: Ibid.
"sits Remus, the defendant": Ibid.
250-pound deputy: *Troy Record* (New York),
November 19, 1954.
"May it please the Court" to **"you must
forgive me":** *Ohio v. Remus,* closing argument of George Remus, 1.
"What is the meaning of insanity" to **"of
necessity, abnormal":** Ibid., 3.
"the unfortunate death of the deceased":
Ibid., 5.
"embryonical condition": Ibid.
"Is there any question in your minds" to
**"ace of the Prohibition Department
—":** Ibid., 5–6.
"This social leper": Ibid., 6.
"And when I see beautiful Mrs. Bruck"

to **"I say not"**: Ibid., 13–14.

"He shouted" to **"bowed himself almost double"**: *Cincinnati Enquirer,* December 20, 1927.

"Some of the things that the unfortunate": *Ohio v. Remus,* closing argument of George Remus, 16.

"After years of incarceration": Ibid., 19.

"And then the high-handed methods" to **"selling good liquor —"**: Ibid.

"Do you folks think" to **"own five senses"**: Ibid., 23.

"The defendant started his life" to **"Mr. Charles P. Taft the Second —"**: Ibid., 24.

"civilized country"; **"what everlasting gratitude"**: Ibid., 29.

"to the tune of three thousand": Ibid.

"if the said defendant goes down": Ibid., 30.

"the deceased, with this moral pervert": Ibid., 41.

"Your time is up now": Ibid., 42.

"Thank you, Your Honor": Ibid.

"into the good graces": Ibid., 47.

"That is the principle upon which": Ibid., 51.

"You have five minutes left": Ibid., 52.

"Let every one of you" to **"the defendant won't flinch"**: Ibid., 55.

"The defendant stands before you" to "Merry Christmas to you": Ibid., 56–57.

With a bow: *Cincinnati Enquirer,* December 20, 1927.

"It was only right at the end": *Anaconda Standard* (Montana), December 20, 1927.

"failed to click": *Cincinnati Enquirer,* December 20, 1927.

offered five possible verdicts: Ibid., December 21, 1927.

"In support of this defense" to "bad moral character": Ibid.

If they hadn't reached a verdict by 1: 15: *Chicago Tribune,* December 21, 1927.

The ballot he wanted: Ibid.

At 2:54 P.M.: *Cincinnati Enquirer,* December 21, 1927.

"Have you agreed upon a verdict?": Ibid.

"We have, Your Honor": Ibid.

horn-rimmed glasses: Ibid.

His skin was pale: Ibid.

"You will give your verdict": Ibid.

"We, the jury, on the issue joined": Ibid.

"Keep quiet! Keep quiet!": Ibid.

He rose unsteadily: Ibid.

"This is American justice": *Chicago Tribune,* December 21, 1927.

"Thank you, thank you!": *Cincinnati Enquirer,* December 21, 1927.

"Sit down, sit down!": Ibid.

"Ha, ha, ha, he, he, he": Ibid.

"Not guilty — hooray! Not guilty — hooray!": Ibid.

"And I don't have the least idea": *Chicago Tribune,* December 21, 1927.

"Thank God!": *Cincinnati Enquirer,* December 21, 1927.

"gross miscarriage of justice": *Chicago Tribune,* December 21, 1927.

"I see that that which we expected" to **"such a mess"**: William Howard Taft to Horace Taft, December 21, 1927, William Howard Taft Papers, LOC.

"Do you know what we termed it" to **"he wasn't last Christmas"**: *Chicago Tribune,* December 21, 1927.

gazing at Remus as she spoke: Ibid.

"As the evidence unfolded" to

"justified in what he did": Ibid.

"Why did you decide": Ibid.

"We felt that Remus"; "One of the factors": Ibid.

"most unruly client": *Cincinnati Enquirer,* December 21, 1927.

"Thank God for a verdict" to **"have to acquit me"**: Ibid.

famed reporter for the *New York World:* William A. Cook, 168.

Remus decided that pictures: Ibid.

enjoy a drink or two: *Times Recorder* (Zanesville, Ohio), February 11, 1928.

"The damnedest thing I ever saw"; "Is that the way": *Cincinnati Enquirer,* December 21, 1927.

"immediately freed": Ibid., December 23, 1927.

"This petition is the most intolerable": *New York Daily News,* December 25, 1927.

"Broadway salaries": *Cincinnati Enquirer,* December 30, 1927.

"merest little appearance": Ibid.

"Twelve Good Men and True": Ibid.

Probate Court Testimony of George Remus: *Ohio v. Remus,* probate testimony of George Remus, 43–44.

The Unfortunate Woman

"histrionic, an actor, and a bad actor at that": *Ohio v. Remus,* testimony of Charles E. Kiely, 122.

"a very dangerous man to be at liberty": Ibid., 183.

"a psychopath": Rosenberg and Armstrong, 240; *Cincinnati Enquirer,* December 31, 1927.

"until such time": *Cincinnati Enquirer,* December 31, 1927.

**representative from the *New York Times:* ** *New York Times,* December 31, 1927.

"Well, what about it" to "a farce": Ibid.

"The alienists had better" to "nine wonders of the world": Ibid.

"Remus elected to profit": *Cincinnati Enquirer,* January 2, 1928.

"When a man of violent": Ibid.

"The most disgusting thing" to **"institutions to hold them"**: Clipping, Willebrandt file on George Remus, 23-1907, NARA.

"Now how about Dodge?" to "Federal Prohibition agent?": Quoted in *Cincinnati Enquirer,* January 2, 1928.

"Now that the Remus trial": Hoover to Luhring, December 28, 1927, FBI/ DOJ file on Franklin Dodge, FOI/PA# 1346338, NARA.

"As to the first lead" to **"General Willebrandt's division"**: Luhring to Hoover, January 12, 1928, Willebrandt file on George Remus, 23-1907, NARA.

"No need": Memorandum to "Mrs. Willebrandt" from J. Edgar Hoover, January 20, 1928, Willebrandt file on George Remus, 23-1907, NARA.

Elston and two deputy sheriffs arrived: *Cincinnati Enquirer,* January 7, 1928.

Remus joined the church choir: *Wisconsin Daily Herald* (Wausau, Wisconsin), January 9, 1928.

three of whom were hired: Rosenberg and Armstrong, 241.

"I am surprised at your stand" to **"my plea of sanity"**: *Cincinnati Enquirer,* February 24, 1928.

"confusion of mentality from worry": *Ohio v. Remus,* testimony of Dr. Shelby

Mumaugh, 66.

"fury and violence": Ibid., 84.

"sane beyond a doubt": Ibid., 11.

"head of a powerful mind": Ibid., testimony of Dr. C. L. Steer, 271.

"deviate": Ibid., testimony of Dr. P. I. Tussing, 207.

pregnancy or menopause: Ibid.

"learned a good deal"; "probably would think it over": Ibid., 198.

"morally and legally wrong": Ibid., 213.

"very cheerful": Ibid.

"I am fifty years old" to "bygones are bygones": Ibid., testimony of Dr. C. L. Steer, 310.

"take care of Dodge": Ibid.

"grandiose ideas": Ibid., testimony of K. L. Weber, 790. 306

"big": Ibid., 835.

"That in itself doesn't mean so much": Ibid.

"react unpleasantly": Ibid., 791.

"It's wonderful"; "I knew they would believe": *Cincinnati Enquirer,* March 31, 1928.

"the fight to keep Remus behind bars": *New York Times,* March 30, 1928.

"It may be"; "We frankly say": Ibid.

"I am leaving for Cincinnati" to "With love, Father": *Cincinnati Enquirer,* June 21, 1928.

"I am very, very happy"; "I shall open": Ibid.

"The unfortunate woman" to **"like a mermaid":** *Washington Post,* April 28, 1938.

A Hammer to the Angels

Easter egg hunt: *Cincinnati Enquirer,* April 20, 1930.

Dodge was indicted: *Lansing State Journal* (Michigan), November 8, 1930.

contradicted reports he'd submitted to Willebrandt: Ibid., November 28, 1930.

who had offered Dodge the position: Cook, 187.

"highly disturbing"; "set the public literally aghast": *Michigan Daily Globe,* (Ironwood, Michigan), August 7, 1933.

perfect for the job: *Akron Beacon Journal,* June 2, 1934.

"gagged, muzzled and prevented": James Yearsley to Willebrandt, February 9, 1928, Willebrandt file on George Remus, 23-1907, NARA.

"human filth of rubbish in America": Cecil F. Bates to Willebrandt, July 26, 1928, Willebrandt file on George Remus, 23-1907, NARA.

"Well, you know Remus" to **"a woman, to accomplish":** A Price Hill resident to Willebrandt, September 3, 1928, Willebrandt file on George Remus, 23-1907, NARA.

the most shabbily dressed man: Brown, 66.

Willebrandt took every precaution: *New York Times,* June 30, 1928.

"Hello, suckers!": Peretti, 109.

"the most outraged and cruelly treated": Ibid.

"Governor Smith's prohibition plan": Ibid.

"whispering campaign": *St. Louis Star and Times,* September 25, 1928.

"Prohibition Portia": *St. Louis Post-Dispatch,* October 15, 1961.

"laid herself open": Quoted in William A. Cook, 182.

"To judge the story of your life": Brown, 168.

"just too much": Ibid.

Willebrandt spent a night driving: Ibid.

"no other woman has ever had": *Los Angeles Times,* July 2, 2000.

"Anyone on the line?" to "It will be best for you": Brown, 175.

"I was intensely *hurt*": Ibid.

more than 160,000 Prohibition-related cases: Ibid., 75.

presented 278 cases before the Supreme Court: Willebrandt, *The Inside of Prohibition,* 239.

"her graceful tailored figure"; "a regular adornment": Brown, 75.

"No political, economic or moral issue": Willebrandt, *The Inside of Prohibition,* 15.

"repulsive facts": Ibid., 55.

"psychological damage": Ibid., 118.

"bad odor"; "folly": Ibid., 132.

Willebrandt choosing all of the furniture: Ibid.

"I do not conduct my private practice": *Baltimore Sun,* November 22, 1930.

She worried not about the press: Brown, 182–183.

"Official investigations into the political beliefs": Ibid., 237.

"You know my affinity" to **"luck for Nixon":** Ibid., 251.

"I realized how many times" to **"things that tarnish":** Ibid., 259.

"pretty cute": Ibid., 260.

A gusty wind toppled her: Ibid., 261.

"flew like the man on the trapeze": Ibid.

"reasonably moderate rate": Ibid., 262.

"care any more": Ibid.

"If Mabel had worn trousers": *Los Angeles Times,* July, 2, 2000.

"They have in their hearts" to **"by our lawmakers":** Charles P. Taft II, "So This Is Justice," *World's Work,* May 1928.

"The utter absurdity of entrusting": Ibid.

"It was," the paper wrote: *Cincinnati Enquirer,* December 4, 1983.

"your petitioner further represents";

"neither the petitioner": *Chillicothe Gazette* (Ohio), August 31, 1929.

Her petition was granted: *Akron Beacon Journal,* October 17, 1929.

On this day, at least: Photo from Sharon Calder.

checked into Columbia Hospital: Email from Sharon Calder, November 19, 2016.

"This well known musician is accustomed": *Marion Star* (Ohio), February 4, 1928.

"The Girl Who Stood By Her Dad": *Detroit Free Press,* January 12, 1928.

she had tired of questions: *The Times* (Munster, Indiana), October 3, 1928.

"a prominent criminal lawyer": *Chicago Tribune,* February 24, 1928.

"best girl": Ibid.

"Meet my little girl"; "She has always been an admirer": Ibid.

the Uptown neighborhood of Chicago: Ibid., February 20, 1987.

filed a motion in probate court: Ibid., June 27, 1928.

fifteen bottles of liquor: *News Leader* (Staunton, Virginia), December 20, 1929.

$3,000: *Cincinnati Enquirer,* October 9, 1931.

$150,000: Ibid., October 20, 1931.

$245,918.40: Ibid., October 6, 1931.

estate of a racetrack magnate: *Indianapolis News,* November 25, 1939.

he sold his mansion: Ibid., October 1, 1934.

a government lien of $34,000: Ibid., October 2, 1934.

lone success was in recovering valuables: *Cincinnati Enquirer,* March 20, 1929.

collect the $10,000 fine: Ibid., October 11, 1931.

$158,255 in unpaid taxes: *The Tribune* (Coshocton, Ohio) December 16, 1928.

"Tell no one I am here" to **"spotlight, you see":** *Washington Post,* April 28, 1938.

"George," the friend called: Ibid.

living in a boardinghouse: William A. Cook, 198.

"Another Gatsby Passes": Hotchkiss and Meyer, 34.

with a few hard blows: Ibid.

wild and sobbing: Willis, 139.

ABOUT THE AUTHOR

Karen Abbott is the *New York Times* best-selling author of *Sin in the Second City, American Rose,* and, most recently, *Liar, Temptress, Soldier, Spy,* named one of the best books of the year by *Library Journal* and *The Christian Science Monitor.* A native of Philadelphia, she now lives in New York City. Follow Karen at karenabbott.net.

The employees of Thorndike Press hope you have enjoyed this Large Print book. All our Thorndike, Wheeler, and Kennebec Large Print titles are designed for easy reading, and all our books are made to last. Other Thorndike Press Large Print books are available at your library, through selected bookstores, or directly from us.

For information about titles, please call:
  (800) 223-1244

or visit our website at:
  gale.com/thorndike

To share your comments, please write:
  Publisher
  Thorndike Press
  10 Water St., Suite 310
  Waterville, ME 04901